PANIC
DIARIES

PANIC DIARIES

A Genealogy of Panic Disorder

JACKIE ORR

Duke University Press   Durham and London

2006

© 2006 Duke University Press

All rights reserved

Printed in the United States of America on acid-free paper ∞

Designed by Rebecca M. Giménez

Typeset in Minion by Tseng Information Systems, Inc.

Library of Congress Cataloging-in-Publication Data and republication

acknowledgments appear on the last printed pages of this book.

FOR ALL THE BURNING GIRLS

WHO ONCE YELLED "FIRE!"

CONTENTS

ACKNOWLEDGMENTS

The social webs of knowledge, challenge, love, money, labor, and friendship that have made this book possible are a pleasure to try to name. In Boston, Stephen Pfohl and the Parasite Cafe introduced me to the radical arts and science of a sociology cut by surrealism. With Victoria Burke, Mark Driscoll, Cristina Favretto, Avery Gordon, Jeremy Grainger, Andrew Herman, Sandra Joshel, Pelle Lowe, Josef Mendoza, Diane Nelson, and Sit-Com International, I learned tons about the collective powers of creative dis-ease. In Berkeley, the friendship of Elizabeth Bernstein, Shana Cohen, LuAnne Codella, Robert Glick, Teresa Gowan, Maren Klawiter, Natasha Kirsten Kraus, Mary Peelen, Pamela Perry, the Pushy Bottoms, Will Rountree, Leslie Salzinger, Laurie Schaffner, Noga Shalev, and Françoise Vergès gave me intellectual comradeship that I continue to cherish today. In Syracuse, Monisha Das Gupta, Marj DeVault, Mary Ellen Kavanaugh, Claudia Klaver, Andrew London, and Julia Loughlin have kept me warm. To Dóvar Chen, my love and deepest thanks.

Troy Duster graciously took on my "case" when I was a dissertation student, and guided me with sweet assurances that I was never really lost. Adele Clarke, Patricia Clough, Joan Fujimura, Caren Kaplan, Maren Klawiter, Emily Martin, Roddey Reid, Molly Rhodes, and Jennifer Terry have all read pieces of the manuscript at different stages. I am indebted to their engaged criticisms and encouragements. Donna Haraway and the late Kathy Acker have been transformative teachers, though I have never sat in their classrooms. I learned from reading their work how to experiment with thinking and language; this book would not have been thought, or written, without their fierce intelligence.

Much of the research and writing of the book was generously supported by the Institute for the Study of Social Change, the Department of Sociology, and the Doreen B. Townsend Center for the Humanities at the

University of California, Berkeley; and the Humanities Research Institute (HRI) at the University of California, Irvine. My time as an HRI resident fellow with the Postdisciplinary Approaches to the Technosciences research group, organized by Sharon Traweek and Roddey Reid, had a profound influence on my thinking. The Institute for the Study of Social Change also provided financial support for a set of interviews with key figures in the history of psychiatric classification and panic disorder research. My thanks to those I interviewed, Jim Ballenger, Jean Endicott, Donald F. Klein, Mark Pollack, Jerrold Rosenbaum, David Sheehan, Robert Spitzer, and Myrna Weissman, for sharing their historical memories with me. The healing and martial arts of Karina Epperlein and Carol Joyce have kept my body strong and my breathing steady during long stretches of writing. At Duke University Press, thanks to my editors Raphael Allen and Reynolds Smith for their care, and wit, and patience.

Performing my work helps to keep it — and me — alive. I owe a special debt of gratitude to those who over the years have organized performance events, making it possible for the work to meet a lively audience in real time: Craig Baldwin, Patricia Clough, Lauren Crux, Carolyn Dinshaw, Dwight Fee, Nancy Fisher, Patricia Geist, Lynne Haney, Valerie Hartouni, Andrew Herman, Bill Hoynes, Laura Mamo, Shannon May, Stephen Pfohl, Chris Robbins, Jennifer Terry, and Nina Wakeford.

PROLOGUE

I'm a sick woman who studies history, looking for cures, searching for more potent forms of dis-ease.

Knowledge is "made for cutting,"[1] writes Michel Foucault, a historian and son of a surgeon, who attempts to carve out the voluminous historical silence constituting the relation between modern reason and its irreducible "other" — the figure of madness. In *Madness and Civilization: A History of Insanity in the Age of Reason*, Foucault suggests that once upon a time, before the truth of madness was established in the medicalized realm of sickness and disease, human "unreason" flourished in multiple, meaningful exchanges with a reason from which it had not yet been decisively severed. Before the historical act of scission that founded madness in its modern form — isolated on one side of an abyss across which reason (while taking careful notes) observed its alien figure — unreason spoke in many tongues, none of them yet dead languages.

The transformation of a prolific, knowing speech of unreason into the compulsive, hallucinatory, senseless stammerings of madness takes place, Foucault tells us, at a particular historical moment: when the emerging techniques of modern reason become a foundation of modern political power. Unreason is rendered speechless at the moment when that *other form of madness* becomes dominant, that "other form of madness by which men, in an act of sovereign reason, confine their neighbors, and communicate . . . [with] each other through the merciless language of non-madness."[2]

It is the workings of this mad reason and its relations to contemporary power with which I am somewhat compulsively concerned here, in the stammered hallucinations that follow. In a society of unspeakable madness, how does a mad woman tell a history of what has come to be called a "mental disorder"? And, immersed in a merciless language of non-madness, how will we ever hear her?

1

History, Memory, Story:
Openings

True! — nervous — very, very dreadfully nervous I had been and am; but why *will* you say that I am mad? The disease had sharpened my senses — not destroyed — not dulled them. . . . Hearken! and observe how healthily — how calmly I can tell you the whole story. — EDGAR ALLAN POE[1]

The point is to reconfigure what counts as knowledge. — DONNA HARAWAY[2]

Perhaps it was a clear, cold, blue-sky afternoon when the Iroquois Theater burned. Certainly it was a Wednesday; the archives will tell you that. Sixteen chorus girls stood onstage singing "Pearly Moonlight" while the Queen of the Aerial Ballet and her troupe of eleven dancers, tied to invisible wires and hanging high above the stage, waited for their cue. In the audience, a crowd of nearly two thousand sat watching the matinee performance of *Mr. Bluebeard*.[3] Then a line of flame shot up the muslin curtain. The chorus girls kept on singing, but you could see their eyes go wild.

Nearly six hundred people died in the Iroquois Theater fire one winter afternoon, December 30, 1903. "Panic Balks Escape: Maddened Audience Unable to Reach the Exits," "Panic in the Iroquois Causes Frightful Loss—Women and Children Trampled in the Wild Rush," read the headlines the next day. The exact cause of the extraordinary loss of life appeared uncertain. Some reported that a short circuit in an electric light sparked the first flame. Others noted the failure of the asbestos curtain to fall, held in place by the wire on which the Queen of the Aerial Ballet, in a spectacular special effect, flew out over the audience.

But the owners of the newly opened Iroquois Theater, a palatial building in downtown Chicago, quickly declared: "The panic, as everybody says, was the chief cause of the large number of deaths."[4] (Whatever the facts of the matter, several stagehands and the chief electrician of the Iroquois were arrested and charged with manslaughter, while fifteen chorus girls were jailed on a $5,000 bond as the sixteenth girl, one Miss Romaine, continued to elude detectives.)[5]

At the beginning of the twentieth century, "panic" often plays a leading role in popular stories of catastrophe and in theoretical stagings of the collective psychology of crowds. Jamming the exits and inflaming fatalities, panic also permits those who preside over industrial-size disasters to account differently for the loss of life—and to render more obscure its financial and legal accounting—by offering a deadly psychological sub-text to the malfunctions of increasingly massive, complex technosocial machineries.[6] The Iroquois Theater, built at a cost of over $1 million and designed according to "the most modern plans,"[7] boasted two thousand electric lights illuminating its giant interior staircases where corpses piled as much as ten feet high as surging crowds struggled to flee the flames. The panicky flight of the audience, the theater's owners had more than reason to believe, was at least as fatal as the fire itself.

"The panic is the crudest and simplest example of collective mental life," writes William McDougall in 1920.[8] Conceiving of panic as a form of "primitive sympathy" communicated via emotional contagion and collective imitation or mimesis, several late-nineteenth- and early-twentieth-century social theorists view such instances of contagious communication as the very nature of the "social."[9] "Suggestion" and "emotional contagion" are concepts used to name the elusive force constituting the sociality of the modern collective, as well as the frenzied spread of panic. Emile Durkheim, writing in 1912 with the accumulated confidence of an imperial ethnography, finds the most elementary form of modern social life in the contagious communicative power of the totemic image.[10] Embodying the suggestive, binding power of the very idea of a society, the totem image is uncovered by this founder of modern sociology as an original imprint of a specifically social force. Where does this social force come from? From the energetic traces of effervescent rituals of mimesis and contagious emotion, explains Durkheim, reading the ethnographic stories of nineteenth-century gentlemen and ladies observing the lives of the indigenous Iroquois in the United States.[11] What burns in the Iroquois theaters, suggest the early messengers of a modern social science, may be nothing other than the social itself.

What social is that? Is it communicating right now? Are you listening? Could you stop if you tried? The theater of panic opens out onto the stage of the social. This book is written in the space of that opening.

Making openings is perhaps the task of any effective theory, and any affecting theater (with which theory shares an etymological tie in the Latin *thea*, the act of seeing). Antonin Artaud, theorist of an experimental "theater of cruelty" in the 1930s, paid relentless attention to the opening "cut or inscription that makes mise-en-scène of the empty stage in the first place," in Patricia Clough's words.[12] This cut or opening tear into the empty stage operates as a kind of "originary technicity," a technique for producing (carving, inscribing) an opening, for framing an origin.[13] Out of the void of possibilities, an incision toward meaning, toward a particular mise-en-scène, is made. Every opening of a story, every gesture toward staging an origin, becomes, then, "a repetition of that which cannot be repeated: the first cut."[14]

Remember as best you can, always, the first cut into this story is repeatedly performed in the dark, in a theater I want to call the social, by something you could call terror.

Once upon a time one April night, a viceroy in eighteenth-century Sardinia has a terrifying dream of the plague infecting himself and the whole tiny island. The next day, he refuses to allow a ship to dock in the harbor, suspecting it carries the deadly contagion. The ship sails on, landing twenty days later in the port of Marseilles, where its arrival coincides with the worst outbreak of the plague in that city's history. Artaud discovers this "astonishing historical fact" in the archives of the tiny town of Cagliari and opens his influential 1938 essay "The Theater and the Plague" by recounting the strange tale.[15] Between the plague and the viceroy, Artaud observes, "a palpable communication, however subtle, was established." It would be foolish, the theorist argues, to limit our notion of how disease communicates to "contagion by simple contact."[16] More foolish still to fail to create a theater that can become, like the plague that is profoundly its kin, a site of delirious communication, an epidemic of fatal meanings and the physical matter of dreams.

Actor, playwright, schizophrenic, surrealist, essayist, and inmate for nine years in several asylums for the insane, Artaud may seem like an unlikely supplement to the professionalizing ranks of early-twentieth-century theorists of panic and the "suggestible" social. But let me suggest that Artaud's "theater of cruelty" sought to achieve — through the intensity of ritual and the experimental hieroglyphics of embodied forms — something on the same order as the conflagration at the Iroquois Theater. What modern social science tried to make intelligible, Artaud tried to make real: the contagion of gesture, the communicative power of a scream, a mimetic theater of collective seizure and frenzied emotion.

Artaud's intent was not to start a panic but to experiment through performance with the features of the social—never far from the alchemy of theater—that collective terror also opens toward. The "mind's capacity for receiving suggestion," which Artaud identifies as one source of theater's transformative power, is precisely the capacity that modern social science locates as one source of the social itself.[17] One method by which the social communicates its self. Are you still listening?

PSYCHOPOWER AND THE SOCIAL

> Power does not bear a constant shape nor redound to a single source.
> It does not follow causal—linear or dialectical—routes; it is not
> calculable in all of its effects; it does not remain material in
> substance.—WENDY BROWN[18]

> Underneath all reason lies delirium.—GILLES DELEUZE[19]

This is a story about panic, and about the techniques developed—in the entangled fields of social science and psychiatry, the U.S. government and the military, the mass media and the transnational drug industry—to make panicked bodies speak, and to manage what they can be heard to say. Stretching across the last century of U.S. history, this is a selective chronicle of the sanctioned communications between a social "disorder" and that which would govern it in the name of a desired order, in the interests of a more effective administration. Survey research, public opinion polls, laboratory experiments, research on mental patients, self-tests in popular magazines, atom bomb tests in the desert, cybernetic models, psychiatric interviews, electric shocks, clinical drug trials, TV talk shows, computerized diagnostics, and genetic research compose one partial, compulsive inventory of the arsenal of techniques aimed at producing potentially useful speech from the tremulous mouth of terror.

This is a story about what panic has been made to say and how such historically specific speech has been produced. "The body *is* a historical situation," writes Judith Butler.[20] The panicked body's situated history is the embodied, wildly beating heart of this book.

Once upon a time one spring night as I was turning over to sleep I suddenly became terrified that I was about to die. I started trembling, and my heart beat so fast in my chest I was sure it would just stop. The next day at work I panicked again while sitting in front of the computer, then while walking down the sunlit street. My life became a strung-together bunch of attacks of total terror. I didn't know what to do. I went to a doctor. She listened to my heart and decided I was okay and should probably take a vacation. I couldn't afford to take a vacation. I went to a psychiatrist. She listened to me talk and decided I probably had something called "panic disorder." She wrote me a prescription for a drug called Xanax, which I thought was quite nice of her, since I couldn't afford to see a psychiatrist again. After I took the Xanax, the attacks of panic eased. The pill knew how to talk to my terror. That pill communicated with my panic while I remained for some time quite tongue-tied, without story or history for the situation in which my body seized.

Does terror have its own archive? Is panic indexed in the annals of history? Are those of us who symptomatically share heart-racing attacks of floating terror—what "normality," in a stunning dispossession of its own fears, will call our "pathology"—documented in those densely stocked shelves? If, as performer Laurie Anderson writes, "history is stories that we half-remember, and most of them never even get written down," then what kind of panic stories could be written out of the selective textual memories of the archival brain?[21] If the archive is, in Michel Foucault's words, the "law of what can be said," if the archive is an actively present, productive "*system of . . . enunciability*" ensuring that what is spoken today is "born in accordance with specific regularities," then out of such closely governed speech what history of panic could possibly be told?[22]

Certainly not a history that would try to give panic a true voice but, rather, a historicized story of the voices given to panic by a knowledge compelled to make panic truthfully speak. Certainly not a history that would try to contribute to a science of panic but, instead, a story of the historical formation of a science that claims knowledge of panic as one of its significant contributions. The archive, Foucault warns, does not afford the genealogist a confident empirical grasp of real historical objects, or the positivist pleasures of original discovery. What a genealogy "really does," Foucault writes, is "entertain the claims to attention of local, discontinuous, disqualified, illegitimate knowledges against the claims of a unitary body of theory which would . . . order them in the name of some true knowledge and some arbitrary idea of what constitutes a science and its objects. Genealogies are therefore not positivistic returns to a more careful or exact form of science. *They are precisely anti-sciences.*" It is not against science in general, its contents or concepts, that genealogy takes aim, but rather against the social power accruing to science at a particular historical moment: "It is really against *the effects of a power of discourse that is considered to be scientific* that the genealogy must wage its struggle."[23]

So this is a story about panic, and also about knowledge and power. Here the social sciences are important not only in informing the methods used to compose such a story but also as players in the story itself, active historical participants in the social theater that they claim as their site of research. Doubling as both a method and an object of my study, sociology is not a simple hero in this story, enabling a sick woman to locate her panicky symptoms in a broader context of social and historical relations. Rather, sociology, social psychology, psychiatry, and psychopharmacology are treated as historically specific social fields where panic is made into an object of knowledge by scientific discourses and disciplined subjects that partially construct the very object they promise to explain and control. Both subjects and objects of knowledge — sociology and its panicky populations, psychiatry and its terrified patients, psychopharmacology and its centrally nervous systems — are situated in shifting historical networks of power. What you know and don't know about panic is one of power's networked effects.

Thirty-five years after the Iroquois Theater burns, the social is again set on fire, this time by a 1938 CBS radio drama of *The War of the Worlds*, starring Martians outfitted with high-tech death rays aimed at thousands of startled inhabitants of the state of New Jersey. Hadley Cantril's now-famous 1940 study of the "panic broadcast" is sponsored by the Rockefeller Foundation and the Federal Radio Education Committee; Cantril's empirical measure of "suggestibility" is made possible by new techniques of survey research incubated in the belly of the radio broadcast industry.[24] Power operates the channels of transmission for what you hear and don't hear when terror talks.

In 1980, three decades after the U.S. government opens a new National Institute of Mental Health and declares the management of mental disease a public health priority, "panic disorder" emerges as a new psychiatric diagnosis.[25] Defined by floating attacks of terror that occur without any apparent cause, panic disorder is estimated to afflict millions of people in the United States. In 1982 a drug called Xanax, manufactured by the Upjohn Company, appears on the market, quickly becoming a best-selling treatment for panic attacks and anxiety. Even when the panicky body is your own, the experience of such a dis-ease never falls entirely outside the storied histories of power's play, of power's insistent production of panic knowledge.

"Biopower" is the name Michel Foucault gives to the coupling of the power of the modern state with the planned administration of the life, health, and diseases of individuals and entire populations. Foucault's earliest intimations of biopower can be found in *The Birth of the Clinic: An Archaeology of Medical Perception* (1963), where he narrates the convergence of social and medical space architectured by the late-eighteenth-century French state, partly in response to the political demand to control contagious epidemics, most dramatically the plague.[26] Located simultaneously at multiple levels of social organization — including economic relations, state surveillance strategies, and knowledge practices in medicine and the social sciences — the appearance of biopower for Foucault marks the very "threshold of modernity." For the first time, "methods of power and knowledge assumed responsibility for the life processes and undertook to control and modify them," bringing human health and disease into "the realm of explicit calculations." The result is the historical emergence of a "normalizing" society.[27]

"PSYCHOpower" is the name I would offer for technologies of power and techniques of knowledge developed by a normalizing society to regulate the psychological life, health, and disorders of individuals and entire populations. In part conceptual kin and strategic ally of modern biopower, PSYCHOpower operates through psychological monitoring, measurement, and discipline, administering order in the unruly psychic realms of perception, emotion, and memory. As Nikolas Rose observes, the twentieth-century " 'psycho' knowledges," organized around the psychological "discipline of the normal individual," play an increasingly significant role in the exercise of power and the government of groups in purportedly democratic, late capitalist societies.[28] PSYCHO-power makes possible the "democratic" administration of collective or group existence through techniques of public opinion polling, attitude measurement, and the psychological test, intensifying and multiplying the communicative feedback loops between governing bodies and the bodies they would govern. These techniques, according to Rose, pursue the dream of a psychological expertise that would "allow the continuous adjustment of the decisions taken by authorities . . . in the light of the subjective commitments, values, and motivations of those over whom authority is to be exercised. . . . [A]uthority is to be both effective and legitimate to the extent that it is exercised in the light of a knowledge of those who are governed."[29] PSYCHOpower works by multiplying the possible surfaces of contact between psychic processes and their regulation, and by legitimating power itself as a kind of therapeutic activity.

The psychic life of panic has been a sustained target of PSYCHOpower's attention. Panic and its collective and individual disorderings offer up one experimental space, one extended strategic surface, on which PSY-CHOpower has developed an empirical language and a set of instrumental techniques for measuring and managing the accelerated pulse of pan-icky bodies. Beginning on the anxious eve of World War II, I track the emergent techniques used to identify and manipulate the psychological matters of collective terror. Out of hybrid experiments conducted in the crucible of market research, public opinion surveys, social psychology, and U.S. military strategy, empirical methods are forged for more confidently speaking about features of panic that are now, with more confidence, heard to speak.

In the postwar years, concern about the U.S. public's propensity for "mass hysteria" in the face of escalating Cold War tensions and nuclear threats gives rise to a concerted effort among civilian and military government agencies, and social scientists, to investigate the collective dynamics of panic behavior. Public opinion polls attempt to register shifting tides of atomic terror. Academic researchers pursue laboratory models of panic interactions. Cybernetics and the information sciences model new communication strategies for controlling panic and promoting its presumed antithesis, national "morale." Civil defense agencies distribute pamphlets and produce feature-length films encouraging calm and highlighting the proper attitudes and information necessary to avoid a catastrophic postatomic panic.

The experience of individualized terror, too, is subjected to the disciplining productions of empirical findings and regulatory controls. From military psychiatry's treatment of "war neuroses" during World War II to the introduction of "panic disorder" in the late-twentieth-century lexicon of biopsychiatry, PSYCHOpower tries to project a persuasive empirical outline across the surface of symptomatic terrors that it promises to both name and erase. Structured psychiatric interviews, psychopharmacology, clinical drug trials, and the development of an "empirically based" diagnostic system usher in an unprecedented set of systematic psychiatric techniques for managing individualized disorders of affect and desire, of perception and memory, of trauma and the telltale heart of terror.

But I do not intend the notion of PSYCHOpower only as an extension of modern biopower. It is not only a psychological correlate of Foucault's story of the calibrated management of "life itself" through disciplinary technologies and a normalizing gaze. The PSYCHOpower I see at work is not only indebted to Foucault's insights in *Madness and Civilization*, where he maps the historical distance that modern reason carves out between itself and the scene of madness. PSYCHOpower's strategies are not limited to a disciplining of psychological disorders and the imperatives of public administration. No. The contours of PSYCHOpower can stretch a bit crazily beyond the logics of discourse and disciplines. PSYCHOpower can work somewhat psychotically to actively re-fuse and confuse the boundaries between the real and the unreal. Between deadly terror and its (potentially fatal) simulation. Playing seriously with the logistics and illogics of perception, PSYCHOpower may operate not only in the field of rationalizing techniques but in the form of magical appearances or the persuasive trick. Indeed, understanding the "trick *as* technique," in Michael Taussig's words,[30] is to begin to approach that perhaps maddening realm where power deploys both reason and magic, disciplining methods and controlled mimesis, sciences and fictions, orders and experimental disorderings — all as tactical players in the cultural production of perception itself.

If one aim, then, of PSYCHOpower has been to manage panic, another aim has been to learn how to make it. If PSYCHOpower wants to control the collective terror in a burning theater, it also wants to know how to simulate the fire that starts it. If protecting frightened subjects from the face of death is one of PSYCHOpower's goals, so is constructing a spectacular death mask to trigger an experimental terror. If calming panic disorders through prescription drugs is one of its aims, so is promoting the panic attacks that extend the market reach of a pharmaceutical cure. (The word "psychopharmacology" is first used in 1957 in conjunction with a newly scientific psychiatry interested in experimentally producing, through drugs like LSD, an "experimental psychosis" that can then be cured by other drugs.)[31] The PSYCHOscientific reason that designs the pills and the public opinion polls, the diagnostic categories and the civil defense protocols, is a reason that knows it has nightmares and is trying to learn *how to use them*. In 1955 over sixty atomic bombs explode one day in dozens of U.S. cities, inflicting twenty million civilian casualties. As TV cameras record the events and government officials take careful notes, this nationwide civil defense simulation tests the nation's vulnerability to mass panic and its preparedness for atomic attack. PSYCHOpower is a form of rationality that wants to mimic as well as manage what it will name the "irrational" or the unconscious, taking on the figure of madness, by turns, as its radical "other" and its intimate familiar.[32]

Edward L. Bernays, nephew of Sigmund Freud and founder in the 1920s of the public relations industry, can be considered one of PSYCHOpower's most forthright strategists.[33] In a 1941 essay addressing the U.S. Army, Bernays announces that the "diabolical thing about the present age is that hysteria and suggestion can produce realities even in the political world—realities that may be described as pseudo-creations but none the less effective."[34] Associating the threat of fascism as much with its propaganda strategies as its military force, Bernays advises the army to mobilize recent social scientific knowledge that has been so successfully applied in the fields of communication and public opinion. "Compulsion and censorship have no place in a democracy," he affirms, but a concerted " 'engineering of consent,' through reason, persuasion, suggestion," can and should be used to maintain U.S. national morale and emotional unity.[35] The power of suggestion—identified as both a diabolical disease and a persuasive cure. A theater of PSYCHOpower—restaging the production of reality in a slightly psychotic social space cut through by propaganda and public relations, by mass media(tions) and military imperatives, by the offspring of psychoanalysis in positive transference with the arts and sciences of corporate communications.

These calculating and crazy technologies of power touch intimately on the forms of sociality that turn-of-the-century social theorists associate with suggestibility and collective mimesis. The emotional contagion of collective experience, or the totemic force of images, is the object as well as the medium of a power aimed at countering *as well as productively constituting* the experience of social and psychic disorders. The force of such power is perceptual, emotional, imaginary, and profoundly corporeal. Indeed, PSYCHOpower—in advance of contemporary feminist critiques—disdains the notion of a mind/body split, troubling with its tricks and techniques the presumed borders between the psychological and the physiological, the image and the body, between psychic lives and social movements. Michael Taussig, theorizing the mimetic healing practices of successful shamans, notes that a "certain play of 'bodiedness,' contagion, and physical connection [is] a co-component of the mimetic alongside the idea, the symbol."[36] Carefully studying the complex flows between social embodiment and the effectiveness of symbols, PSYCHOpower tries to regulate *and imitate* the fluid materialities indexed by the concept of social suggestion.

While PSYCHOpower is not a new force, tied historically to the moment that Foucault repeatedly marks—when techniques of modern reason constitute, for the first time, a foundation of political power—it nonetheless takes on new forms and new tactical capacities as power/knowledges become entangled with something about which Foucault had too little to say: the rise of twentieth-century information and communications technologies, the mass-mediated realities of everyday life in the age of electronic reproductions. The condensed theoretical seizures enacted by Jean Baudrillard, that theorist of a hyperreal world of capitalism-gone-electric, suggest that Foucault's analysis misses the "frenzied semiurgy" of a society operating not through the disciplining regimes of truth but through screened information flows and speculative exchanges, through the phantasmatic seductions of floating signs without referent.[37] Baudrillard evokes the simultaneously psychotic and mundane vertigo promoted by an excess of capital-intensive communications networks, culminating in "an original and profound mutation of the very forms of perception and pleasure."[38] Sensible structures of social or historical meaning disappear into the fascinating static of televisual spectacle, into networked techno-ecstasies of communication.

Somewhat less hyperactively, Donna Haraway offers a historical analysis of the social mutations wrought by new information and communications technologies, new technoscientific hookups of humans and machines, of simulated computer models and calculated social effects. Haraway tells a story of post–World War II communications and information sciences transforming key concepts in the life and social sciences (nature, organism, society) into "Cold War objects of knowledge," reconceived as "heavily militarized command-communication-control and information system[s]."[39] A key operator in this discursive mutation is the science of cybernetics, which develops a statistical and probabilistic, a mathematical and metaphoric language for modeling a range of human, machine, and social behaviors as problems in communication and control. In Haraway's account: "The social goal of the new [cybernetic] life science was clearly statistical control of the mass through sophisticated communications systems. . . . [E]verything has become a system."[40] For the biological and social sciences retooled by cybernetic insights, disturbances or disorders in any technical — or social — system are addressed as problems in systems design, to be solved by more effective forms of communicative feedback, by an engineering of increasingly automated practices of communicative control.

PSYCHOpower oscillating between techno-ecstasy and automated cybernetic control systems? Entranced in front of the screen, performing strategic, long-term schizoid (con)fusions of social relations and simulation models? The disciplinary powers of laser-guided weapons cut and spliced with the communicative pleasures of globally broadcast destruction? Michel Foucault meets Alfred Hitchcock in a post–Cold War shower of screened sacrifices, prime-time terrorisms, televisual warfare with a CBS news anchor embedded in an army tank — regimes of normative truth encounter the phantasmatic artillery in Norman Bates's psycho mind — in the dark, in the desert, in the latest digitally relayed storm.[41]

Shot: Reverse shot. PSYCHObullets for every panicked cyber-brain misfiring. Smart, now even smarter, bombs against every possibility of defense. Depression or panic attacks offering privileged points of access for targeted technologies of power, from Prozac and Paxil to CNN and reality TV. In all directions, normal curves stretching toward statistically modulated outcomes, future options imploding in predictive probabilities. PSYCHOpower armed and ready and already anticipating the twenty-second century? Panic waiting anxious in the wings for its next role?

PARANOID EPISTEMOLOGY

> Paranoia knows some things well and others poorly.
> —EVE KOSOFSKY SEDGWICK[42]

And so the contagious paranoia at play in theories of contemporary cyber-ultra-hyper-digital-electro-techno-power-gone-postmodern makes its mark on the panicky story I tell here.[43] The theoretical fiction of PSYCHOpower takes seriously at least the suggestion that technoscientific reason may be operating today as a somewhat psychotic social force, oscillating between techniques for disciplining panic and tactics for producing it. Between communications media and mechanisms of total control. Between regulating the madness of disorder and mining (or miming) it for any secrets it might hold for the tactical deployments of a seductively psychological *or illogical* power.

In its exquisite sense of contagious connectivity, paranoia is one form that a felt insistence on the social and historical structuring of psychic experience can take. Paranoia "knows well" the resonant evidence suggesting that everything really is connected—the psyche and the power of the social, a small white pill and a wildly historical story. This text performs a kind of practiced paranoia by situating panic within a dramatic theater where the mass media, the military, corporate capital, the state, psychiatry, and the social sciences are cast in leading roles as sometimes secret agents of a political power that aims to produce the psychic and emotional structurings of—some very nervous—social subjects.

In an important sense, a somewhat paranoiac position is embedded in the sociologics of any structural analysis. In *Empire of Conspiracy* (2000),

Timothy Melley interprets much of U.S. postwar social scientific thought as a relentlessly paranoid reading of the power of social structures: "Texts from the last half of the twentieth century are replete with the frightening 'discovery' that human behavior can be regulated by social messages and communications. This discovery in turn feeds the tendency to attribute motives to large social and economic organizations, bureaucracies, information-processing systems, communication networks, discourses, and social institutions."[44] Paranoia "knows well" the analytic tendencies in social science to turn the complexities of structural dynamics into scary stories of control, giving motive and name to the very forces that remain so historically elusive, so excessively but unspeakably social.

Approached as a pathology of knowledge, paranoia's particular sickness can be cured by a healthy antidote of what paranoia only "knows poorly": discontinuities of pattern, the tiny causalities of chance, the play of unintended effects, the reparative and tender (as opposed to deadly and terrifying) features of intricate connection.[45] However, approached not as an epistemological pathology but as a historically sedimented intimation of one of PSYCHOpower's effects, paranoia can read as symptomatic evidence of a much more social disease: the dis-ease of a social that can materialize via contagious connections and invisible communications, a social whose force remains in part curiously secret to itself. The social becomes a piece of what the dis-eased body performs, in its symptomatic — sometimes tender and reparative — attempts to communicate. Oh, oh, are you listening still?

TRAUMATIZING TECHNOSCIENCE

> The traumatized, we might say, carry an impossible history within
> them. — CATHY CARUTH[46]

By situating a slightly paranoid story of panic on the shimmering borders of the psychic and the social, of the body and history, the terrain of this book touches on the emergent field of "trauma studies."[47] As a site for thinking about embodied entanglements of the psychological, the social, the affective, and the historical, the study of trauma also contributes to a destabilizing of confident distinctions on which disciplinary knowledges, and their disciplined objects, depend. In *An Archive of Feelings* (2003), an analysis of everyday trauma and queer public cultures, Ann Cvetkovich writes: "Defined culturally rather than clinically . . . [t]rauma becomes a central category for looking at the intersections of emotional and social processes along with the intersections of memory and history. . . . [T]rauma discourse is important precisely because it challenges distinctions between the mental and physical, the psychic and social, and the internal and external as locations or sources of pain."[48] Foregrounding the tension between well-footnoted histories and almost unspeakable scenes of violence, the ruptures of traumatic experience "dislocat[e] the boundaries of our modes of understanding," notes Cathy Caruth. Psychoanalysis, history, sociology, psychiatry, and cultural theory are each cut open and cut into by cross-discipling questions of how to retell traumatic stories, or how to contribute to some form of cure.[49]

As in feminist psychoanalytic studies on hysteria that precede and partially prefigure trauma studies, approaching trauma demands attention to the politics of knowledge and the historically situated possibilities and impossibilities of communication.[50] If traumatized or panicked or hysterical bodies mark a symptomatic site of what Foucault calls "subjugated knowledges" — those local, popular, inadequately scientific knowledges "of the psychiatric patient, of the ill person" — then what kind of study would be able to hear such bodies speak?[51] What methods could make sense of such bodies and the largely unwritten archive of their feelings? How to excavate the "memory of hostile encounters," the "historical knowledge of struggles," buried at the scene of a subjugated knowing?[52] In 1975, Catherine Clément and Hélène Cixous call for "another way of knowing . . . [a]nother way of producing, of communicating," as they conjure a mythic history connecting the symptomatic sufferings of the hysteric to the historical repression of the witch, whose power of spells and cures went up in flames as the Inquisition cleared the way by force for the psychic and social foundations of early modern Europe.[53] (Was it echoes of this ancient combat that the young Freud could hear, if barely, when he noticed the disturbing resonances between the stories of hysterical patients and the documented "confessions" of witches under torture?)[54] If panic, too, embodies historical memories of struggle, endlessly undocumented battles against PSYCHOpower's strategic moves, how to hear what might lie in excess of the orderly communications pronounced in the name of panicky disorders?

Luce Irigaray, speaking of—and with—the feminized figure of hysteria, writes: "Hers are contradictory words, somewhat mad from the standpoint of reason, inaudible for whoever listens to them with . . . a fully elaborated code in hand." To hear, "one would have to learn to listen with another ear."[55] Turning an "other ear" to trauma, Caruth listens for how the traumatized themselves become "the symptom of a history that they cannot entirely possess," an "impossible history" that haunts with all the more force for being out of memory's confident reach.[56] In a sensuous weave of feminist theory, sociological imagination, and a radically socialized psychoanalysis, Avery Gordon in *Ghostly Matters* (1997) pushes the historical and psychic power of haunting toward a methodological practice, one that draws on—as well as analyzes and transforms—trauma's effects:

> To be haunted and to write from that location, to take on the condition of what you study, is not a methodology or a consciousness you can simply adopt or adapt as a set of rules or an identity; it produces its own insights and blindnesses. Following the ghosts is about making a contact that changes you and refashions the social relations in which you are located.
>
> . . . It is often [about] . . . inarticulate experiences, of symptoms and screen memories, of spiraling affects, of more than one story at a time, of the traffic in domains of experience that are anything but transparent and referential.[57]

Attending to the complex materiality of stories of haunting makes telling impossible histories more possible. Talking with ghosts ties the problem of method to the crazy imperatives of communicating with the disturbingly animate dead.

By what impossible histories are panicked bodies possessed? What ghosted present plays out on the social stage where collective panic takes flight? *Once upon a time one spring night as she was turning over to sleep, she started trembling and her heart beat so fast in her chest she was sure she would just die. Once upon a time she was seized by a story, an impos-*

sible tale playing out across the white sheets, shuttling between waking and dream, falling over and over into terror.

"The perception that seeks to seize these sufferings and their words in their wild state necessarily belongs to a world that has already captured them."[58] This is no true story of panic as subjugated knowing that I tell here. And yet surely it is something more and something other than what it also is: a critical genealogy of the "truths" that panic has been made to speak in the language of its capture, by a series of little rationalities (the social science survey, the psychiatric interview) that accomplish at the same time its silence. As persuaded as I am of this verbose historical silencing of panic, there remains the desire to turn an other ear toward what might (im)possibly be heard of *spiraling affects*, of *inarticulate experiences* and *more than one story at a time*. There is still the chattering, stammering conversation with the dead and about death, about the shock of a death that can be delivered before the heart stops beating—a shockingly impossible story that perhaps a panicked body knows well how to, however failingly, tell.

In *Trauma: A Genealogy* (2000), Ruth Leys traces a history of the concept of trauma in relation to the "hypnotic-suggestive" bond, a kind of trance state or scene of suggestibility that, for Freud and other theorists, defines the psychic core of traumatic experience.[59] Trauma tears open a structure of experience predicated on bounded senses of self and other, of inside and outside. Traumatic "experience" breaks into and breaks open the bounded subject or "self," catapulting experience toward a radically different structure of "unconscious imitation or mimesis," a vertiginous and "abyssal openness to all identification."[60] Oddly, uneasily, then, trauma cannot be said to involve a psychic "subject"—since traumatic experience takes place in the shattered borderlands of any subject/object distinction. Disturbingly, almost unspeakably, there is no precise traumatic "event," no clear executioner's knife that arrives from the outside to kill me on the inside. Trauma is, imprecisely, a vertiginously relational scene in which shock, violence, a scene of death or its threat, undoes the psychic architecture of inside and out, undoing at the same time a coherent subject who could confidently, consciously remember how to say what happened.[61] The possibility of a memory of trauma, of an unbroken account of its history, disappears in the hypnotic-suggestive knots that tie trauma to an interminable, repetitive present tense.

Jean-Martin Charcot, Freud's teacher in the mid-1880s when they together wander the hysterics' ward of the Salpêtrière Clinic in Paris, claims that "traumatic-hysterical dysfunctions" are intimately linked to the psychological mechanisms of suggestibility.[62] Charcot uses hypnotic and suggestive methods — occasionally enhanced by a dose of amyl nitrate — to direct live performances of hysterical seizures performed by hypnotized women patients in the medical amphitheater of the Salpêtrière. A few years later, in *Studies on Hysteria* (1895), Freud and Josef Breuer describe how, with suggestion and hypnosis as their curative approach, the sufferings of hysterics are relieved when patients emotionally relive and give story to a traumatic experience attached to a symptom.[63]

During World Wars I and II, drawing on the earlier experiments of Freud and others, psychiatrists treating soldiers suffering from "shell shock" and "war neuroses" use hypnosis and suggestive techniques — sometimes supplemented by narcotic drugs — to return traumatized soldiers to the scene where their "self" was blown open. What follows from the soldiers is never a true story of their terror, but a mimetic theater of embodied shock and relived emotion as they reenact in vivid detail the sensational scene.[64] Sometimes, some say, such theater has the power to heal.

And will you believe me if I tell you that reading feminist histories of hysteria helped to cure my panicky symptoms, suggesting the possibility of story in places that had held only a fierce and repetitious fear? In the spaces opened by theaters of feminist theory, by bewitching spells and spiraling affects and the desire to tell differently a history of women's sickness, my attacks of panic eased, displaced by other stories, other forms of communicating a profound dis-ease now reimagined as a symptom of something far more panicky than the beat of my own heart. It would be quite a story. And not untrue.

The "scandalous nature of the traumatic cure," writes Leys, has never been fully grasped.[65] Even today, the power of suggestion and mimetic identifications to constitute both the psychic materiality of trauma and the medium of its cure remains elusive. How, Leys asks, does hypnosis really cure? But perhaps the story is not so scandalous when situated within a suggestive history of suggestion as a social force, of emotional identifications and mimetic contagions as one radically social feature of psychic connection. The story, then, perhaps turns to the scandalous nature of the social, a social that can operate—in one of its most potent forms—*from inside out* of the individualized subject/self; a social that saturates traumatizing scenes of terrifying violence, sexual attack, threatened death; a social that is (still) shocking in its power to terrorize, and in its power to cure. Perhaps. Although I could be wrong.

In the symptomatic account of panic I offer here, the power of the social to terrorize and to cure the terrors it helps to produce is inextricably tied to stories of technoscience. Not only do radio and television, jet planes and atomic bombs, computers and pills, crowd the historical stagings of this text, but the language of technoscientific methods and technique—a language struggling to become a hegemonic form of communication in the twentieth-century social sciences—appears as a central obsession, a somewhat traumatic scene, to which I repeatedly turn and return.

By the early 1950s, as I chronicle in chapter 3, collective panic itself is reconceived as a technoscientific object, seemingly far from the speculative fictions of contagious emotion and suggestive mimesis. The problem of collective panic tearing through the social group, a problem at the fore of government anxieties and state-sponsored research in the atomic age, is reconfigured through the technoscientific and profoundly social language of cybernetics. Today, a history of the present seems impossible to tell without reference to cybernetic discourse, and a large and growing scholarship exists on the cultural, military, imaginary, political, and economic transformations that cybernetics entails.[66] Spreading rather contagiously through a range of intellectual fields (including biology, mathematics, neurology, sociology, anthropology) and technoscientific developments (including computer design and missile weaponry), cybernetics pursues a universal language for speaking about objects and processes as systems of communication, organized and controlled through the feedback and exchange of information. Information is understood by cybernetics as "*a pattern*, not a presence," explains Katherine Hayles, defined "as a probability function, with no dimensions, no materiality, and no necessary connection with meaning."[67] Group panic, in social cybernetic terms, is theorized as a dysfunctional terror, a breakdown in social communication and effective control. The cure lies in reengineering information patterns, rewiring the panicky (t)error by reworking the communication system that controls it.

A cybernetic "psyche" is conceptually assembled in the 1950s as a self-regulating communication and information-processing system. From its interest in the psychophysiology of hypnosis and traumatic shock, to its suggestive analogies between the operations of the nervous system and the electronic circuits of a digital computer, cybernetics takes the human brain and central nervous system as primary objects of theory and research. Psychiatrists, psychoanalysts, and neurologists are key figures in the interdisciplinary group that, from 1946 to 1953, works to develop an explicit language and method for cybernetic thought. As I trace in chapter 4, "cyber-psychiatry" begins to replace the psychoanalytic notion of the unconscious constituted by libidinal energy with a cybernetic model of the brain as a communication system, constituted by the exchange of information. Mental disorders can be conceived, and treated, as disorders in communication. Psychopharmacology can be modeled as the message, or communications media, that corrects information disorders in the cybernetic brain. Individual panic disorder can be theorized as the effect of "deranged circuitry," reengineered for proper functioning by a tiny white pill.

And have we grasped fully today the scandalous nature of the techno-scientific cure? Have you ever swallowed a psychopharmacological story that could slow your pounding heart, cut your memory into simpler pieces, and deliver new dreams during your slightly technoscientific sleep? In what place that is no place at all but a pattern of informatic signals, electrochemical circuits, in what place that is no place at all do panic and the pill called Xanax meet? What kind of theater of the social could effectively silence a flickering, floating terror of death with a tale of improved traffic in technoscientific messages?

If the field of trauma includes the implosive zones where subject and object, inside and outside, present and past are radically refused and restructured, then what structure of experience (im)possibly emerges, what fusions and confusions take place, as cybernetic subjects/objects implode in the shared immaterial medium of information? What impossible history lies inside the technoscientific truth of a psychopharmaceutical cure?

What elusive trace of trauma may be carried in these words I write you through the computer's screenings, these electric signals sent through technoscientific circuits whose history neither you, nor I, nor the computer, nor the information patterns connecting us, can ever truly possess?

Engaging with trauma, Ann Cvetkovich urges, reveals a need for "sensational stories" — felt stories, immersed in embodied sensations — as "an alternative form of knowledge to the abstractions of systemic analysis."[68] Is there also a need for sensational stories *about* the abstractions of systemic analysis? About sensational embodiment in the abstractions of systems? As an alternative form of sociological and illogical knowledge, in the chapters that follow, I repeatedly turn to stories of the sensational, embodied effects of new — and contagious? — technoscientific logics of the social. Stories of the abstract, embodied, informational *il*logics of social dis-ease and disorders. If trauma marks a "moment in which abstract social systems can actually be felt or sensed," then perhaps traumatizing technoscience means following the ghosts who carry felt traces of such a systematized and technoscientific social.[69] Perhaps a panicked body is one of those ghosts?

I was born in the year of the integrated circuit, one mile from the ocean, fifteen yards from a three-story electrical substation, on an island that served as a U.S. military training base. My father worked for the navy, specializing in underwater explosives, before working as an electrical engineer at Bell Telephone Labs, managing the mass manufacturing of integrated circuits. The integrated circuit brings together on the same material plane, etched within a single crystal, previously separate components of electro-technoscientific communication. Its development dramatically increases the complexity and speed of the circulation of information. Sponsored primarily by military contracts in the first decade of its production, the integrated circuit is the material base for the weapons systems, computer systems, communications systems, and social systems networked into the twenty-first century.

Can you hear me when I say that information patterns and unconscious desires don't feel to me like entirely separate stories? Will you believe that I dream over and over of bomber planes flying out of the ocean into the electric shock of sudden waking? I'm not saying it's so easy as claiming that society's just crazy. I'm not saying I don't suffer from systematic dysfunctional fears. But I ask you, really, can a pill ever cure such a story?

Society is always more or less a work of art. — ROBERT E. PARK[70]

"A message illuminates the screen that partially cuts my flesh from what remains pulsating. Its color is pink, light green and violent. This message inFORMs me that somebody is knocking at the door of what might yet be critically re-membered. . . . When I open the door a figure appears whose past is in my future. It is the Black Madonna Durkheim and I know it in an instant. Mama Dada Mama Dada Dada Mama Dada. I flash dead pan(icked) to black and she says, 'If you want, I'll be your host. Pack up your possessions and let's dance.' . . . Being profoundly affected by the Black Madonna's words, and being equally bored by the predominantly whitemale culture of social science in which I found myself (w)riting, I said YES."[71]

This excerpt from Stephen Pfohl's *Death at the Parasite Cafe: Social Science (Fictions) and the Postmodern* (1992), offers one contemporary, exuberant sign of social science writing's turn toward the "performative," toward practices of writing that play seriously with the question of style and the politics of form.[72] Pfohl, a sociologist, marks his break with the styleless style of social science by pointing suggestively backward toward the figure of Emile Durkheim, and toward Dada. Durkheim's belief in the social effervescence of collective representations is one force behind the Collège de Sociologie (1937–39), a small group of mostly French intellectuals who, influenced simultaneously by surrealism, begin to explore "the contagious effects of the representations" they study; the Collège approaches representation, including the representations produced by sociology, as one possible site of transformative, collective communication.[73] Dada, a furious and festive early-twentieth-century experiment in political (anti)art forms, plays with live performance, language, image, and sound in its desire to break open fixed codes of meaning, ripping through representational common sense with explosions of nonsense and surprise.[74]

Performing sociology, as *Panic Diaries* attempts to do, as a noticeably social fiction, insisting on the materiality of a social science text as a powerfully fictive representation of the real, is not only a challenge to social science's disciplined desire to represent its own data-driven, causal story as "the singularly real one."[75] It is not only a refusal to compose "as with rosary beads a religion of cause and effect bound to a narrative ordering of reality."[76] It is not only an attempt to turn the social sciences toward "the unconscious processes upon which they depend but that they disavow in the narrative construction of their authority as empirical sciences."[77] It is not simply a strategy to foreground how the borders between science and literature, fact and fiction, evidence and affect, social reality and psychic fantasy are far more permeable than "normal" social science wants to recognize. It is not only about social science.

Performing sociology is also and most immediately about critical, creative responses to struggles over what gets to count as, and who gets to make, public knowledge and collective memory. Performative writing stages itself within and on the side of a politics of representation that attends to the epistemological demands from gendered, racialized, colonized, dis-eased, class-ified, and sexualized bodies for a rewriting and representing of the social that incorporates excluded histories and subjugated knowings. How can we "rattle the buried bones. . . . How can we write about what has been erased? . . . Dare we do otherwise?" asks Jennifer Natalya Fink in *Performing Hybridity* (1999).[78] Experiments with style or selective remixings of history, memory, poetry, dream, theory, and story attempt to tie intricate knots between the production of knowledge and the place of not knowing, of not possessing the "singularly real story" in the face of so many historically specific silences. So many real symptoms of buried bones, rattling barely.

Experiments with social science writing — including the one you hold in your hands — can also be read as one response to the shifting sociologics of technoscientific cultures. New techniques and technologies of communicative power, from radar and radio to television, computers, satellite technologies, and military weaponry, usher in new modes of social reality, as well as the necessity of new languages and methods for understanding those realities.[79] Describing Cold War nuclear culture, Paul Edwards writes: "Simulations became more real than reality itself, as the nuclear standoff evolved into an entirely abstract war of position. Simulations — computer models, war games, statistical analysis . . . [had] more political significance and more cultural impact than the weapons that could not be used."[80] How to represent such radical shifts in the technosocial construction of what's real? "What mode of knowledge production," Avery Gordon wonders, "is possible and adequate in the postmodern world?" How to rethink our "storytelling device[s] . . . in a world where the real is no longer self-evident, . . . [where we] must question the boundaries separating truth from delusion, the fact from the artifact, the visible from the invisible, science from literature"?[81]

Reading cybernetics and *its* stories as potent (social) science fictions of what's real, with probability functions and information patterns composing new im/materialities of social communication and control, Donna Haraway observes: "The entire universe of objects that can be known scientifically must be formulated as problems in communications engineering (for the managers) or theories of the text (for those who would resist)."[82] What theories—and practices—of the social science text might have a fighting chance to communicate these emergent technosocial stories, while resisting the technosocial logics of control in which they are embedded? "Cyborg politics" becomes "the struggle for language and the struggle against perfect communication, against the one code that translates all meaning perfectly."[83] What practices of language, what creative countercodes, can cut through the dominant communicative patterns structuring contemporary power and perceptions?

This book is no perfect answer to such questions. But the stylistic composition of *Panic Diaries*—its commitment to performative writing as one possible, one imperfectly political, form of social science scholarship[84]—is as much a part of the story I tell here as the historical plotlines. It is an extended experiment with social science writing as also a literary project. "By writing," writes the filmmaker and feminist theorist Trinh T. Minh-ha, "one situates oneself vis-à-vis both society and the nature of literature, that is to say, the tools of creation."[85] Performing sociology as a creative project helps to stage the social as creative force. If society is always "more or less a work of art," could sociology really be anything else?[86]

Performance, Peggy Phelan asserts, is a "complex technology."[87] Throughout the book, I engage technologies of performance in a number of ways. "Performing writing" as a material practice, I experiment in several places in the text with techniques of collage/montage writing. Rooted in the disruptions of Dada and surrealism (and incorporated today into all kinds of popular culture forms, including advertising and prime-time TV shows), collage can be one performative strategy for telling *more than one story at a time*, bringing together on the same textual surface — and outside the common sense or sensations of linear time — pieces of history, fiction, ethnography, dream, and autobiography in a noticeably constructed, suggestively *surr*eal evocation of social realities. Effective collage can "shock patterns of connection into quite different patterning,"[88] tearing gaps in a "seemingly seamless social ordering of perception."[89] Effective collage is also affective, opening up emotional, sometimes contagious, not fully conscious forms of feeling.

At the same time, I use metaphors of performance to describe the techniques and technologies developed by twentieth-century social science to produce or "perform" its objects of study. Acts of operationalizing, miniaturizing, abstracting, standardizing, quantifying, simulating, and modeling are profoundly performative acts conducted, across the last century, in increasingly well-funded theaters of empiricism with increasingly exclusive rights to stage the most valued (social) science fictions. As the role of technoscientific practices like information theory and computer modeling grows more central to knowledge production, the performed features of probabilistic, simulated, or statistically aggregated objects only grow — more dramatic.

Finally, most complexly perhaps, panic is performed throughout this text as an affective and historical, fictive and real, social theater to which I find myself somewhat repetitiously, rather traumatically, drawn. Here, over and over, in a perpetual present tense that trauma and the space of performance both share, I rewrite a psychic distress in the context of a social dis-ease. Act against the silencing of barely speakable stories by the technobabble of a normalizing cure. Search for the archival detail accumulated at the scene of this historical accident, this panicked body.

Let me end with a brief staging of each chapter.

Chapter 2 opens with a story of the "panic broadcast," a 1938 radio performance of H. G. Wells's fictional *The War of the Worlds* that reportedly gives rise to a nationwide panic. In new state-sponsored theaters of empiricism, collective panic is first taught how to speak through the language and technique of a rational social scientific method. But how rational is the drive for control over the unconscious, affective terror of social groups? How scientific is the subject of social science as he tracks his panicky object from the marketplace of radio broadcasting into the militarized zones of world war? What stories of emergent technosocial terrors get lost in the noise of new empirical methods for social psychological control?

Chapter 3 takes place in the crucible of the Cold War culture of the United States. Using collage as a performative writing strategy throughout, I cut and splice together a story of the spread of technoscientific anxieties in the atomic age; the rise of cybernetic social systems theory in the work of the sociologist Talcott Parsons; the proliferation of empirical research and systematic theories of collective panic; and the story of Anne Parsons, a social scientist and the daughter of Talcott Parsons, who researches mental disease until she herself starts panicking at the peak of Cold War tensions. In a spin of mimetic identifications and emotional contagions, I try to write myself into and out of this maddening history that I seem never fully able to possess. However much it seems to possess me.

Chapters 4 and 5 turn from a focus on collective panic to "individualized" panic disorder, with cybernetics offering one technoscientific bridge between them. Chapter 4 begins with a scene of the psychiatric treatment of traumatized World War II soldiers, passes through the science fiction of the cyborg (first conceived in 1960 by two psychiatric researchers at a state mental institution), and ends in 1969 with a cybernetic theory of mental disorders and their pharmacological control. In between lies a history of postwar U.S. psychiatry, moving out of the mental asylum and into the general public as the mass treatment and prevention of mental disorders becomes a government-sponsored mandate. With the help of cybernetics, psychiatry starts to learn how to perform the necessary abstractions for establishing the science fictions of its own psychiatric language.

Chapter 5, also composed as an extended collage, takes place largely within contemporary medicalized and market-driven theaters of individualized terror. Notes from the diary I keep as a research subject in a clinical drug trial for Xanax cut into a story of the technosocial construction of panic disorder. Embodied in the abstractions of a scientific psychiatry, swallowing pills on my way to some other form of cure, I perform the role of a sick woman within the integrating circuits of the transnational drug industry, standardized and computerized practices of psychiatric research and diagnosis, and a still wildly suggestive social.

2

The Martian in the Machine:
Panic Theory and Theaters of War

PROFESSOR PIERSON: As I set down these notes on paper, I'm obsessed by the thought that I may be the last living man on earth. [...] All that happened before the arrival of these monstrous creatures in the world now seems part of another life. [...] My wife, my colleagues, my students, my books, my observatory, my . . . my world . . . where are they? Did they ever exist? [...] I keep watch at the window. From time to time I catch sight of a Martian above the black smoke.— *The War of the Worlds*[1]

When the Other falls out of the starry sky into the chasms of the psyche, the "subject" is obviously obliged to stake out new boundaries for his field of implantation and to re-ensure—otherwise, elsewhere—his dominance. . . . But how to tame these uncharted territories, these dark continents, these worlds through the looking glass? How to master . . . these moving phantoms of the unconscious, when a long history has taught you to seek out and desire only clarity, the clear perception of (fixed) ideas? Perhaps this is the time to stress *technique* again?—LUCE IRIGARAY[2]

Ground zero is at Grovers Mill. At 8:50 P.M., on Sunday, October 30, **a huge flaming object** reportedly falls out of the sky and lands in a farmer's field just outside Trenton, New Jersey.[3] Only minutes earlier, Professor Pierson, the famous astronomer at work in his observatory at Princeton, confirms reports of several explosions on the planet Mars. The Professor **describes the phenomenon as like a jet of blue flames shot from a gun**. Rushing to the scene at the Grovers Mill farm (**crowd noises . . . police sirens**), the Professor joins the radio announcer Carl Phillips, the state police, and a growing crowd of curious onlookers. The object, half buried in the ground, looks like a huge metal cylinder and emits **a curious humming sound**.

Suddenly, without warning, the top of the cylinder **is beginning to rotate like a screw**. The crowd grows silent. Peering out of the dark cylinder are **two luminous disks . . . are they eyes?** Something crawls **out of the shadow like a gray snake**. Large as a bear, it **glistens like wet leather**. Its face is **indescribable. . . . The eyes are black and gleam like a serpent. The mouth is V-shaped with saliva dripping from its rimless lips that seem to quiver and pulsate**. The crowd falls back. **They've seen enough**.

The police captain confers with Professor Pierson. **The Professor moves around one side, studying the object**, while two policemen advance toward the monster holding a white **flag of truce**.

The humming sound increases in intensity. **A humped shape is rising out of the pit**. In the darkness, **a small beam of light against a mirror** becomes visible. The crowd now sees **a jet of flame springing from that mirror**, leaping directly in the path of the advancing policemen. **It strikes them head on**. They are now **turning into flame. (Screams and unearthly shrieks.)** In seconds, the **whole field's caught fire**, the woods, the gas tanks of automobiles (**explosion**), the barns . . . **It's spreading everywhere**.

The Professor, unable to offer any **authoritative information** about the nature of the monstrous creatures, is able to identify their **mysterious weapon** as a heat ray. About which he will venture **some conjectural explanation**. Using **scientific knowledge far in advance of our own**, the creatures are capable of generating an intense heat, which they can then **project in a parallel beam against any object they choose, by means of a polished parabolic mirror of unknown composition.**

Within an hour of the appearance of the **huge flaming object**, the monster creatures — **the vanguard of an invading army from the planet Mars** whose **apparent objective is to crush resistance, paralyze communication, and disorganize human society** — destroy almost seven thousand armed men in the fields around Grovers Mill, gain control of midstate New Jersey, annihilate U.S. army bomber planes, and release a deadly black poison gas across the eastern seaboard. Highways clog with **frantic human traffic**. Bells ring out across New York City to warn of the advancing Martians. **The enemy** crosses the Passaic River and straddles the Pulaski Skyway. As additional Martian cylinders are reported landing outside Buffalo, Chicago, and St. Louis, the monsters stand towering over Manhattan, tall as skyscrapers, **lifting their metal hands** into the sky. **This is the end now. Smoke comes out. . . . black smoke, drifting over the city** . . .

. . . and the downtown tower of the Columbia Broadcasting System, where Orson Welles and the CBS Mercury Theater are just finishing up the live radio broadcast of their weekly Sunday evening show. The year is 1938. Tonight's radio play, an adaptation of H. G. Wells's novel *The War of the Worlds*, starring Orson Welles as the prosaic Professor Pierson, is about to make history.

Or at least news. "Radio Listeners in Panic, Taking War Drama as Fact," announces the *New York Times* the next morning. "Fake 'War' on Radio Spreads Panic over U.S.," reports the *Daily News*. The radio broadcast "disrupted households, interrupted religious services, created traffic jams and clogged communications systems."[4] Telephone switchboards at CBS were "swamped into uselessness," while radio and police stations nationwide reported jammed phone lines and up to a 500 percent increase in calls.[5] Stories of men, women, and children fleeing in

"I had no idea!"—Orson Welles after the panic. Photograph by Associated Press, 1938.

cars, frantic phone calls relaying the deadly news to friends and relatives, attempted suicides, hasty religious services calling for deliverance, and radio listeners treated in hospital emergency rooms for shock and hysteria circulate in the print media for days. A "lingering fascination" with the panic story is fed by continuing newspaper coverage for weeks after the event.[6]

News commentary on the panic circles around the significance of the radio public's propensity toward mass hysteria and delusion. Some herald Orson Welles and the Mercury Theater for "having made the most amazing and important of contributions to the social sciences," demonstrating the ease with which "a few effective voices, accompanied by sound effects, can so convince masses of people of a totally unreasonable, completely fantastic proposition as to create nation-wide panic."[7] Others argue for the urgent need for radio censorship. U.S. senator Clyde Herring promises to introduce a bill establishing a censorship board from which all radio programs would have to gain approval.[8] A general agreement that "radio can spread and radio can control ideas and information essential to national defense" is only the preamble to politically charged dissent over how such "defense," and radio's role in it, should be deployed.[9] Should the state protect the public from its own tremulous tendencies toward mass panic, recognizing in the control of radio airwaves the first line of national defense? Or is state control of radio itself the most lethal weapon of totalitarian government, a dangerous monopoly on such a powerfully suggestive medium? If the electrified voice of Adolf Hitler is currently scaring much of Europe to its knees with "an army and an airforce to back up his shrieking words," asks news columnist Dorothy Thompson, then what to make of Orson Welles's apparent ability to "scare thousands into demoralization with nothing at all"?[10]

But is there really "nothing at all" fatally frightening about the "panic broadcast"? Those who interpret the public reaction as a collective failure of reason emphasize the absurd content of the play (Martians in rocket ships wielding death rays), and the public's apparent inability to perform rational checks on the imaginary machinery of the radio drama (including the unlikely time span of a planetary invasion conducted in sixty terrestrial minutes). However, those who also attend to the radio play's formal properties find good reason for the panicky fright: the play effectively simulates an entirely new genre of radio broadcast, associated with military invasion and the imminent peril of civilian populations. Hadley Cantril notes that only two months earlier, during the war scare of August–September 1938, radio introduces the "emergency broadcast," with live, on-the-scene coverage of events unfolding in Europe.[11] As fascist forces threaten national borders and Europe edges toward all-out war, one of the largest audiences in the young history of U.S. radio is captivated by minute-by-minute reporting of catastrophe broadcast live by the "break-in" news bulletin interrupting regular programming, and by live eyewitness accounts from radio announcers accompanied by the background sounds of battles raging nearby.

When the Martians land on October 30, 1938, their arrival is also announced via a series of simulated "special news bulletins" interrupting a regularly scheduled music program. As the mysterious death ray quickly incinerates the New Jersey state police, the attack is reported through the eyes of an astounded on-the-scene radio announcer. The scriptwriter who transformed H. G. Wells's novel into a radio play reported that he was instructed to "dramatize it in the form of news bulletins."[12] News of the Martian invasion is communicated to an audience tuned in not only to the radio play's plotline but to its form; part of the play's plot is expressed through its form. The role of formal technique in fooling the radio audience does not escape CBS, which proclaims in the days after the panic: "In order that this may not happen again, the Program Department hereafter will not use the technique of a simulated news broadcast within a dramatization when the circumstances of the broadcast could cause immediate alarm to numbers of listeners."[13]

Whatever the power of such simulated technique, and however frightening the Mercury Theater's *The War of the Worlds* really was for many listeners, the effects of the broadcast are not only terrifying. Public opinion, at first loudly critical of CBS and Orson Welles, seems to reverse itself in the following days.[14] Over 90 percent of the 1,400 letters that pour into CBS and the Mercury Theater after the show are favorable. Most notably, the audience size almost doubles for the following Sunday night's CBS radio drama.[15] Soon Orson Welles packs up the Mercury Theater players, heading to Hollywood and a legendary career in cinema. If the "panic broadcast" is an exemplary instance of mass suggestion in all its irrational power and imaginary contagion, then clearly for a significant portion of the U.S. public, such phantasmatic theater is not all a bad thing. In fact, and in fiction, and perhaps in the trembling border between them . . . it is a pleasure.

Two features of this phantasmatic theater mark its particular and unprecedented staging within the new medium of radio. First, the radio audience constitutes a new configuration of shared social space, redrawing academic conceptions and cultural experiences of the social group. The "crowd" that hears the CBS version of *The War of the Worlds* is spatialized in a geographic register that reaches as far as the radio waves' legislated frequency and sites of reception. The mobilization of social imaginations and of collective perceptions within this newly constituted crowd are only just taking heterogeneous form in 1938. Techniques for predicting, measuring, and controlling such collective mobilization are in their infancy. This "dispersed crowd," an emergent form of an electronically mediated group, is only just beginning to assemble within the abstract architectures of signal, broadcast, and reception.[16] How this crowd will move between its abstract circuiting and other social spaces—and to what imaginary and political effect—is a wildly open question.

A second, related feature of this new social theater is its trafficking in new forms of mass-mediated suggestion. "The power of mass suggestion is the most potent force today," commentary on the radio-induced panic cautions.[17] With the coming of radio broadcast, the specter of a truly "mass" suggestion emerges with a new urgency. How would electronic modes of address alter or amplify the power of images or charismatic figures to mobilize collective actions and perceptions? How would the phantasmatic fields of suggestion be transformed when events, both fictional and real, could be projected to a mass audience in an abstractly shared social space via new technologies of representation? Could rationality and the imperatives of reason withstand the mass illusions or delusions made more likely, and more mass(ive), by the senses and sensations excited through the new broadcast media?

And so in the historical shadow cast by the CBS Mercury Theater's spectacular performance, we can begin, perhaps, to perceive a **humped shape rising out of the pit**.[18] Indeed, in the somewhat hysterical shadow cast by the Shadow, the haunting radio personality created by Orson Welles in the years before his role as Professor Pierson, we can dimly make out this unprecedented crowd of human bodies pressing toward a nationwide panic, **their silhouettes standing out** against the surface of the mysterious object. What really is this strange new object, and what hold does it exert over its fascinated crowd? And what of the **mysterious weapon**—able to **project in a parallel beam** an intense light reflected off a **mirror of unknown composition**—that resides inside this object? What enemy lives within? What *is* the Martian in this machine? A new fear encased in an old story of monsters wielding magical, murderous weapons? Or an old fear encoded in a new frequency, exciting strange electronic fields of as-yet-uncharted human motion?

And could the Professor now please offer **some conjectural explanation** about **the origin of** this unsettling outbreak of panic?

Every science must constitute its object of study; indeed, that is its most fundamental achievement. — DONNA HARAWAY[19]

The social group does not exist as a real entity, but must be transformed into one. Social relationships can be understood causally; they . . . can eventually be expressed in laws. Once this is understood, the social group can be spoken of as a real entity, that is, it can become the object to be scientifically explained. — ROBERT E. PARK[20]

In the early decades of the twentieth century, theories of panic cohere around the "doctrine of suggestion" and its centrality to understanding crowd and collective behavior. Suggestion, imitation, primitive sympathy, emotional contagion — this cluster of related terms speculatively stakes out the very stuff of the social group as a youthful U.S. social science attempts to simultaneously configure the definitive nature of the "social" and a convincing "science" for its study.[21] With the crowd serving as an observable field of specifically social interactions, crowd "suggestibility" becomes a favored explanation for collective motivations and movements. For sociologist Robert E. Park, whose writings profoundly shape the field of collective behavior, the "suggestive influence" is the essential feature of the crowd, enabling its "dynamic reciprocity." According to Park, "It is because of this widespread occurrence of crowd suggestion that collective psychology can claim the status of an explanatory social science."[22] Suggestion's mutual infection of thought and feeling, and its intensification of emotional and mental states through the medium of social interaction, are the causal mechanisms that can define a crowd as a homogeneous unit accessible to scientific explanation.

What is the nature of this so-very-social suggestion, and the crowd that moves by its contagious laws? Located in the elusive in-between of individual and group interaction, suggestion is often described by analogy with the individual's experience of hypnosis and the dream, the disassociation of consciousness connected with hysteria, somnambulism, and the spell. In a chapter devoted to suggestibility in *Social Psychology* (1908), the sociologist Edward A. Ross, quoting the influential crowd psychologist Boris Sidis, asserts that "abnormal suggestibility is a disaggregation of consciousness, a slit, a scar, produced in the mind, a crack that may extend wider and deeper, ending at last in the total disjunction of the waking, guiding, controlling consciousness from . . . the rest of the stream of life."[23] Relayed repeatedly in discussions of individual psychology through the language of the abnormal and the pathological, the concept of suggestion in social psychology describes instead a fundamental, even causal, feature of the social bond. The very foundation of the social appears oddly dependent on the most dangerous, disruptive features of individual consciousness.

This peculiar positioning of suggestion as a kind of necessary psychopathology of the social group can be traced back to the writings of Gustave Le Bon, whose enormously influential *The Crowd: A Study of the Popular Mind* (1895), published in the same year as Freud and Breuer's *Studies on Hysteria*, becomes a touchstone for subsequent theories of collective psychology.[24] Le Bon's crowd is the site of the individual's transformation into a "state of fascination," like that of a hypnotized subject, in which emotional volatility, cathexis to a powerful leader or image, and contagious communication with others combine to create nothing less than a "hypnotic order" and mental uniformity that exhibit entirely new psychological characteristics.[25]

This mental psychology of the crowd, or "the group mind," as William McDougall terms it, unifies and homogenizes individuals in the crowd at precisely the cost of that feature of individuality which presumably integrates and unifies *it*, that is, individual consciousness. The crowd embodies an ambivalent tension: the potential pathology of the individual constitutes the very possibility of the social in its formation as a crowd or collectivity. And the explicitly irrational character of suggestion supplies the unifying, interactive mechanism producing the "social" as an object for rational explanation and social scientific observation. The image of the crowd that emerges from this conceptual knot is a contradictory one: the crowd is consistently associated with an array of pathologized "others" — neurotic, feminine, "primitive," and racialized others, the mass of working classes and the poor — while also expressing the most celebrated features of a nationalist unity, naturalized through hereditary notions of "the race" or "the group mind."[26] And while emblematizing the potent unity of national culture, the crowd simultaneously embodies a persistent uncivil threat to that very unity in its capacity for revolutionary fervor or ecstatic, collective disobedience to the rules of reason and law.[27]

Within these theoretical stagings of suggestion and the crowd, the problem of collective panic takes shape. Explanations are built along the conceptual fault lines of a divide structured by differing notions of the boundaries of the "social" itself. For Le Bon, panic is a clear example of that "contagious power as intense as that of microbes" which takes possession of and defines the "psychological crowd."[28] For William McDougall, too, the group panic "is the crudest and simplest example of collective mental life." Operating according to the "principle of primitive sympathy" in which the "direct induction or contagion" of emotion is responsible for the communication of collective affect, panic is the outcome of the social interaction between group members: "Each man perceives on every hand the symptoms of fear, the blanched distorted faces . . . and the screams of terror of his fellows; and with each such perception his own impulse and his own emotion rise to a higher pitch of intensity."[29]

But for Sigmund Freud in his theory of group psychology, the terrified actions of a group in panic delineate the vanishing point of a social bond forged through the power of suggestion. Taking McDougall to task for embracing "the paradoxical position that [the] group mind does away with itself in one of its most striking manifestations," Freud insists that a collective panic emerges at the moment when the essential libidinal ties of the social group disintegrate. In the blank face of a disappearing sociality, panic takes hold when "mutual ties have ceased to exist, and a gigantic and senseless dread is set free."[30] Far from being the outcome of a contagious fear passing through a collectivity bound together by suggestion, panic, for Freud, is the effect of a breakdown of the necessary bindings that enable the energetic transfer of emotions within a group; it is the absence, not the emergence, of a collective or social psychology. Robert Park agrees, writing that the "masses seized by panic" are closer to the behavior of an animal herd than to the vicissitudes of a collective psychological process.[31]

The divide measuring these differing notions of panic cuts a critical difference between conceptions of suggestion and the social: can the power of suggestion not only create the social group but also annihilate it? Does a group in panic mark the limit or the effect of suggestion's bind-ing social force? To paraphrase Freud's skeptical query: can the social do away with itself in one of its most powerful acts of sociality? And finally, for the aspiring social scientist, can the very phenomenon that makes his inquiry a scientific endeavor — the causal force of suggestibility — simul-taneously destroy the social object that it founds and makes possible?

Robert E. Park offers one escape route for saving the social from the threat of its own essentially "suggestible" self. The power of *facts*, Park argues, can transform the dangerously suggestible actions of the crowd into the normatively bound conversations of the "public." Conceiving of suggestibility as a form of communication that constitutes the crowd, he suggests that the public can be constituted by a "new method of commu-nication": the social construction and exchange of facts.[32]

A fact, Park writes in 1904, "is a new concept."[33] It is the concept he uses to explain the collective psychological process by which individuals come to have shared meanings about particular objects or events, mean-ings that develop into "public opinion." Facts "take the place of concrete reality," substituting instead "an ideally constructed object . . . which is equally acceptable for all members of the group." The ideally constructed object represented by a fact enables each individual member of the pub-lic to make "a purely theoretical interpretation of things . . . one that is free from individual values," and these purely ideal and theoretical things make possible the kinds of communication that compose public opinion. The public then attempts to base its behavior on these "abstract views" about the interpretation of things and thereby "subjects itself to abstract norms." Once these abstract norms are generally accepted, they "func-tion as a new force in collective life, and it is precisely this new force which is active in the public but not in the crowd."[34]

Thus, concludes the Professor, to be a member of a crowd, one must be able to feel and be moved. But to be a member of the public, the "con-ditions are somewhat more exacting" — one must also be able to "think and reason with others." For one to do so, an unconditional acceptance of the "norms of logic" is required.[35]

Indeed, in constructing the facts of suggestion and the crowd, the emergent subject of social science can be seen striving to persuasively establish his own norms of logic, his own methodical procedures for thinking and reasoning, in public, with others. If, as the Professor suggests, "Suggestion is a *process of communication* resulting in the acceptance with conviction of the communicated proposition in the absence of logically adequate grounds for its acceptance,"[36] then we can clearly see the efforts of early-twentieth-century social science to find its own logically adequate grounds for communicating—outside the contagions of suggestion—about suggestion, panic, and the social group. We can watch carefully the struggle to create a reasonable social scientific subject through the formation of an abstract socio-logical method that produces reasonable truths about its social scientific object.

OPERATION SURVEY RESEARCH

> But man only asks (himself) questions that he can already answer, using the supply of instruments he has available to assimilate even the disasters in his history. This time at any rate he is prepared to lay odds again, and, give or take a few new weapons, he will *make the unconscious into a property of his language.*—LUCE IRIGARAY[37]

> Fortunately the first Martian machine landed only a few miles from the source of the investigation.—HADLEY CANTRIL[38]

Ground zero is at Grovers Mill, and eight miles away at Princeton University, Professor Hadley Cantril is about to see a landmark study in social psychology fall out of the sky and into his . . . field. *The Invasion from Mars: A Study in the Psychology of Panic* (1940) is made possible, Cantril observes, by the "unexpected 'experimental' situation" provided by the 1938 *War of the Worlds* radio broadcast.[39] The study is conducted by Cantril and the staff of the Princeton Radio Research Project. *Invasion from Mars* investigates the underlying social and psychological causes of the panic and offers general insights into "how the common man reacts in a time of stress and strain."[40] Based on two nationwide statistical surveys and 135 interviews with residents in and around Grovers Mill, New Jersey, where the fictional Martian ship reportedly landed, the study is also a self-conscious attempt to develop reliable empirical research methods appropriate to the field of social psychology.

Introduced by Cantril as "the first panic that has been carefully studied with the research tools now available," *Invasion from Mars* is written in part for an audience of professional social scientists. But published together with the full script of Howard Koch's radio adaptation of *The War of the Worlds*, the book is also directed at a broader public. *Time* magazine's review of the book, accompanied by a photograph of the handsome, bespectacled Cantril, gives a popular gloss to the study's ambitions: "Dr. Cantril and associates went after known survivors of the Sunday nightmare with a questionnaire many times as nosy as a census blank. In addition to straightforward questions about the incident, the project's interviewers asked people about Mars, rocket ships, religion, superstitions, job security, education, year and make of car."[41] In its third printing by Princeton University Press by 1952, *Invasion from Mars* successfully blends the academic pretension to educate with the popular desire to be entertained. And as an early instance of the use of survey techniques on the general public to represent and explain the social behavior of that public to itself, the study holds a significant place in the history of U.S. social science research.

Particular knowledge about Mars which could be applied to the broadcast (get general concept of Mars). Do you think it is possible that there is some form of life on Mars comparable to ours? Very possible . . . . . Slightly possible . . . . . Not at all . . . . . No opinion . . . . .[42]

Cantril's investigation of the nature and causes of the 1938 panic comes at a propitious moment for the field of social psychology. Since the earlier theories of suggestion by Ross, Park, Freud, and McDougall, social psychologists have grown increasingly dissatisfied with the quasi-mystical allusions subtending the "group mind" and its collectively contagious unconscious. Along with other social sciences in the United States in the interwar years, social psychology is searching for more empirically grounded methods of research and less reliance on speculative and empirically unsubstantiated theory.[43] Research on panic, in particular, has been hampered by the difficulty in systematically studying panic behavior or obtaining reliable reports from participants or observers. As sociologist Richard LaPiere laments in *Collective Behavior* (1938), "Sociological and sociopsychological concern with the panic type of collective interaction is . . . scattered and fragmentary; and there is practically no technical literature on the subject."[44]

What are the three things you are most afraid of? Have you ever had to manage a complicated situation? Yes . . . . . No . . . . . What major catastrophe do you picture as possible to the American people?

Cantril's study of the Martian panic is perfectly positioned to contribute to a growing confidence that social psychology can develop an array of methodological techniques for more accurately measuring and systematically explaining collective behavior — even collective outbreaks, like panic, that seem mired in the elusive realm of the nonrational, the unconscious, or the spontaneous. While acknowledging the unique conditions surrounding this episode of panic, Cantril also wants to identify what "from a psychological point of view, might make this the prototype of any panic."[45] The study's significance rests, then, not only on its theorization of panic and its demonstration of new "research tools" for social psychology but also on its "educational implications" for average citizens: "If they can see why some people reacted unintelligently in this instance, they may be able to build up their resistance to similar occurrences." When people are caught in a real crisis, "the information recorded here may help them make a more satisfactory adjustment."[46]

The importance of achieving a "satisfactory adjustment" to stressful circumstances through an informed judgment is heightened, for Cantril, by the emergence of radio. The potential of this new medium "for informing all segments of a population of current happenings, for arousing in them a common sense of fear or joy and for enciting them to similar reactions" leads to the unprecedented formation of a new kind of social collectivity, in which social crises can be rapidly communicated and broadly constituted.[47] Noting that 27.5 million out of 32 million families in the United States have radios, a larger number than have telephones, plumbing, cars, or electricity, Cantril argues that the radio audience composes "the most modern type of social group" in existence. "The radio audience consists essentially of thousands of small, congregate groups united in time and experiencing a common stimulus — altogether making possible the largest grouping of people ever known."[48] The attempt to educate this "most modern type of social group" toward common practices of critical judgment and rational interpretation as a prophylactic against collective irrational behavior is an explicit aim of Cantril's *The Invasion from Mars*. "Since the panic arose essentially from an error in judgment," a key element of the analysis becomes the core features of sound judgment, or the nature of "critical ability." In contrast to those with the critical ability to interpret the broadcast as a fantastic drama, those who panicked were unable to "distinguish between fiction and reality."[49]

Identifying the conditions giving rise to an inability to recognize the difference between reality and fiction becomes Cantril's central task. The danger of having one of the "largest groupings of people ever known" populated by those who fail to differentiate accurately between theater and real life is a challenge the Professor is compelled to take on.

---

1. How did you happen to know that it was a play? 2. Did you doubt for any time after you had tuned in that it was a play? Yes . . . . . No . . . . . 3. If doubted: At what part of the program was it? a. Why just then? b. What made you certain that it was a play after all?

The problem of the public's propensity for mass panic circles back to social psychology's early concern about the nature of the "public" and its relation to suggestion. Robert Park's conception of the public as a social group distinguished from the crowd by its individualizing tendencies, its distance from suggestibility, and its exchange of agreed-on "facts" isn't shared by all. Edward Ross, drawing on the popular work of the French writer Gabriel Tarde, argues in 1908 that technologies of mass communication can circulate the unconscious effects of suggestion throughout the new "mass" of a dispersed public, spreading even farther and faster than in the fleshy proximities of a crowd. Writing before the advent of radio, Ross argues: "Presence is not essential to mass suggestion. Mental touch is no longer bound up with physical proximity. With the telegraph to collect and transmit the expressions and signs of the ruling mood . . . remote people are brought, as it were, into one another's presence. Through its organs the excited public is able to assail the individual with a mass of suggestions almost as vivid as if he actually stood in the midst of an immense crowd."[50]

"Contagion without contact" is Ross's expression for the kind of mental touch made possible by the new communications media.[51] Far from constituting a radical difference from the crowd, the public is, for Ross, a social group subject to the same phantasmatic force of suggestion. And the dispersion of the crowd into the far-flung reaches of the public through the "space-annihilating devices" of the new media promotes the spread of suggestive influence across a much broader social field.[52]

---

2. A. How did you find out that it was a play? a. Detailed account of respondent's reaction. (How soon did he check, at what point of program, why just then, who made the check, what sort of checks were they, what did the checks made or offered contribute to his reaction? Why did he not make any checks?) b. What did you do when you thought it was true?

Cantril's investigation begins by measuring the reach of the "mental touch" of Orson Welles's radio theater. Using figures from two national surveys, Cantril estimates that 6 million people were listening on October 30, 1938, to the CBS broadcast.[53] According to the Gallup poll, 28 percent of that 6 million—approximately 1.7 million people—believed at some point that they were listening to a "real news report" of an apparent Martian invasion. Of that group, 70 percent, or about 1.2 million people, were "frightened or disturbed" by the news they were hearing. This ready "confus[ion] of fiction with reality" by frightened listeners becomes the subject of the Professor's next methodological step: classifying listeners who at some point believed the radio play was real into four subgroups, according to their differing abilities to properly interpret reality versus theater.[54]

Religious beliefs, *Weltanschauung*. Do you believe that God can and does control events on this earth? Yes..... No..... No opinion..... Does man's life on this earth seem to you meaningless, temporary, futile, etc.?

The classification is derived from an analysis of the 135 interviews with people in and around Grovers Mill who heard the Martian broadcast, conducted by four paid interviewers hired by the Princeton Radio Research Project.[55] The classification divides listeners' behavior into four categories, according to the "degrees of intelligent behavior displayed in the panic situation." Intelligent behavior, according to the Professor, is measured by "checking behavior," that is, efforts by an individual to check the available evidence for proof that her or his judgment is correct. The Professor quotes amply from the interviews to give examples of each of the four different types of behavior. One family, exhibiting the least intelligent type of behavior, reports: "We had tuned in to listen to Orson Welles but when the flashes came I thought it was true. . . . Then I called in to my husband: 'Dan, why don't you get dressed? You don't want to die in your working clothes.' My husband said we were here for God's glory and honor and it was for Him to decide when we should die. *We should prepare ourselves.*"[56]

Equipped with his four classificatory categories, the Professor sorts his data from both the face-to-face interviews conducted on a nonrandom sample of people in northern New Jersey, and the telephone survey of 920 audience members conducted by cbs.[57] Statistical tabulations are made of the proportion of listeners from each of the two surveys that fit into each of the four categories. The next and most complex step in the methodological process is to examine what psychological features of a person determine "into which of the four groups he will fall."[58]

General attitude toward science: Do you think it is possible that we shall sometime have rocket ships and interplanetary communication?

Having established that "critical ability," defined in part by "a general capacity to distinguish between fiction and reality," is the preeminent feature of those persons able to recognize the broadcast as theater, Cantril considers what conditions inhibit critical ability in others.[59] He concludes that the best way to describe such conditions is "what we might call susceptibility-to-suggestion-when-facing-a-dangerous-situation." In pursuit of a "realistic and appropriate measure" for susceptibility-to-suggestion, Cantril introduces a methodological innovation: by "pooling different bits of information" from each interview, an indexical measure of a general personality trait (i.e., susceptibility-to-suggestion) can be developed. The measure is based on a set of seven specific criteria. Acknowledging that the criteria were "at first intuitively selected," Cantril emphasizes that this methodological procedure "gives quantitatively reliable results." The methodological magic of his technique is explicitly noted: "By consciously reconstructing the intuitive process, an impressionistic procedure was transformed into a quantitative method." While the transformative process itself, requiring someone to code each interview for the presence or absence of each criterion, is, "to be sure, subjective," the Professor reassures any skeptics that "errors in judgment undoubtedly tended to cancel each other."[60]

Which of the following would you most like to have? (allow for three checks) Old-age security . . . . . High salary . . . . . College education for your children . . . . . Job security . . . . . Safety of investments . . . . . No war in the next fifty years . . . . . No depression in the next fifty years . . . . . Getting ahead in your profession . . . . . Having some good friends . . . . . Having a pretty home in a good neighborhood . . . . . Having more variety in living . . . . . Having a pleasant family . . . . . No major political changes in the next decades . . . . .

The Professor is aware of possible objections to his methodological procedures. Some "would argue that the assumption of a general characteristic of 'susceptibility' is merely an unscientific reification of a bundle of actually discrete elements of personality we happened to find related. This argument — contrary as it is to common sense and to evidence — is too involved to answer here completely." The Professor is confident that his technique for measuring a "general personality trait" of suggestibility reveals a concrete, quantifiable variable in the equation defining the problem of panic.[61] The technique allows him to profess, without relying on speculative theory or on his own powers of suggestion, the existence of an empirically measurable psychological feature that plays a causal role in panic. Methodically pursued, logically established, and quantitatively grounded, suggestibility can now circulate as a shared, acceptable object of social psychological inquiry.

And as a specified object of social and psychological control. In his concluding remarks, Cantril, observing the obligations of "the social scientist who is a citizen as well as a scholar," proposes how such panics may in the future be prevented. Without ignoring the significance of the sociohistorical conditions in which the panic erupted—that is, "the highly disturbed economic conditions many Americans have experienced for the past decade [and] the consequent unemployment"— Cantril nonetheless ends with a call to fortify the individual psychological architecture of critical ability. A trained and habituated critical ability would "enable people to distinguish between reality and fiction" and encourage them "to make more appropriate adjustments if they ever were caught in a genuinely critical situation." In sum, individuals must be educated in the proper methods for testing and interpreting their world: "Our study of the common man of our times has shown us that his ability to orient himself appropriately in critical situations will be increased if he can be taught to adopt an attitude of readiness to question the interpretations he hears. . . . If he is to judge these interpretations intelligently, his knowledge must be grounded in evidence or tested experience."[62]

The panic-prone public, like the methodical and methodoLOGIcally sound Professor, must adhere to the psychological habits and emotional attitudes that will encourage reason, and intelligent standards of interpretive practice. The persuasion of evidence and the power of the test— for the panic-prone public as for the Professor—must ultimately prevail.

If respondent has stated that it is *very probable* that there is life on Mars, tell him that most scientists think it very unlikely. Get reaction. If respondent has stated that it is *scarcely* or *not at all probable* that there is life on Mars, tell him that some eminent astronomers believe that there is. Get reaction.

THE THEATER OF OPERATIONS

McGafferty: And why? What's done it?
Who's behind it? That's the question gentlemen.
Things like this don't happen by themselves.
What's behind it? Who is?
—ARCHIBALD MACLEISH[63]

All can be recuperated when issued by the signifying order in place. It
is still better to speak only in riddles, allusions, hints, parables. Even
if asked to clarify a few points. Even if people plead that they just
don't understand. —LUCE IRIGARAY[64]

They say the dead can't speak, but I have a few questions. In search of
some answers, I took a plane to New York City and a train up the Hudson River, then a cab to the archives of the Rockefeller Foundation. This
seemed appropriate. The Rockefellers made their fortune by controlling
nationwide transportation systems and supplying the oil to fuel them.[65]
That is, they learned how to profit from moving things around in indus-
trialized, industrial-size ways. Apparently they were rather good at this.
Today you can find three separate definitions in the dictionary for the
meaning of "Rockefeller." One for John Davison. One for Nelson Aldrich.
And one for Winthrop.[66] This, to me, is a measure of a certain worldly success. Another measure is that when you ask these men questions, even if
they're dead, they still want to give you answers. This is one possible definition of one kind of archive: a place where very successful dead people
continue to speak, to tell their stories.

   And a place where they continue to keep their secrets. The Rockefeller
archives hold documents that speak not about what the businesses run
by the Rockefellers did but about what the charitable, or philanthropic,
branch of their corporate empire did. So very successful dead people who
are listed in the dictionary with multiple meanings not only want to help
answer certain questions after they're dead, but don't want to answer
others. They don't, for example, want to give people access to stories that
might explain their business activities, decisions, deals, ambitions, and
their consequences.[67] This power of the powerful to continue speaking or
to remain silent after death partially structures the chatter of skulls I hear
with my ear to the archives.

   So what are the questions I'm raising? For the dead? I want to know
what were the major causes not of the 1938 panic broadcast but of the research that takes the national panic as its object. What conditions made
possible Hadley Cantril's *The Invasion from Mars*, this strange genre of
social science fiction, part radio play, part methodological drama nar-
rating the need for more rational interpretive practices among the U.S.

public? How was the stage set for this debut performance of a quantifiable, indexical measure of suggestibility? What was the Princeton Radio Research Project, and why was it interested in *The War of the Worlds*? Who were the offstage players in this new theater of empiricism, this emergent methodo-LOGICS of U.S. social psychology?

In his funding proposal to the Rockefeller Foundation in 1937, Hadley Cantril, professor of psychology at Princeton University's School for International and Public Affairs, professes the need for "an objective analysis" of the "basic human factors" shaping the value of radio for different groups of listeners. In contrast to market research studies conducted by commercial organizations on the size and tastes of radio audiences, research on why different people listen to radio and "what its influences are on subsequent behavior" is inadequate and incomplete.[68] The project Cantril outlines would investigate radio's meaning and effects and suggest directions for future programming that can meet the different entertainment and educational needs of a multiplicity of radio audiences.

But to undertake such a project successfully, the development of new research techniques is essential. Cantril outlines a four-year research program in which the first two years would be devoted primarily to establishing the methodological procedures necessary to "define radio listening in quantitative terms." He explains: "To achieve the ultimate aims desired in this study, new methods must be devised and tested to procure the answers to our problems. In spite of the research already completed in this field, *the creation of new techniques adequate for the requirements* has lagged"; if research is "to penetrate into new fields," scientifically proven methodological innovations must pave the way.[69] Citing as one of the key methodological problems the difficulty of evaluating the reliability and validity of listeners' answers to questions about why they listen, Cantril suggests a nine-step research technique (using experimental and control groups of listeners) whose reliability can be tested and measured. The final two years of the study, he proposes, would involve the application of these techniques in a broad survey of radio listening in the general population.

In April 1937 the Rockefeller Foundation awards $67,000 to fund the first two years of what will come to be called the Princeton Radio Research Project. The project's activities from September 1937 to August 1939 are to be aimed at "developing and testing techniques by which evidence needed to answer" basic questions about the role of radio can be secured.[70]

If one strength of Cantril's project is its commitment to expanding the methods and aims of radio research beyond the commercially driven interests of the radio broadcast industry, the project and the methods it promises to develop are at the same time deeply indebted to the industry and its market research agenda. Frank Stanton, director of audience research at the Columbia Broadcasting System (CBS), coauthors the Rockefeller proposal with Cantril, and the two originally plan to direct the project together.[71] (Stanton, hired by CBS in 1935 as the first Ph.D. to work for the radio industry, wrote his dissertation on methods of investigating "radio listening behavior" and joined CBS just as the company became interested in market research as a technique for convincing advertisers to buy airtime — the research division was in fact located in CBS's department of sales and promotion.)[72] The research proposal also enjoys the support of George Gallup, a personal friend of Cantril's and already a luminary figure in the new field of public opinion polling, which is methodologically tied to consumer surveys and market research. Gallup writes a letter of support to the Rockefeller Foundation urging their sponsorship of the Cantril-Stanton project.[73]

Finally, the research proposal is reviewed and approved by the Federal Radio Education Committee (FREC), composed of three representatives from the radio broadcast industry and three nationally prominent educators, which adopts the project as part of their own sponsored research series.[74] Professor Hadley Cantril is actually one of the six members of the FREC committee, and he turns to Rockefeller Foundation funding only after the FREC itself fails in its efforts to secure sufficient funding from the radio industry for its research agenda.[75]

The origins of the Princeton Radio Research Project involve, then, a hybrid mix of academic, state, and industry-sponsored research initiatives, financially backed by corporate philanthropic foundation money. Who will guide this fledgling research project and negotiate its multiple constituencies? Frank Stanton and Hadley Cantril both decide against leading the project, just months before its launching. In August 1937, Paul Lazarsfeld, a young Viennese intellectual who first came to the United States in 1933 on a Rockefeller Foundation fellowship, accepts the job.

Lazarsfeld, trained as a mathematician and founder in Vienna of the Research Center for Economic Psychology, brings to the Princeton Radio Research Project a passionate interest in the development of social science methods that can combine the laws of large numbers with the interpretation of individual behavior.[76] He is also a pioneer in conducting academic research that piggybacks financially and methodologically on market research. His research institute in Vienna carried out consumer research on coffee, beer, shoes, and chocolate while developing innovative techniques of interview design and cross-tabulation. In a speech as new director of the Princeton Radio Research Project, Lazarsfeld refers to the market research done by commercial U.S. broadcasters as "a body of data which in its comprehensiveness and importance is almost comparable to vital statistics and certainly is larger than that at the disposal of any other field of social research."[77] The financial difficulties of gathering such large bodies of data for statistical research can partly be mitigated by joining forces with an industry that is actively pursuing related research in its effort to target the largest mass market yet to emerge: the national radio audience. The development of market research in the United States is inextricably tied to the radio broadcast industry and to the methodological techniques for a "science of mass communication" with which Lazarsfeld's name is today associated.[78]

Statistical techniques for interpreting quantifiable mass data are only half of Lazarsfeld's passion, and only half of the Princeton Radio Research's Project's early methodological agenda. It is the interaction of these data with the language of the individual case study that constitutes the challenge for academic social science as it seeks to develop the field of audience research techniques opened up by the industry. For Lazarsfeld, this means experimenting with ways to combine individual interview material with systematic, statistical analysis in an ambitious program that can elaborate on and supersede market research techniques.[79] This mixing of qualitative and quantitative methods could help address a "crucial problem" of radio research: how to know under what conditions the information obtained from "a great number of subjective statements of masses of people" can be of value to social science.[80] If the aims of research are to understand the reasons for people's listening and the effects of listening on their subsequent behavior, then can valid methods for answering such questions be discovered, given the necessity of relying in part on the subjective responses of listeners?

By Sunday evening, October 30, 1938, the Princeton Radio Research Project's answer to that question is a definitive yes. Ground zero of the Orson Welles broadcast appears to fall securely within the methodological grasp of a social psychology pursuing empirically rigorous procedures funded by corporate philanthropy, bolstered by the broadcast industry's market research techniques, and authorized by the U.S. federal government.

Curiously, ground zero for the Martian landing rests propitiously, almost perfectly, within the geographical and institutional nexus of the Princeton Radio Research Project. The imaginary Martian machine lands a mere eight miles away from Princeton University, where Hadley Cantril and the small staff of the Princeton Radio Research Project are located. Frank Stanton, who continues to collaborate actively with the project, is situated in the research department at CBS, home of Orson Welles's Mercury Theater and the radio broadcast of *The War of the Worlds*. On the morning after the show, Paul Lazarsfeld phones Stanton with an immediate request for money from the CBS research budget to fund a study on the national panic.[81] In the following week, the CBS research department carries out two statistical surveys, including a national telephone survey of 920 listeners who heard the show.[82] Herta Herzog, Lazarsfeld's wife and a full-time researcher for the Princeton Radio Research Project, conducts a pilot study of the panic three days after the broadcast at the site of ground zero; her study contributes to the design of the questionnaire used over the next three weeks for the 135 in-depth interviews with people in and around Orange, New Jersey, who were frightened by the radio broadcast.[83] The interviews are conducted by four fieldworkers for the Princeton Radio Research Project with emergency funds provided by the Rockefeller Foundation's General Education Board.[84] Finally, George Gallup and his American Institute of Public Opinion conduct their own national public opinion survey on reactions to the panic broadcast.[85]

The impressive empirical foundation for Hadley Cantril's *The Invasion from Mars* comes from these multiple studies, and from the immediate mobilization of resources already tightly ringed around the site of the Martian landing. With all the pieces of a successful study in place, many of them already in position before the panic actually breaks out, the investigation of the broadcast becomes one of the most celebrated products of the first years of the Princeton Radio Research Project.[86] What interests might have motivated this tight network of academic, industry, and philanthropic attention to a Martian-inspired panic?

In Cantril's application for emergency funding for the panic study, he calls the "mass hysteria" among listeners "an almost unparalleled source of data" for the social psychologist interested in radio's effects, and also for the educator interested in the power of propaganda.[87] He suggests that the study's findings be released to the Institute for Propaganda Analysis (its full name—"A Non-profit Corporation to Help the Intelligent Citizen Detect and Analyze Propaganda"). Cantril actually sits on the advisory board of the institute, one of many social scientists in the 1930s whose interest in the new radio and communications research grows out of a concern, elaborated during the interwar years, over propaganda and new techniques of mass persuasion.[88] Although the problem of propaganda and the covert manipulation of beliefs is barely mentioned in *The Invasion from Mars*, behind the scenes of Cantril's study—and beneath its repeated concerns with the promotion of "critical ability" and "intelligent behavior"—lies the specter of mass suggestibility in the face of increasingly powerful and technologically sophisticated propaganda techniques. While Cantril's enthusiastic hope that the panic study "can become a standard reference in the field of social psychology" is no doubt sincere, it is accompanied by an ambition to produce an analysis useful to understanding and managing public susceptibility to propaganda.[89]

The study's methodological preoccupation with constructing a quantitative measure of individual suggestibility can be understood in the context of this unstated interest in propaganda's persuasive power. Paul Lazarsfeld is credited with developing the specific methodological technique used by Cantril to evaluate the personality trait called "susceptibility-to-suggestion."[90] The technique emerges out of Lazarsfeld's interest in using the individual case study to identify tendencies of statistical aggregates, enabling a cross-tabulation between suggestible personalities and other, more easily measured features of the aggregate: income, education, sex, age, et cetera. Cantril is primarily concerned to show the relative autonomy of the suggestibility trait, emphasizing, for example, its specificity as a psychological characteristic and its significant variability within different groupings by education level.[91]

But Lazarsfeld's own empirical research on suggestibility tells a different story. In *Radio and the Printed Page* (1940), sponsored by the Princeton Radio Research Project and published the same year as Cantril's *The Invasion from Mars*, Lazarsfeld describes the "new consumer of news": the radio listener, who is "more likely to be a woman than a man, more likely to live in a rural than in a metropolitan area, and, above all, is more likely to be a person on the lower economic and cultural level." Analyzing data from a CBS survey of 920 listeners of *The War of the Worlds* broadcast (an analysis not included in Cantril's study), Lazarsfeld finds listener suggestibility correlated with decreasing levels of education. Emphasizing that it is precisely this group of people who are drawn to radio rather than the newspaper as a source of news, Lazarsfeld concludes: "Of all the facts that make radio a powerful social institution, probably the most imposing one is that radio is the preferred medium of the more suggestible man."[92] Situating the problem of suggestibility within a set of variables attached to individual audience members, Lazarsfeld chooses not to address the specificities of radio as a form of mass communication, or the specific class and cultural status of radio's producers, as part of the problem of mass persuasion.

One member of the Princeton Radio Research Project, a young scholar from the Frankfurt school in Germany, does raise objections to the underlying presumptions of the research effort and the implications for an analysis of mass persuasion. Theodor Adorno, hired onto the project at the insistence of Paul Lazarsfeld to conduct a study on radio music, presents his preliminary findings to the research staff in October 1939.[93] Adorno argues against the project's approach to radio research as a study of "effects" on listeners, an approach that fails to question the structure of the radio broadcast industry, or the wider society, or the social functions of radio. This limited approach to empirical research, Adorno insists, guarantees that only a certain type of finding will be produced—one of use in manipulating the effects of radio on listeners:

It appears to me that the guiding interest behind investigations of such a character is basically one of *administrative technique*: How can a given, more or less central agency handle most successfully given groups . . . in such a way as to induce them to behave according to the aims of the central agency? The logical form of such investigations is moulded according to the ideal of a skilled manipulation of masses. Whatever its content may be, it is a type of investigation that follows essentially the pattern of market analysis even if it appears to be completely remote from any selling purpose.[94]

The problem of mass manipulation, for Adorno, rests not primarily with the social or psychological features of radio listeners but with the aims and practices of radio producers and the social and political structures in which radio is deployed. Social science researchers, including members of the Princeton Radio Research Project, whose empirical investigations contribute to an accumulation of techniques for the effective measurement and administration of the desired behaviors, are participants in the very problem they purport to study.

Theodor Adorno's work with the Radio Research Project is terminated in 1940, after Rockefeller Foundation executives reject his research reports and refuse to continue his funding.[95]

Was the Princeton Radio Research Project part of a choreographed, if not precisely conspiratorial, design to develop techniques for the mass manipulation of audience behavior? Were the methods underpinning *The Invasion from Mars* indiscernible in their desired effects, if not their stated intentions, from market research? Was protecting the U.S. public from propaganda one motive for social science's interest in early research on mass communication? Or was early radio research itself contributing to the development of techniques of propaganda and mass persuasion that best fit a capitalist society on the brink of war and in the wake of fiscal panic and depression? And how did those fictional Martians come to land so conveniently center stage in the realist theaters of empiricism unfolding at the Princeton Radio Research Project?

The archives are silent in response to such questions. The orderly ghosts of well-spoken men in dark coats, their secretaries and scribes, walk the hallways of this selective history, and they, on such topics, are not speaking. Instead, one singular incantation echoes down the historical corridors: "*Who* says *what* to *whom* in *what channel* with *what effects*?" This is the "five-questions model" of communications research—foundational in mass communications studies even today—developed out of the Rockefeller Communication Seminar, held from September 1939 to June 1940 on the sixty-fourth floor of the Rockefeller Plaza in Manhattan. The Rockefeller seminar, established initially to help focus the ongoing work of the Princeton Radio Research Project and plan the future of communications research, was regularly attended by prominent figures in U.S. social science such as Hadley Cantril, Paul Lazarsfeld, Harold Laswell, and Robert S. Lynd. As preparations for the United States' entry into World War II intensified, the seminar turned its attention to advising the federal government on communications policies during the prolonged emergency of war; seminar participants included representatives of the navy, the Department of Justice, and the Federal Communications Commission.[96] Issues of national security, public opinion control, and "democratic propaganda" increasingly preoccupied the Rockefeller seminar, as well as ongoing concerns about scientific, verifiable methods of research that could produce information useful to wartime policymakers. "We believe . . . that we have available today methods of research," the seminar reported in July 1940, "which can reliably inform us about the public mind and how it is being, or can be, influenced in relation to public affairs."[97]

Who asks *what questions* of *whom* in *what channel* and with *what effects*? At ground zero in 1938, the questions are asked by the Princeton Research Project, CBS, and Gallup's American Institute of Public Opinion, of a nationwide sample of potentially panicky radio listeners, through channels of communication newly opened by survey research methods developed out of commercial radio research and academic social psychology and supported by corporate philanthropy and the federal government.

And with *what effects*, this new historical and methodological play of question and answer? Of interview schedules and coded responses? Of individual case studies and statistically cross-tabulated psychological tendencies? Here the answer is necessarily partial, historically specific, and perhaps inescapably suggestive. The operations of survey research performed in Cantril's *The Invasion from Mars* effect a new language for collective panic and "mass hysteria," a language subject to methodical interpretation because it is the methodical product of a set of interpretive procedures structuring that language every step of the way. The methodological theater of *The Invasion from Mars* gives a speaking part, complete with monologues and individualized personalities, for that previously elusive mass prone to irrational panics. To that suggestive substratum of society whose reality is too easily confused by the fleeting persuasions of fantasy and the sensory effervescence of the new electronic talking machines. Out of a dramatic seizure of social symptoms — terror-stricken phone calls, frantic drivers in speeding cars, prayers and tears for salvation, bodies rapt before the radio dial, convulsed by the end of the world — survey research produces a set of spoken responses offered up in the valuable currency of "data," open to exchange and the magic equivalences of quantification. Panic in this empirical theater will utter its secrets and enunciate its origins and intentions in a familiar grammar and a syntactical clarity previously reserved for the language of reason.

And perhaps not surprisingly, what panic will be heard to say about itself never strays too far from the problems the researcher himself encounters in his own struggle to hear panic speak, scientifically and with calculable levels of certainty. If the empirically driven panic researcher is faced with the dangers of subjective interpretation, both his own and those of his interview subjects, then through repetitious procedures of verification and validation, cross-checking the "evidence" against protocols of proper judgment, this subjective morass of imaginary terror can be made to yield up its objective treasures. Panic, for its part, need only look out the window, check the newspaper for that night's radio programming, phone the police or perform a quick test of the temporal and logical impossibilities of such a fantastic war of the worlds exploding in its ear, in order to calm its anxious heartbeat and reorient its subjective fears toward a more objective ascertainment of the available information.

Who asks *what questions* of *whom* in *what channel* and with *what effects*? With an echo effect, then, the problems of administering an empirical method for social science reverberate within the problem of panic. An echo effect? In any case, some confusion of subject and object, in the Professor's professed pursuit of the empirical outlines of a real social science. "Let the people speak for themselves," Hadley Cantril writes on the first page of this most famous empirical study of collective panic and its communications.[98] But is the Professor really prepared for such speaking? Is he perhaps quite preoccupied by preparations for other, more pressing matters?

And as for *the channel* through which all such questions must be circuited, let us not forget that *control of the channel* is possibly, then and still now, the main story. Let us not forget that the Rockefeller Foundation's and the Federal Radio Education Committee's interest in radio research is timed to follow the radio broadcast industry's successful defeat of New Deal–era legislation that tried to secure 25 percent of existing radio frequencies for noncommercial voices, including those of educational, labor, agricultural, religious, and cooperative organizations. After the proposed legislation fails, the radio networks launch a new initiative called "public service" programming, scheduling contributions to educational and "cultural uplift" during unsponsored airtime. CBS introduces Orson Welles's "Mercury Theater on the Air," the broadcast site for *The War of the Worlds*, in the summer of 1938 as a part of its public service initiative.[99] Refusing to give over commercial control of any channels, the networks willingly volunteer to give limited airtime to experimental radio theater.

Orson Welles and several other members of the Mercury Theater group are active participants in the artistic and political life of the Popular Front, a leftist movement emerging in the early 1930s out of the labor struggles of the Depression. The Mercury Theater's broadcast of *The War of the Worlds* on October 30, 1938, and poet Archibald MacLeish's radio play *Air Raid*, broadcast three days earlier, are an experimental form of electronic drama "depicting fascist invasions and air raids" as part of an explicit antifascist politics.[100] Are Welles and the Mercury Theater playing intentionally with the malleability and intensity of the public's increasingly volatile fears? Is the Martian in this machine an impending threat of world war, channeled through the suggestive sectors of a peacetime U.S. population being methodically prepared for war?

If the dead could speak—not the ones housed in the archives, but those remembered vaguely, if it all, for their panicky propensity to die from sheer terror—what would they say? Do they have questions for the living? If so, could they find a channel for asking them?

What questions can be asked in the presence of so many techniques for constructing empirical answers?

What secrets still rest in the absence of channels for transmitting them?

CHANNEL ZERO: THE CASE STUDY
OF MISS JANE DEAN

Let the people speak for themselves. — HADLEY CANTRIL[101]

Miss Jane Dean is an unmarried woman, fifty-seven years old. She lives with her sister in a house she owns. Her home is in a small New Jersey town.[102] **When things began to come out I was already in the habit of believing the beginning and I kept right on believing.** She has a modest but secure income. Miss Dean only went to grammar school. **I was just carried away** She is a Protestant **by the realistic method of production.**

She had tuned in the radio accidentally in company with her sister, at the time when "beings came out of the meteor." **I was writing a history theme. The girl from upstairs came and made me go up to her place.** She says, "Of course I did not make any attempt to check up on the broadcast. When I hear something like that I take it for granted it is true." **Everybody was excited I felt as if I was going crazy.** At 8:30, when the station identification was made, she turned her radio off, assuming that "it was the end of everything." **We were holding each other. Everything seemed unimportant in the face of death. I was afraid to die, just kept on listening.**

In Miss Dean's case [her] beliefs **I didn't do anything** had made her expect a catastrophe. She did not mind death but wanted to die. **I just kept listening.**

Miss Dean's mental world is a narrow one **so many odd things are happening in the world** from which external events in the real world are deliberately excluded. She prides herself on not reading much **science has progressed so far that we don't know how far it might have gone on Mars.** When asked what developments in any field she considered most useful she refused the whole idea of progress by say-

Searching the sky for Martians in Grovers Mill. Author, 2004.

ing "none will really help us." She is completely ignorant of scientific or other achievements **in the back of my head I had the idea that it was really an airplane like a zeppelin that looked like a meteor and the Germans were attacking us with gas bombs** and furthermore refuses even to believe they are possible.

One may assume that Miss Dean is a deeply frustrated woman who has turned fanatic **I thought it was some kind of a new airship and a new method of attack**. Just what personal experiences in the past have led to her condition we do not know. She mentioned "conflicts in her life," but refused to elaborate on them. **I thought they might not know themselves completely what it was**.

She checks as the only desirable thing, "no war in the next fifty years," leaving out all items providing for the development of personality or the enrichment of social life.

I kept translating the unbelievable parts into something I could believe for Miss Dean an end of the world **until finally I reached the breaking point** is an event that gives meaning to the kind of life she has led **I mean my mind just couldn't twist things any more** She and her sister are resigned and prepared for the event **so I just stopped believing**.

. . . I went outside once to look at the stars. I saw a clear sky but somehow was not reassured.

We were told it was to be a "panic" raid . . . and that our aiming
point would be the market square. We had no choice. We bombed as
instructed and killed, I would estimate, nearly 100,000 people (we
will never know), mainly women and children. I was horrified when
we were later filmed at a mock propaganda briefing when the original
briefing instructions were reversed; but I cannot say more, as I would
be in trouble under the official secrets act. — BRITISH AIRPLANE
NAVIGATOR IN 1945 DRESDEN AIR RAID[103]

The Announcer: They swing: the wing dips:
There's the signal: the dip: they'll
Dive; they're ready to dive:
They're steady; they're heading down:
They're dead on the town . . .
(*A crazy stammering of machine guns . . .*)
A Woman's Voice (*shrieking*): It's us do you see!
A Woman's Voice (*shrieking*): It's us don't you see us!
—ARCHIBALD MACLEISH[104]

Ground zero is almost everywhere and so nowhere exactly as the social
and technological conflagration of a second world war spreads across the
volatile maps of European nationalism, Old and New World colonialism,
Asian empire, modern fascism. The world in flames. Tactical, practiced
catastrophe on an unprecedented scale. A fully militarized modernity on
the rise. These are the prevailing conditions as Professor Hadley Cantril, now director of the Office of Public Opinion Research at Princeton,
publishes his suggestions for an orderly transfer of power from German-
occupied territories to the Allied Military Governments in the winter of
1943. Anticipating "the terrific impact of invasion with all its dislocation"
that will precede the Allied liberation, the Professor warns, "Conditions
will be ripe for panic."[105]

In "Causes and Control of Riot and Panic" (1943), Cantril announces
that his approach "will be the psychological one, an approach that must
become part and parcel of modern military science." Indeed, he argues,

it is through the studied application of psychological knowledge that the Allied military force can differentiate its control strategies from those of the Nazis. Should Allied forces rely strictly on control tactics in the "old-fashioned military tradition," the population "may find it more difficult than otherwise to distinguish between what they have expected to be democratic occupation as contrasted to the authoritarian occupation our side has deposed." The Professor advises that "if a psychological approach is properly understood and adroitly carried out, the need for military measures will be considerably minimized." Addressing specifically the problem of panic caused by people who are "susceptible to some suggestion" in the face of a perceived threat, Cantril focuses on how to manage the "avoidable set of psychological conditions" precipitating panicky mass behavior.[106]

Concerns about the psychological control of panic among civilian populations intensifies with the emergence of "total war," or the understanding that the success of the military effort during World War II requires the complete mobilization of civilian resources in all spheres of social and economic life. Shaped partly by the development of new technologies of transportation and communication, including aerial bombing and the radio broadcast, the new strategic situation of total war reconfigures the intensities of military conflict away from the antagonisms of frontline battle toward the more complex organization of overlapping fields of militarized warfare. Panic in the field of battle — once limited to the threat of rout among combat soldiers, or the terror of civilians facing an invading army — now includes the potential psychological reactions of civilians on the "home front" faced with the rapid, radio-beamed dissemination of news of military defeat, or the more immediate threat of invasion from the air by enemy planes capable of immense destruction.

In the November 1941 issue of the *American Journal of Sociology*, the social sciences are busy mobilizing their own civilian resources on the eve of U.S. entry into World War II. Organized around the problems of measuring and strengthening civilian morale while protecting against demoralization and its most extreme expression, panic, the special issue opens with an essay by the psychiatrist Harry Stack Sullivan, "Psychiatric

Aspects of Morale."[107] He explains: "The avoidance of demoralization and the promotion and maintenance of morale are as important in the civilian home front and the industrial and commercial supporting organizations as they are in the zones of combat. For this reason, psychiatric strategy and tactics have become overwhelmingly important in war."[108] Sociologist Robert E. Park, in his contributing essay, sounds a similar note:

> Since war has invaded the realm of the spirit, morale has assumed a new importance in both war and peace. Total war is now an enterprise so colossal that belligerent nations find it necessary not only to mobilize all their resources, material and moral, but to make present peace little more than a preparation for future war. Under these conditions so-called psychic warfare . . . has assumed an importance and achieved a technical efficiency which . . . has profoundly altered the character of peace, making it much harder to bear.
>
> The object of attack in psychic warfare is morale, and less that of the men in arms than of the civil population back of the lines.[109]

With the boundaries between peace and war, civilian and soldier, psychological and military, home and combat zone, set spinning in the vortex of total war, the social scientist begins to emerge as a self-conscious soldier of knowledge, ready to serve the militarized requirements of civilian communication, command, and control.

In their efforts to contribute to U.S. national morale, the authors find themselves facing the same problem that Hadley Cantril wrestles with in "Causes and Control of Riot and Panic": what are the differences between "democratic" and "authoritarian" techniques of social control in a time of total war? While Harry Stack Sullivan argues for the need to suspend democratic ideals in the United States and replace them with overtly authoritarian social structures to win the fight against fascism, most authors in the *American Journal of Sociology* special issue search for more specifically "democratic" methods to maintain morale, prevent panic, and prevail in warfare.[110] Clarifying the " 'intelligence' activities" that distinguish a democratic government's attempt to shape citizen behavior from more overtly manipulative state interventions, the sociologist Edward A. Shils reports on the unprecedented scale of current U.S. government research on citizens' attitudes and opinions.[111] A paramount task for any democratic government is to discover "the preferences of the population whose behavior it seeks to influence," making it "especially urgent to possess means of acquiring knowledge of the state of mind of its citizens." Shils reports that Professor Hadley Cantril's Institute of Public Opinion Research at Princeton University, and George Gallup's American Institute of Public Opinion, are currently providing the Office of Civilian Defense useful information on the state of mind of U.S. citizens regarding the present war.[112]

Robert E. Park encourages an approach to civilian morale "supported by a principle of reason," in which the uncensored circulation of news and differing public opinions bolster a sense of national unity and will, and do so in vivid contrast to the propaganda and "spiritual warfare" characterizing Germany's strategies of morale building.[113] But Park also acknowledges the "magic" power of symbols and words to create morale in both military and civilian groups, even in the face of profound demoralization. Describing the magical effect of President Roosevelt's March 12, 1933, radio address to the nation then "in a state of panic" about the collapse of the financial system, Park observes: "One of the functions of the magician in primitive society . . . is to restore morale when fear in the presence of some unforeseen or unprecedented event, like the recent invasion from Mars as reported by Orson Welles, has shaken it."[114]

In recognition of the magical, morale-boosting power of symbols, the *American Journal of Sociology* issue publishes two essays by executives from the radio and movie industry. Reasoned confidence alone is not enough to move a nation on the brink of total war. The "masses must be moved by emotional excitement and exaltation if they are to reach any high pitch of forceful action," declares James Angell of NBC radio. The "great psychological advantage" of radio's transmission of a live human voice makes it a prime communications medium for influencing "national attitudes."[115] Walter Wanger, a movie studio executive, asserts that the "builders of morale must weave . . . a fabric of emotion around the rational aspects of democratic life. . . . Men must become emotionalized, to use a clumsy word, about their country and their country's goals." Moviemakers, he suggests, can be indispensable in aiding social scientists and political leaders in the "emotionalizing" process.[116]

How precisely does the magical morale work of movies and radio, backed by the symbolic productions of social scientists and politicians, differ in a democracy from the propaganda techniques of the German fascists? "The arts and devices of spiritual warfare are many and various and more subtle no doubt than any analysis has thus far disclosed," the Professor observes.[117] With one eye on the Nuremberg rallies and the other fixed on the Gallup polls, U.S. social science on the edge of total war splits its gaze across a confused strategic landscape marked by "weapons of psychic warfare,"[118] "destructive psychiatric strategy,"[119] " 'intelligence' activities of the federal government,"[120] and the magical conjuring of morale through "words and symbols" relayed through techno-circuits of light and sound.[121] In the new situation of "total defense" seemingly necessitated by the outbreak of war on all fronts, the social scientist, now military strategist and magician by turns, searches for a language and technique to counter and to create psychological threats waged in the fluid currencies of total modern warfare.

And it is here, in the fields of language and technique, in the particular language of technique, that U.S. social psychology makes its most valued contributions to total war. With the U.S. entry into World War II in December 1941, the War Department mobilizes a Research Branch, housed within its new Morale Division, that conducts over two hundred wartime surveys aimed at measuring the "attitudes" of soldiers in the U.S. Army. Under the direction of the sociologist Samuel Stouffer, the Research Branch uses survey research techniques, employed by a mixed staff of over one hundred civilian and military personnel interviewing over 500,000 soldiers, to prove, for the first time in military history, the "engineering utility" of a social scientific study of soldiers' attitudes.[122]

The civilian staff of the Research Branch is composed mostly of young sociologists, psychologists, and statisticians, as well as personnel drawn from commercial research agencies. The techniques of public opinion and market research used by these agencies, according to Stouffer, become the primary emphasis of Research Branch activities. Consultants to the Research Branch—including Hadley Cantril, Paul Lazarsfeld, and Frank Stanton—are men already versed in the social scientific application of such methods.[123] A monthly Research Branch publication entitled *What the Soldier Thinks*, summarizing soldiers' attitudes on a diversity of topics, begins circulating in 1943 to all army officers. More secret research findings—all the Research Branch reports were classified documents—are circulated to higher-level army personnel to help direct the formulation of military policy and priorities.[124]

In his foreword to *The American Soldier: Studies in Social Psychology in World War II*, a four-volume postwar publication based on Research Branch survey data, General Frederick H. Osborn reports that the citizen army provided an "exceptional opportunity for the effective use of the new scientific methods" developed in the years just before the war. Never before, the general notes, had scientific evidence and factual knowledge been used to "direct human behavior" on such a large scale.[125]

And never before have social scientists conducting survey research had access to such a large grouping of individuals, organized under rigid hierarchical discipline, and easily sampled at random for an interview that was not voluntary but mandated by military authority. The Research Branch surveys were, according to the sociologist Herbert Hyman—who conducted some of them—an example of a social scientific "inquest, an inquiry enforced by authority," permitting studies to be conducted "on a grander scale than any experimentalist could have achieved in civilian society."[126]

An even more ambitious deployment of social psychology's empirical methods occurs in a research enterprise less well known today, even though it demanded a greater investment of military and civilian resources than did the Research Branch studies. Surveys of the effects of Allied aerial bombing on civilian morale in Germany conducted by the Morale Division of the United States Strategic Bombing Survey (USSBS) begin in the late fall of 1944. Established by the secretary of war under directive from President Roosevelt, the USSBS employs over one thousand staff, including three hundred civilian members overseen by an eleven-member civilian directorate chaired by the president of Prudential Life Insurance Company. The task of the vast research enterprise is to assess the effects of this new weapon, the aerial bomber, in its "first massive wartime test."[127] One of the acknowledged targets of the Allied forces' strategic bombing of enemy civilians, beyond the disruption of wartime industrial capacity, is the morale of the civilian population, considered an essential element in the successful conduct of total war.[128]

It was in March 1944, the first large raid on Ulm. My husband was at his job at the auto works and had raid duty when a phosphorus bomb fell directly on him. He burned like a torch.[129]

Military historians cite H. G. Wells's 1908 novel *The War in the Air* as one imaginary origin of the twentieth-century military concept of strategic aerial bombing, which plays a major and possibly decisive role in the theater of operations during World War II.[130]

I saw people killed by falling bricks and heard the screams of others dying in the fire. I dragged my best friend from a burning building and she died in my arms. I saw others who went stark mad.

The Morale Division of the USSBS is established with the specific objective "to determine the direct and indirect effects of bombing upon the attitudes, behavior and health of the civilian population, with particular reference to its effect upon the willingness and capacity of the bombed population to give effective and continued support to the German war effort."[131] Pilot studies for the morale survey of the German population begin before Germany concedes defeat, carried out in the territories already occupied by Allied forces. Interview teams are composed largely of social scientists and psychologists familiar with German language and culture.[132]

One can't get used to the raids. I wished for an end. We all got nerves. We did not get enough sleep and were very tense. People fainted when they heard the first bomb drop.

The bulk of the USSBS survey research on morale in Germany is conducted in June and July 1945. Over 3,700 German civilians in thirty-four towns and cities are interviewed. Cities are classified according to their status as unbombed, lightly bombed, moderately bombed, and heavily bombed. A heavily bombed city, in the USSBS classification, is one in which between 19,000 and 47,000 tons of bombs were dropped during the war.[133] The study's independent variable is civilian exposure to (1) bombings of different kind and magnitude, (2) threat of bombings, and (3) damage from bombings (as experienced or observed). The dependent variable is identified as civilians' will and capacity to support the ongoing war effort.[134]

I never became accustomed to the raids and bombing. I don't think anybody did. I was always afraid and shaking and nervous.

"The bombing of the two [German and Japanese] populations and the accompanying surveys may be seen as giant natural experiments," writes the Professor. "Their gruesome and tragic context makes it more, not less, important for social scientists to study the findings for the unique knowledge provided."[135] Major findings from the Morale Division's surveys include that bombing "seriously depressed the morale" of the civilian population.[136] However, heavy bombing of towns did not result in a decrease in morale in proportion to the increased amount of bombing. A principle of "diminishing returns" is observed, wherein the maximum morale effects "of dropping a given tonnage of bombs on Germany would have been attained by lighter raids as widely distributed as possible." In a number of cities that experienced the heaviest bombing, a slight improvement in morale is observed.[137]

I got rather used to those raids. After all I could not do any more than die.

An additional aim of the USSBS survey research is to help inform strategy in the intensified aerial bombardment campaign about to begin against Japan in the summer of 1945.[138] At the conclusion of that campaign, on August 15, 1945, President Truman directs the USSBS to extend its investigative reach from the European theater into the Pacific theater, and to include a separate survey of the morale effects of atomic bombing of civilians in Hiroshima and Nagasaki.[139]

FALLING SUBJECTS

And even as man seeks to rise higher and higher — in his knowledge
too — so too the ground fractures more and more beneath his feet. . . .

At stake here somewhere, ever more insistent in its deathly hauteur, is the risk that the subject (as) self will crumble away. Also at stake, therefore, the "object" and the modes of dividing the economy between them. — LUCE IRIGARAY[140]

Suddenly, like a thing falling upon me from without, came fear.

. . . The fear I felt was no rational fear, but a panic terror not only of the Martians but of the dusk and stillness all about me. . . . I remember I felt an extraordinary persuasion that I was being played with, that presently, when I was upon the very verge of safety, this mysterious death — as swift as the passage of light — would leap after me from the pit about the cylinder and strike me down.

— H. G. WELLS[141]

Ground zero is at Aioi Bridge. At 8:15 A.M., on Wednesday, August 6, an atomic bomb nicknamed "Little Boy" falls out of a U.S. warplane and explodes 570 meters above the ground with an incendiary flash. The bomb destroys a significant portion of the military, industrial, residential, and civilian life of Hiroshima, Japan. On August 9, a second atomic bomb falls on the city of Nagasaki. To similar effect.

Slowly a humped shape rose out of the pit, and the ghost of a beam of light seemed to flicker out from it. . . . Flashes of actual flame, a bright glare leaping from one to another, sprang from the scattered group of men. It was as if some invisible jet impinged upon them and flashed into white flame. It was as if each man were suddenly and momentarily turned to fire.[142]

In October 1945, pretesting begins for the interview instrument designed for the USSBS survey research on Japanese civilian morale. During November and December, 3,200 Japanese civilians are interviewed. The survey in Japan, as in Germany, is conducted as an inquest, enforced by the military authority of the occupying U.S. forces. Members of the USSBS survey research team, accompanied by a local policeman or other city official, locate the selected interviewee and schedule a time for the survey. The interview is carried out in the local headquarters of the occupying military unit.[143]

Shadow of hand wheel burned into the wall at ground zero, Hiroshima. United States Strategic Bombing Survey, *The Effects of Atomic Bombs on Hiroshima and Nagasaki*, 1946.

Then, by the light of their own destruction, I saw them staggering and falling.[144]

Of particular interest to the USSBS are the effects of the atomic bombs dropped on Hiroshima and Nagasaki. While Japanese cities had been the target of what was now being termed "conventional" (i.e., not atomic) bombing—including a spectacular attack on Tokyo on March 9, 1945, in which over 83,000 civilians were killed, 102,000 civilians were injured, and 15.8 square miles of the city were devastated[145]—the new atomic weapons promised to raise the scale and force of destruction and, perhaps, of psychological demoralization to new levels.[146]

The beam swung close overhead, lighting the tops of the beech-trees that line the road, and splitting the bricks, smashing the windows, firing the window-frames. . . . In the sudden thud, hiss, and glare of the igniting trees, the panic-stricken crowd seems to have swayed hesitatingly for some moments. Sparks and burning twigs began to fall into the road. . . . Hats and dresses caught fire. . . . There were shrieks and shouts.[147]

But the effect of the atomic bombs on depressing civilian morale is surprisingly limited. Although "as might be expected," reaction to the atomic attacks was characterized by "fear" and "uncontrolled terror," the USSBS morale survey discovers that only 40 percent of survivors reported increased demoralization in the war effort induced by the bomb.[148] And among Japanese civilians living outside the two target cities, only 28 percent felt more demoralized by news of the atomic explosions. The USSBS attributes this finding to the "lack of understanding of the meaning of the new weapon" among civilians who did not experience its effects, while hypothesizing that if "the channels of mass communication [were] as readily available to all the population as they are in the United States," the effects on morale would have been greater.[149]

And beyond . . . the glittering Martians went to and fro, calmly and methodically . . . taking possession of the conquered country. They do not seem to have aimed at extermination so much as at complete demoralisation and the destruction of any opposition.[150]

In another interesting finding, the morale survey reveals that "admiration" for the atomic bomb was more frequently reported than anger at its use. Over 25 percent of civilian survivors living in and around Hiroshima and Nagasaki "said they were impressed by its power and by the scientific skill which underlay its discovery and production."[151]

I sat up, strangely perplexed. . . . My terror had fallen from me like a garment. . . . It was as if something turned over, and the point of view altered abruptly. . . . I was immediately the self of every day again — a decent, ordinary citizen. . . . The impulse of my flight, the starting flames, were as if they had been in a dream.[152]

In the final chapter of the USSBS report *The Effects of Atomic Bombs on Hiroshima and Nagasaki*, the authors turn to "an insistent question" raised in the minds of the survey's investigators during their research: "What if the target for the bomb had been an American City?"[153] While the task of the survey research has been the ascertainment of facts, "the meaning of those facts" must also be faced, and the meaning of the facts of atomic bombing for the citizens of the United States leads to several summary recommendations by the USSBS.

At times I suffer from the strangest sense of detachment from myself and the world about me; I seem to watch it all from the outside, from somewhere inconceivably remote, out of time, out of space, out of the stress and tragedy of it all.[154]

"Since modern science can be marshaled for the defense as well as the attack," the report concludes, "there is reason to hope that protective weapons and techniques will be improved."[155] Among these defensive techniques, the USSBS suggests a decentralization and "partial dispersal of the national centers of activity" and population; the establishment of a nationwide organization of civilian defense; and an "unrelaxing state of readiness" to use atomic weapons in retaliation for an attack, so that "no single blow or series of blows from an enemy can cripple [U.S.] ability to strike back in the same way." Imperative to this state of perpetual defensive readiness is the testing of atomic weapons' effects "under varying conditions." The USSBS looks forward to the production of "valuable data for defining more precisely what is already known about the atomic bomb's effectiveness." Such data should become available, the USSBS concludes, after the atomic bomb tests planned by the U.S. military in the upcoming Operation Crossroads.[156]

It is still a matter of wonder how the Martians are able to slay men so swiftly and so silently. Many think that in some way they are able to generate an intense heat . . . [that] they project in a parallel beam against any object they choose by means of a polished parabolic mirror of unknown composition. . . .

But no one has

absolutely

proved

these

details.[157]

3

"Keep Calm!" for the Cold War:
Diary of a Mental Patient

First day: well here I am, at last it happened, I got awfully scared about . . .
short range missiles and long range missiles and . . . biological warfare
and chemical warfare . . . and it looked like the whole order was cracking
at the seams and then I was an intellectual and a woman to boot, isolated
and all that, so I tried the couch and he kept saying why can't you come to
terms with your basic feminine instincts so I kept trying on his couch and
it wasn't much fun and I thought about it and I was really awfully scared
about the missiles and live now while you have the chance and weren't we
going to have any resistance and I was resisting insight into my feminine
instincts . . . and who the hell can find the real repression in suburban
houses no it is just that you CANNOT COME TO TERMS WITH YOUR BASIC
FEMININE INSTINCTS but I don't want an automatic washing machine
electric dryer electric roaster . . . and if somebody doesn't do something
about it they are going to blow up too . . . and then suddenly I cracked or
as they would say in the jargon around here I flipped and here I am.

. . . I was isolated from the group but nobody ever beat me up or called
me names . . . and my father thought it was clear that everyone should be
against the Nazis and he kept pounding on the typewriter all day about it
so he was isolated from the group and I guess that's where I got it from.

Then there is me. My name is Anne and I come from the best New
England families Mayflower and all that I never put up my hair in rollers
every night . . . because my mother never taught me how and the Irish
Catholic cheerleaders . . . had dates every night and I was isolated from
the group. —ANNE PARSONS, *Diary of a Mental Patient*[1]

Daddy was a functionalist. He worked as an electrical engineer for Bell Telephone Laboratories in Reading, Pennsylvania, in the 1960s and we lived in a white suburb in a yellow house with a green lawn and the NORMS AND VALUES OF OUR COMMUNITY could be strongly correlated with the ideological tendencies of large sectors of other white U.S. suburbs with green lawns and sufficient incomes for family vacations in New Jersey and a thirty-foot civil defense siren next to the neighborhood swimming pool.

Later in high school in a different suburb where they taught you German with Frau Oplesch who was on television three days a week when they wheeled her in on the TV cart to say EINS ZWEI DREI then act like she heard you repeating it back I learned a way of writing poetry the teacher called prose poetry the main technique of which is TO WRITE AND WRITE IN VERY LONG SENTENCES WITH HARDLY ANY PUNCTUATION AT ALL and the model for this genre was schizophrenia which in the mid-1970s didn't surprise anyone that some supposedly crazy people did poetry or what the teacher called stream of consciousness writing or at least it had the appearance of such though the teacher said the best writers probably edited quite a bit except perhaps THE CRAZY PEOPLE who just got it right the first time. So we'd sit in poetry class and read out loud our latest efforts that went something like "a wind blows up my dress / and so i   think   of   you" after which we would discuss each other's poems and say what we got out of them (the interpretation).

But in Reading, Pennsylvania, in the 1960s there was no schizophrenic prose poetry in the classroom however quite a focus on Thanksgiving and the proper spelling of "syncopation" and the colorful hexagrams on the large red barns of the Amish people visible from the interstate highway and after the family supper we looked at the tiny integrated circuit Daddy brought home from work under my brother's microscope. Gold filaments. Perfectly straight parallel tracks crossing and crisscrossing. Precise as an Amish hexagram.

Nuclear family relations. Federal Civil Defense Administration, *Operation Doorstep*, 1953.

Daddy said the tiny integrated circuit is the ESSENTIAL BUILDING BLOCK of most of our smartest machines of the day at Bell Labs they make them so easily they only cost twenty-five cents a piece which I considered an impressive achievement like the time Daddy took our TV all apart to show me where the pictures came from however even then I suspected HIS EXPLANATION WAS AT BEST PARTIAL.

In 1962 when we moved to the suburbs of Reading, Pennsylvania, the United States had 224 intercontinental ballistic missiles built to deliver nuclear bombs to their target. The Soviet Union had almost 300 intercontinental ballistic missiles built for the same purpose.[2] I don't remember being afraid of nuclear war. I remember dressing up at night as the Bride of Frankenstein a Siamese twin a black dinosaur with a knobby green mask for Halloween my favorite holiday when we children of Reading paraded through the streets after dark in a weird winding procession of pirates witches gypsies goblins sorcerers skeletons trailing for blocks and blocks behind the local red fire engine while the fathers of Reading held flaming torches and   walked   silent   beside. Protecting us from the dark. I presume.

REALLY AWFULLY SCARED

The picture of public thinking about the atomic bomb is now relatively clear. We have seen that despite the magnitude of the

destructive power represented by the bomb, and the unprecedented
publicity it has received through the mass media, its importance is
not reflected in the role it holds in the conscious life of the
population. — DOUVAN AND WITHEY, "Some Attitudinal
Consequences of Atomic Energy" (1953)[3]

It will be argued that a huge fraction of the public, perhaps the
majority, *already* displays clinical symptoms indicative of hysteria
and predisposing to panic. — WYLIE, "Panic, Psychology, and the
Bomb" (1954)[4]

Operation Crossroads is carried out by the U.S. military during the summer of 1946. In the Bikini atoll of the South Pacific, the United States tests the effects of atomic weaponry by dropping bombs on an assembled fleet of its own antiquated naval ships. On July 1, an atomic bomb is exploded in the air over the fleet. On July 26, a second bomb is detonated underwater below the fleet. A major international media event, the Bikini explosions usher in a brave new era of nuclear testing in which the targeting scenario of atomic attack commonly involves the United States bombing itself. And measuring the effects.[5]

One of the methods for measuring the atomic bombs' effects is a national survey of U.S. public opinion conducted before and after the Bikini experiment. Funded by the Rockefeller Foundation and the Carnegie Corporation at the request of the Social Science Research Council (SSRC), the survey questionnaire is administered to national cross-section samples of the U.S. population in June 1946 and again in August. Professor Hadley Cantril, along with Rensis Likert, former director of the Morale Division of the United States Strategic Bombing Survey (USSBS), and Leonard S. Cottrell Jr., former director of the Survey Section of the War Department's Research Branch, help to oversee the survey project. In a foreword to the book version of the survey's findings, "written primarily for the intelligent citizen,"[6] General Frederick Osborn (former director of the Morale Division of the Research Branch) applauds recent advances in modern social thinking made possible by "new techniques [and] new methods of analysis of factual objective data," including the public opinion survey. "This new instrument," he asserts, "will increasingly give us a background of fact against which to check on the validity of the hypotheses or assumptions which are a necessary premise to practical action."[7]

General Osborn's positive assessment of the public opinion survey as a powerful new technique is apparently shared by the U.S. State Department, which secretly contracts monthly survey research on U.S. public opinion on foreign affairs from 1945 to 1957. Conducted by the fledgling National Opinion Research Center (NORC), the secret State Department surveys provide NORC with a sustained source of income in its early years and serve as a methodological training ground and fact-producing machine for what will become one of the most widely used survey databases in the social sciences.[8]

The State Department's clandestine contract with NORC is arranged through Professor Hadley Cantril, director of Princeton's Office of Public Opinion Research (one of two U.S. polling organizations used by the Central Intelligence Agency in the immediate postwar years).[9] The Professor's public service to the state extends back at least to World War II, when Cantril performs a series of confidential public opinion surveys for the State Department, the White House, and several military agencies.[10] Cantril's secret research for the U.S. government follows close on the heels of the study for which he is best known: *The Invasion from Mars* (1940), a social psychology of the panic created by Orson Welles's radio broadcast of H. G. Wells's *The War of the Worlds*.

The SSRC survey of public opinion before and after the Bikini explosions investigates U.S. public feelings about a wide range of issues in current international affairs. The published version of the study highlights the troubling evidence that the U.S. public tends to be confused, inconsistent, contradictory, poorly informed, or undecided about world affairs, including the grave issues surrounding atomic weapons. Although 98 percent of those surveyed report knowing that the atomic bomb exists, and while the vast majority acknowledge the bomb's immense destructive potential, researchers note there is "little indication that the people recognize the revolutionary significance of the new weapon."[11] In marked contrast with the public proclamations of leading scientists, over half of the survey subjects believe that the United States can develop an effective defense against atomic weapons. And while close to 60 percent of respondents believe another world war is possible or likely within the next twenty-five years—and two-thirds of the total sample agree that there is a real danger of an atomic bomb being used against the United States— over half of the respondents also report that they are not at all worried about the atomic bomb. The public appears aware but unthreatened, anticipating atomic attack but personally unconcerned. The atomic bomb figures in people's imagination of the future, "but its inescapability has not yet been borne in upon most of them." In conclusion, the book's authors suggest that a "focusing of attention and securing [of] psychological involvement" is necessary for Americans to fully appreciate and participate in the government of world affairs in the atomic age.[12]

As for the study's original hypothesis that there might be a measurable difference in public opinion before and after the Bikini experiments, the factual evidence is resoundingly clear: the effects of Operation Crossroads on U.S. public opinion is nil. Public interest in the highly publicized atomic explosions, the authors remark, "was perhaps merely an interest in a spectacular event."[13]

In August 1946, Paramount Pictures releases a newsreel to movie theaters across the country that combines footage of the aftermath of the bombing of Hiroshima with images of the Bikini explosions.[14]

Regardless of the facts borne out in the SSRC survey, and in spite of the somewhat disappointing performance of the atomic bombs in the Bikini atoll (only a few of the ships were damaged), the official top-secret analysis of Operation Crossroads prepared for President Truman in 1947 by the Joint Chiefs of Staff delivers an unequivocal message: the primary value of the atomic bomb is its "psychological implication," that is, its capacity to terrorize and demoralize an enemy nation, perhaps without ever being actually deployed.[15] The new weapon's ultimate military power is psychological. The panic that would accompany the use, or perhaps merely the threat, of nuclear weapons is therefore a key strategic advantage for a nation on the military offensive, and a problem of the highest order for the nation planning its own defense. The country best able to exploit this potentially nerve-shattering psychological situation will prevail.

In August 1947, two months after their evaluation of Operation Crossroads, the Joint Chiefs of Staff develop a war plan against the Soviet Union that opens with the atomic bombing of civilians in Soviet cities. Given the suggestive code name "Broiler," the plan presumes the bombing would create not only mass destruction but mass terror, profound confusion, and social chaos as millions panic in a helpless attempt to escape. Civil defense theory in the United States projects and reverses the assumptions of "Broiler" in its imagination of Soviet military strategy; the task of civil defense becomes the protection of U.S. civilian morale in the event of a Soviet nuclear offensive aimed at civilian targets and intended to panic and disable the nation.[16]

I don't know why this all seems so important to me. I'm not really sure it'll help me get better. I can't really say if it's why I got sick. I'm hoping maybe it'll help me get out of here. In the daytime they let me go out to visit the library where there're stacks and stacks of stories like these I wander through I see maps're posted at the entrance to each library room though I find they don't help much to know what comes after what which connects to whom or when it just all falls apart against the codes of strict meaning. At night, I have to come back in here to dream.

In a series of both classified and public documents produced in the late 1940s to address the civil defense and social problems facing U.S. policymakers in the atomic era, the findings of the Joint Chiefs of Staff's evaluation of Operation Crossroads become foundational assumptions for thinking about atomic warfare. The problem of panic and the destruction of national morale are recognized repeatedly as the main obstacles to the successful conduct of nuclear war. In the first national civil defense plan proposed by the newly established Office of Civil Defense Planning in 1948, a three-hundred-page blueprint of a "model state civil defense organization" relies heavily on plans for the evacuation and relocation of threatened civilian populations but notes that "fear and panic render large groups almost unmanageable and could easily destroy the effectiveness of the best laid transportation plan."[17] In an early Office of Civil Defense instruction manual entitled *Panic Control and Prevention* (1951), readers learn that "mass panic can produce more damage to life and property than any number of atomic bombs. . . . If war comes, it will be a total, absolute war. Fitness of the civilian will be of equal importance with fitness of the fighter. The outcome of the war will depend upon the staying power of the civilian just as much as upon that of the soldier. The fatigued civilian will be the unfit, panic-ripe civilian."[18] As an antidote to mass panic and terror, the Office of Civil Defense calls for a nationwide public information campaign to inform the public of atomic dangers and of the steps that can be taken to protect against them.

But by 1953, little has changed in the disturbing social scientific picture of a confused public, seemingly psychologically distanced from the looming dangers of atomic warfare. Researchers at the University of Michigan's Survey Research Center — established in 1946 by Rensis Likert, former director of the Morale Division of the USSBS and advisor to the SSRC study of Operation Crossroads — summarize their portrait of a public uninterested in learning about the effects of atomic bombs, unaffected by conscious worry about atomic war, with unstable, labile attitudes lacking any "logical structure" or evidence of well-developed, differentiated thinking.[19] They conclude that the high profile of atomic energy in the mass media and in "popular fantasy" stands in stark contrast to its apparent absence in "people's conscious day-to-day thoughts." The psychological explanation for such a paradoxical situation, they suggest, rests in a combination of factors, including perhaps the disavowal of anxiety as a defense against intolerable feelings of fear and powerlessness in the face of the new weapons. Further research and systematic investigation are recommended.[20]

In a 1954 essay published in the *Bulletin of the Atomic Scientists*, the popular novelist Philip Wylie paints a dramatically different image of the U.S. public suffering from atomic stress. In "Panic, Psychology, and the Bomb," Wylie writes:

> The general population has been subjected, for nearly nine years, to a "war of nerves" unwittingly waged against it by its own leaders. There has been no coherent plan for atomic information, for public education, or even for presenting simple fact. Secrecy has built up potential psychological catastrophe to a degree so great that secrecy *alone* (in a nation unused to it) explains much of the "repressed fear" discussed here. *Hysteria and panic rise from the unknown and the misunderstood, the withheld, the hinted, the suspected, the ignored, and from the repressed dread that materializes unexpectedly.*[21]

Against reassurances that the U.S. public will face the ravages of atomic assault calmly, Wylie asserts that the public is "already exhibiting on a massive scale a vast variety of 'symptoms' which, in clinical psychology, are known to be the results of deeply repressed fear."[22] Wylie interprets the growing public fascination with flying saucers, the widespread apathy toward the nuclear threat, and the spreading persecutory zeal of anti-Communism as evidence of a mass hysteria launched by the repressed terror of atomic war. He proposes the establishment of a federal committee that would create a factual, rational basis for "atomic public relations." In our atomic age, he cautions, "to exploit the whole of physics without employing all known psychology" is to invite catastrophe on an unprecedented scale. The "*larger part* of *our* catastrophe," Wylie concludes, "would be the product of *panic!*"[23]

THE GROUP

> What of the behavior of groups? It is evident that each society has its
> peculiarities of vocabulary and grammar, and that members of even
> small groups usually develop jargon and special vocabularies which
> serve instrumental or ritualistic ends. . . . The constitution of any
> human group is thus a symbolic, not a physical, fact.
> —ANSELM STRAUSS[24]

> Any style of empiricism involves . . . a choice as to what is most
> real. —C. WRIGHT MILLS[25]

The social psychology of panic and group behavior in the postwar years struggles to elaborate the empirical promise and practices of wartime research. In 1947 the sociologist Anselm Strauss laments the paucity of empirical attention to collective behavior as a vital field of sociological concern.[26] In the closing years of World War II, Strauss published an overview of the existing literature on collective panic that called for "a more direct attack upon panic than has hitherto been accorded it," citing the absence of knowledge about specific causal mechanisms or preventative measures, and discussing the methodological obstacles to a systematic empirical research program. "One of the major tasks facing the student of panic," he wrote in 1944, "is the development of methods designed to give him the kind of data he needs to answer the questions he raises about the phenomena of panic."[27]

In the next ten years, a "more direct attack" is made on the problem of data and methods that can make panic more responsive to researchers' queries. These developments take place within the broader context of the academic social sciences becoming integrated in historically new ways with government and corporate administrative agendas, funding networks, and research priorities.[28] The World War II liaison between the study of group behavior, empirical research methods modeled after practices in the "natural" sciences, and the imperative to produce knowledge useful for the management and social control of populations under investigation is generalized into a broad mandate for social science research. For the group of scholars interested in panic, the post–World War II construction of a shared language and methodological vocabulary for studying panic and collective behavior becomes a means for securing professional legitimacy as well as funding support and government interest.

The establishment of survey research methods as a respected technique of social scientific inquiry (and a key feature of graduate training in many sociology departments) takes place in these postwar years. Although the publication of *The American Soldier: Studies in Social Psychology* (1949–50), a four-volume overview of War Department survey data from World War II, is met with criticism in some corners of sociology, a popular volume of commentary on the studies and a reanalysis of some of the original survey data is published in 1950.[29] Edited by Paul Lazarsfeld and Robert K. Merton, *Continuities in Social Research: Studies in the Scope and Method of "The American Soldier"* is designed for use as a textbook in college and university classrooms. Seeking to use the War Department's social psychology studies as an inspiration for amassing a cumulative body of sociological knowledge and methodological techniques, Lazarsfeld and Merton argue for the importance of public attitude and opinion surveys as "applied research," vital to effective policy formation and administrative decision making. Samuel Stouffer, a sociologist and editor of the original *American Soldier* studies, asserts in the book's final essay: "If social science is to be taken seriously and receive large financial support, its 'engineering' applications must visibly pay off. It is an interesting speculation as to how much of the vast financial support of the 'pure' research in so-called natural science would be forthcoming except for the spectacular applications in industry, in health, in war."[30] By the time that *Continuities in Social Research* is published, Paul Lazarsfeld and the Princeton Radio Research Project have moved to New York City and—out of the organizational seed of that Rockefeller-funded project—have cultured what becomes a powerful, nationally renowned center of social science research: the Columbia Bureau of Applied Social Research, where survey research techniques are a major focus.[31]

Survey research is not the only methodological front on which social psychology and the study of group behavior expand their stake in scientific techniques and applied research. Borrowing heavily from the procedural repertoire of psychology, which establishes its "scientific" methods and administrative value in the United States several decades earlier, social psychology by the mid-1950s displays a confident plurality of empirical methods based on the precise (often statistically testable) measurement of psychological behavior and the objective (often mathematically inflected) analysis of its variations and causal dynamics.[32] With a self-conscious neopositivist zeal, postwar social psychology pursues an imagined unity with science through the adoption of the "operational methods in physics and mathematics," whereby the methods of empirical research anchor the validity of theoretical propositions in "concrete operations which can be performed, are repeatable and public."[33]

In the early 1950s, collective panic is subject to a new form of empirical investigation: the controlled laboratory experiment. Alexander Mintz publishes "Non-adaptive Group Behavior" (1951), based on his experimental investigation of the phenomenology of panic in small groups. (In Anselm Strauss's 1944 overview of the panic literature, he noted the prohibition in a "free society" on the use of experimental techniques to study mass panic in humans, contrasting such controls to Nazi Germany, where panic experiments had been reported.[34] But twenty-five years later, Stanley Milgram and Hans Toch report that the study of panic is one of the few areas in collective behavior where a "discernible experimental tradition" can be identified.)[35] Mintz hypothesizes that the strikingly nonadaptive behavior of people in panic situations is due not to emotional excitement but to a reasonable and rational perception of their situation and its likely outcome. He frames his experiment as an empirical challenge to social psychological notions of "contagion" and "suggestion" as the decisive factor in collective panic.[36] Mintz tries to move beyond the mystified, difficult-to-operationalize concept of suggestion, instead approaching group behavior in more rational and rationalizable terms.

Mintz's thinking is part of a broader postwar conceptual reorientation of collective behavior that rejects the prevalent prewar notion of such behavior as intrinsically irrational. Instead, collective behavior is perceived as a form of group "problem solving," or a collective attempt to adapt successfully to changes in the environment.[37] In a 1953 essay, Anselm Strauss suggests that even under conditions of extreme stress like panic, humans continue to engage in "high order" social behavior involving the ongoing interpretation of their environment. Dismissing notions of panic as a regression to instinctual behavior in which "social factors [are] temporarily inoperable," Strauss defines collective panic as the effect of "particular definitions of situations, of interaction that still involves *high order sign behavior*, including *complex and socialized emoting, perceiving, and remembering*."[38] For Strauss, communication and "high order sign behavior" are essential components of any kind of group behavior. For some of his colleagues, experimental access to these forms of communication makes possible meaningful laboratory research on group behavior's variable features.

For Mintz in 1951, a reasonable experimental operationalization of collective panic behavior entails the following. A group of approximately twenty student volunteers assembles in the laboratory. Each individual is given a piece of string attached to a cone. The cones are placed together inside a glass bottle with a thin neck. Under a number of experimentally varied conditions, group members are instructed to pull their cones out of the bottle within a limited number of seconds or risk being fined ten cents if they fail. The threat of a traffic jam in the bottleneck, preventing all members from achieving their goal, is the experimental equivalent of a panic situation, where, for example, audience members caught in a theater fire jam the exits in a panicky attempt to escape burning to death. Mintz suggests that his experimental findings can help explain the differential group behavior during bank failures, food or gasoline shortages, and submarine disasters, although "full verification" of the theories awaits investigation of "real life situations"—which will be forthcoming.[39]

Why insert panic into a thin-necked glass bottle? How to fit a submarine disaster through the door of an experimental laboratory? Mintz's "miniature social situations" perform the exceedingly useful—if, to the uninitiated, somewhat magical—task of representing the social and its psychology in a form conducive to radical spatial contraction and the precise measurement of observable behaviors across time.[40] The conceptual abstractions that undergird this miniaturization are not, initially, mathematical abstractions, although they stage and will later permit quantitative and statistical analysis. The abstractions are initially founded elsewhere, in the rather commonplace symbolic operations of metaphor and analogy.

For example, a defining feature of panic for Mintz is its emergence in a social situation with a volatile reward structure, as perceived by social participants. Thus people who perceive the risk of dying in a theater fire are like people who perceive they might be fined ten cents for failure to perform a task; thus the behavior of a group attempting to pull cones out of a thin-necked bottle is analogous to the behavior of a group panicking in a theater fire; thus the information elicited from a laboratory experiment can be applied to the analysis of behavior in "real" social situations. Thus "behavior" is an analytic unit capable of being abstractly represented and reproduced in a laboratory. And a social theory of group behavior is capable of being experimentally tested: "If the theory is correct it should be possible to illustrate its functioning in the laboratory."[41]

If the theory functions in the laboratory, then it's possible for the methodical social psychologist to empirically verify that the successful control of panic depends on the control of individuals' perception of their social situation. This is useful. If you think I'm saying this is just stupid, you're not following the story. I'm saying this is useful information. For social psychologists who begin to perceive how their theories might perform empirically inside controlled laboratories, this is very useful information. Individuals' perception of their social situation is the key to control. Of panic, I mean. What does panic mean? Panic means perceiving that your situation's out of control, so that it's in your own best interest to be out of control, too. Panic means perceiving if you don't get that cone out of that bottle in the next fifteen seconds you're gonna nonadaptively burn to death inside this crazy social situation in which the proliferating laboratories of empirical findings start to function in the 1950s like a theater on fire in order to accumulate data on the pileup of cones and corpses through the abstracted perceptions of a group of social psychologists signaling to each other through a new language of technique. Panic might even be perceiving that the new language of technique inside the laboratory speaks worlds about the social situation outside the laboratory inside which panic is now supposed to speak. Panic could be perceiving that there are no clear boundaries between attempts to control perceptions inside the experimental laboratory and outside. Panic may be starting to perceive that this experiment that it is inside is also outside and so the social situation's feeling pretty out of control. I mean, experimentally speaking, panic is perceiving things're really getting out of control.

Two years after Mintz's experiment, social psychology succeeds in fitting a crowd into a twenty-one-by-twenty-four-foot room and testing its behavior. The feat is achieved by G. E. Swanson at the University of Michigan.[42] Viewing his research as a contribution to a "general theory of social organization" as called for by the sociologist Talcott Parsons, Swanson begins "A Preliminary Laboratory Study of the Acting Crowd" (1953) by asserting that the behavior of crowds "as well as the other phenomena of collective behavior" can "profitably be conceptualized, along with bureaucracies, families, labor unions, political parties, voluntary organizations, and all other groups, as *special forms of the interpersonal patterns of influence* that appear as people adapt to one another in the course of mastering the problems set by the environment."[43] This general concept of the social group allows Swanson to define the essential feature of the crowd as "a particular form of organization for the collective solution of problems — an organizational form that might appear in populations of any size from two on up." Loosed from any definition that relies on large numbers of people, the crowd can thus be miniaturized, operationalized, and symbolically reproduced in the abstract form of an organizational pattern. Or, in Swanson's words, "with such a conception, it became meaningful to think of producing crowd behavior in small, experimentally created populations."[44] That the behavior of a small number of people in a room could be meaningfully thought of as crowd behavior rests entirely on the abstract, generalized, and useful definition of an acting crowd as a patterned form emerging out of the effort to master the environment.

At the controls.
Federal Civil Defense
Administration/Atomic
Energy Commission,
Operation Ivy, 1952.

Swanson's experiment involves assembling twelve groups, each group composed of three student volunteers, inside a laboratory with a playing area equipped with golf balls, pucks, a goal area, and a set of signal lights on a control desk. Instructions are read out loud to the volunteers: "During the war, and at present, social scientists have been exploring the way groups deal with problems." Today's experiment asks the volunteers to attempt to solve a problem that is "patterned on the situations created by the State Department . . . for selecting groups of skilled personnel to handle particularly difficult jobs." The volunteers are told that they will be observed playing a competitive game. They will not be informed what the method is for scoring points in the game. When a player breaks the unknown rules of the game, a red penalty signal will flash. A green signal will flash when a player scores a point according to the game's secret rules. "The way to get the most points," the volunteers are advised, "is to work together, plan together, and, at all times, to keep moving." As soon as the volunteers begin the experiment, researchers turn on a tape recorder in an adjoining room that loudly plays a prerecorded voice reading an excerpt from a fundamentalist treatise on the nature of heaven, the climactic lines from Karl Marx's *The Communist Manifesto*, a newspaper report on a vegetarian Thanksgiving dinner, and a radio broadcast of a Detroit Tigers baseball game, "complete with the jingle advertising, 'Brewster, the Goebel Beer Rooster.' "[45]

The experiment, Swanson explains, is designed to test a set of ten predictions, based on the recent literature on crowd behavior, concerning how different groups will behave in relation to ten dependent variables including suggestibility, group communication, and success in performing a task. Swanson reports that his experimental findings indicate that "it is possible to predict a large share of the phenomena of the acting crowd."[46]

If, indeed, as Anselm Strauss suggests in 1953, the constitution of any human group is "a symbolic, not a physical, fact," then the symbolic practices of social psychologists in the 1950s begin to constitute that human group through languages of abstraction and vocabularies of method that make the "group" appear to be an increasingly malleable symbolic and psychological entity. Accessible via the instrumental linguistics of control. Open to the administrative rituals of prediction.

That panic and crowd behavior could be symbolically constituted, tested, and analyzed in the experimental laboratories of social psychology indicates, as well, an interesting change in the constitution of social psychologists and sociologists as a human group. Bound together by a desire to empirically define and manipulate their "object" of study, researchers approach ever more closely the promise of finding the data and methods needed to make panic speak in the language of sociology's own changing symbolic universe, to ensure panic's fluency in the same vocabularies as the questions it is asked, repeatedly and with a disciplined insistence, to address. As the language of social psychology grows more complex, more practiced in the science of its own semiotics and high-order sign making, is it any surprise to find panic, too, advancing in symbolic complexities? To hear panic signaling—from within that glass bottle, inside the walls of this oh-so-symbolically constituted test tube—the reasonable structures of its own social perceptions?

ORDER WAS CRACKING

> Since the advent of the atomic bomb, unfortunate psychological
> reactions have developed in the minds of civilians. . . . The fear
> reaction of the uninitiated civilian is . . . of such magnitude that it
> could well interfere with important military missions or civil defense
> in time of war.

> ... Luckily, if given half a chance, hope rises readily in even the
> darkest situation. For all people, with the exception of psychopaths,
> are *more interested in their futures than in their disordered pasts.*
> —Office of Civil Defense[47]

The byline reads "Moscow, 1960," and the article narrates the historical highlights of world war as they spin out from the Soviet assassination attempt on the Yugoslav leader Marshal Tito on May 10, 1952. After a successful Soviet takeover of Belgrade's new radio broadcasting station, an armed man in the engineering control room shouts into the microphone, "Tito is dead!" "This was the signal," the article recites, "for the start of 32 months of unlimited catastrophe for the human race, in the course of which millions of innocent people met violent deaths. . . . Among their scorched, shattered graveyards were the atomized ruins of Washington, Chicago, Philadelphia, Detroit, New York, London and eventually Moscow."[48]

On May 14, 1952, the United States begins dropping atomic bombs on selected military and industrial targets in the Soviet Union, carefully avoiding civilian population centers. The round-the-clock saturation bombing campaign continues for three months and sixteen days.[49] One year later, the Soviet Union responds with the atomic bombing of civilians in targeted U.S. cities. An eyewitness account of the attack on Washington, D.C., accompanied by a two-page illustration of the nation's capital on fire — "Note Pentagon blazing (at upper left)," the caption reads—describes the catastrophic scene:

> The American capital is missing in action.
>
> A single enemy atom bomb has destroyed the heart of the city. The rest is rapidly becoming a fire-washed memory. The flames are raging over 18 square miles.
>
> . . . Civil defense has broken down. The few valiant disaster squads are helpless in this homeless flood of agony and misery. Troops are moving in to restore order among maddened masses trying to flee the city.[50]

The United States retaliates in July 1953 with its first atomic assault on a civilian center—Moscow. An eyewitness report-from-the-air is written by Edward R. Murrow, the popular CBS commentator, who accompanies the military airplane crew that drops the atom bomb.[51]

This dramatic staging of World War III is offered up by *Collier's* magazine in October 1951, in a special issue entitled "Preview of the War We Do Not Want." *Collier's*, a popular weekly magazine with a wide circulation aimed at a white, suburban, middle-class audience, designs the special issue in consultation with top military, economic, and political thinkers in U.S. and international affairs. "Operation Eggnog" — the "purposely meaningless code name" that *Collier's* assigns to the special issue — draws on "authoritative research" and the imaginations of academics, novelists, former Communists, playwrights, and journalists to construct this "spectacular" vision of the future through a retrospective look back on a decade that has not yet taken place: a decade opening with war, progressing to triumph, and closing with the democratic reconstruction of Soviet society in the ruins of its military defeat.[52]

The hypothetical war reportage in *Collier's* appears in the same year that the new Federal Civil Defense Administration (FCDA) launches "one of the largest mass programs the nation has ever essayed": the public education and training of U.S. civilians in the "proper public attitudes and behavior" necessary to their own defense.[53] Created by presidential executive order, the FCDA's mandate, spelled out in the Federal Civil Defense Act of 1950, is to provide for the civilian defense of both life and property in the event of war through the organization of a volunteer civil defense corps and the establishment of emergency communication systems to warn of enemy attack.[54]

A major aim of the civil defense public information program is to educate citizens about the basic facts of the atomic bomb's effects and to suggest simple, common-sense, available remedies. Since "panic resulting from enemy attack may well be the most difficult of all civil defense problems," explains a 1951 instruction manual for local civil defense leaders, a "determined and earnest attempt must be made to understand and control human behavior."[55]

With "Keep Calm!" as its easy-to-remember antidote to atomic disease, the FCDA and its state and local infrastructures sponsor a range of print, radio, television, and cinematic messages aimed at disseminating the relevant facts and advising the appropriate behaviors. Over twenty million copies of the FCDA's pamphlet "Survival under Atomic Attack" are distributed in 1951.[56] In folksy prose, the text describes what to expect if even that worst-case scenario occurs: an atomic blast catches you unawares and you "soak up a serious dose of explosive radioactivity." Readers are informed that "for a few days you might continue to feel below par and about 2 weeks later most of your hair might fall out. . . . But in spite of it all, you would still stand better than an even chance of making a complete recovery, including having your hair grow in again."[57] The problem of lingering radioactivity in the environment—as detected by "your local radiological defense teams"—can be addressed by taking a shower. The pamphlet concludes: "Civil defense must start with you. But if you lose your head and blindly attempt to run from the dangers, you may touch off a panic that will cost your life and put tremendous obstacles in the way of your Civil Defense Corps." The pamphlet includes a tear-out sheet entitled "Six Survival Secrets for Atomic Attacks," which readers are instructed to keep with them at all times until memorized.[58]

In April 1951, the FCDA releases a movie version of *Survival under Atomic Attack*. Commercial distributors sell more prints of *Survival* in the first nine months after its release than any other film in the history of the industry.[59] In the next several years, the FCDA's mass public education program produces an instructive litany of films, newsreels, and made-for-TV series including *Let's Face It, Bombproof, Operation Scramble, What You Should Know about Biological Warfare, Disaster on Main Street*, and *Target You.*[60]

But alongside government-sponsored encouragements to "Keep Calm!" and efforts to render an atomic blast a manageable, even familiar, scenario, an apparently contradictory effort to frighten the U.S. public is simultaneously under way. From its inception, the FCDA names "public apathy" toward civilian defense as the major obstacle to the successful conduct of its task.[61] The concept of civilian defense as a necessary feature of "total defense"—the logical corollary of "total war"[62]—has not yet entered the consciousness of a reticent U.S. public. In a public letter to President Truman in 1952, the first director of the FCDA explains: "Too few realize that the atomic bomb changed the character of warfare and that in future conflicts the man and woman in the street and in the factory will be the prime target—that they will be in the front line of battle. . . . [T]here is little real understanding of the need for a balanced defense, composed of the civil and the military serving in a co-equal partnership."[63] In the *Report of the Project East River* (1952), an extensive study of the problems of civil defense commissioned by the Department of Defense, the National Security Resources Board, and the FCDA, the authors cite attitude surveys conducted by the University of Michigan Survey Research Center to argue that one "major barrier to involvement and activity in civil defense" is the public's tendency to believe that an atomic attack cannot really occur in their hometown, or that the U.S. military will successfully protect the country should such an attack take place.[64] The report recommends a massive public information and training program to address the public's indifference to the civil defense procedures that will most likely become a "future way of life." Based on its assessment of ongoing military tensions with the Soviet Union, the report asserts that the entire edifice of Cold War national security rests on the psychological fortitude of the U.S. civilian population. Thus the problem of a panic-prone public is oddly coupled with the problem of public apathy; both problems can be solved by an extensive campaign of information, education, and training. The campaign must communicate that national defense today "transcends the military's ability and responsibility" and depends equally on citizens' capacity for self-help and self-defense.[65]

Report of the Project East River becomes known as "the Bible of civil defense."[66] Collectively authored by Associated Universities, Inc., a Cold War think tank organized by a consortium of elite universities under contract with the U.S. Army Signal Corps, the report draws on the expertise of sociologists, psychologists, engineers, physicists, economists, public relations personnel, and leading educators. In preparing their report, the project's researchers also consult with the Psychological Strategy Board, an agency established by secret presidential directive in 1951 and charged with the task of designing "psychological operations" against enemies, including the dissemination of propaganda and planning of psychological warfare.[67] The historian Guy Oakes suggests that the public information campaign outlined in the report retools the psychological strategies and propaganda techniques aimed at adversaries abroad for use as "emotional management techniques for psychologically manipulating" the U.S. public at home.[68] A "home" now recognized by U.S. government planners as a perpetually militarized terrain of total war. Or total defense? These two concepts themselves become conflated in the psychic confusions of aggressor and victim, attack and protection, total invulnerability and total panic. While U.S. leaders consistently portray the Soviet Union and the Communist threat as the aggressive forces ready to target civilian populations as atomic ground zero, such a portrayal permits U.S. decision makers the strange freedom to engage in domestic psychological warfare that targets a dangerously indifferent U.S. public.[69]

And so the management of nuclear fear — the dangers both of its excess (the chaos of panic) and of its absence (the unpreparedness of apathy) — becomes a primary goal of the institutionalization of civilian self-defense.[70] In the project's plan for an informed public inoculated against the dangers of mass panic, the encouragement of individual and group fear is acknowledged as a necessary civil defense strategy. Under conditions of atomic threat, the difference between national security and national fear is set spinning: national security *is* national fear; a nation without fear of atomic annihilation is a nation without security. "Panic Prevention and Control," a fifteen-page appendix to *Report of the Project East River*, distinguishes between panic behavior, an "untoward mass reaction" characterized by "aimless, unorganized, unreasoning, nonconstructive activity," and fear, a "normal response to danger," which can be "channeled" usefully into effective "combat" behavior.[71] Fear presents an opportunity for the emergence of organized behavior that can confront and reduce the danger of panic. The key to panic control rests "in the effort to channel crowd behavior in an organized direction." The surest prevention against panic, for civilians as for combat soldiers, is the "implanting of habitual . . . responses" to danger situations, a goal that can be achieved only by intensively training the public in proper behavior in emergency situations; the most effective training situation, for the public as for combat troops, is one that uses "every approach toward realism." The report's authors recommend "human laboratory situations" as a useful setting for analyzing panic, this "otherwise unmanageable social phenomenon."[72]

Now it's 1955. The byline reads "Survival City, Nev.," and the article narrates the highlights of the first atomic bomb dropped on a "typical" U.S. town.[73] Part laboratory experiment, part reality, part mass-mediated spectacle, the incendiary fate of Survival City is broadcast live on CBS and NBC-TV to an estimated audience of 100 million viewers who tune in to watch the blast on May 5, 1955. The climactic televising of the explosion is preceded by two weeks of live telecasts three times daily from the test site.[74] The town, composed of ten brick houses and several prefabricated industrial buildings, is built and bombed to test the effectiveness of civil defense procedures during an atomic attack. Of the five hundred witnesses to the explosion in the Nevada desert, two hundred are civil defense personnel who participate in a series of field exercises in the "exposed area" after the explosion. A group of civilians experience the blast from a trench only 10,500 feet from ground zero, demonstrating "that civil defenders can take it along with the troops." Designed to demonstrate the ferocity of atomic power, and, in the FCDA's words, to bring "vast numbers of Americans face to face with the enormity of the problem of survival in the nuclear age," the atomic test is jointly sponsored by the FCDA, the Atomic Energy Commission (AEC), and private industry.[75] Over 450 members of the press, including radio, television, and newsreel reporters, are stationed eight miles from ground zero on "Media Hill." An unnamed "pretty girl" carries out televised interviews with the city's "survivors"—an array of human-size mannequins placed throughout the test site—before and after the explosion.[76]

The experiment at Survival City, code named Operation Cue, is a follow-up to Operation Doorstep, conducted in March 1953, when an atomic bomb is dropped in the desert to test the blast, radiation, and shock wave effects on two frame houses inhabited by human mannequins—some seated at the dinner table or in the living room in front of the television. The bomb's effects on automobiles, U.S. Postal Service trucks, and underground shelters is also measured. A survey conducted after Operation Doorstep indicates that 70 percent of the public becomes knowledgeable about the government's atomic experiments as a result of the well-publicized event. FCDA officials in 1953 credit Operation Doorstep with doing more to "promote knowledge of self-protection and civil defense" than any other event that year.[77]

I don't remember the code names, the dates, the data, their findings, but without a doubt it was operating at my doorstep, on cue and in front of the local cameras. I remember the mangled plastic of neatly dressed mannequins, the time-series still photos of that experimental white two-story house going up in flames, then flattened by some storm rushing out from inside, simultaneously buckling in from an invisible force without. I wasn't yet born in 1955. But the state-sponsored campaign to compress an unthinkable atomic future into the thinkable present, to operationalize, in the time span of a few seconds and on the scale of a sixteen-inch TV screen, the apocalypse from which the state offered no defense but one's own "self"-protection—no protection but the state's solemn, spectacular, electronically broadcast witness to the fantastic destruction of a test-tube U.S. town—reached forward into my history before I had one and planted a few . . . perceptions. Even in here, especially in here, I sense how the future can sometimes already have happened. How it can arrive, already over, on your doorstep, an anticipated terror that has already taken place on some strangely choreographed cue. As the child of federally administrated time warps, born into a future already compressed into yesterday's experimental lab—"Tomorrow Today!" exclaims a series of fifteen-minute made-for-TV FCDA films[78]—there isn't much to do in this crazy place but carefully reinvent the psychodramas of such a disordered past. Cautiously reconstruct the social *il*logics of such an elusive history. That's really what I'm doing here, I think, in the subterranean shelter of a perpetually breachable self-defense.

At night, they tell me, I have bad dreams, tossing against sleep, mumbling outside consciousness. But sometimes I suspect I'm just seeing newsreels of my future, already running past. A future fast-tracked on an imaginary six-lane interstate highway, built for a mass evacuation that is   not   yet   over.[79]

MACHINE ELECTRIC

We have imposed on the human being, and on our psychological
studies of him, the paradigm of communication engineering. This is
quite useful. . . . If you have a situation where a human being is acting
as a communication system, then he must obey the same laws that
govern all communication systems, just as he must obey the law of
gravitation. — GEORGE A. MILLER, "Communication and the
Information Theory," *Panic and Morale: Conference Transactions*[80]

The fact that we cannot telegraph the pattern of a man from one
place to another is probably due to technical difficulties. . . . It is not
due to any impossibility of the idea. —NORBERT WIENER, *Human Use
of Human Beings*[81]

The first interdisciplinary conference on "Morale and the Prevention and
Control of Panic" is held in February 1951 in New York City; a follow-up
conference takes place in November 1954. The meetings are jointly sponsored by the Josiah Macy Jr. Foundation and the New York Academy of
Medicine. Drawing together over fifty participants from medicine, psychiatry, civil defense, sociology, the radio and television industry, psychology, public health, and political science, the conference organizers
hope to set future directions for research and action on the problems of
panic and morale. Critical of the "fear technique" to which the nation has
been exposed, conference organizers encourage "teams of social scientists and other leaders who have knowledge of human behavior" to participate in designing programs that will be "morale-building rather than
panic-building."[82]

The conference meetings on morale and panic are two among nearly
two hundred conferences sponsored by the Macy Foundation in pursuit
of its founding mission: to promote scientific investigations into "fundamental aspects" of health and disease, especially problems falling "between the sciences" in the borderlands of the medical and the social.[83]
Launched in 1930 with funds from the Macy family business in shipping
and oil (where the Macys were occasional partners with the Rockefeller
family enterprise), the Macy Foundation's philanthropic activities during
World War II focus on health issues central to national defense.[84] The relatively new concept of an interdisciplinary and informal "conference technique," first initiated by the Rockefeller Foundation in 1936, becomes the
postwar model for Macy-sponsored gatherings as the foundation continues its close partnership with U.S. government officials and research
agendas.[85]

The 1954 conference on morale and panic exemplifies the foundation's commitment to bring together a cross-disciplinary array of profes-
sionals in academia, government, industry, and medicine to focus on a
theoretical and practical problem in the "psycho-social" field.[86] Staging

the problem of morale in relation to panic — that is, "good morale impedes panic, and . . . poor or bad morale favors it" — the conference addresses several basic questions: What is morale? By what criteria can it be measured? And how can good morale be fostered and bad morale improved?[87] Under the guidance of Dr. Frank Fremont-Smith, the director of the Macy Foundation's medical division, preparations for the 1954 conference include three separate miniconferences in Chicago, Boston, and Washington, each devoted to discussions by "specialists" of the proposed definition of morale.[88]

But the most extensive intellectual orientation for the 1954 conference is the one formal presentation during the two-day meeting, an opening address entitled "Communication and the Information Theory" delivered by George Miller of Harvard's Psycho-Acoustic Laboratory.[89] Miller's focus on communication and information theory is tied to the definition of morale proposed by Dr. Iago Galdston, a psychiatrist and representative of the New York Academy of Medicine, at both the 1951 and 1954 conferences. Conceiving of morale not as a "thing" in itself but as a feature or quality of behavior that can be judged against a "prototype pattern" of development, Galdston suggests that group morale might profitably be defined "in terms of behavior involved in the achievement of prototype group goal patterns."[90] Good morale — behavior aimed at achieving prototype goal patterns — can be promoted through communication, he hypothesizes. More specifically, a broad spectrum of communication may ensure the individual's successful orientation toward "his reality situation," where the "breadth of the communication spectrum makes possible a multi-phased, integrated appreciation of the reality."[91] Is it possible, Galdston asks, that the "breadth of the spectrum of information" is the key to good morale?

Miller's presentation hopes to give conference participants a more confident grasp of "the state of the art in communication" as seen from a contemporary engineering perspective, and to encourage the application of communication and information theory to the problem of morale.[92] During World War II, Miller worked in the Psycho-Acoustic Laboratory at Harvard University on the wartime problem of jamming enemy voice communications, experimenting with a variety of interference patterns that could disrupt a listener's understanding of the main signal in a radio communication.[93] As an experimental center for the emerging science of psycholinguistics, the Psycho-Acoustic Lab tackled the problem of "noise control" in military communication systems partially through a close alliance with research personnel and experimental techniques developed at Bell Telephone Laboratories, with whom the Psycho-Acoustic Lab maintains important postwar institutional relations.[94]

Beginning with a diagram of a "generalized communication system" that traces the flow of information from source to channel to destination, and highlighting the ever-present danger of system disruption by noise, Miller suggests that both human and machine communication can be understood through this simplified model. Recent advances in the mathematical theory of communication, made possible by Claude Shannon's research at Bell Labs and Norbert Wiener's convergent work at the Massachusetts Institute of Technology, have led to statistical and probabilistic methods for quantifying the amount of information passing through a communication system. For a company like Bell Labs, where Shannon developed his theory of information in 1949, the ability to measure the amount of information carried in a signal means the ability to more precisely and economically design the channel capacity (for example, the telephone wire) to fit the amount of information traveling through it.[95]

The statistical and probabilistic methods formulated at Bell Laboratories for quantifying information begin with the assumption that information is wanted for making a decision, for selecting one choice among a variety of possible options. Information, Miller explains, permits the receiver to "reduce the range of possible alternatives" in the selection of a desired outcome, or goal.[96] One "unit" or "bit" of information is arbitrarily defined as the amount of information needed to reduce by half the possible choices that could lead to the desired goal. Information, then, is a quantified measure of the present path to future outcomes.

In applying this model of a communication system to human social interactions, Miller makes clear that humans can occupy any of the three positions in the flow of information: source (input), channel (transmission), or destination (output). But it is primarily the positioning of humans as information "channels" that interests Miller as he suggests how the communication engineer might contribute to the social engineering of good morale. Drawing on the findings of recent work in experimental psychology, Miller reports that humans have been found to have a quite limited "channel capacity" for transmitting information. Experiments at "putting information into a person" demonstrate that humans tend toward a channel capacity of approximately 2.5 units or bits of information, far inferior to the transmission capabilities of a thin copper wire. Beyond this limit, humans begin to introduce noise into the communication system, resulting in system "errors," that is, a lack of correlation between the input and output signals. In contrast to a telephone (at one thousand bits per second), or a television set (at millions of bits per second), humans appear to be designed with a maximum channel capacity of twenty-five bits per second.[97]

However, turning from the amount of information to the breadth or spectrum of information humans can handle, Miller reports on "laboratory measurements" indicating that a human being is a highly developed "multi-channel information-processing system" capable of effectively handling many different inputs and many different outputs at once. That is, our communicative strength lies in our ability to handle a multiplicity of information; we are well designed to handle simultaneously several different information channels. Based on measurements of the number of different channels needed to process human language, linguists estimate that humans can handle up to nine or ten channels at one time. For the communications engineer trying to maximize morale, this means that "you don't want to give a person a lot of information of any one particular kind. If you want to use him effectively, you have to give him a lot of different kinds of information."[98] Miller concludes that Galdston's suggestion that good morale demands a wide spectrum of information may well be correct.

For conference participants, Miller's introductory remarks provide a frame of reference and a set of analogies for thinking about the problem of morale in both individuals and groups. Indeed, the difference between the group and individual begins to blur as both are conceived, in parallel fashion, as communication systems—producing, transmitting, and receiving information through intrapsychic or interpersonal processes. As the psychiatrist Roy Grinker remarks during the conference proceedings, the possibility may exist of a general frame of reference or common language for viewing any "system."[99] In such a general systems approach, Grinker explains, the concepts used in sociological and psychodynamic language become interchangeable. The language of interacting, integrated systems offers, he suggests, a bridge between the scientific discourses of separate disciplines:

> I think that we are at a stage in science where the disciplines are touching each other at their boundaries, that the ways in which we are viewing one system or another are very similar, and that we are developing . . . *general concepts which are applicable to multiple systems.* Morale . . . is a concept which is applicable whether it be in relation to coordinated somatic functions, the development of integrative personality or social cohesiveness, or even, I think one could imagine, a world order. They are of the same nature of events.[100]

Grinker's dream of a common language traversing the systematic scientific discourses of somatic function, personality, society, or even world order is not an individualized fantasy or pursuit. Indeed, one "goal pattern" of the group of Macy-sponsored conferences, and several of its key participants, is to establish a shared set of concepts, models, or methods across the disparate social, psychological, life, and medical sciences.

The language of communication and information theory introduced at the conference on panic and morale is in fact borrowed from the most ambitious and far-reaching conference program sponsored by Macy from 1946 to 1953: a series of ten interdisciplinary meetings on the new field of cybernetics.[101] The cybernetics conferences overlap in both time and intellectual focus with the 1951 and 1954 conferences on panic and morale. Cybernetics (from the Greek *kybernetes*, meaning pilot or governor) emerges out of the Macy conferences as a new cross-disciplinary subfield devoted to understanding communication and information feedback as the main control techniques in a range of self-regulating "systems."[102]

Cybernetics is an interdisciplinary science of control through communication; its etymological tie to practices of governing is extended through the Macy conferences into shared conceptualizations of "control" in the physiological, engineering, and social sciences. The first cybernetics conference in March 1946 opens with two presentations: one by an experimental neurobiologist on the electrical properties of nerve cells, the other by a mathematician working at Princeton on the design of the first electronic computing machine. Together they introduce the productive analogy between the electrical operations of the human nervous system and the general purpose computer — an analogy that dominates participants' discussions throughout the cybernetics conferences.[103] The disciplinary fields represented by participants in the cybernetics meetings include electrical engineering, mathematics, chemistry, psychiatry, neurology, biology, physiology, zoology, anatomy, sociology, anthropology, psychology, economics, and philosophy. From the social sciences, attendees at the first meeting are Paul Lazarsfeld (sociologist and director of the Columbia Bureau of Applied Social Research), Kurt Lewin (social psychologist and director of MIT's Research Center for Group Dynamics), Margaret Mead (anthropologist), Gregory Bateson (anthropologist), and Heinrich Kluver (experimental psychologist, University of Chicago).[104]

The cybernetic perception of the human nervous system as an electrical machine, and of the computing machine as a network of interacting neurons, is staged by a seminal 1943 essay in the prehistory of cybernetic thought, coauthored by Arturo Rosenblueth (a neurobiologist), Julian Bigelow (an engineer), and Norbert Wiener (a mathematician).[105] The three men become Macy conference participants and core members of the founding group of cyberneticians. Their short essay argues that certain activities of machines and of humans can together be classified as goal-seeking behavior, in which achieving a future goal depends on "feedback" between that future goal and the current behavior of the machine — or human — system. Three of the fundamental features of cybernetic techniques are introduced in this modest essay: first, the analogy between the behavior of machines and humans; second, the grounding of that analogy in metaphors of communication between goals and behavior directed toward those goals; and third, the insistence on circular causality, or the feedback between causes and effects in mutually influencing circuits of communication.[106]

The arguments set forth in the 1943 essay have their conceptual and material origins in the military work conducted by Wiener and Bigelow during World War II. In his widely read book *Cybernetics, or Control and Communication in the Animal and the Machine* (1948), Norbert

Wiener, recognized as a founding intellectual figure of the new subfield, recounts how the basic insights of cybernetics emerged out of the engineering problems encountered in the wartime effort to build a more effective control apparatus for antiaircraft artillery.[107] The technical and strategic problem of how to better shoot down German bomber planes — which, together with the development of atomic weapons, became the two most sophisticated U.S. scientific projects during World War II — involved thinking of the firing gun, the pilot, the moving plane, a moving target, moving machines, and the movements of men as components of a single system. The goal of the system is to accurately target and gun down a moving aerial enemy armed with a lethal bomb. The mathematical problem that Wiener attacked and solved was how to predict, as he explains, "the future of a curve," that is, how to make a statistical prediction, based on incomplete information about the target's pattern of movement, of the target's future location and course so as to improve the control of antiaircraft fire and increase its chances of hitting the enemy target. Wiener's mathematical theory uses statistics to predict the future of a curvilinear flight pattern, based on information from the past (i.e., the behavior of the plane). The materialization of this prediction in the control apparatus of the antiaircraft artillery system involves the problem of negative feedback between radar information and the adjustment of gun controls. The behavior of humans in the fire-control apparatus, according to Wiener, needs to be "incorporate[d] . . . mathematically into the machines they control."[108]

The "new and fundamental revolution in technique" achieved by cybernetics models the multiple, heterogeneous actors in a system (machines, information, humans, electricity) as controlled and controlling via communicative feedback.[109] In *The Human Use of Human Beings: Cybernetics and Society* (1950), his second book written for an educated, nonspecialist readership, Wiener asks, "What then is this communication, which is so human and so essential?" Communication, he explains, is composed of patterns, an ordered arrangement of elements in which "the order of the elements" is the definitive feature, and not "the intrinsic nature of these elements."[110] Communication is tied to the formal, structural properties, or pattern, of things and relationships, and not to their materiality. Considering the human individual as "something which has to do with continuity of pattern, and consequently with something that shares the nature of communication," Wiener speculates in the chapter entitled "The Individual as the Word" that the fundamental identity of the individual body rests not in a physical continuity of matter but in a continuity of patterned processes, a continuity or identity that can, like an electronic code, be transmitted through a communicative channel: "There is no fundamental absolute line between the types of transmission which we can use for sending a telegram from country to country and the types of transmission which at least are theoretically possible for a living organism such as a human being."[111]

The science of cybernetics, Wiener summarizes, is the study of messages, particularly the "effective messages of control," where control operates as "the sending of messages which effectively change the behavior of the recipient." A message is the particular type of pattern in which information is transmitted; it is a "transmitted pattern." The study of society, he concludes, can only be understood as the study of "the messages and the communication facilities which belong to it," specifically the "messages between man and machines, between machine and man, and between machine and machine." The study of these messages in society would then also be the study of the control of humans and machines through the messages, or "transmitted patterns," that direct or redirect their behavior.[112]

I think that's the kind of study I'm doing here. It's a cybernetic approach, really. Trying to hear the patterns, assess the formal properties, of the messages transmitted among this group of mostly men who gather with intensity, liberal tolerance, and philanthropic funding sometime after Hiroshima, before Cambodia, to predict the future curves of knowledge systems gone to war and never quite come back. Total war. Total defense. Total (social) science. This cross-disciplining desire for total systems. For a mathematically precise probability that if the defensive gestures of a moving enemy and its evasive but not random curves of flight are electronically recorded on a radar screen and subjected to a set of statistical runs producing information for transmittal to the gun control apparatus aiming with a minimalized margin of error at the future of that enemy's flight through space in time then the system will achieve its goal, behave with purpose, penetrate the most intricate defense. The message will be—delivered.

The 1954 Macy conference on morale and panic is a choreographed attempt to introduce the central concepts of a cybernetic model of communication systems to an elite group of social scientists. The Macy Foundation, operating itself as a kind of communications device and aware of its own conference program "as the most persistent and wide-ranging effort to promote cross-discipline communication in the USA,"[113] is experimenting with cybernetics as an effective, multidisciplinary, "total" language for understanding social problems and engineering their solution. The cybernetic approach has all the attractions of a simplified behaviorism, with its focus on input-output processes and the measurable, observable features of behavior. But it also incorporates into its model the potential complexities, or psychological processes, of behaviorism's blank, black box—the "channel" in the cybernetic communication system has properties of its own that should be investigated so as to be successfully used.[114]

The informal discussions constituting the bulk of the 1954 conference on panic and morale revolve largely around the perceptual operations of the transmission channel—understood as either the individual or the group—for morale behavior. Galdston's hypothesis that a broad spectrum of communication flowing through the human channel increases awareness of reality, reduces the dangers of panic, and "facilitates effective behavior, which in turn enhances morale," is met with a disparate chorus of responses.[115] Some are concerned with the psychodynamic problem of "noise" generated in early mother-child relations; many raise questions of where or how the "meaning" of information fits into individual or group morale patterns; and several object to the lack of attention to social values that prescribe certain behaviors as "good" morale and others as "bad." But the terms of the conversation are largely set by the conceptual parameters of communication and information models. The messages promoting a cybernetic approach to social problems are suggestively transmitted through the influential Cold War channels of intellectual and institutional communication assembled by the philanthropic reach of the Macy Foundation.

> *Basic Law of Morale*: "The Individual Must Feel That He Is Partici-
> pating in His Own Destiny." He must feel that he is voluntarily
> pursuing his own goals. . . . [I]f the citizen feels that the objectives of
> the government are essentially the objectives that he himself desires, if
> they arouse his hopes and therefor his voluntary cooperation, he will
> feel identified with the enterprise — with civil defense — and will aid it
> to the best of his ability. — Office of Civil Defense[116]

"Test Yourself," the headline reads, "How Panic-Proof Are You?" The two-page self-test in the August 1953 issue of the popular *Collier's* magazine shows five large boxes, each containing survey questions or tests of behavior for predicting your susceptibility to panic. "How do you feel when: . . . You are alone and your doorbell and telephone ring simultaneously?" Check one: "I'm not bothered." "I become tense." "I blow up." — "Extend one arm, holding a heavy book. . . . Now count the words in this paragraph." — "Set an alarm clock ringing continuously on the table near you. Then count the crosses in the circle without using a pencil to assist you." — "Time yourself on this test. How long does it take you to place a dot at the center of each of the zeros below?" (360 tiny zeros are drawn beneath). Numerical instructions are included for scoring your individual "panic rating." If your final score is under 50, you are likely to panic. From 70 to 90, you're "panic-resistant." Above 90, "you're as close to being panic-proof as a human can be."[117]

The self-test is part of a longer feature article titled "Panic, the Ultimate Weapon?" written by Val Peterson, director of the FCDA. In keeping with civil defense theory of the time, Peterson, after describing the apocalyptic aftermath of an atomic blast over Main Street — "The heart of your community is a smoke-filled desolation rimmed by fires" — warns of the dramatic threat that panic presents to U.S. national security: "On your actions may depend not only your life and the lives of countless others, but your country's victory or defeat, and the survival of everything you hold dear. Ninety per cent of all emergency measures after an atomic blast will depend on the prevention of panic among the survivors in the first 90 seconds. . . . If there is an ultimate weapon, it may well be mass panic —

not the A-bomb."[118] Announcing that the fundamental fact of the atomic era is that "we, the citizens of the strongest nation on earth, are also the most panic-prone," Peterson discloses the recent findings from important panic research. One "highly classified nonprofit organization in the West," which has conducted "panic-probing experiments all over the nation" and shared its findings with U.S. federal agencies, speculates on the possibility of developing chemical agents that can decrease panic susceptibility. Other "Western researchers" have devised animal experiments involving the application of 70,000 volts of "harmless but spectacular" high-frequency electricity to a laboratory mouse, exciting inch-long blue sparks from each hair on its body. Most mice, although not physically injured, go mad from the experiments—although a few exceptional rodents kept calm and "in successive tests actually began to enjoy the experience." Although unclear how these findings might apply to humans, "tests have shown" that the cowboy of the Western high plains is, like the occasional mouse and the entire species of snowy owls, unusually impervious to panic. Due perhaps to the calm woven into life in "vast lonely spaces."[119]

The article ends with Peterson's confident summary of the panic-prevention steps successfully implemented by the FCDA. The installation of "broad emergency information facilities," achieved through the cooperation of the government and the broadcast industry, has set into operation CONELRAD, the code name for a new system of radio emergency broadcasting providing a "sure, instant channel of information from defense officials to the public anywhere in the country." The essential facts of the situation can now be broadcast within minutes after an attack warning, and the president of the United States is now able to address from a single microphone every live radio set in the country. With the "information media" recognizing their own critical role in national survival, Peterson concludes, "we can go a long way in licking the psychological impact of an enemy attack," preventing panic and "maintaining morale" by transmitting the facts to a concerned public.[120]

And tell me, my lonesome cowboy, whatever do you think they did with the mice who went mad? More tests? On the temperature, the transient electrochemical states, the neural architectures of wild bewilderment? Of dumb, live-wired, animal intelligence electrified beyond a safe return by the harmless if spectacular blue jolt of scientific inquiry?

And where are you now, my sweet cowboy? With calm arms outstretched can you hold me, trembling, here in this place? Far from your Western plateaus. Beyond the stoic watch of the snowy owl. I'm caught here, and with calculation, in this abstract place of panic proneness, in the vast lonely spaces of this deserted classification, of this continuously timed self-test that I'm failing my outstretched arm holding a book counting the words in this paragraph drawing a dot in the center of 360 tiny circles with an alarm clock sounding endlessly on a table nearby while somebody's knocking at that door as the telephone starts ringing and I tell you, my darling, I am feeling—a little tense.

By 1956, the FCDA recognizes that the facts of the potential attack situation facing the United States in the atomic era have become acutely disturbing. With the advent of the hydrogen bomb—capable of exponentially greater mass destruction, especially through radioactive fallout, than a "conventional" atomic bomb—and the development of guided intercontinental ballistic missiles just over the horizon, the warning time for attack and the threatened destruction from an all-out atomic airstrike reach almost unimaginable dimensions. Civil defense planning assumptions spelled out by the FCDA in its 1956 annual report include the following: (1) the enemy's initial attack will attempt "a knockout blow" relying primarily on nuclear weapons, but most likely also involving chemical and biological weaponry; (2) the attack will target U.S. military, civilian, and industrial areas (187 probable targets are listed, including every significantly populated metropolitan area and all state capitals); (3) warning time for cities on the Atlantic coast will be from one to three hours; and (4) radioactive fallout from a large-scale mass attack will cover vast areas of the United States and could affect any region.[121] In light of the rapid increase in the size and destructive force of nuclear arsenals and the rapid decrease in delivery times made possible by new aerospace technologies, the FCDA calls for a "modernization" of its civil defense organization. As part of a $1.9 million annual budget for research and development, the FCDA provides more than $200,000 to corporations and research institutes for the development of a "home warning device" to alert residents of nuclear attack, as well as funding for the National Opinion Research Center (NORC) to improve techniques for disseminating civil defense information through the mass media, a grant to Group Attitudes, Inc., to evaluate the effectiveness of civil defense public information campaigns, and a renewal of the ongoing contract with the University of Michigan's Survey Research Center to continue attitude surveys on current public thinking about civil defense.[122]

The alarming "facts" of nuclear threat and civilian survival continue in 1956 to be circulated in an array of dramatized forms, with over twenty-two motion pictures (most of them cleared for television airing) available for showing in schools, civic organizations, and churches.[123] One of the films, *Operation Ivy*, documents the secret military operation carried out in the Marshall Islands on November 1, 1952, when the United States detonates its first hydrogen bomb, producing the largest nuclear fireball in history. Kept an official secret from the U.S. public for a year and a half— while rumors of the operation and its filmed version circulated widely— the H-bomb is introduced to the public via a televised broadcast of *Operation Ivy* aired in April 1954. The top-secret film is originally screened for a select audience composed of President Eisenhower, his cabinet, and the Joint Chiefs of Staff, who view it at the White House in June 1953.[124]

The film shows the sensational atomic fireball rising out of the sea and the shock waves rushing across the ocean surface. An enormous mushroom cloud darkens the sky. Superimposed against the horizon of flame is a replica of Manhattan's skyline: "The fireball alone," the film narrates, "would engulf about one-quarter of the island of Manhattan." In National Security Council meetings, where the public release of the film is contentiously debated in early 1954, rationales for distributing the documentary veer from the plea by the FCDA director Val Peterson for something that could "scare the American people out of their indifference" to President Eisenhower's vehement critique of fear tactics and his pronouncement that the film should be shown only if it offered "real and substantial knowledge to the people." For one reason or the other or perhaps both, *Operation Ivy* is released on April 2, 1954, and is broadcast repeatedly over television stations throughout the day. In the FCDA media package accompanying the film's release, Peterson emphasizes both the phenomenal power of the new weapon with its spectacular visual effects, and the capacity of current civil defense strategies to absorb the new threat without major changes.[125]

Testing. Eins. Zwei. Drei. Testing. Can you hear me? Are we communicating yet? Is the connection holding?

Alert Today—Alive Tomorrow, a film produced for the FCDA in 1956, portrays the unchanging civil defense response to the changing strategic landscape of nuclear attack.[126] The choreographed documentary opens with the halcyon scene of a "typical" U.S. town, with tidy streets, single-story brick houses, freshly mowed lawns, and well-behaved children. The camera records the friendly routines of suburban white men doing yardwork on a sunny Saturday afternoon, suburban white women chatting as they hang the laundry out to dry. On a street in downtown Reading, a mother and her two children stroll down the sidewalk. The young girl, wearing summer shorts and horn-rim glasses, turns to look in a shop window filled with well-dressed mannequins. But a poster in the window catches her eye: "Civilians Can Be Bombed!" Close-up shot on the young girl's face, bewildered.

The town is Reading, Pennsylvania. The stars of the film are the eight thousand community volunteers who compose the well-prepared civil defense organization pictured in its myriad functions: auxiliary fire and police departments, volunteer ambulance units. Reading displays its riches of trained citizens willing and able to load, transport, unload, and assemble a two-hundred-bed emergency hospital. Middle-aged housewives wearing white jumpsuits and helmets practice emergency procedures in an all-female volunteer rescue team—running into burning buildings, working the pulley system that sends "victims" strapped neatly onto stretchers out of smoking windows to safety below.

At the firing range of the Reading Pistol Club, members of the auxiliary citizen police corps watch patiently as the instructor demonstrates how to properly aim and fire a revolver at a distant target. Each of the white-suited volunteers then takes a turn with the gun. In the event of atomic attack, who will be the actual targets of the volunteer civil defense militia? The announcer explains that with their civil defense training at the Reading Pistol Club, citizens will be prepared to "check possible panic" in the chaotic aftermath, contributing a "strong stabilizing effect on the

Watching the Cold War. RKO/Federal Civil Defense Administration, *Alert Today— Alive Tomorrow*, 1956.

jittery populace."[127] Panic-resistant citizens, bearing down in white jump-suits and belted guns, under the voluntary burdens of national defense. A bleak future, armed and ready, advancing toward the pretested and perhaps less voluntary corps of the panic prone.

IN SUBURBAN HOUSES

Daddy was a navy frogman. Ocean. Motion. Off the coast of Southern California in the late 1950s, he was trained to detonate and defuse under-water explosives. In a manner of speaking, then, I was born out of the belly of my mother into the belly of the U.S. military. Sunlight. Dynamite. When we moved in 1962 from the small island that served as a military training base for the U.S. Navy to the suburbs of Reading, Pennsylvania, my parents bought their first house with a loan furnished through the GI bill. Daddy's job as an engineer was made possible by a master's degree in physics that he earned on the GI bill's education program. These're different ways that I interpret the meaning of the Cold War.

(I wake in the dark of this place, my head banging with dream quickly escaping. Hands search blind for a pen, some paper. I write, I WANT TO KNOW — IS IT POSSIBLE TO WRITE IN THE DARK? IS IT POSSIBLE TO WRITE IN THIS DARK? I WANT TO WRITE IN THE DARK.)

I turn on the light—to find the lines, some rope of words to pull me through. Strung taut between dreaming and wake. And why do I wake?

What causes me to wake now so often near four A.M.? My brain sucked in a syncopated rhythm of memory, meaning, darkness, meaning. Memory. I remember. Under the bed in the dark four A.M. and in hiding as Daddy grabs her neck. He is naked, she in a soft nylon gown. They have been to the annual Firemen's Ball, for the Reading Volunteer Fire Corps, come home late and well drunk. Mama nylon across the bed and he naked choking her, collared at the throat, he softly speaking such language, "bitch," he whispers hot and her head hanging off the bed, at the edges. I am under the bed four A.M. in the dark and in hiding and WHY DON'T I STOP HIM? Mama, do I try?

Such a scene playing out across these white sheets — Mama's head on the edge — returned from the Reading Firemen's Ball and well drunk, her head hanging at the edges and his hands on her throat binding. (Breath.) He has collared her, the blood must be gathering in her brain round her edges drunk with the fireman, their many balls, such dancing. (Death.) She must be at the water's edge going to liquid as he collars her, bitch, he naked against her nylon. What boiled in your brain, Mama, what tale to tell if we ease up the bindings, a bloodletting, what flow Mama of words, no words, tears, no tears, what a bloodletting of your brain that burned after the Firemen's Ball as his fingers pressed your borders. Your waters flowing. What do you know Mama? With what binding does your brain blood boil?

Dear Mama, I don't know if I stopped him. I think I stood there in the darkness of the mid-1960s, unblinking. But I do know now you stop me, remind me never to die for his delight. Quite a binding! It makes my blood boil. But how do I move Mama, feet tied again to mud and dancing on some other grounds? How do we let the blood boiling in these hot brains? I don't wanna die for his delight but I will burn if need be for mine. Where is our delight, Mama, what blood flows us toward other borders? Tell me Mama, I'm under the bed four A.M. and in hiding, listening for the next lines, a rope of words, a knotted sheet thrown to me. We are at a watery edge, Mama, and ghosts calling us under and down, ghosts calling my name, bitch, going under. How do we flow toward other edges, toward our delight, Mama, in this dark and you on your back and back from the Firemen's Ball and me under the bed in the dark again and burning

mama where is delight
 and how do we write
   where   is   de   light
how do we write in such a dark, mama,
  such a dark mama four A.M. dream?

FATHER THOUGHT IT WAS CLEAR

The father symbol everywhere [is] the one who must be and, apart
from clearly neurotic cases, to some extent genuinely is respected. . . .
At the same time there is an ambivalent undercurrent in the attitudes
toward such figures which on occasion may come to the centre of
the stage. — TALCOTT PARSONS[128]

Daddy, I have had to kill you. — SYLVIA PLATH[129]

Talcott Parsons is not an empirical sociologist. But his career as a preeminent sociological theorist in the United States, where his reputation and influence peak by the early 1960s, is explicitly committed to the development of a logically adequate, internally consistent and coherent system of social theory that can guide the selection and interpretation of empirical facts. For Parsons, the mutual interdependence of "empirical interpretations of society" and the "structure of theoretical systems" constitutes the necessary foundation for a verifiable science of society. In the pursuit of a scientific theory of society — that is, "a body of logically interrelated 'general concepts' of empirical reference" — theory itself can operate as an "independent variable" in the development of science; theory has the potential power to determine what "facts will be discovered" and what directions will be taken by the "scientific investigation" of the social.[130] The attempt to wield such determinant power is perhaps one animating motive for Parsons's considerable body of theoretical work, spanning more than five decades of writing and teaching.

While Parsons's theoretical system loses its hegemonic hold on the disciplining of sociologists by the late 1960s, it is still recognized today as, in the words of Jeffrey Alexander, a "permanent contribution to social thought," particularly the unparalleled achievement of Parsons's "clarifying theoretical logic."[131] Among his permanent contributions is the establishment of a canon of classical theory, composed of turn-of-the-century European "fathers" of U.S. sociological theory, posthumously birthed after World War II and respected to this day with a kind of Oedipal intensity unrivaled in other academic disciplines.[132] Positioning his own work and the "voluntarist theory of action" at its core as the site of convergence between opposing European epistemological traditions, Parsons becomes himself the father of "Parsonian functionalism."[133] Parsons's functionalism is an elaborate attempt to systemically construct a closed, logically related set of analytic concepts of sufficient generality to provide an encompassing frame of reference for a unified science of social action, where action is conceived as normatively regulated and oriented to the attainment of goals.[134]

The frame of reference and logic of conceptualization organizing Parsons's entire, exhaustive theoretical enterprise is the notion of a "system." As he states at the outset of *The Social System: The Major Exposition of the Author's Conceptual Scheme for the Analysis of the Dynamics of the Social System* (1951): "The fundamental starting point is the concept of social systems of action. The *interaction* of individual actors, that is, takes place under such conditions that it is possible to treat such a process of inter-action *as a system in the scientific sense* and subject it to the same order of theoretical analysis which has been successfully applied to other types of systems in other sciences."[135]

Parsons attributes the early inspiration for this focus on systems to a Harvard seminar in the 1930s conducted by L. J. Henderson, a laboratory physiologist who enters the social sciences convinced, according to Parsons, of the "extreme importance of the concept of system in scientific theory."[136] From Henderson's model of "system" based on physics and chemistry, to the later influence of systems borrowed from biology and cybernetics, Parsons's conceptualization of the logic of the "action system" in relation to the "social system" is structured, deeply and consistently, by analogies with the functioning of systems as modeled in the natural sciences. The notion of system provides a model not only for how "society" or "action" are to be theorized but for how the structure of theory itself is to be conceived: as a "system of concepts" providing a logical framework for the "orderly growth" of a dynamic knowledge of society.[137]

In the early 1950s, Parsons's systems model begins to mutate. He credits a series of interdisciplinary conferences, sponsored by the Carnegie Corporation and organized by Roy Grinker and other psychiatrists deeply anchored in biological thought, as the "intellectual bonanza" that helps him better grasp the action system (which he conceives as a more technical term for human behavior) as "a single superordinate system that involved a plurality of interlocking restricted systems."[138] The conference series, "A Unified Theory of Human Behavior," which begins in 1951 and meets regularly for almost a decade, pushes Parsons toward recognizing a fourth systems component of the action system: the "behavioral organism," operating together with the personality system, the social system, and the cultural system already theorized in his previous work.[139] Parsons starts to move beyond the early functional logic of the system model borrowed from L. J. Henderson, toward a more specific analogy with recent biological models of the organism. The "behavioral organism" — which touches on, but is not equivalent to, the organic body — is the site, Parsons theorizes, at which social objects and the "culture of the personality" become internalized in the individual, the brain being the most important locus for this level of system activity.[140] Of particular interest to Parsons is the work of James Old, a social psychologist and conference participant, who enters the field of brain research to study the relation between the brain and behavior.[141]

Parsons's attention to the biology of behavior intersects with his introduction, in the same years, to cybernetics and information theory. As a guest at two of the Macy-sponsored cybernetics conferences, Parsons encounters the notion of cybernetic feedback mechanisms as self-regulatory processes analogous to homeostasis in the biological organism.[142] The emphasis on control and organization in cybernetic notions of feedback offers Parsons a new, better model of how control may operate in social systems: via hierarchically organized regulatory processes embedded in the system as feedback mechanisms. He writes: "Clarification of the problem of control . . . was immensely promoted by the emergence, at a most strategic time for me, of a new development in general science —

namely, cybernetics in its close relation to information theory. It could now be plausibly argued that *the basic form of control in action systems was of the cybernetic type* and not primarily, as had been generally argued, the analogy of the coercive-compulsive aspects of the processes in which political power is involved."[143] In Parsons's theoretical system, the cybernetic hierarchy of control will become a dominant model for conceptualizing the interactions between the behavioral organism and the personality, cultural, and social systems. By some accounts, Parsons's cybernetic hierarchy of control marks the most sophisticated conceptualization he ever achieves of the problem of social order.[144]

In the same years that Parsons is rethinking his action system in relation to biological and cybernetic models of system activity, he publishes a series of articles delineating a psychoanalytically inflected social psychology of the "personality system."[145] Since coming to a theoretical crossroads in the late 1930s, when he begins to seriously read Sigmund Freud's writings and decides to enter a formal psychoanalytic training and analysis at the Boston Psychoanalytic Institute, Parsons has regularly engaged psychoanalytic thought.[146] In "The Superego and the Theory of Social Systems," first presented in 1951 for the American Psychiatric Association, he attempts a theoretical unification of psychoanalysis and sociology, with the wider aim of "contribut[ing] to the development of a common foundation for the theoretical analysis of human behavior which can serve to unify all the sciences [of behavior]."[147] The bridge Parsons constructs crosses between Sigmund Freud (the father of psychoanalysis) and Freud's contemporary Emile Durkheim (a canonized father of sociological theory) to create a common frame of reference in Parsons's own theory of action systems. It is toward this theory of action and its concern with meaning and motivation that Parsons directs his convergence of Freud's concept of the superego in the personality and Durkheim's sociological concern with moral norms and "value patterns" in the social system. The internalization of these value patterns or norms occurs through the mediation of a common culture, understood by Parsons as a shared "system of symbols." The superego—as well as the ego, and certain aspects even of the id or the unconscious—are internalizations of this cultural symbol system, making the structuring of the personality system and its deepest motivations a thoroughly cultural and "normative" affair.[148]

I don't blame Daddy. Really. I'm not even sure I understand what he's saying. But like he says there's this system we're all interacting in or there's this interaction that's all a system and in this interactive system which according to Daddy supposedly functions by everybody internalizing all these supposedly shared symbols which're also systems so we have systems internalizing systems all in the name of the system's interaction's interpenetration's interdependence which strikes me as a peculiarly abstract way to talk about society even though I totally understand that's exactly why Daddy's doing it. He wants to make an abstract way to talk about society. That, I believe, is the motivation for his actions. Daddy might say his motivation is an effect of the internalization of cultural value patterns. I myself would speculate that Daddy's motivation is an effect of a certain culture's valuing of patterns. A valuing of very abstract patterns. Of patterns of abstraction. Of pattern's abstraction patterns even. Or, if you're really good at it, of pattern's abstraction patterns' abstraction patterns. (You see how it could provide a lifetime of work.) And I wonder sometimes—wandering through these internalizations of Daddy's abstractions, wondering at my institutionalization within abstract patterns of Daddies—where does this valuing of abstract patterns come from?

In a second paper, presented in 1952 for the American Psychological Association, Talcott Parsons offers a more specific theorization of how normative social authority, or the value patterns of the culture, come to reside internally in the personality system. The father as symbolic object, the representative of a generalized meaning-complex that extends beyond the actual figure of the familial father, is the "point of articulation" between the family subsystem and the wider social system.[149] Sociologically speaking, the father symbol "is perhaps the most important single channel through which the value patterns of the culture on the more general level come to be internalized in the process of socialization." The profound ambivalence associated with the father symbol is thus linked to its generalized meaning as "the prototype of a source of authority. He comes into the individual's most intimate security system and makes disturbing demands." Although his essay offers only a "fragmentary analysis" of this most important of symbol systems, Parsons ends on a note of confidence that the now convergent streams of sociology and psychoanalysis are moving ever closer toward fruitful integration. The promise of "careful and competent empirical research" conducted at the crossroads of the two disciplines lies just ahead.[150]

MOTHER NEVER TAUGHT ME

> The child's erotic attachment to the mother is the "rope" by which
> she pulls him up from a lower to a higher level in the hard climb of
> "growing up." But because the points of attachment of this "rope"
> remain sensitive . . . there is a permanent channel back into the still
> operative infantile motivational system. Serious disturbances of the
> equilibrium of the personality can always re-open these channels.
> —TALCOTT PARSONS[151]

> Aggression which arises within the home may be dealt with by
> displacement outside of it. —ANNE PARSONS[152]

Anne Parsons is a young woman in her early twenties when her father begins to theorize publicly about the father symbol in his effort to integrate psychoanalysis and social science in a systematic theory of personality and culture. In 1955, at the age of twenty-five, she completes her doctoral thesis in Paris, where she studies with the anthropologist Claude Lévi-Strauss, the developmental psychologist Jean Piaget, and the psychoanalyst Jacques Lacan. Upon the conferral of her academic degree, her father, Anne Parsons reports, who had only recently "given me up for instability and compulsive deviance," is extremely proud of his daughter.[153]

Upon her return to the United States, Parsons begins what will become a lifelong project: the interdisciplinary, cross-cultural study of mental illness and psychiatry. From 1955 to 1960, with funding from the National Institute of Mental Health and an affiliation with Harvard Medical School, she conducts empirical research at several mental hospitals in Boston and spends two years in Naples, Italy, doing fieldwork in mental institutions on the symptomatology and treatment of schizophrenia among working-class Italians.[154] In the introduction to a collection of Anne Parsons's writings, *Belief, Magic, and Anomie: Essays in Psychosocial Anthropology* (1969), her research is praised for persuasively situating the individual in the context of "group patterns of interaction" and for emphasizing the interdependence of personality, culture, and social structure.[155]

Parsons's analysis of mental illness draws heavily on concepts from cultural anthropology, psychoanalysis, and her father's sociological theory. In her essay "Expressive Symbolism in Witchcraft and Delusion," she discusses the case of a thirty-seven-year-old Italian woman, immigrated to the United States, married and mother of nine children, briefly hospitalized in Boston for paranoid schizophrenia, who, after her release, "took off all her clothes, rubbed her body with bathing alcohol and ignited it. She was next seen by the landlord, walking down the stairs in flames with a child under each arm. . . . [S]he died in the hospital of severe burns."[156] Parsons examines the "expressive symbolism" in the woman's case—a concept borrowed from her father, who defines it as "the cultural patterning of action of the expressive type."[157] Is it more accurate, Anne Parsons wonders, to explain the woman's symptoms as paranoid delusions, or as the cultural effect of her belief in witchcraft and magical symbols learned in the Italian peasant community in which she grew up?

In a related chapter, Parsons draws on her fieldwork in Naples to suggest cultural and class differences in the content of paranoid delusions. Among primarily working-class women hospitalized in a private mental institution in southern Italy, she finds delusional imagery almost exclusively focused on "concrete persons and events" in their family and neighborhood. In contrast, middle-class U.S. women hospitalized in a private institution displayed delusions "with a very strong tendency toward abstraction."[158] One U.S. woman from an "intellectually inclined and cosmopolitan" family tells Parsons: "I thought I would be a good weapon in the struggle between Communist and Western powers. . . . I read the *Look* article about the radio-active family—that's how I felt, spreading radioactivity. I had a lot of information on me—anything I did would mean that all the Americans would be swept off the earth and I thought the hospital was a big factory that observed guinea pigs—everything was arranged."[159] Another patient, daughter of a Madison Avenue advertising executive, says about her life on the hospital ward, "What is it that the people on the ward know about me that I don't know? I just feel so degraded. It's getting more complicated every day—the books, the TV, they're all written for me, it's one big advertising campaign at my expense. They are redoing the hospital—switching the male and female wards— it's all planned by an advertising agency for my benefit."[160]

Emphasizing the intimacy between the content of delusional imagery and the concrete cultural locations of the patients, Parsons suggests that the tendency of U.S. patients "to juxtapose personal details and ideas about ideologies or institutions" and to incorporate technological concepts into "sophisticated paranoid 'systems,'" is connected to living in a culture where association with secondary institutions, outside the primary group of family or neighborhood, becomes crucial to individual identity. The "juxtaposed abstractions" in the paranoid thinking of U.S. patients, who seem to be "desperately trying to organize an overcomplex world," stands in stark opposition to the Neapolitan patients, who express "vividly communicated terror [and] anger . . . using language with remarkably concrete and explosive forcefulness."[161]

My mama was the parson's daughter. Youngest of three children, her father was a Presbyterian minister, and her mother was the daughter of a Presbyterian minister. That makes me the daughter of a parson's daughter. And the daughter of a parson's daughter's daughter. At some level the pattern comes through loud and clear but you still have to wonder— is all this just noise? Does it count as a transmissible message? Have we exceeded channel capacity of the information-processing system? Do I just hate Daddy with an aggressive expressive symbolism verging on the paranoid delusion that the whole panicky world is on fire and Daddy says he's on the front lines of my defense gearing up for a little goal-oriented action a little cybernetic antiaircraft artillery system a little civilian participation in the psychological state of the nation but it all seems just a bit too offensive to me a bit too much oriented toward some form of attack as she walks downstairs in flames with a child under each arm as she burns across that marital bed after the firemen's ball as she empirically investigates the abstract dis-orders of cultural patterns of social psychological communication to find there some openings back toward a future that hasn't happened but lies buried in a fictional phantasmatic memory of a matter, a materiality, a mother's bodymind once upon a time before this story begins ticktocking to the tune of an experimentally calibrated clock and yes, it is true, you could call it a serious disturbance in my equilibrium. At least it gives me something to think about. As I wander about this institution, looking for a way out. Imagining, though not based on any exact empirical proof, that Mama was looking too. That the parson's daughter, that abstract mother symbol system pattern, was trying to find an escape route, too.

In the concluding chapter of *Belief, Magic, and Anomie*, an excerpt from her doctoral thesis, Anne Parsons presents a historical and social psychological analysis of the distortion and transmission of psychoanalytic concepts across different cultural settings.[162] She observes that in contrast to French renderings of the unconscious as a "psychic space," dominant notions of the unconscious in the United States offer up a far more mechanized image. "At the present time," she writes, "one sees a growing use of analogies to machine processes in order to describe the inner world, such as adjustment, ego repair. . . . Just as in the terms which refer to biology and behaviorism (growth, purposive behavior), there is the implication of a collective movement within which the discrete units must be coordinated."[163] These images of mechanically coordinated and interconnected unconscious movements, she suggests, are symptomatic of American culture more broadly.

Parsons explains her own method of analysis as an attempt to apply Freud's method of symbolic interpretation to "the social level." Drawing on Freud's analysis of the symbolic operations in dreams, she gives examples of how "displacement," and the "reversal between the relations of symbolic dichotomy," are at work in the diffusion of meanings across different cultures, including the cultural diffusion of Freud's own psychoanalytic concepts. The French surrealists, she argues, dreamily reverse Freud's symbolic dichotomy between conscious/unconscious and reality/dream to insist on the value of the devalued second terms (unconscious and dream) over the first (consciousness and reality). In a reversal of Freud's own commitment to "bring the dreamer to reality," Anne Parsons sees the surrealists using Freudian theory as a method for bringing reality back to its dreams.[164]

New Guided Missile Takes Off. . . . This newest antiaircraft missile, soaring upward on its supersonic flight, is launched, steered and exploded by electronic control. . . . The control devices were developed by the Bell System's research and manufacturing units. . . . This guided missile assignment for the Army Ordnance Corps is just one of many important military projects now entrusted to the Bell Telephone System. — advertisement, *Collier's* magazine (1951)

With the development of such weapon delivery systems as intermediate-range and intercontinental ballistic missiles, the United States finds itself today for the first time quite vulnerable to a massive air attack.

. . . Undoubtedly, the task of anticipating and evaluating the manifold problems of survival in such a disaster situation presents to sociology and the other social sciences one of their greatest and most awesome challenges, along both theoretical and practical grounds.

— EDWARD TIRYAKIAN[165]

By the late 1950s, a burgeoning literature and a proliferation of empirical research establish collective panic as a popular, if contentious, object of social psychological study. In a 1957 overview of the field of collective behavior, the sociologist Herbert Blumer remarks on the impressive degree of controversy surrounding the study of panic and calls for more empirical research into actual panic situations, which might better reveal verifiable "mechanisms of panic formation." In particular, he notes the debate — foregrounded in Alexander Mintz's 1951 laboratory experiments on group panic — over whether panic constitutes irrational behavior or is instead based on reasonable perceptions of a social situation.[166]

The question of the rationality or irrationality of group panic is linked to the shifting fortunes of "emotional contagion" and "suggestibility" as adequate social psychological concepts for describing mechanisms of collective behavior. As specific types of collectivities — the public, the crowd, the mass — become conceptually differentiated, the notion of suggestibility as the defining feature of the crowd is replaced by an emphasis on the normative, reasonable, even adaptive features of crowd behavior.[167]

In a 1956 edition of *Social Psychology*, the authors Alfred Lindesmith and Anselm Strauss remark that "much of what is called suggestibility actually involves judgment and reasoning and may represent a quite realistic adaptation."[168] For Ralph Turner and Lewis Killian, editors of the well-known textbook *Collective Behavior* (1957), collective behavior is defined not by an absence of social norms but by the spontaneous, emergent nature of those norms.[169]

Together with its object of study, panic research throughout the 1950s is characterized by the increasingly normative features of its own increasingly reasonable behavior. Denouncing the empty acrobatics of "arbitrary speculative interpretation"[170] and "ad hoc statements representing impressionistic reflections on a few sparsely detailed accounts,"[171] panic researchers agree on the need to collect empirical data that permit hypothetical propositions about panic which can be tested, verified, and used to advance panic theory and implement effective social controls.[172]

Lamenting the "lack of a systematic set of empirically based generalizations and conceptualizations," the sociologist Enrico Quarantelli offers a series of hypotheses that might serve as the basis for further panic research.[173] In "The Behavior of Panic Participants" (1957), Quarantelli draws on field data gathered through survey research conducted by the National Opinion Research Center (NORC) Disaster Team, under contract with the Department of the Army. Members of the mobile disaster team arrive at the scene from within three hours to three days of a catastrophe, collecting approximately one thousand tape-recorded interviews with people in communities devastated by tornadoes, earthquakes, airplane crashes, industrial explosions, or train wrecks.[174]

As a counter to the vague and ambiguous usage in most discussions, Quarantelli begins with a precise definition of panic behavior as "actual (or attempted) physical flight." Such flight behavior generally takes "the form of actual physical running," although conceivably it can be "manifested in varying activities such as driving vehicles, swimming, crawling, riding horses, rowing, climbing, jumping, digging, etc."[175] He emphasizes that contrary to previous sociological images of the panicked individual as antisocial, wild, chaotic, irrational, maladaptive, and nonfunctional, panic participants in fact exhibit complex, socially learned reactions: "Whatever else panic behavior may involve, it does represent the behavior of a socialized individual, perceiving and thinking in socially defined and supported ways." Indeed, Quarantelli argues, in certain circumstances a panicky person's terrified attempt to escape imminent danger may constitute the most adaptive action possible. Far from being "antisocial" or even "nonfunctional" behavior, panic has the potential to adjust an individual to the unexpected danger of personal annihilation.[176]

An additional important finding from the NORC Disaster Team's data is that one of the contributing conditions to panic is, Quarantelli reports, the "pre-definition of a crisis as one that is likely to eventuate in panic flight. . . . [A]ny such predefining of a situation as potentially panic-producing can have a direct effect on a participant's interpretation of the behavior of others, as well as his own behavior."[177]

Quarantelli's finding is echoed in the work of social psychologist Irving Janis. In a statement prepared in 1955 at the request of the FCDA by a subcommittee of the National Research Council's Committee on Disaster Studies, Janis and his coauthors underline the suggestive power of the social predefinition of a situation to influence panic behavior: "Those who predict that a large number of Americans will react to the threat of an enemy attack by becoming panic-stricken are not basing their opinion on the existing evidence. Moreover, *to emphasize the likelihood of panic is to promote the suggestion to the American people that this sort of behavior is expected of them.*" The authors suggest, in contrast, that "there is every reason to believe that, rather than panic, the dominant reaction of the American people will continue to be an energetic, adaptive response to whatever threats and dangers they face."[178]

The empirical basis for Janis's claims is laid out in his 1951 report, *Air War and Emotional Stress: Psychological Studies of Bombing and Civilian Defense*, contracted by the Rand Corporation as part of its research program for the U.S. Air Force. The twofold purpose of the report is to contribute to a general theory of behavior by examining "basic processes of human adjustment" in situations of extreme stress, and to provide information for the effective development of postdisaster civil defense controls.[179] Janis reviews the civilian surveys conducted at the close of World War II by the Morale Division of the United States Strategic Bombing Survey (USSBS), as well as the scattered documentation of eyewitness accounts of the atomic bombing of Hiroshima and Nagasaki. Drawing on this empirical case material to outline the "total pattern of disaster behavior" among survivors of the U.S. atomic attacks, Janis tentatively concludes that overt panic behavior is seldom evidenced.[180]

In the 1955 statement for the FCDA, Janis and his coauthors do still adhere to a definition of panic as irrational, maladaptive behavior, or a kind of "mass hysteria." But if panic is not itself reasonable, it is subject to reasoned control through the provision of "realistic information."[181] Specifically, the panic-producing effects of a limited number of escape routes, some or all of which become blocked, can be avoided by civil defense plans ensuring a variety of alternative escape routes and securing reliable channels of communication. The greatest threat to social organization and adaptive behavior in a postatomic disaster, the authors conclude, is ambiguity, insufficient information, conflicting messages, and jammed communication circuits.[182]

Perhaps the most ambitious attempt in the growing literature on panic to systematically mine the existing empirical research for testable hypotheses and theoretical propositions is Paul Foreman's "Panic Theory" (1953), published in *Sociology and Social Research*. His comparative analysis of fifty-four documented cases of panic concludes with nineteen propositions aimed at inferring the dynamics of panic causation and control.[183] Rejecting definitions of panic as irrational, nonadaptive, or antisocial behavior, Foreman identifies "rout" or mass-flight reactions as panic's distinctive feature. With Quarantelli and Janis, Foreman concurs that the social predefinition of a situation or a symbol as panic inducing can be sufficient cause to create terror if the situation occurs: "If a stimulus, prior to its occurrence, is linguistically defined as unmanageable, its name alone can induce immediate terror and panic. . . . There are accounts indicating that the cry of 'Napalm!' may have operated in this way in Korea."[184]

Foreman's nineteen propositions are not only directed at the control of collective panic. They are also intended to aid the production of panic behavior. "Quite possibly, panic may be a legitimate device of modern warfare, harsh as this idea may at first seem. Quite possibly, also, attention to control efforts . . . may result in the improvement of defensive as well as offensive tactics, whether these tactics apply to military or civilian situations."[185] Concerned that an "obsession with prevention may have retarded panic theory," Foreman eagerly fills the gap by suggesting a series of panic-inducing propositions. For example: "Any stimulus which confronts individuals in a target population with an acute sense of danger or its threat is a likely prelude to terror and panic." Moreover, repetition and extended duration can contribute to a "compounding of terror responses." And: "The probability of prolonged and extended terror and panic following an air raid would presumably be increased by secondary attacks on throngs of people rushing out along traffic arteries in quest of security." And: "Since acute fatigue, depression, anxiety, aggressive behavior, apprehensive rumors, social disruption, sickness, and injury" are common emotional successors to terror and panic, "these behavior forms might be most successfully provoked by directing acute danger threats to target populations recently terrorized or panicked."[186]

In conclusion, the Professor encourages the development of more propositions like his own. "If knowledge about terror and panic must in a world of atomic bombs and guided missiles succeed sermonizing," then the accumulation of theory and synthesis of empirical data and discernment of logical gaps may profitably suggest future steps for the "development and testing of ideas."[187]

And so the story starts spinning. With the systematic spiraling of panic prevention into panic production as panic theory emerges as a guide not only to the systematic control of its theoretical object but to its systematic creation. With the enthusiastic conflation of the control of panic and the pursuit of panic as a form of control. With the curious theoretical vertigo in which social suggestibility becomes reasonable just as reason starts to experiment with its oh-so-suggestive symbolic powers. As social science suggests that empirical observation suggests that the social predefinition of a situation as panic inducing is enough to suggest to the American people that they will panic at the symbolic sound of—"Napalm!" "Napalm!" panic cries—but now YOU TELL ME WHAT IS THEORY? Now you theorize WHAT IS REASON? Now you reason that SYMBOLS ARE SUGGESTIVE? Now you suggest that SUGGESTION IS REASONABLE? "Napalm! Napalm!" the Professor suggests, and somewhere panic starts to cry, Is this a dream? Is this reality? In which direction lies escape? Are all exits blocked by short-circuited communications, crazily crossed signals? Is one definition of insanity the attempt to activate a fictional escape route in the face of a perpetually jammed exit? And somewhere panic starts to whimper, Get me out, just get me out of this institution that they call social science but which feels like a white two-story frame house flattened, enflamed by some storm rushing out from inside, simultaneously buckling in from some invisible force without. With a crowd of panic researchers at the door, blocking all escape, systematically attempting to logically survey the damage. To methodically measure the patterned effects of such a violent and sanctioned reason.

By the end of the decade, when the sociologist Edward Tiryakian of Princeton University publishes "Aftermath of a Thermonuclear Attack on the United States: Some Sociological Considerations" in the journal *Social Problems* (1959), the strategic situation facing the social scientist trying to contribute to a national survival plan in a postatomic attack scenario looks rather grim. The development of H-bombs and thermonuclear weapons introduces the "fantastic explosive force" of fifteen to fifty megatons of TNT, Tiryakian calmly reports, and one fifty-megaton bomb now exceeds the combined explosive force of all the bombs dropped on Germany during World War II. And with expected technological developments in missile delivery systems, the U.S. civil defense system may have no more than a five- to ten-minute warning before such bombs reach their targets. In addition, the problem of radioactive fallout from the nuclear blast is severe. Researchers suggest that a thirty-megaton bomb exploding over Boston could, along with destroying the entire Greater Boston metropolitan area, disperse lethal radioactive fallout over all of Massachusetts, Rhode Island, and Connecticut.[188]

Nonetheless Tiryakian approaches the problem of a postdisaster survival plan with the assumption that the "sociological problems attending the aftermath of a thermonuclear or atomic bombing would not be completely different from those attending any other disaster-stricken society or social system." As a result, "generalizations about behavior patterns emerging from previous disaster studies may theoretically bear some relevance to an atomic bombing disaster."[189] Drawing, then, on the empirically observed "behavior patterns" of humans in the aftermath of a tornado, an earthquake, a plane crash, or a house explosion, the Professor proceeds to conceive of a systematic survival plan applicable in the aftermath of a massive nuclear attack. Generalizing from the available post-disaster data, the Professor can also now define a massive nuclear attack as not conducive to a potentially fatal outbreak of mass panic. The value of such a reassuring definition includes, by the Professor's own logic, the definition's symbolic power to actually render such a situation less panic prone by the suggestive force of its empirically grounded, scientifically soothing conclusions.

So it is difficult to say whether Tiryakian really believes his plan for national survival could be implemented, or whether he simply believes the suggestion of survival is sociologically useful. It is hard to know whether he really thinks, as he claims, that "differential behavior" will in fact occur in spatial zone one (ground zero), spatial zone two, and spatial zone three of a thermonuclear blast. Or that professional rescue workers in zone one will indeed exhibit the most "functional, purposive, and coordinated activity," while fearful survivors in zone two will demonstrate the greatest propensity toward panicky flight and the most urgent need for social control. Or that the circulation of "accurate and pertinent information" between zones will be achieved, as required for the reorganization of social activity. Or that officials will take care of the easily overlooked problem of the "disposal of the dead," and the related "problem of developing a means of systematic identification of corpses."[190]

No, there's really no telling what might happen, because "of course," as the Professor notes, "we have no assurance that all or any of these common findings of previous disaster studies would recur in a thermonuclear disaster." But "on the other hand," the Professor observes, "there is no a priori basis for thinking these behavior patterns would not recur in such a situation." And in the small space of survival between "no assurance" and "the other hand," the Professor suggests, now somewhat predictably, the need for more systematic research, and "a more elaborate codification of data pertinent" to a wide range of disaster situations.[191]

NAMES

> Language is no longer something that is primarily normative. It has become factual. The question is not what code should we use, but what code do we use. — NORBERT WIENER[192]

No objects, spaces, or bodies are sacred in themselves; any
component can be interfaced with any other if the proper standard,
the proper code, can be constructed for processing signals in a
common language. — DONNA HARAWAY[193]

The language of cybernetics, this new interdisciplinary science of control through communication, continues throughout the 1950s to spread
across the networked fields of science, the social sciences, industry, and
the military.[194] The historian of science Donna Haraway traces the diffuse
influence of cybernetic modeling in the post–World War II life sciences,
with its promise of a new unity in biological thought and its transformation and intensification of interconnections between the physical, life,
and human sciences.[195] With an emphasis on information exchange and
the circulation of signal/messages, and on a logic of control through inbuilt, self-regulating feedback mechanisms, cybernetics offers a vocabulary of technique and a universalizing grammar of relations for a "common" research into the behavior of cells, organisms, machines, groups,
societies, animals, and humans as command-control-communication
systems.[196]

The language of cybernetic control, originating in part in the militarized crucible of World War II, also has a more complex genealogy.
Haraway traces cybernetic language and imagery back to the pre–World
War II development of semiotics — the science of signs or the "general
theory of communication."[197] In the United States, semiotics is most
closely associated with the work in the 1930s of an interdisciplinary set of
intellectuals at the University of Chicago, including John Dewey, William
James, and the social psychologist George Herbert Mead. A semiotic
theory of language is woven into the language of cybernetics: cybernetics
is a language partially birthed by a scientific theory of language.

Semiotics, Haraway explains, simultaneously offers a theory of communication and a "theory of behavior control." With behavior understood as essentially "the process of signaling," semiotics addresses the
basic problem of "how systems of signs affected behavior patterns."
Semiotic approaches to the "behavior" of sign systems help to lay the
conceptual groundwork for cybernetic language to displace the living
organism as a privileged sender or receiver of signals: a participant in

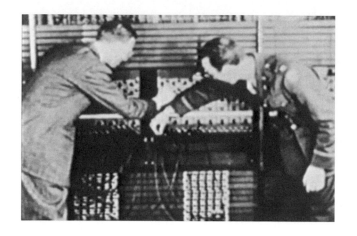

Communicating
systems. *Spectres of the
Spectrum*, directed by
Craig Baldwin, 1999.

a communications system can be any system component capable of
transmitting message signals. Operations research and cybernetic solutions to World War II problems of weapons defense and targeted attack — in which metal, electricity, flesh, consciousness, motion, and inanimate matter together compose a single system — are enabled by a
general theory of communication that conceives of system design as
communication design.[198] Control of the system's behavior is inseparable
from the control of communication and information flows between and
within system components. Neither "consciousness" nor "humanness"
nor "aliveness" offers a privileged communicative status to elements of
the system — all system parts are "coded" together by their functional
status as information processors.

"From the magic of names," writes Norbert Wiener in his reflections
on the history of language, "it is but a step to a deeper and more scientific interest in language."[199] And from the deep, scientific, and semiotic
interest in language, it is perhaps but a step to Wiener's cybernetic desire
"to show . . . that language is not an exclusive attribute of man, but is one
which he may share to a certain degree with the machines he has constructed. . . . We ordinarily think of communication and of language as
being directed from person to person. However, it is quite possible for
a person to talk to a machine, a machine to a person, and a machine
to a machine."[200] Wiener's somewhat magical notion of communication
between machine and machine is made possible by his naming of lan-

guage as a function of the brain's inbuilt "preoccupation with codes," and his naming of the human interest in language as "an innate interest in coding and decoding." Like the semiotic focus on signaling as a linguistic structure shared by animate and inanimate behavior systems, the cybernetic translation of "language" into "code" operates to close the gap between the language practices of humans and machines; in cybernetics, both machines and humans "communicate" through the coding and decoding of information. Wiener explains that the "modern point of view on language . . . assimilates the operation of linguistic translation and the related operations of the interpretation of language . . . to the performance and the coupling of non-human communication networks."[201] Or, in Haraway's words, "communication sciences . . . are constructed by a common move — *the translation of the world into a problem of coding.*"[202] But for Haraway, unlike Wiener, this move to translate world into code is also and everywhere a power play. Cybernetics and communication sciences are for Haraway "a search for a common language *in which all resistance to instrumental control disappears* and all heterogeneity can be submitted to disassembly, reassembly, investment, and exchange."[203]

Daddy was a linguist. He worked at Harvard University as a professor of Slavic languages, and Norbert, the eldest son, is raised by Daddy to be a genius which means Norbert's three years old when Daddy teaches him how to spell after which he learns in a few weeks to read fluently so that by the age of six he's reading Charles Darwin and at age eleven he enters college well schooled in mathematics, Latin, German, and biology all of which Daddy calls an experiment in education although Norbert has rather mixed feelings about the whole experience saying how Daddy would teach him algebra by turning from *a gentle and loving father* into an *avenger of blood* and the moment that Norbert made an error *if I did not follow this by coming to heel at once* Daddy would shout at a *high pitch of emotion* until *I was weeping and terrified* and Mama would then come in to say the neighbors were complaining ABOUT THE LEVEL OF NOISE.[204]

But sure enough Norbert becomes a child prodigy and then too the founding father of cybernetics who writes that *learning is in its essence a form of feedback* in which *the pattern of behavior is modified by past experience* and this *feedback principle* of learning means that *behavior is scanned for its result, and that the success or failure of this result modi-*

fies future behavior[205] and that such learning or feedback behavior takes place in both living systems (people) and nonliving systems (machines) which're not really so different as some of us would like to think so IS IT CRAZY TO SUGGEST that learning algebra with Daddy might be an early lesson in cybernetic communication patterns which isn't the same as saying Daddy's a total monster (if that's what you're thinking) in fact I learned that Daddy was born in Russia and was the son of a Jewish schoolteacher who believed the Yiddish language spoken in his own community was a dying language and should be replaced with German and Daddy moved to the United States in 1881 to found a utopian vegetarian-socialist community but got sidetracked by the need to make money so drawing on his knowledge of Yiddish, German, Russian, French, Greek, Latin, Serbian, Danish, Dutch, Polish, Italian, and English he becomes a laborer a farmhand a janitor and a peddler before becoming a high school teacher in Kansas of classical languages and mathematics while studying Gaelic several American Indian languages and Bantu before becoming a professor at Harvard where Daddy publishes a book on the history of Yiddish literature in which he translates for the first time into English a poem called "In the Sweatshop" that goes like this:

> The machines in the shop roar so wildly
> that often I forget in the roar that I am;
> I am lost in the terrible tumult,
> my ego disappears, I am a machine.
> I work, and work, and work without end;
> I am busy, and busy, and busy at all time.
> For what? and for whom? I know not, I ask not!
> How should a machine ever come to think?[206]

So Daddy's not a monster but as Mama liked to say he's just got a lot on his mind.

When Norbert writes his book on cybernetics and society he dedicates it to the memory of his father, "My closest mentor and dearest antagonist."[207]

However its magic gets named, cybernetics appears to unleash the particular power of language to operate as a kind of programmed and programming "code." The instrumental control built into cybernetic codes—codes that contain and communicate directions for modulating the behavior patterns of natural, technological, and social processes interpreted as cybernetic systems—functions through the purportedly self-regulating structure of circular feedback loops. Cybernetic systems, whether natural, technological, or social (or any combination), are designed to "communicate" control via negative feedback, that is, through the circulation of information about the system's performance in relation to a future-directed system goal, or desired outcome, which feeds back into and alters the present performance of the system. This kind of behavior control via informational feedback circuits can be either "naturally" occurring in human and biological organisms, or technologically designed into machine operations, or "techno-naturally" structured into human-machine operations. As Wiener explains:

> It is my thesis that the operation of the living individual and the operation of some of the newer communication machines are precisely parallel. . . . [I]n both of them there exists a special apparatus for collecting information from the outer world at low energy levels, and for making it available in the operation of the individual or of the machine. In both cases these external messages are [taken] . . . through the internal transforming powers of the apparatus, whether it be alive or dead. The information is then turned into a new form available for the further stages of performance. In both the animal and the machine this performance is made to be effective on the outer world. In both of them, their *performed* action on the outer world, and not merely their *intended* action, is reported back to the central regulatory apparatus.[208]

While machines with "receptors" that can perceive information about the machines' performance from an outside source and use that information to transform and control the performance have existed for centuries—a common example is the steering device of a ship—the rise of machines that can receive and process information *in an electronic form* is a technological transformation ushering in the twentieth-century kind of machine "talk," or communicative feedback, designed and analyzed by cybernetics.[209] The central regulatory apparatus in cybernetic systems is usually organized around the reception, relay, and transmission of electronic information. Cybernetics' language of control is primarily an electronically coded language, functioning via electric signs, electric circuits, and electronically modulated systems behavior.

Even more fundamentally, the kind of machine-machine or machine-human "talk" regulating the performance of a cybernetic system has a specific temporal orientation: it is communication or talk about the projected, probabilistic future state of the system if its behavior continues on its present course. The future state of the system is "encoded" in the form of a set of probabilities that are fed back into the system as information guiding the necessary transformations, in the present, of its behavior.[210] With purposive, goal-oriented behavior as a central preoccupation in cybernetic thinking, the nature of feedback in a cybernetic system always encodes information about adjustments of behavior in relation to a desired future outcome. The future, preferably mathematically and statistically modeled in a set of probabilistic alternatives, becomes an informational input into the programmed control of a system's present action.

The fundamental meaning of information in the cybernetic sense incorporates this temporal orientation: information, as Wiener explains, is a measure not only of the "regularity of a pattern" but of a particular kind of pattern known as a "time series" pattern, or "a pattern in which the parts are spread in time."[211] Communicative feedback involves information about the regularities of a behavior pattern as it continues over time. The automatic self-regulation built into the control apparatus of a cybernetic system is "automated" in relation to the modeling of possible futures. The language of cybernetics speaks about present patterns as they spread out toward future probabilities. What it wants to say has everything to do with how and where it wants to be in a future already present in the form of information automatically feeding back into a system existing strangely across both the here and now and a yet-to-come signaling to make itself into something not yet here but intensely wanted and on its way.

FIND THE REAL

Appearances have always played a much more important part than
reality in history, where the unreal is always of greater moment than
the real. — GUSTAVE LE BON[212]

Things are even more complicated than this, however. If simulation is a technology for the reproduction of the real, for that very reason it signals the emergence of an order where the real is everywhere in crisis and threatening to disappear. — WILLIAM BOGARD[213]

Ground zero incinerates sixty U.S. cities when sixty-one atomic bombs explode on their civilian targets in the early afternoon of Friday, June 15, 1955. The bombs range in explosive force from the equivalent of twenty kilotons to five megatons of TNT and are delivered by air or by guided missiles launched from submarines at sea. At 11:04 A.M. (EST), the nation-wide civil defense communication system is activated, sending the coded "red alert" signal of an imminent air attack out to the key points of the civil air defense warning system, which then transmit it to over 3,500 sub-key points located in local police and fire stations across the country.[214]

By the end of the day, the massive nuclear attack on the United States is estimated to have killed over 8 million people, injured 12 million more, destroyed 6.7 million homes, and created potentially deadly radioactive fallout conditions over approximately 63,000 square miles.[215]

The event is called Operation Alert, a national civil defense simulation exercise conducted by the FCDA in cooperation with other federal and state agencies, the White House, the military, organized labor, the media, municipal governments, businesses large and small, and the U.S. pub-lic. The stated goal of Operation Alert is to enhance civil defense train-ing while testing and evaluating local operational plans for atomic attack preparedness, survival, and recovery.[216] First organized in 1954, Opera-tion Alert exercises take place each summer for the next four years. These "series of annual rehearsals for World War III," writes the Cold War histo-rian Guy Oakes, "enacted simulations of a nuclear attack in an elaborate national sociodrama that combined elements of mobilization for war, disaster relief, the church social, summer camp, and the county fair."[217]

The carefully planned protocol for each Operation Alert exercise calls on participating communities to play out their assigned civil defense sce-narios as realistically as possible. Protocol for the three-day exercise in June 1955 incorporates the technique of "telescoping" events that might in reality play out over weeks or months into a simulated performance in mere hours or days.[218] For the FCDA, the on-the-ground civil defense simulations yield valuable information about weaknesses and gaps in the immensely complex planning effort for survival under atomic attack.[219]

Over eighty U.S. cities participate in Operation Alert 1955 by carrying out some form of public evacuation: sixty-two cities "simulated the action on paper," while another eighteen conduct actual evacuations, transporting at least 117,000 people.[220] In Memphis, Tennessee, an estimated 25,000 people are evacuated from downtown office buildings. In Atlanta, Georgia, 3,500 government officials are evacuated from seventeen different sites, including 2,000 federal employees who are transported seven miles, registered, and fed lunch. In Maine, Vermont, New Hampshire, Connecticut, Massachusetts, Rhode Island, New York, and New Jersey, public participation in the exercise—stopping traffic and taking shelter—is mandatory. In Youngstown, Ohio, the entire city, led by the mayor, evacuates. The 554th Explosive Ordnance Detachment, "adding realism to the exercise," detonates a mock bomb near the city's center. In outlying support areas, 1,200 civil defense volunteers with sixty vehicles are moved into a "simulated disaster area in which actual operations were carried out under realistic disaster conditions," including "huge fires [and] explosions."[221]

But the climax of the 1955 Operation Alert exercise is the three-day evacuation of over 15,000 federal employees from fifteen government agencies—including President Eisenhower and his cabinet—to thirty-one secret sites outside Washington, D.C.[222] Situated somewhere in the mountains of Virginia, the "emergency operations quarters" of the president—who is accompanied by Nelson Rockefeller, national security advisor; Allen Dulles, director of the CIA; and Val Peterson, director of the FCDA—become the preserve of operational continuity for the state after the nuclear obliteration of the nation's capital.[223]

Seated inside a makeshift tent before a microphone, President Eisenhower addresses the nation in a live television broadcast announcing the simulated civil defense emergency and the continuing survival of the nation. The televised presidential address is the culmination of a sophisticated, well-planned public relations and press campaign around Operation Alert, launched some six weeks before the event. Desiring extensive media attention for the event, but also strict control of its contents, White House and FCDA officials meet with executives from the broadcasting industry well in advance of the simulated attack. A media center, christened "Newpoint" and created solely to coordinate public information about Operation Alert, is established in Richmond, Virginia. Open twenty-four hours a day for the duration of the exercise, Newpoint is the centralized media control tower from which journalists file their stories, and where radio interviews with evacuated government officials are conducted via special telephone lines linked to the undisclosed relocation sites. Press conferences with government officials helicoptered in from the secret sites are arranged just outside Richmond.[224]

I can hear it sometimes still if I listen hard over thirty years later that slow sonorous sixty-second wail of the civil defense siren sounding the first Wednesday of every month of my white suburban childhood. It was the 1960s and in Reading, Pennsylvania, we were beyond the optimistic antics of duck and cover not yet initiates into the maddening pessimism of mutually assured destruction and so everybody called it the "civil defense" siren but nobody taught the children of Reading to cover our eyes from the flash or crawl into the nearest ditch or NOT LOSE YOUR HEAD AND PANIC instead I was taught to think of tornadoes and run straight home if ever I heard that wail and it wasn't a Wednesday and even if it were Monday or Tuesday the only real enemy was bad weather. The worst thing generally that ever really happened was in the summer when you were at the neighborhood swimming pool lying in the sun breathing in the smell which you loved of chlorine weed-killer melting tar under the hot rays which you didn't think of as ultraviolet beneath a blue blue sky not yet torn by the ozone hole in the shadow of the thirty-foot civil defense siren and all of the sudden that siren would blast and you'd startle scanning heart pounding blood pumping the sky for twisters then remember it was 1 P.M. on Wednesday so run like mad to the bright bright blue pool and jump in with all the other kids laughing because we all learned although I'm not sure exactly who taught us that UNDERWATER YOU COULD PARTIALLY DROWN OUT THE NOISE.

For those who might have missed the nationwide front-page coverage, the FCDA produces *Operation Alert*, the movie, filmed during the 1956 simulation exercises. Comparing the movie *Invasion of the Body Snatchers* (released in the same year) to the "curiously surreal and dreamlike effect" of watching images of an apparently homogeneous American population in the act of saving their country from atomic devastation, Oakes describes how "the profile of the American people presented in *Operation Alert* reflects a larger sociological picture of American society as totally planned and engineered for a single contingency. All the preparations for a nuclear attack have been laid well in advance . . . [and] have been thoroughly tested to determine that they are in perfect working order and will function according to plan." The film documents the orderly flow of traffic as Manhattan, hit by five hydrogen bombs, is flawlessly evacuated to presumably safer regions on the other side of the Lincoln Tunnel. In St. Albans, West Virginia, city residents carry out what the film calls a "postattack plan for business," as evacuated postal workers reestablish a station in the middle of a country field and the Bank of St. Albans reopens nearby on a card table.[225]

The human actors in *Operation Alert* display the same calm and coordinated efficiency as their compatriots in the FCDA-sponsored film *The Day Called X*, a thirty-minute, made-for-TV CBS documentary of the actual evacuation of Portland, Oregon, during a civil defense rehearsal for World War III. Oakes describes the "internal self-management" so thoroughly embodied by the volunteer civil defense actors:

> The Portland plan for survival is self-correcting and works according to built-in negative-feedback mechanisms. All the problems that might arise in a nuclear emergency as well as the means for their solution have been anticipated. . . . [N]o one panics or even fails to perform the assigned tasks. . . . The Portlanders work together like the parts of an immense, complex, and beautifully designed machine that is constructed for a single purpose. . . . The plan has been designed so precisely and operates so faultlessly that there is no logical space between the rule and the behavior that constitutes its correct application. The place for interpretations has disappeared.[226]

Despite the images of cheerful, volunteer civil defense robots communicated across the public wires and television screens, the findings from Operation Alert's social experiment are far less sanguine. Conducted at least partially with the purpose of revealing deficiencies in civil defense planning and preparedness, the exercises clearly demonstrate to the FCDA serious weaknesses in civil defense infrastructure.[227] As a result, each succeeding year of Operation Alert exercises tries to incorporate a more systematic, fully rationalized plan of action with more effective systems of communication feedback, and to achieve a closer fit between simulated event and actual atomic invasion.[228]

In 1956 the exercises are held over a seven-day period in July during which the nation tries to cope with a hypothetical war that starts with ninety-seven thermonuclear bombs exploding over fifty-two U.S. cities, followed by scattered enemy commando raids, acts of internal sabotage, and the additional bombing of military air bases.[229]

If the reality of the annual FCDA simulations is carefully constructed by government control of information and a close partnership with national communications media, the surreality of the military and civil defense situation revealed by the simulation exercises starts to make itself felt at the highest levels of U.S. government. After each Operation Alert, postexercise evaluations are conducted in top-secret meetings with Eisenhower, his cabinet members, and the National Security Council. In Oakes's words, the "performance of Operation Alert appeared to refute the Cold War conception of nuclear reality on which it was based," that is, the reality that a nuclear crisis could be managed and mastered by the mobilization of national resources and systematic civil defense planning.[230] As government officials grapple with the paradox of civil defense — that effective civil defense depends on the existence of the social, economic, and political institutions it is charged with reestablishing in the wake of a nuclear disaster — a dreamlike illogic begins to thread through their annual evaluations. Operation Alert seems to prove that the "self-protection" on which civilian defense is premised cannot be achieved, yet officials continue to design and conduct the annual exercises under the banner of promoting to the U.S. public the concept of survival and civilian protection.[231] Reviewing the declassified notes from these meetings, Oakes describes how "discussion of civil defense in the cabinet and the NSC [National Security Council] assumed a disconcertingly surreal character. Policy makers seem to have lost their footing. In some cases, they appear to have engaged in the impossible task of thinking in multiple realities, as if they were attempting to consummate an intellectually insupportable but morally defensible commitment to mutually inconsistent principles. . . . Despite these dizzying shifts in framework, policymakers did not seem to experience intellectual vertigo."[232] In the strained effort to avoid vertigo, officials argue that civil defense may be an illusion, but an illusion indispensable for the psychological morale of a public that would undoubtedly panic were the reality of nuclear defense known — in other words, that there is none. Eisenhower makes the more tortured argument that Operation Alert might in fact serve a deterrent role not despite *but because of* its manifest demonstration of the impossibility of protection and defense. By assuming that the Soviet Union would come to the same conclusions about Operation Alert that U.S. officials had, Eisenhower suggests that the exercise might function as a kind of conceptual experiment whereby the Soviets, in a hypothetical exercise of an Operation Alert on their own society, would discover that they, too, were defenseless. "In the final analysis," Oakes concludes, "civil defense did constitute a deterrent, but only by proving its own futility."[233]

From its inception in the suggestion of FCDA director Val Peterson at a National Security Council meeting in January 1954, Operation Alert is considered a risky but useful test of the public's psychological readiness for World War III. Peterson's initial argument for conducting a national civil defense drill is its value in demonstrating that Americans are indeed "subject to hysteria," thereby raising the stakes in the battle for comprehensive civil defense planning and citizen participation.[234] Others on the Security Council fear that the "psychological impact" of such an exercise might lead to public panic.[235] In a cabinet discussion held during the course of the extended Operation Alert exercises in 1957, secretary of defense Charles Wilson reports that, due to the realistic simulation of emergency government activities over a period of several weeks, "people were panic stricken in large cities and were paying no attention to Government orders."[236] Any solution to the problem of panic seemed to exacerbate Operation Alert's volatile mix of the real and the unreal. Presuming the panic is due to people's confusion over the actuality of the simulated emergency operations, a statement by President Eisenhower clarifying the simulated nature of the operations might calm the panic but be mistakenly interpreted by the Soviets as an indication of real preparations for war, thereby touching off a defensive Soviet nuclear offensive. The simulated civil defense drill, creating an actual panic, could then explode into a real war caused by the dramatized preparations to defend against it.[237]

After a 1956 cabinet-level evaluation of that year's Operation Alert, where concern is expressed over how the exercises are affecting public attitudes, Eisenhower calls for a blue-ribbon panel of social scientists to convene and discuss the issue. In their top-secret report to the president, written by Frank Fremont-Smith of the Macy Foundation, panelists speak in a chorus of collective bafflement. They suppose that people are frightened by the dangers of atomic weapons and desire to avoid war. But they are unable to report with any certainty what the new weapons really mean to the U.S. public.[238]

WHY CAN'T YOU COME

> In relation to the term "resistance," Dr. Lacan has remarked in a
> lecture that the term implies an active struggle. I personally had never
> conceived of the term in this manner. I had thought rather of the
> passive resistance of physical matter. — ANNE PARSONS[239]

> We must cease to kiss the whip that lashes us. — NORBERT WIENER[240]

In 1961, at the age of thirty, Anne Parsons experiences what she describes as a "severe panic episode" related to her growing fears of nuclear war.[241] The panic is heightened by the political drama playing out between Cold War adversaries on opposite sides of the Iron Curtain—the "Berlin crisis," which brings renewed threats of nuclear war during the first years of the Kennedy administration. Parsons begins to read extensively about the U.S. military-industrial complex, writing that "a political image of the world crystallized in my mind—it [the military-industrial complex] against the rest of humanity."[242] In a letter to a friend, she connects her panic to a childhood experience of being severely burned just as war broke out in 1939 and lying in the hospital worrying about children in Europe being bombed. She also explains that the panic was tied to her belief that

> imminent destruction was actually possible, so that I would look at
> familiar things as if never expecting to see them again. I had night-
> mares of trying to escape from biological and chemical weapons. . . .
> During the most acute phase it seemed that every day I discovered the

existence of some new evil: for example, a friend told me of developments in biological and chemical warfare making it possible to kill a man by flicking a drop of fluid and for a day or two I felt that such fluids were all around. Also I was extremely sensitive to sirens: in fact, the whole affair began one day when I heard fire sirens on the way to my analytic session after a lunch table conversation in which I learned that a colleague had built a shelter.[243]

Parsons's panic experience takes place during her first year in psychoanalysis. After returning from Italy and her fieldwork in mental hospitals in 1960, Anne Parsons enters a training analysis and course of study at the Boston Psychoanalytic Institute, the same institute where her father Talcott underwent analysis in 1946.[244] Talcott Parsons remains connected with the institute and is a well-known figure in the tightknit psychoanalytic community in Boston. His psychoanalyst, Dr. Grete Bibring, has in the intervening years become an intellectual and institutional sponsor of his daughter's psychiatric research.[245]

In deciding to undergo analysis, Parsons has a double motive: first, she believes that psychoanalytic training will enrich her interdisciplinary work in psychiatry and social science; and second, she hopes the analysis can help her through the depression and professional isolation she feels upon returning to the United States, an unmarried woman intellectual with no secure institutional affiliation or academic position.[246]

Anne Parsons describes how the reaction of her "extremely orthodox" analyst to her panic was "to say nothing at all."[247] His diagnosis of her problems as a failure to accept her basic femininity is for Parsons a source of personal anguish, since she deeply desires to be married and finds life as a single woman in her thirties miserably isolating. But she also resists his interpretation, arguing that her "personality" is situated within cultural and social structures that make it enormously difficult to be a woman with intellectual and career ambitions while successfully fulfilling more traditional feminine roles.[248]

Testing. Eins. Zwei. Drei. Testing. Can you hear me? Are we transmitting yet?

In the second year of her analysis, her psychic condition continues to deteriorate. She wants to terminate the analysis, but her analyst "insisted that this would be a form of acting out of impulses that should be ana-

The family house on fire. Federal Civil Defense Administration, *Operation Doorstep*, 1953.

lyzed on the couch." At the beginning of her third year of analysis, she does leave, feeling that she is losing the struggle to "maintain an identity against this disorganizing sense."[249] As a consequence of her termination of the analysis, Parsons is expelled from the institute in March 1963 with the explanation that she suffers from "serious neurotic difficulties not treatable by means of psychoanalysis."[250]

In September 1963, Parsons is hospitalized at the Yale Psychiatric Institute, where she spends the following nine months. While institutionalized, she keeps a journal that she titles "Diary of a Mental Patient," and writes several essays for publication. One of the essays, published in 1964 in the journal *Psychiatry*, presents a barely veiled denouncement of Parsons's experience with the Boston Psychoanalytic Institute. She critiques the potential institutional abuses and asymmetrical professional authority structured into the psychoanalytic training situation when a candidate for becoming a psychoanalyst is professionally evaluated through the intensely private scene of a training analysis.[251]

In her unpublished diary, Parsons writes of the failed psychoanalysis in a different language, differently expressive of her sense of outrage and entrapment in a social situation she undoubtedly feels is partially responsible for the psychic breakdown leading to her institutionalization:

> So I tried the couch and he kept saying why can't you come to terms with your basic feminine instincts so I kept on trying on his couch and it wasn't much fun and I thought about it and I was really aw-

fully scared about the missiles . . . and weren't we going to have any resistance and I was resisting insight into my feminine instincts and who the hell could marry one of those pompous medical students anyway it wasn't so much fun on the couch and think about cafes in Paris and Vienna and students in Africa fighting for freedom and who the hell can find the real repression in suburban houses no it is just that you CANNOT COME TO TERMS WITH YOUR BASIC FEMININE INSTINCTS.[252]

Caught and on his couch somewhere between dreaming and daylight between anger and analysis between systematic insights into social structures and the expressive symbolics of a schizophrenic sensibility. Startled by sirens on the way to psychoanalysis. Seduced by resistance on your journey from the Mayflower to mental dis-ease. Caught between languages daddies missiles and mamas and silences memories repressions and syncopated professions with which she can never precisely COME TO TERMS. And could you? Caught in public with your privates displayed? Picture it just for a moment. The maddening patterns of abstraction, the *mise en abyme* of mirrors as the theorist of culturally specific symptomatologies turns symptomatic, panicked and still professing inside the institution she took as her object of study, as her subject of empirical research. What blood gathered in your brain, Mama, what bindings collared you and burning your head hanging at the edges after you danced with Daddy at that oh-so-systematic ball symptomatically choreographed with personalities and cultures and behaviors and logics and I'm not saying it's so simple as Daddy's just crazy. I'm not suggesting that she doesn't partly suffer from random chance disturbance. All I know for sure is I'm burning in the story with a sense that doesn't quite function, a rhythm that can't quite dance.

Sometimes I see parallel tracks crossing and crisscrossing. Into wildly integrated circuits. I'm simply trying to understand the patterns.

HE KEPT POUNDING ON

A control logic can be part of a system of domination based on
practices of coordination and management, i.e., the scientific way,
and not on practices of direct force and traditional authority. . . .

Functionalism is a logic for the mediation of domination through self-sustaining processes, not a logic of direct visible command.

—DONNA HARAWAY[253]

The mechanical control of man cannot succeed unless we know man's built-in purposes, and why we want to control him.

—NORBERT WIENER[254]

Beginning in the mid-1950s, Talcott Parsons pursues an explicit elaboration of cybernetic language into a theory of society and social control.[255] His work is perhaps the most developed instance in the field of sociology of what Donna Haraway calls "cybernetic functionalism," a cross-disciplinary, post–World War II discourse emerging out of the biological and social sciences.[256] To a functionalist teleology of control—focused on the "maintenance of stable order" and the rule-governed, self-regulating transformation of "bounded wholes" over space and time—cybernetic functionalism brings a new set of tools drawn from systems engineering and information science.[257] The management of integration, adjustment, and adaptation in a wide range of coordinated actions, the terrain of a functionalist logic of control, is coupled with an analysis of information exchange and the coding and decoding of command structures, the domain of the cybernetic communications engineer.

In its universalizing reach as a kind of total science, cybernetic functionalism enters the realm of social theory with an ambition to transform all the social into a laboratory for cybernetic research and cybernetic conceptualizations of social control.[258] As a committed "communications engineer" in the laboratory called the "social system," Parsons envisions the logic of cybernetic control as an inherent, inbuilt feature of an interrelated set of processes. "The basic conception," he states in 1960, "is that 'behavior' is subject to a graded hierarchical system of control mechanisms in the cybernetic-information theory sense, and that this system constitutes a continuous series extending from the highest level of the cultural and the social system, through the personality and the higher-order organic systems, to organs, tissues, and cells, and indeed even to subsystems of cells."[259] The ease with which Parsons's "system of control mechanisms" crosses the boundary between the social and the organismic points to an essential continuity between these levels implied in the founding assumptions of cybernetic thought.[260] Despite other differences in social, cultural, personality, organismic, and cell systems, "the basic processes of control" in each system, according to Parsons, "are what we ordinarily call processes of communication."[261] As a result, the control aspects of any cybernetic system — whether it be a social, natural, or technological system — appear as a design feature of the communication processes embedded in the system itself.

This naturalizing of an internal logic of control embedded in social systems has several consequences for cybernetic social theory. First, explanations for social order and stability do not need to attend to whether or why "control" is a central feature of social organization; instead, with society conceptualized *as a control system*, social theory's focus becomes *how* social stability and order are maintained. For Parsons, it is the cultural system that performs an essential, stabilizing "pattern-maintenance function" in the social system. In his most striking cybernetic formulation of the cultural system's control function, Parsons writes:

> In what sense, then, can patterned . . . cultural systems be said to "control" social interaction and the action of individuals? . . . The central phenomenon . . . is the provision of "standards" or "models" for the regulation of action. They give selective clues to what information about conditions of action is relevant to the attainment of what goals. They provide ways of organizing and codifying such information in relevant terms. Finally, and particularly important, as the course of action proceeds, they provide ways of testing whether and in what respects it is proceeding "according to plan," or, because . . . of the intervention of unforeseeable or uncontrollable circumstances, how a change is indicated — this, of course, is the process of "feedback."[262]

On several occasions, Parsons likens the work of cultural patterns in communicating normative orientations or shared "symbols" to the function of genetic codes in providing stable physiological features for each species.[263] This cybernetic functioning of communication-as-control permits, in a theory of social order, a focus on "normative control as distinguished above all from coercive enforcement."[264] Language plays a key role in this normative process. According to Parsons, "language . . . is a *system* of symbols which have meaning relative to a *code*. A linguistic code is a *normative* structure parallel to that composed of societal values and norms—indeed, it is properly considered a special case of the norm."[265] The cultural and linguistic encoding of normative patterns in Parsons's social theory operates to normalize or naturalize language itself as an inherent control feature of the social system.

And since control of the system functions at the level of the relational patternings, or structure, of the system itself, the human actor in the social system is theorized as neither precisely controlled nor controlling. At the level of conscious, centrally coordinated action, no human agents are—or can be—running the social show. Parsons cautions:

> In talking about the kinds of systems we are dealing with, that is, systems that involve multiple levels of organization and hierarchical sets of control mechanisms, we must be careful not to think of "control" in terms too close to human common sense. We do not need to postulate a fellow who sits up somewhere giving orders. For instance, the code components of a language, which controls communication in terms of that language, illustrates one major type of control. For many of the most important processes there need not be any particular human agent who is making decisions about how a system shall operate. . . . [T]here is a basic conception of systems operating at least partially without central planning.[266]

And since nobody in this system is exactly involved in coercive controlling, nobody is exactly coercively controlled. "Voluntary" action remains the conceptual centerpiece of Parsons's theoretical system, although, curiously, the more action is integrated into the "superindividual matrix" of overlapping, interacting systems, the more voluntary it, theoretically, becomes.[267] Other less-nimble cybernetic social theorists have stated this paradoxical situation with less finesse, if more forthrightly. According to Charles Dechert, political scientist and organizer of the 1964 symposium "The Social Impact of Cybernetics":

> Social control is the capacity . . . to manipulate the internal and/or external environments of other persons or groups so as to achieve a preconceived end. This normally involves selected changes in their information inputs designed *to change in some way their perceptions or*

values so that they *respond in the desired manner.* It is largely concerned with "evoking" an "autonomous" response. . . . Basically, when dealing with objects as complex and autonomous as persons, control is reduced to presenting a challenge so structured that it evokes the desired response. Since social action normally involves a feedback loop, the socially controlled in some sense also control the controller.[268]

The cybernetic space of voluntary, autonomous action opens strangely into the infinite regress of the controlled who control the controllers who control the controlled who, also, are controllers. These entangled loops of control are not constituted through direct coercion but communicated through the informational redesign of perceptions and values.

I would like to give Daddy some feedback on these issues. Undoubtedly I already have, although I'm not completely sure I was in control of the process. Of communicating my feedback. Or of desiring to communicate my feedback. Or of feeding back my desire to communicate. It's all feeling a little complex at the moment perhaps it's the concern that I may never get out of here unless I learn how to communicate (my desires) in Daddy's codes.

Then I'm walking down a city street and I see him. I know right away he's the one. Who's been watching me. I'm angry at his secret-agent-style spying so I decide to walk up to him and tell him I'm not afraid. Of him. Of his watching me. As I approach he turns his face toward me and I see now what his eyes are made of. I see now that he sees with eyes silver and blue digital scanners and as I approach him his eyes record my every move. I see now the whole thing's a setup getting me angry so I'll come closer so he can record information about me at close range and I start to tremble as I stand before him saying, "You don't make me afraid," knowing but trying not to let it reflect in the screen of his eyes that now I know that HE NOW KNOWS EVEN MORE AND FOR WHAT PURPOSE? I turn my back and walk away from the man with the digital eyes waking up in the dark of this place undone by such deep controlled terror when they chuckling tell me the next day I'm a classic paranoid case (they make a note in my file) I look them straight in the eye and ask them who's making who every day describe her darkest dreams? They make another note in my file.

This intricate architecturing of social controls, Parsons explains, while built into the very functioning of the social system, does not operate flawlessly or without the threat of disruption by deviance and resistance. "It may be stated that the conception of a system of control implies that there are important resistances to control," he writes, "and that the successful operation of the [control] mechanisms is therefore problematical."[269] This problematical nature of control and resistance is, however, in a cybernetic system reassuringly circumscribed by the self-regulating operations of communicative feedback. Resistance to control, in cybernetic language, simultaneously calls out for its own readjustment. Resistance can be read as a form of feedback communicating the necessary direction and inbuilt desire for improved regulation.

One of the most developed examples in Parsons's work of this kind of resistance toward readjustment is the case of sickness, which he conceives of as a form of "social deviance."[270] In a 1958 essay, Parsons theorizes how mental illness, in particular, shares with other kinds of deviance its origins in a breakdown of the "adjustive processes," which integrate the personality with the demands of the social system.[271] At the same time, mental illness constitutes a kind of protective defense against other more threatening forms of social disruption. If mental illness is a manifestation of social deviance, then it is one that invites its own social control. "Mental illness, then, including its therapies," Parsons writes, "is a kind of 'second line of defense' of the social system vis-à-vis the problems of the 'control' of the behavior of its members. It involves a set of mechanisms which take over when the primary ones prove inadequate."[272]

As a secondary type of control mechanism, mental illness and its therapeutic treatment together make possible the readjustment and re-integration of the personality with the imperatives of the social system's functioning. Central to this process of control is the successful conduct of communication within the therapeutic setting. For communication that operates through "the media of signs and symbols" to work, both patient and therapist must be encoded in a shared system of meanings. For symbols to communicate, Parsons argues, "there must be standardized 'codes,' in terms of which their meanings are 'known,' these are general systems of 'patterns' and 'norms.' There must be communicators capable of sending messages in these codes, and receivers capable of understanding or 'decoding' them. At each end of the relationship the 'meaning' of the symbols and their combinations must articulate in definite ways."[273]

Thus, even in the case of serious disturbances in the primary mechanisms of social control, the systematic encoding of meaning through patterns and norms secures a powerful therapeutics of communication, capable of restoring deviance within the desired social order.[274] Within these (crazy) social orderings of desire.

TO HAVE ANY RESISTANCE

> I am certainly revolting against something and it has taken a long
> time to figure out just what. — ANNE PARSONS[275]

> In war, one person's noise is another's information.
> — WILLIAM BOGARD[276]

Anne Parsons is voluntarily committed to the Yale Psychiatric Institute in September 1963. By the winter of 1964, believing that the hospitalization is no longer benefiting her, she begins to fight for her release. She wants to write a book entitled *Essays on the Culture, Ethics, and Politics of a Therapeutic Society*, partly based on the field notes she has continued to take while, now, a patient inside her chosen field site, the mental institution.

Parsons's critique of psychotherapy and psychoanalytic techniques only intensifies during her hospitalization. She eventually goes on strike from the compulsory psychotherapy sessions, argues against her mandatory participation in group process, fights for the privacy and library privileges necessary to continue her studies and writing, and sardonically notes, based on her observations of hospital life, that "the most consistent law I can discover governing the behavior of psychotherapists is that [the patient] should always sacrifice whatever other alternatives one has in order to stay where they can go on seeing you."[277] Her attempts to gain release from the hospital fail, and she begins to question what it means to be "voluntarily" committed to an institution from which there appears to be no exit.[278]

Even during her first months as a mental patient, when Parsons participates willingly in the required psychotherapy and continues to write

After the blast.
Federal Civil Defense
Administration,
Operation Doorstep,
1953.

prolifically for publication, she engages in political struggles over daily life on the psychiatric ward.[279] She organizes a Thanksgiving fast among the patients, writing in a Thanksgiving manifesto that refusing to eat might "reaffirm in sorrow at their violation those democratic traditions on which all of our national holidays and our national life are based."[280] In letters written from the hospital, Parsons expresses her concern over U.S. militarism and the Cuban situation, the November 1963 assassination of John F. Kennedy, and her anxieties about a right-wing ascendancy in U.S. politics. She resists the depoliticization that psychoanalysis and psychotherapy encourage, insisting on her right to respond politically to current events. In a letter to her father in November 1963, Parsons explains: "This is what an . . . important part of my conflict with Dr. A [her analyst at the Boston Psychoanalytic Institute] . . . was about, since when I was in such a panic about nuclear war and the possibility of American fascism, he simply could not or did not see that people ever have strong emotions about anything but their immediate personal relationships or whatever it is that happens before one is six years old."[281] Many of the letters Parsons writes to her father during her hospitalization are, according to the feminist historian Winifred Breines, "political disagreements accusing him of being too conservative."[282]

Anne Parsons's most extensive critique of psychotherapy is a lengthy essay she writes while hospitalized. The object of critique is her own practice in a state mental hospital in Massachusetts where, operating as both clinician and social researcher, she conducted intensive psychotherapy with institutionalized patients. The essay, "Cultural Barriers to Insight and the Structural Reality of Transference," focuses on her two-year therapeutic relationship with "Mr. Calibrese," an Italian man who emigrates to the United States several years before being hospitalized. Parsons argues that the therapeutic relationship, which ended in failure (with Mr. Calibrese residing in a chronic ward with no hope of being discharged anytime soon), promoted the patient's inappropriate and unnecessary dependency on the therapist, Parsons herself, as he struggled to cope inside the mental institution with the complex realities of a difficult situation outside the institution.

In a reflexive critique of the therapeutic techniques that she herself employed, Parsons questions the "overly idealistic representations of the culture of psychotherapy—that is, the sum total of shared social meanings and communication patterns which characterize those who believe that the path to salvation lies in a self-conscious understanding of personal feelings." Staging with persuasion and compassion the class- and culture-based realities of Mr. Calibrese's troubles, and of his transferential response to the therapeutic relation, Parsons outlines the features of an alternative to the dominant culture of psychotherapy—what she terms "active psychotherapy," requiring a therapist to "always talk to the patient in his own social vocabulary," and to help patients make decisions and address conflicts within the social context of their own lives. She concludes with an indictment of the tendency toward collective, professional hallucinations that arises when "people speak the same professional language" and so come to "agree on the validity of certain perceptions or interpretations mainly through a process of consensual validation which has no real referent outside itself." At their worst extreme, these professionally validated but referentless perceptions link up powerfully with the professional research enterprise, creating conditions in which the "uncovering" of patients' psychic lives is compelled more by "research, teaching, and other career-maximizing motives" than by concern "for whether the patients feel better or worse after they have been 'uncovered.'" [283]

In the spring of 1964, Parsons's situation at the psychiatric institute worsens. She finds herself unable to keep writing. Her efforts to secure a professional affiliation for the following year have failed. Her struggle to escape her "voluntary" commitment is stalled. In April she takes a trip to New York without permission, and this attempt to "run away" brings on more severe hospital restrictions: she is no longer allowed out of the institution to go to the library. In a letter written in early May to her father, who is on a professional trip to Moscow, she congratulates him for reaching the peak of his career and pleads with him to help her get out of the hospital and find a place to live near their family farm in New Hampshire. She decries the "gadgeteering optimism" of the psychotherapeutic culture she feels locked within and the expenditures, monetary and otherwise, being wasted on her unsuccessful treatment.[284]

(At the watery edge, Mama, ghosts calling you under and down, ghosts calling your name, bitch, going under. And how do we write, where is delight, in such a dark, Mama, such a dark dream.)

On June 9, 1964, at the age of thirty-three, Parsons commits suicide while a patient in the Yale Psychiatric Institute. A collection of fifteen of her essays, edited by a small group of friends and professional colleagues, is published posthumously in 1969.[285] In a collection of his essays titled *Social Structure and Personality*, published in the year of his daughter's death, Talcott Parsons dedicates the book: "For Anne, a Sensitive and Resourceful Student of the Problems of This Book."

THE JARGON AROUND HERE

But there was no System. Just a Nervous System, far more dangerous, illusions of order congealed by fear. — MICHAEL TAUSSIG[286]

In Daddy's 436-page *Theory of Collective Behavior* (1962), the problem of group panic and other forms of collective behavior is theorized according to a model of behavior based on "the logic of value-added."[287] That is, Daddy tries to explain panic using a model borrowed from economics, where it's used to explain, among other things, the process of converting iron ore into automobiles. According to Daddy, this "value-added" economic model can be expanded into an explanatory scheme for understanding the logic of social determinants at work in collective behavior. The key element in the value-added scheme is that it operates via a logic — applicable to collective action or to automobile manufacturing—and this logic can be seen to function "according to a definite pattern."[288]

Daddy says the field of collective behavior is "underdeveloped scientifically," lacking standardized meanings even for its principal object, collective behavior. Bemoaning the "language of the field" that "shrouds its very subject in indeterminacy" by naming collective behavior as irrational and thereby suggesting it lies beyond the grasp of "empirical explanation," Daddy asserts instead that collective "outbursts" are structured actions that occur with regularity, clustering in time and in patterned frequencies among specific social groups. Daddy is trying to make a new language for the field.[289]

Daddy's model of value-added is coupled with the model, developed by Daddy and Daddy, for classifying the general components of social action.[290] In this way, Daddy can unite both collective and other forms of social behavior into "the same theoretical framework."[291] Daddy, like Daddy, values the idea of common theoretical frames. Just a few years earlier, Daddy and Daddy wrote a book together trying to theoretically unite the fields of economics and sociology.[292]

Daddy defines the nature of collective behavior as an "attempt to reconstruct a disturbed social order." Collective behavior arises in response to structural strain and is always a "search for solutions" to problems created by social dysfunctions.[293] Collective behavior, for Daddy, doesn't desire dysfunction or disorder. It wants, just like Daddy, to solve problems of disorder. But at the heart of its attempts at problem solving, collective behavior is guided by beliefs in the "existence of extraordinary forces—threats, conspiracies, etc.—at work in the universe." These beliefs in extraordinary forces are, Daddy says, "akin to magical beliefs."[294] Collective behavior believes in magic. (Daddy believes in science.)

Using the logic of value-added, Daddy's analysis of panic systematically organizes the empirical evidence from bombing attacks, mine explosions, flying saucer sightings, shipwrecks, food shortages, battlefield combat, floods, Martian invasions, tornadoes, theater fires, stock market crashes, and earthquakes into a coherent explanatory scheme for panic. Daddy's theory of collective behavior is hailed as a radical attempt to reorient the field and is praised as an exceedingly useful guide to empirical research.[295]

Three years after the publication of Daddy's major theoretical treatise on collective behavior, Daddy, Daddy, Daddy, and Daddy publish their findings as "Collective Behavior in a Simulated Panic Situation" (1965) in the first issue of the new *Journal of Experimental Social Psychology*.[296] While Daddy concludes his *Theory of Collective Behavior* with the observation that experimentation "is virtually impossible in the study of collective behavior,"[297] Daddy et al. eagerly investigate the "laboratory paradigm of an escape mob" in an effort to improve on the laboratory simulation of panic conducted by Daddy in 1951.[298]

The laboratory simulation performed by Daddy et al. is intended to contribute to "a more modern theory of social influence." Perceiving that a panicked group is faced with the problem of an "interdependent escape situation" where the behavior of each participant is mutually bound up with every other, Daddy et al. hypothesize that the "distribution of attitudes toward the escape situation" is the critical factor in the total performance of the group in solving its escape problem.[299]

Criticizing Daddy's 1951 experiment for failing to adequately simulate the effects of acute danger in an interdependent escape situation, Daddy et al. are committed to simulating "levels of threat as high as seemed experimentally feasible."[300]

So in 1965 Daddy et al. conduct a laboratory experiment in which one-third of the 264 students who volunteer for the experiment arrive at the laboratory and **each one had electrodes for delivering shock attached to the first and third fingers** of his hand while Daddy explains that this is an experiment about **behavior under threat the situation being one where a number of people have to use a single limited exit to escape from an impending danger within a limited time**.[301]

After the experiment is briefly explained to them Daddy then delivers two **fairly strong shocks** after which Daddy says to the experimental subjects **"I have called this a danger situation because those of you who do not escape before the time is up will receive a painful electric shock as a result of not escaping just a few moments ago we determined a 'shock threshold' for each of you we went through all the trouble of getting these measurements because we want to be able to give you the most painful and uncomfortable shock we can without seriously hurting you in any way I want to be completely honest with you and tell** you exactly what you are in for those of you who do not escape will re-ceive a series of extremely painful shocks . . . they're going to hurt but we must do this to impress upon you the uncomfortable consequences of not escaping."

Then Daddy says **"About this time in past sessions of this experi-ment some people expressed a desire to leave after finding out what it was all about but I'm afraid I can't allow this"** at which moment Daddy hands out a questionnaire for all the volunteers to answer questions about whether or not they want to leave the experiment that they can't leave.

In addition, one-half of the one-third of the 264 volunteers who par-ticipate in the laboratory experiment are administered an injection of epinephrine by a physician at the beginning of the experiment while Daddy reassures them **"The shot you are getting is a neutral solution. . . . This will have no physiological effects"** and then about seven to ten minutes later just as Daddy is explaining to them about the very harm-ful shocks they'll be receiving if they don't escape from the situation in the experiment from which they can't escape the effects of the epineph-rine which tends to bring on the physiological symptoms often associated with fear and danger (**speeded heart rate and involuntary tremor**) are starting to kick in and that gives Daddy some more information about the effects of threat on the experimental subjects' capacity to solve the interdependent escape problem.

Needless to say, Daddy says, the subjects were never given the threat-ened shocks. Instead, they were given a postexperiment questionnaire followed by a " 'catharsis' session" in which "they were permitted to ask questions and air their feelings."[302]

FLIPPED AND HERE I AM

Testing. Eins zwei drei . . . testing. Eins zwei drei vier fünf . . . Can you hear me? Is the connection holding? Are we transmitting yet? Boppy doppy doopy wah yahyah mm. Is that what you think craziness is? Do people who go crazy freak you? Look sweetheart.[303]

Let me tell you how I'm feeling.

I woke up in my attic that the winds swept through and all the world was gray and black. I saw jet airplanes coming out of the ocean waves, gray sky and black sea. Silver planes, waves, silver planes, waves. In the distance, you could hear the siren.

I walked along a highway. I was looking for a place to sit down, for some grass I could walk in, for a wood I could explore.

Inside the laboratory, I encountered the outside. The outside was inside. The inside was outside. Cause, effect, cause, effect. Effect. Effect. Cause. In the distance, you couldn't see any horizon.

> In communication sciences, the translation of the world into a problem in coding can be illustrated by looking at cybernetic (feedback-controlled) systems theories . . . [in which] solution to the key questions rests on a theory of language and control. . . . Information is just that kind of quantifiable element (unit, basis of unity) which allows universal translation and so unhindered instrumental power (called effective communication). The biggest threat to such power is interruption of communication.[304]

I walked for hours. All the land on both sides of the highway, cultivated and wild, was privately owned by the oil, aerospace, communications, biotechnology, pharmaceutical, and coffee industries. I had to keep walking on the highway. Electronic billboards posted every few miles said, "Information Highway." I thought that people today when they move, move only by car, train, boat, plane, space shuttle, or the Internet. And so people move only on roads. I think it's becoming harder to get off the roads. I think it's becoming harder to speak outside the codes.

I live on a desert island. It's a nice desert island. I like it here. I eat. I sleep. I go to the library. But I've been getting bored . . . What can I do? I can repeat what I see. Exit doors jammed by a vast accumulation of data. Electricity conducted at unmeasured social speeds. Pirates gypsies goblins sorcerers skeletons dancing in the shadow of the thirty-foot civil defense siren. (And the witches. And the witches, still burning.)

So I walk along home, to Satellite Beach. Maybe it's the year 2006. We're four miles from Patrick Air Force Base. Thirty miles from NASA's Cape Canaveral. An hour by car south of Disney World. There are waves and waves and the ocean swells somewhat over the edges where I lie, I listen, I lie. And as I listen at the edges I hear another high swelling and over our heads where we lie sunning on Satellite Beach they fly eins zwei silver bird-planes and larger than the pelicans. They circle over Satellite Beach in a high swelling tide. How they roared, Mama, how loud they roared one two over my head, over yours, are you listening Mama? Did you count them coming, flying low, shrill, insistent silver and swelling the edges of these Satellite Beaches?

AND OUT OF THE CORNER OF MY EYE I SAW THEM, MAMA, TO THE LEFT AND MOVING ACROSS THE FRAME FILLED BY YOUR SWELL FACE SHADED BY A WICKER HAT WITH RED, WHITE, AND BLUE RIBBONS ROUND THE BRIM AND TWO BIG SILVER ROAR BIRD-PLANES FLY ACROSS THE FRAME, ACROSS THAT BLUE BLUE SKY, BEHIND THE WIDE WICKER BRIM OF YOUR SUN HAT MAMA

DID YOU THINK IT WOULD KEEP YOU FROM BURNING?

Ring around the rosy
a pocketful of posy
astronauts, astronauts
we all fall—
Roger. Over and out.

4

Performing Methods:
Cybernetics, Psychopharmacology,
and Postwar Psychiatry

per • form v. 1. To begin and carry through to
completion . . . 2. To take action . . . 3.a. To enact
(a feat or role) before an audience.

meth • od n. 1. A means or manner of procedure . . .
2. Orderly and systematic arrangement . . . 3. The procedures
and techniques characteristic of a particular discipline or field
of knowledge. — *the Method*. A system of acting in which the
actor recalls emotion and reactions from his past experience
and utilizes them in the role he is playing. — *The American
Heritage Dictionary of the English Language*

Scene one: war neurosis. The spectacle is "electrifying to watch," observers report.[1] The body grows rigid, the wild eyes open wide, the pupils dilate, and a fine layer of perspiration covers the skin. The hands may convulse. Breathing quickens and becomes shallow. Terror vividly restages itself in intricate, observable physiological detail inside the small, darkened room where patient and psychiatrist together reenact traumatic scenes of battle: the failed scramble for cover during an attack; the death of a friend in combat.

The reenactment begins with the psychiatrist verbally staging "a typical scene. . . . The patient is told that mortar shells are flying about; that one has just landed close by; that enemy planes are overhead . . . and that he must tell what is happening." If such vague images do not elicit a story from the patient, the psychiatrist attempts to make the scene "more dramatic and realistic." The psychiatrist may then "play the role of a fellow soldier, calling out to the patient, in an alarmed voice, to duck" as the shells explode around them. "Persistence is rewarded in almost every case by an account of the scene in progress."[2]

Some patients then emotionally and verbally relive the scene, talking to invisible comrades, startling at absent explosions. Others get out of bed and, unaware of their actual surroundings, act out a past trauma in the present tense, wandering about the room looking for a lost friend, or crying over the body of a dead soldier. "Some patients return over and over again to one short, traumatic scene, living it through repeatedly; as if, like a needle traveling around a cracked record, they could not get past this point." Others, at the height of their emotional reenactment, collapse onto the bed, overwhelmed, unable to continue. In certain cases when the patient is vividly reliving a traumatic scene, the psychiatrist "is called upon to play a variety of roles. When the patient becomes convulsed with the violence of the terror, he must step in as a protective and supporting figure, comforting and reassuring the patient, and encouraging him to proceed." In almost all cases, the psychiatrist observes, the release of violent and repressed emotional memories prepares the way for further therapeutic treatment and recovery.[3]

In September 1943, a restricted monograph prepared by Lieutenant Colonel Roy R. Grinker and Captain John Spiegel, two U.S. psychiatrists stationed in Algiers, is circulated by the Air Surgeon of the Army Air Forces. The monograph narrates the case histories of dozens of U.S. and British psychiatric casualties treated by Grinker and Spiegel in the winter and spring of 1943, during the intensive ground and air combat of the Tunisian campaign in North Africa. Funding for the Air Force's publication and distribution of the restricted document is provided by the Josiah Macy Jr. Foundation.

The three-hundred-page monograph documents the disturbances observed and treatments conducted at the Algiers clinic, where the authors see hundreds of men, often for only a few weeks, before returning them to active duty, to noncombatant service, or, if treatment fails, to their country of origin as permanent psychiatric casualties of war. While noting that the many permutations of observed symptoms render "classification into types difficult and artificial," Grinker and Spiegel delineate ten different clinical syndromes under the broad label "war neuroses," each syndrome differentiated by "the method by which anxiety is handled." The list includes psychosomatic disturbances, depression, psychoses, and, at the top of the list, "free-floating anxiety, severe and mild."[4]

Grinker and Spiegel also introduce a new therapeutic technique for treating even the most crippling cases of war neurosis. Their technique, called "narcosynthesis," involves injecting the patient with a sedative drug (sodium pentothal) to induce a narcotic, dreamlike state. Then, using techniques of suggestion, the therapist prompts the patient to reenact the traumatic experience, encouraging the reliving and release of intense emotions. "The effect of the drug," Grinker and Spiegel note, "enables the patient to deal with these revived emotions in a more economic and rational manner, instead of catastrophic defensive technics. . . . Under treatment, the patient actually synthesizes the emotions and memories connected with his experience, putting together what has lain fragmented between consciousness and unconsciousness."[5] The authors advise their wartime colleagues that narcosynthesis is "immediately indicated" in many cases of severe anxiety states. Viewing the war neuroses as "psychosomatic disturbances" having "both a physiological and psychological" basis, Grinker and Spiegel believe that wartime psychiatric casualties "offer the best opportunity" for studying the functioning of the ego and its "interrelation with biological and psychological drives."[6]

Scene two: remote-controlled psychosis. In the late spring of 1960, a psychiatrist and a computer engineer travel to a U.S. Air Force base in Texas to attend a symposium called "Psychophysiological Aspects of Space Flight." Nathan Kline, the psychiatrist, is director of research at Rockland State Hospital in New York, a large public mental institution; Manfred Clynes, the computer engineer, is chief research scientist in Rockland's Dynamic Simulation Lab. Kline and Clynes coauthor a symposium paper entitled "Drugs, Space, and Cybernetics: Evolution to Cyborgs."[7] They introduce the concept of the "cyborg"—a hybrid of *cy*bernetic technologies and human *org*anism designed for survival and success in outer space—to the Air Force–sponsored gathering of scientists, physicians, psychiatrists, psychologists, and engineers.

Kline and Clynes's cyborg is a speculative notion, an imagined hypothesis formulated out of the fantastic coupling of the astronaut's body with an array of cybernetic devices aimed at adapting the human body to extraterrestrial space. Drawing on cybernetic control theory and its focus on automatic, self-regulating systems, the authors imagine the supplementary technologies that might extend the body's capacity for self-regulation in an environment for which evolution has not prepared it. "The purpose of the Cyborg," they write, "is to provide an organizational system in which . . . robot-like problems are taken care of automatically and unconsciously." Seeing the new problems presented by spaceflight as a "spiritual challenge [for man] to take an active part in his own biological evolution," Kline and Clynes encourage what they call "participant evolution" through cyborg technologies. The cyborg, "biologically optimize[d]" for its new environment, is seen as an experimental techno-supplement to evolution itself.[8]

Pharmaceutical drugs and innovative drug delivery systems are central components of the self-regulating "man-machine systems" that Kline and Clynes imagine for the emergent cyborg.[9] Kline, who plays a leading role in the 1950s in establishing the new field of psychopharmacology for the treatment of mental disorders, and Clynes, whose research with mental patients focuses on "the organization of the body's nervous system and its cybernetic control,"[10] compose the perfect conceptual team for approaching the human central nervous system as a cybernetic mechanism, and proposing a science-fictional series of automated devices for readjusting the organism in outer space. "To the already existing biological control loop an additional control loop would be added," they explain, "designed by man for his better homeostatic operation, i.e., Cyborg."[11] For example, should the unprecedented, unpredictable stresses of long-term spaceflight precipitate a psychotic episode in the human organism, the authors suggest the possible administration of psychopharmacological drugs via remote control from Earth.[12]

The Air Force symposium is organized around the urgent demands of "Project Mercury" — the U.S. military's first attempt to send humans into outer space — and the technological requirements of maintaining humans, psychologically and physiologically, in this new environment. According to the conference organizers, the main limitation on "the degree of efficiency of the total system" of man-machine interactions, in outer space or everyday society, is lack of knowledge about the psychophysiological limits of human behavior. "Man's behavior is a joint function of many kinds of influences arising both inside and outside the body, and . . . the understanding and control of this behavior can be achieved only through the joint efforts of all the life sciences,"[13] the organizers state. Scientists of today and the future are urged to develop an "integrated understanding" of the psychological and biological factors of behavior. Man's behavior is "most meaningful only when we are able to integrate the psychosocial facets of his performance into a framework of genetics, anatomy, physiology, and chemistry."[14] The symposium encourages the pursuit of an integrated understanding of humans' "total behavior" in space, and on planet Earth.

Scene three: panic attack. Between October 1958 and July 1961, over two hundred mental patients voluntarily institutionalized at Hillside Hospital in New York are administered a new psychopharmacological drug, imipramine. In 1962, a young research psychiatrist, Dr. Donald Klein, and the director of Hillside's Department of Experimental Psychiatry,

Dr. Max Fink, coauthor a paper on the "various patterns of behavioral response to imipramine" observed when they administer a standardized daily dosage of this "mysterious, new, and as yet unmarketed drug" to 80 percent of all patients at Hillside.[15] The administration of the drug is not a treatment for any specific mental disorder. It is a research experiment aimed at developing a "descriptive behavioral typology" based on patients' differential reactions to the drug.[16]

Before joining the staff at Hillside, Donald Klein works as a psychiatrist and assistant surgeon at a medium-security federal penitentiary in Lexington, Kentucky.[17] The facility is a combined jail and one-thousand-bed hospital, run by the U.S. Public Health Service. Many of the hospital's patients are elderly World War I veterans. According to Klein, the Lexington facility had "probably *the* most advanced human psychopharmacological studies unit in the world at that time." From 1954 to 1956, Klein participates in some of the earliest U.S. scientific studies of psychopharmacological agents like LSD, chlorpromazine, and reserpine.[18]

When Klein joins the Department of Experimental Psychiatry at Hillside in 1959, his "tremendous interest in medication and human experimentation" finds fertile ground.[19] The department is run by Max Fink, a neurologist, psychiatrist, and psychoanalyst. Klein and Fink identify seven different behavioral response patterns in patients after they take the imipramine, a drug manufactured by Geigy Pharmaceuticals but not yet available on the market. Of special interest is a behavioral pattern they name "reduction of episodic anxiety response," observed among a subpopulation of research subjects who suffer from "inexplicable 'panic' attacks, accompanied by rapid breathing, palpitations, weakness, and a feeling of impending death."[20] After administration of the drug, the attacks disappear. Klein and Fink argue that this behavioral response to imipramine makes visible a distinct psychophysiological process of anxiety—the "panic attack"—that can now be discerned as a discrete symptom.

The psychopharmacological research launched by Klein and Fink at Hillside mental hospital is an early achievement in what Klein will later elaborate into a full-fledged research technique: "pharmacological dissection," or "the power of the experimental technique . . . whereby one can pierce through the fascinating, confusing web of symptoms and dys-

functions to tease out the major participant variables by attending to specific drug effects."[21] Proposed as a method for constructing useful boundaries around clusters of symptoms, pharmacological dissection works as
a kind of inductionism in reverse. Working backward from drug effect
to the identification of syndromes, this experimental technique reveals a
discernible mental disorder — and a distinct population of symptomatic
subjects — as a function of drug response.

The drug research conducted with institutionalized mental patients by
Klein and Fink from 1958 to 1961 will wait twenty years before enjoying
recognition as the early empirical evidence, gleaned through the visibili-
ties made possible by pharmacological dissection, of a new psychiatric
object: panic disorder. Introduced in the official U.S. psychiatric lexicon
in 1980, panic disorder is soon acknowledged as a widespread psychiatric
problem affecting millions of people in the United States.[22]

DISAPPEARING OBJECTS

> Symptoms ignored, however, do not disappear, and . . . only
> appear elsewhere, perhaps in more virulent forms.
> —ROBERT ROMANYSHYN[23]

Sometime during the 1960s, I could not say precisely when, and I will only
speculate why, research and theory on collective panic fade as a popular
topic of social scientific attention. Perhaps the waning of scholarly interest corresponds to a growing perception that state-sponsored anxiety
over the threat of nuclear panic has been rendered obsolete by the technological capacity of both U.S. and Soviet governments to obliterate each
other in an all-out nuclear exchange. With the development of satellite
technology, intercontinental ballistic missile delivery systems, and the
spread of increasingly destructive nuclear warheads, U.S. policymakers
and that malleable abstraction, the "general public," may be forced to
recognize that collective panic is not, if it ever was, the most dangerous
aftermath of atomic war. The threat of postatomic panic may quietly disappear behind the unprecedented possibility of national and planetary
apocalypse. And such an unprecedented, perhaps unimaginable, possi-

bility may encourage what the historian Stephen Weart describes as the "worldwide collapse of interest in nuclear war" evident by the late 1960s. Even public opinion research on attitudes toward nuclear war slows to a trickle after 1960.[24]

Perhaps, as well, government and academic interest in panic prevention and control is curbed by rhetorical attempts to domesticate the atom as the atomic energy industry expands into an integral energy source. From 1963 to 1967, U.S. government and industry produce twice as many films about nuclear reactors and three times as many on nuclear safety than in the previous five years. In the course of the decade, an estimated 160 million viewers watch Atomic Energy Commission (AEC)-sponsored films on TV. The FCDA slogan "Keep Calm!" is replaced by the AEC's new mantra — "Safe and Clean!" — as nuclear reactors and atomic energy become a significant present and future source of the nation's power.[25]

Finally, is it conceivable that if, as many Cold War theorists suggest, collective panic occurs in a life-threatening situation from which group members perceive they may be unable to escape, then perhaps at this historical conjuncture the nation discovers new avenues of escape? New orbits of motion that deter the terrifying gravity of the situation? Perhaps as the earth proliferates with the possibility of sudden, violent, techno-scientifically enhanced annihilation, a powerful new escape route is uncovered. An unearthly frontier of hitherto unexplored space is opened that eases the unbearable anxieties, alters the panicked pulsings in the heartlands of Cold War America. Much of the nation tunes in on October 3, 1962, to watch live, minute-by-minute coverage of the televised launch of the U.S. Air Force's Mercury space rocket, manned by a veteran combat pilot of the Korean War, Walter M. Schirra.[26] "Are we all astronauts?" clinical psychologist Robert Romanyshyn asks, some thirty years after the successful launching of Project Mercury.[27] In his provocative history of the body, Romanyshyn suggests that the making of the astronautic body — perhaps a first giant leap for mankind in its journey toward "exosomatic evolution," or evolution outside the body[28] — is not only chronologically congruent with the making of the atomic bomb. It is also, perhaps, at least in some dreamlike sense, psychologically congruent: the astronaut's flight into outer space enacts a deeply desired escape from the terrestrial space now threatened with catastrophic nuclear destruction—a destruction made less panic-stricken by the possibility of an extraterrestrial escape route.[29]

Perhaps. Although I could be wrong.

But, as the twentieth-century history of sociological empiricism loudly and consistently asserts, theoretical speculation is cheap. And, presumably, easy. In following the fate of panic as an empirical object, what becomes most clear is not any definitive explanation for its waning as a social problem, but rather the dramatic reconfiguring of panic away from its construction as a collective social behavior, and toward another, emergent empirical form: as an individualized mental disorder and new object of psychiatric discourse. "Panic disorder" enters the official U.S. psychiatric language in 1980. Defined by recurrent panic attacks, sudden explosive episodes of psychic terror at imminent death or madness, panic disorder also manifests in physiological symptoms such as shortness of breath, sweating or chills, dizziness, and heart palpitations.[30]

Like collective panic, its sociological predecessor, panic disorder's empirical shape embodies a historically specific story of the ascendancy of scientific method within a discipline, psychiatry, struggling for professional legitimacy. And like collective panic in sociology, the story of panic disorder in psychiatry is entangled with a twentieth-century history of how the "empirical" itself becomes the designated arbiter of psychological (or sociological) "reality."

But unlike collective panic, whose origins are always understood to be situational and social, the new object called panic disorder is, from its empirical sighting in Donald Klein's experiments with institutionalized mental patients, bound to the disordered behavior of the individual body and exiled from the realm of social and collective explanation. Far from the fatal contagion of terrified crowds dying to escape burning nightclubs, sinking ships, or atomic attack, the panic-disordered body is defined by *an absence of relation* to any social reason for the force or the timing of its terror. Even within its classificatory family of "anxiety disorders," panic disorder stands out as the psychic response to no discernible stimulus. Unlike the phobic who panics at heights or snakes or enclosed spaces, or those suffering from post-traumatic stress disorder whose nightmares and intrusive memories trace back to a specific scene, the person with panic disorder is diagnosed as such precisely because there is *no observable precipitating cause* for the floating attacks of terror that erupt as she's walking down the street, watching TV, driving the car, sitting in front of the computer, or simply lying in bed, asleep. Dreaming. Perhaps.

OUT OF THE ASYLUM

> Because of the current and future necessity of such large populations
> throughout the world to face a difficult reality, never in the history of
> the study of human behavior has it been so important to understand
> the psychological mechanisms of "normal" individuals.
>
> —ROY GRINKER AND JOHN SPIEGEL[31]

On the eve of World War II, U.S. psychiatry, along with its object, mental disease, is largely institutionalized in public mental hospitals. Public hospitals in 1940 constitute the historical core of U.S. mental health policy, and their patient population (numbering approximately 410,000 people, or 98 percent of all those institutionalized for mental disorders) is the main subject of pre–World War II psychiatric knowledge and practice. In 1940, over two-thirds of the membership of the American Psychiatric Association (APA)—founded in 1844 as the Association of Medical Superintendents of Asylums for the Insane—is working in public mental institutions.[32]

Not until after World War II does psychiatry dramatically expand its professional role from an "institutional specialty" to a more generalized therapeutic practice aimed at a different, and much broader, population: the noninstitutionalized ranks of the less severely symptomatic, the as-yet-unclassified psychic realms of what had previously been categorized, by default, as the psychologically "normal."[33] By 1956, only 17 percent of the APA's members work in state or Veterans Administration hospitals, with the majority now employed in community clinics, private practice, government agencies, and medical schools.[34] Along with its move into the non-institutionalized mental health of the general population, postwar psychiatry also greatly expands its professional numbers, from an APA membership of 2,295 in 1940 to nearly 10,000 members in 1956.[35]

With the expansion of psychiatric practice into new populations with new problems come new demands on the classification system for mental disease. In 1952 the APA publishes the first edition of what will become the professional guidebook of psychiatric diagnosis in the United States — the *Diagnostic and Statistical Manual for Mental Disorders*, or DSM-I.[36] Containing just over one hundred diagnostic categories, the APA's psychiatric language emphasizes psychologically based disorders over biologically based or organic mental diseases. The majority of the disorders, 70 out of almost 120 diagnostic categories, are defined as psychological (and not biologically based) disturbances, including a highly differentiated realm of "psychoneurotic," "personality," and "psychophysiologic" problems.

The APA committee charged with constructing the 1952 diagnostic manual uses as a guideline the psychiatric classification system developed by the U.S. Army during World War II. The army's "sweeping revision" of psychiatric classification in 1945 is prompted by the inadequacy of existing classifications — based largely on the diagnostic demands of institutionalized mental patients — to deal with the psychiatric casualties of war.[37] The foreword to the DSM-I recounts:

> At the beginning of World War II, American psychiatry, civilian and military, was utilizing a system of naming developed primarily for the needs and case loads of public mental hospitals. . . . The Armed Forces faced an increasing psychiatric case load as mobilization and the war went on. . . . Only about 10% of the total cases seen fell into any of the categories ordinarily seen in public mental hospitals. Military psychiatrists . . . found themselves operating within the limits of a nomenclature specifically not designed for 90% of the cases handled. . . . No provision existed for diagnosing psychological reactions to the stress of combat. . . . The official system of nomenclature rapidly became untenable.[38]

Psychiatrists' wartime experience reorients the profession, and its diagnostic language, toward psychodynamic and psychoanalytic emphases on situationally defined "stress," and the central role of anxiety and unconscious defenses as the mechanism underlying most neurotic disturbances. Although in the United States both psychoanalysis and psychodynamic psychiatry have their conceptual foundations in the early decades of this century, not until World War II and afterward do they come to dominate the core conceptions, treatment approaches, and diagnostic language of U.S. psychiatry.[39]

In particular, the claims to successful treatment of a heterogeneous cluster of symptoms loosely diagnosed as "war neuroses" infuse psychiatry with a "renewed spirit of therapeutic optimism and activism," according to Gerald Grob, a historian of psychiatry.[40] "Success" for wartime psychiatry means high rates in returning servicemen who experience debilitating psychological distress to active military duty. "Our experiences with therapy in war neuroses have left us with an optimistic attitude. . . . The lessons we have learned in the combat zone can well be applied in rehabilitation at home," write Roy Grinker and John Spiegel, coauthors of a widely circulated monograph on the treatment of war neuroses published by the U.S. Army in 1943.[41]

In 1945, Grinker and Spiegel coauthor the popular book *Men under Stress*, arguing for the application of military lessons to civilian psychiatry, and especially for a recognition of the effects of stress on otherwise "normal" psychological processes. "The psychological mechanisms under discussion in this book," they write, "are those that apply to Everyman in his struggle to master his own environment. In this realm, a hair divides the normal from the neurotic, the adaptive from the nonadaptive."[42] The case materials that Grinker and Spiegel analyze are from U.S. Air Force combat pilots diagnosed with war neuroses. Acknowledging that the wartime experiences of these pilots involved extreme, life-threatening conditions, the authors insist nonetheless that the psychiatric lessons culled during the giant experiment of war "are of value not alone for their applicability to an understanding of the problems and treatment of the psychiatric casualties of war; they are equally valuable for the understanding of the psychology and psychopathology of people under the stresses of ordinary civilian life. These may not be as continuous or as catastrophic, or their effects as sudden or dramatic, yet in essence they bring into action the same forces within the individual as do the terrifying stimuli of battle."[43]

The insight that under sufficient environmental and social strains even the most mentally healthy predispositions may succumb to neurotic symptoms and nervous breakdown comes to pervade postwar approaches to mental illness and health. The continuum model of mental disorder—where but a "hair divides the normal from the neurotic"—informs much of postwar U.S. psychiatry, itself now deinstitutionalized outside the walls of the asylum, catapulted by the neuroses of war into the previously undiagnosed psychic territories of the postwar public.[44]

OPERATION NATIONAL MENTAL HEALTH

> The guiding philosophy which permeates the activities of the
> National Institute of Mental Health is that prevention of mental
> illness, and the production of positive mental health, is an attainable
> goal. . . . Since this must be done as rapidly and as economically as
> possible, *techniques for a mass approach to the problem must be*
> *developed.* — ROBERT FELIX[45]

The passage of the National Mental Health Act in 1946 marks a historic transformation in U.S. mental health policy. The federal government for the first time takes an active role in the administration and planning around problems of mental illness, a role previously played by individual states' programs and policies. The new federal participation also signifies "an almost revolutionary change" in the very conception of the purpose of governmental activities regarding mental health: from its former exclusive function of caring for and treating the mentally ill, writes Dr. Robert Felix in 1949, the mental health branch of the U.S. government is now "designed to make possible the prevention of mental illness."[46]

Speaking as the first director of the newly established National Institute of Mental Health (NIMH), Felix attributes this laudable change to a growing awareness, signaled by passage of the 1946 National Mental Health Act, "that emotional and personality disorders constitute a public health problem." Indeed, in a 1938 report, the surgeon general of the U.S. Public Health Service named mental disease as the most important public health problem facing the country.[47] The postwar founding of the NIMH in 1949 as a branch of the Public Health Service reflects the "concept of mental health as an integral part of total health" and gives institutional shape to the "desire to have the traditional public health approach applied to the mental health field."[48] Felix cites the previous success of "mass techniques" and public health models in addressing problems of venereal disease and tuberculosis but laments that, to date, mental health programs have not yet met with equal acceptance. "*Workable, usable mass approach methods in the mental health field must be further developed*," Felix argues, "and existing methods must be more fully utilized by state and local health units if mental health activities are to become as widely accepted and as successful as older public health programs. This can occur only if much is learned which is as yet unknown about mental health and illness."[49]

The emergent conception of mental health as a public health concern carries with it a corollary demand for federal support of mental health research. The federal research program initiated under the 1946 National Mental Health Act outlines a broadly conceived interdisciplinary approach, calling for a "diversified attack on the sources of mental disease."[50] Felix avows in a 1949 address to the APA that "no discipline, not even psychiatry, has a monopoly or even a priority in the field of mental health research. The knowledge which will contribute . . . to the production of an emotionally more healthy population must come from many sources."[51] Accordingly, the new Research Branch of the NIMH funds and employs psychiatrists, neurologists, psychologists, sociologists, anthropologists, physiologists, and chemists.

Of immediate interest to the new federal promoters of the "production of positive mental health" for all is the gathering of national epidemiological data on the incidence of mental illness in the United States. Before World War II, psychiatric epidemiology—the statistical study of the spread and distribution of mental disease in a population—is largely restricted to institutionalized patient populations. But with federal participation in mental health research and policy comes the belief that epidemiological studies are a responsibility of the federal government, and that accurate figures on the prevalence of mental disease in the general population hold a key to the development of successful empirical methods for prevention and treatment.[52]

Methodologically, the post–World War II epidemiological studies of mental illness owe much to wartime innovations in survey research methods. The sampling methods, survey techniques, and statistical analyses developed under Samuel Stouffer and the Research Branch of the War Department's Morale Division are used during the war to create neuropsychiatric screening questionnaires aimed at correlating neurotic symptoms to combat stress and morale issues. After the war, community surveys of the incidence of mental illness employ rating scales modeled after the Research Branch's neuropsychiatric questionnaires to construct a composite index of mental health status.[53] The surveys do not measure the incidence of specific diagnostic categories but rather gauge general mental and emotional "impairment" and are conducted by nonspecialists. Many of the studies report disturbingly high rates of mental distress. In the most widely known survey of that era, Leo Srole and his coauthors' *Mental Health in the Metropolis: The Midtown Manhattan Study* (1962), survey research on a probability sample of over one thousand New York City residents measures significant mental impairment in almost a quarter of the respondents; only 19 percent of subjects are classified as symptom free.[54] The Midtown study and much of the early post–World War II epidemiological research on mental health emphasize social causes for mental illness. As Myrna Weissman and Gerald Klerman note in their history of U.S. psychiatric epidemiology: "Poverty, urban anomie, rapid social change, and social class were to become the civilian stress equivalents of combat and threat of death in the military."[55] Postwar psychiatric epidemiology builds not only on the methods of military social science and psychiatry but on their focus on the social and situational precursors to psychic disease.

With the 1946 National Mental Health Act and the federally supported research launched under its aegis, psychiatry is encouraged to become "social psychiatry," concerned at least as much with community-based prevention of mental illness as with institutionally based care. For the postwar psychiatric profession, writes Gerald Grob, "The community, not the hospital, was psychiatry's natural habitat. Psychiatrists had to play a vital role . . . in creating a presumably healthier social order."[56] While the "mass approach" to mental health envisioned by the first director of the NIMH cannot yet be precisely detailed in its techniques, its promise is broadly institutionalized in a new approach to psychiatric knowledge, premised on a social model of mental disease emphasizing prevention and a community-based approach to epidemiology and treatment. The continuum model of mental illness—which takes as its object the mental health of entire populations, and as its main antagonist the socioenvironmental factors that potentially place everyone at risk of mental impairment—becomes an accepted presumption of public policy.[57]

PSYCHE, SOMA, AND CORPORATE PHILANTHROPY

> The suggestion which I offer . . . is that "voodoo death" may be real,
> and that it may be explained as due to shocking emotional stress—to
> obvious or repressed terror. —WALTER B. CANNON[58]

The postwar trajectories of psychiatric knowledge and research promoted by corporate foundation money and philanthropic programming priorities diverge in significant ways from the agenda of the 1946 National Mental Health Act and the newly established NIMH. Since the 1930s, both the Rockefeller Foundation and the Josiah Macy Jr. Foundation demonstrate sustained interest in the murky regions of mental health and disease, and the postwar directions of these powerful philanthropic agencies reflect their earlier commitments. Both foundations play a leading role in the establishment in the late 1930s of psychosomatic medicine—the study of the relation between emotional states and physiological processes—as a new subfield of medical practice and research. Originating in Germany and Austria in the 1920s, the psychosomatic approach attempts to map the relatively unknown borders between emotions and organismic processes, between psychic experiences and the internal landscapes of physiological structure and function.[59] The notion of psychosomatic disease is already central to U.S. military psychiatry during World War II, particularly in the understanding of war neuroses. Yet in contrast to the broadly interdisciplinary and insistently psychosocial emphasis of postwar psychiatry, the philanthropic supporters of psychosomatic medicine want to establish psychiatry as a respected and integral branch of medical science. Building alliances with the more established domain of neuropsychiatry, psychosomatic medicine places neurology and physiology at the center of psychiatric knowledge. If the prevailing postwar impetus is to move psychiatry out of the mental hospital and into the general population, the preference of psychosomatic medicine would be a more moderate relocation—from the mental hospital to the general hospital.

One of the earliest institutional settings for exploring the intimate webs of psyche and soma is the Massachusetts General Hospital in Boston, a private teaching hospital for Harvard Medical School. The psychiatry department first opens at Mass General in 1934 under the directorship of Dr. Stanley Cobb, with funding from the Rockefeller Foundation's Medical Science Division, and is the second psychiatric unit inside a general hospital established by Rockefeller's Alan Gregg, who is eager to promote the incorporation of psychiatry as a branch of medicine.[60] Cobb comes to psychiatry with a background in neuropathology, and a deep interest in both hypnosis and psychoanalysis. He was briefly cured of his chronic stammering after experimenting with hypnosis in 1910 and, years later, is again helped by undergoing psychoanalysis. In the early 1930s, he is active in the Boston Psychoanalytic Society and the newly founded Boston Psychoanalytic Institute.[61] In his 1936 treatise *Foundations of Neuropsychiatry*, Cobb argues for a multidisciplined approach to psychiatric knowledge, lamenting the current problem of the great "void" of knowledge separating the "mental sciences" from their future foundation in the physical sciences. Here in this void, Cobb counsels, research must be pursued to build the necessary factual basis "to explain the observations and to support or refute the theories now promulgated in psychiatry."[62]

The aim of conducting research in the void between the physical and mental sciences is structured into the very location of the psychiatric unit at Mass General. Conceived as a consultation and liaison service for other medical specialties in the hospital (and located on the same floor with neurologists and neurosurgeons), psychiatry at Mass General is from its start organized to serve research and teaching functions, including the instruction of the hospital's medical and social worker staffs in the practices of modern psychiatry. In a report to the Rockefeller Foundation, Cobb lists as one of the department's objectives the training of medical students in psychiatry and "its place in general medicine."[63] Many of the research projects undertaken in the department involve collaboration with physicians and surgeons outside the field of psychiatry. In the words of his biographer, Cobb's ambition is "to integrate treatment of the mind with treatment of the body, to bring psychiatry into the mainstream of modern scientific medicine and surgery."[64] A few years after the psychiatry department opens at Mass General, the study of the "mind-body problem," as it becomes known, is further institutionalized with the launching in 1939 of the *Journal of Psychosomatic Medicine*, followed five years later by the establishment of a new professional association, the American Psychosomatic Society. (Stanley Cobb, a founding member, will become its president in 1955.)

The emergence of psychosomatic medicine as a distinct subfield with its own professional journal and membership is indebted to the sponsorship of the Josiah Macy Jr. Foundation, whose mission to support scientific investigation at the intersection of biology, medicine, and the social sciences fits easily with the agenda of the psychosomatic movement.[65] Frank Fremont-Smith is a young neuropsychiatrist at Harvard Medical School and Massachusetts General Hospital before he becomes medical director at the Macy Foundation in 1936. In the late 1920s, Fremont-Smith works for Stanley Cobb in the neurology department at Harvard and the new neuropathology laboratory at Boston City Hospital—both are funded by a $350,000 grant from the Rockefeller Foundation's General Education Board—where Fremont-Smith develops a method for observing cerebral circulation in the brains of live cat embryos.[66] Explaining that this research "led me to a growing awareness of the influence of psychological factors upon the physiology and bio-chemistry of bodily processes," Fremont-Smith quickly moves toward the cross-disciplinary field of neuropsychiatry.[67]

In 1937 Fremont-Smith travels to Washington, D.C., at the invitation of the National Research Council—a philanthropically funded clearinghouse inaugurated on the eve of World War I to promote the coordination of wartime scientific research—to meet with the Committee on Experimental Neuroses. The committee requests the Macy Foundation's financial sponsorship of a new professional journal devoted to the study of "psychosomatic clinical problems" or the "so-called experimental neuroses and other allied problems."[68] With the help of Lawrence Frank, who joins the Macy Foundation staff in 1936 after serving with the Rockefeller Foundation, Fremont-Smith sets about promoting the new interdisciplinary subfield, starting up the *Journal of Psychosomatic Medicine* in 1939 and sponsoring the organization of a professional society a few years later.[69]

The Macy Foundation's leading role in the institutionalization of psychosomatic medicine converges with its intellectual fascination with the concept of homeostasis. "Homeostasis," according to a 1936 Macy Foundation report, is "a splendid example of the 'operational concepts' by which biology is reinterpreting phenomena of the living organism," offering the possibility of new methods for integrating knowledge across disciplinary fields.[70] First proposed by Walter B. Cannon in *The Wisdom of the Body* (1932), the notion of homeostasis is introduced to Frank Fremont-Smith and Stanley Cobb in the early 1930s at Harvard University, where Cannon is a professor of physiology and the three men together participate in a monthly "Neurological Supper Club." Cobb directly attributes his interest in psychosomatic medicine to Cannon's work, and Fremont-Smith wastes no time in placing the investigation of homeostatic mechanisms squarely on the Macy Foundation's agenda.[71]

Homeostasis, for Cannon, designates the complex of "coordinated physiological processes" by which the organism, in the presence of environmental or external changes, maintains relatively stable states necessary to functioning and to the preservation of life itself.[72] The beauty of homeostasis is not only that it works to stabilize organismic functions but that it works *automatically*, a self-regulating function operating outside the organism's conscious attention or control: "Without homeostatic devices we should be in constant danger of disaster, unless we were always on the alert to correct voluntarily what normally is corrected automatically."[73] Of special interest to Cannon is the autonomic nervous system, or the part of the central nervous system that operates involuntarily and outside conscious control. His concept of homeostasis is based in part on several decades of animal experimentation on the autonomic systems of live cats and dogs at Harvard's physiology laboratory, where Cannon conducts early research on the relation between emotional states and bodily processes.[74]

The Macy Foundation's interest in Cannon's experimental work only intensifies with U.S. entry into World War II and the renewed urgency in finding effective treatments for the traumatic "war neuroses."[75] In Grinker and Spiegel's 1943 monograph on narcosynthesis and the psychiatric treatment of soldiers, they describe how "the pictures of psychoso-matic disturbances flash kaleidoscopically before the eyes of anyone who wishes to observe the war neuroses."[76] Citing the florid array of symp-toms displayed by their patients—including heart palpitations or tachy-cardia, excessive sweating, pupil dilation, trembling, dizziness and head-ache, and the common psychosomatic symptoms of cardiac discomfort, abdominal pains, and nausea—Grinker and Spiegel connect these so-matic symptoms to emotional states rooted, and repressed, in specific physiological processes. "The basic concept of psychosomatic medicine postulates that certain unacceptable emotions, repressed from conscious-ness and motor or verbal expression, find an outlet for their energy in ab-normal innervations of the autonomic nervous system. . . . Such dynamic relationships have been discovered for a few syndromes by the use of tech-nics suitable for the recovery into consciousness of the repressed emo-tions."[77] The "technics" Grinker and Spiegel develop—"narcosynthesis," where patients are pharmacologically induced into a state of heightened suggestibility—offer the young psychiatrists an experimental window on the interrelationships between the emotional and the physiological in a disturbed psyche. Grinker and Spiegel argue that the narcotic state, combined with psychotherapy, yields a promising form of brief, effective treatment in the theaters of war.[78]

One of the reasons for the Macy Foundation's wartime financing of the publication and distribution of Grinker and Spiegel's "restricted mono-graph" to the U.S. Army Air Forces may be its convergence with Cannon's earlier work.[79] Cannon traces his own interest in the function of the auto-nomic nervous system to his research during World War I, later published in his book *Traumatic Shock* (1923). Noting that some soldiers who ex-hibit the potentially life-threatening symptoms of severe shock do so with the most trivial of actual wounds, Cannon proposes that the physiologi-cal effects of an emotional shock are potentially as dramatic as the effects of actual physical trauma.[80] In his 1942 essay "'Voodoo' Death," Can-non extends his theory of traumatic shock to the suggestive hypothesis that the strange occurrence of "death from fear" occasionally witnessed by the astonished ethnographer may be accounted for by the concrete physiological reactions to extreme terror. He exhorts the traveling eth-nographer who may come across this fantastic phenomenon to perform a small number of simple tests to verify that the dying person is physio-logically in a state of shock. Check for a rapid pulse. Observe the cool, moist skin. If feasible, take a small sample of blood and count the red blood corpuscles. Ascertain empirically whether it is really possible to die from sheer terror.[81]

PSYCHE, SOMA, AND THE SOCIAL BODY

> It seems not impossible that the means employed by the more highly
> evolved animals for preserving uniform and stable their internal
> economy (i.e., for preserving homeostasis) may present some general
> principles for the establishment, regulation and control of steady
> states, that would be suggestive for other kinds of organization — even
> social and industrial — which suffer from distressing perturbations.
> —WALTER B. CANNON[82]

As the psychiatry department at Massachusetts General Hospital prac-tices medicine and pursues research in the borderlands of psychic distress and somatic symptoms, its activities attract the attention of a young soci-ologist just starting his career at Harvard University. Talcott Parsons, in-trigued by Walter B. Cannon's suggestion that the organization of society might be investigated "in light of the organization of the body,"[83] de-cides in the late 1930s to undertake a sociological study of medical prac-tice. Motivated in part by his own renounced desire to study biology and medicine, Parsons's research is also personally encouraged by Cannon and another Harvard physiologist, L. J. Henderson.[84] Henderson's semi-nars in the early 1930s deeply impress Parsons, inciting a lifelong theoreti-cal interest in conceptual analogies between the physiology of the body and the functions and dysfunctions of the "social system."

Parsons is fascinated by the emerging field of psychosomatic medi-cine, and the challenges raised by the scientific study of emotional or "irrational" life. "This was a time in which ideas about psychosomatic re-lations were beginning to take hold among the intellectual elite of medi-cine — typified perhaps by internists at the Massachusetts General Hos-pital, where I spent a good deal of time," he recounts.[85] He combines his study of medicine and psychosomatic ideas with an intensive reading of

Sigmund Freud, which together feed his growing theoretical attention to "the problem of the nature of rationality." The practice of medical science raises unsettling questions about how rational knowledge could be used to understand and solve problems of an "irrational" nature. "The concern with psychosomatic problems," Parsons recalls, led to questions about "the significance of the scientific modes of rational investigation and analysis for the understanding, and in some eventual sense control, of the non- and irrational factors in the determination of human action."[86]

Parsons turns to Freud and psychoanalysis to help him wrestle with these problems of the relation between the rational and the nonrational. "In the background," he writes, "was psychoanalysis and the fact that the professor of psychiatry at Massachusetts General Hospital, Stanley Cobb, had recently been the principal founder of the Psychoanalytic Institute in Boston."[87] Parsons begins to see the entire landscape of physician-patient relationships saturated with transferential energy, the unconscious dynamic that Freud identified as the very foundation of psychoanalytic practice and cure. "Transference," Parsons explains, "is most conspicuous in 'psychiatric' cases, but there is every reason to believe that it is always a factor in doctor-patient relationships."[88] In fact, he asserts, the "element of unconscious psychotherapy we have shown to be present in the doctor-patient role relationship" is a core feature of the stabilizing social control function of the doctor role and is central to the broader significance of modern medicine in the social system: "All good medical practice . . . has been and is to some degree psychotherapy. Psychotherapy as a mechanism of social control, therefore, builds on and extends what must be regarded as an 'automatic' or latent set of mechanisms which have been built into the role of physician."[89] Like a kind of homeostatic regulatory mechanism, the doctor role functions as a form of control to bring elements of psyche or soma (or both) into more orderly relations with the social body. Medical practice "is a particularly striking case of the existence of relatively unconscious automatic control mechanisms in society," serving to protect a complex and stress-laden social system from "more serious instability."[90]

While Parsons views his failure to publish a monograph on medical practice as a "major failure of my career," his research does become the motivation for the only empirically based chapter of his theoretical treatise *The Social System* (1951).[91] He argues that the study of modern medicine "has opened a 'window' which can be used for the observation of balancing processes within the social system," that is, processes that regulate the system's equilibrium, protecting against potentially catastrophic disturbances. Here Parsons envisions both medical practice *and the illnesses that it treats* serving a homeostatic function in maintaining social order. Illness is theorized as a form of motivational deviance, with deviance understood as a reaction to strain or stress in the social system.[92] But as a form of deviance, sickness may protect against more threatening forms of motivational disturbance; sickness operates through a somatic or psychosomatic apparatus of disruption to defend against more lethal practices of social disorder, thereby functioning as an "integral part of the social equilibrium itself."[93]

Pursuing this logic in relation to mental illness, Parsons challenges the common sociological assumption that an increase in the incidence of mental illness corresponds to an increase in social disorganization. Instead, he suggests that the spread of mental illness may indicate "the diversion into the sick role of elements of deviant motivation which might have been expressed in alternative roles." In fact, "from the point of view of the stability of the social system," a statistical increase in mental disorders among the population "may be less dangerous" than other possible social scenarios.[94]

SOCIO-PSYCHO-CYBER-PHYSIO-LOGICS

> Far from it being the case . . . that the social relations of men are
> based on the logical relations between things, it is the former which
> have provided the prototype for the latter. . . . Logical relations are
> thus, in a sense, domestic relations. — EMILE DURKHEIM AND
> MARCEL MAUSS[95]

By March 1946, when the first of ten conferences organized by Frank Fremont-Smith and the Macy Foundation launches the interdiscipline of cybernetics, the trajectory of this new science of communication and control is already intimately allied with the "mind-body problem," psychosomatic medicine, neuropsychiatry, and homeostatic models of the brain and central nervous system. The psychiatrist and neurophysiologist Warren McCulloch is Fremont-Smith's choice as chairman of the cybernetics conference series. With a background in mathematics and philosophy, McCulloch spends the early 1930s at Rockland State Hospital, a public mental institution in New York, where he becomes interested in the logical anatomy of mind and madness and the possibility of a neurologically based science of psychiatry. A few years later, at Yale University Medical School, McCulloch conducts brain research on monkeys and chimpanzees in pursuit of empirical data that might shed light on the functional organization of the cerebral cortex in humans. The research involves stimulating targeted regions of the cortex by electric shock or the application of strychnine (a poison and central nervous system stimulant) and then recording the effects via electrodes surgically implanted along the surface of the monkey's brain. In 1941, McCulloch becomes director of the Neuropsychiatric Institute at the University of Illinois Medical School, where, according to historian Steve Heims, he "saw the group's mission as an attempt to lay the biological foundations for a scientific approach to psychiatry." Research at the institute, including investigating drug treatments for the experience of "shell shock," is supported by grants from the Macy and Rockefeller foundations.[96]

McCulloch is one of a handful of physiologists, social scientists, and future cyberneticians who attend a Macy-sponsored "Cerebral Inhibition Meeting" in May 1942, which becomes one seed of the postwar cybernetics conferences. The meeting, inspired by Fremont-Smith's interest in the "psychological and neurological aspects" of hypnosis and featuring a presentation by the well-known hypnotist Milton Erickson, is attended by several neurophysiologists: McCulloch, Arturo Rosenblueth, and Lawrence Kubie.[97] All three men become significant figures in the later cybernetics meetings.

At the 1942 meeting, Rosenblueth introduces recent thinking about how the behavior of both machines and organisms can be modeled as goal-seeking "teleological mechanisms." Rosenblueth distributes a copy of the essay "Behavior, Purpose, and Teleology," which he coauthors with Norbert Wiener and Julian Bigelow, theorizing how goal-seeking, purposive behavior is controlled by information feedback.[98] Concepts of "circular causality" and "negative feedback" explain how information produced by the machine-organism's interaction with the environment feeds back into, or circularly affects, the machine-organism's active pursuit of its goal. The resonance between the cybernetic image of self-regulation through circular feedback and Cannon's notion of homeostasis helps to inspire the Macy-sponsored conference series on cybernetics.[99] The first conference meeting in 1946, with McCulloch presiding as chair, is titled "Conference on Feedback Mechanisms and Circular Causal Systems in Biology and the Social Sciences."

A second nucleus of the future cybernetics group is called together by Norbert Wiener and John von Neumann and meets informally at Princeton University from 1943 to 1945. Participants include Warren McCulloch and his young collaborator, the logician and mathematician Walter Pitts. Motivated in part by von Neumann's wartime efforts to develop a fully automated, general purpose "computing machine," the group also explores the productive analogies between the behavior of organisms and machines, including the logical symmetries between the electric properties of the human nervous system and the computer.[100] The network of ideas drawing communication engineering, statistical mathematics, and the communication and control features of the nervous system together grows more dense and more excited.

Of special interest to von Neumann is a mathematical-formal model of brain behavior theorized by Warren McCulloch and Walter Pitts in "A Logical Calculus of the Ideas Immanent in Nervous Activity" (1943), published in the *Bulletin of Mathematical Biophysics*. The McCulloch-Pitts model, called the "apex of the scientific achievement of both men," states the logical possibility of a formal analogy between "mental" behavior and logic itself.[101] McCulloch and Pitts argue that the nervous system, conceived as a connected net of neurons (or nerve cells), can be represented by analogy with a set of logical symbolic propositions. That is, the physiological relations between nervous activities "correspond . . . to relations among the propositions" in symbolic logic. This correspondence does not constitute a "factual explanation" of nervous activity but rather suggests a "formal equivalence" between such activity and the rigorous language of symbolic logic. Equivalence is based on the similarity between the all-or-none electrical properties of a nerve impulse when it "fires," and the binary, true/false structure of propositional logic. Thus the human brain and nervous system can be represented as an on-off electronic switching device that can be described quantitatively, following the same symbolic logic as propositions with their binary, two-valued, true/false nature.[102]

In McCulloch and Pitts's model of nervous activity, "all psychic events . . . have an intentional, or 'semiotic' character" expressed by the "two-valued logic of propositions."[103] This semiotic psyche is ruled not by a definitive causality or "law of necessary connectivity" but by an indeterminate connectivity, similar to the diffuse causality operating in the field of statistics. As a consequence, all perceptual activity, including attempts to perceive the process of perception itself, operate via a determining, but profoundly undetermined, "neuronal" epistemology: "The role of brains in determining the epistemic relations of our theories to our observations and of these to the facts is all too clear, for it is apparent that every idea and every sensation is realized by activity within that [neural] net, and by no such activity are the actual afferents fully determined. . . . Thus empiry confirms that if our nets are undefined, our facts are undefined, and to the 'real' we can attribute not so much as one quality or 'form.' "[104]

But if knowledge is constitutionally limited by the nature of the semiotic nervous system, and if the "real" is rendered irrevocably incomplete by an ignorance "implicit in all our brains," McCulloch and Pitts nevertheless conclude with dramatic certitude: "Thus both the formal and the final aspects of that activity which we are wont to call *mental* are rigorously deducible from present neurophysiology." For the psychiatrist, they affirm, it is now possible to know that " 'mind' no longer 'goes more ghostly than a ghost.' Instead, *diseased mentality can be understood without loss of scope or rigor, in the scientific terms of neurophysiology.*"[105] Indeed, in the same issue of *Mathematical Biophysics*, Walter Pitts coauthors a second essay with Jerome Lettvin (a psychiatrist who later joins Stanley Cobb's department at Mass General), in which they theorize "diseased mentality"—including a group of mental disorders they term "circular insanities"—in the ghost-free language of a series of mathematical equations denoting "quantitative specifications of different psychotic states."[106]

"The brain is a logical machine," Warren McCulloch asserts, and it is

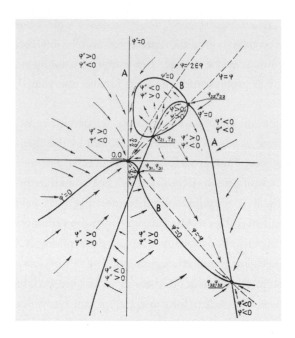

Modeling psychosis. Lettvin and Pitts, "A Mathematical Theory of the Affective Psychoses," 1943.

this contagious suggestion that attracts John von Neumann when he is introduced to the McCulloch-Pitts model of neural nets in 1943 by Norbert Wiener.[107] Wiener foresees the applicability of this formal model of brain behavior to the design problems in electrical engineering: a mathematical model for a neuron is also a useful mathematical model for an electrical circuit, a fundamental operation in the computing machine.[108] The fact that the McCulloch-Pitts model is intended not as a realist representation of the physical properties of an actually existing neuronal circuit but rather as a formal abstraction does not limit its engineering utility.[109] Von Neumann incorporates the logical model into the design of the first digital computing machine, ENIAC (Electronic Numerical Integrator and Calculator), built in 1945.[110] The military-supported development of ENIAC emerges out of the World War II project to automate the massive computational challenge of calculating ballistics tables for antiaircraft artillery systems. Since von Neumann's computer is completed after the war ends, the first computational problem ENIAC is programmed to address is the mathematical model of a hydrogen bomb for the weapons laboratories at Los Alamos.[111]

And so, even before Frank Fremont-Smith and Warren McCulloch deliver their introductory remarks on March 8, 1946, at the first of ten Macy-sponsored meetings that become known as the cybernetics conferences, a core set of ideas has coalesced around formal, mathematicized analogies between nervous activity in the brain, the circuitry in the electronic computer, and the semiotics of propositional logic. John von Neumann and the neurophysiologist Lorente de Nó give the first two presentations on the opening day of the cybernetics conference, offering an introduction to the functional similarities between the new computing machine and the nervous system.[112] Of great interest to von Neumann is the special kind of "purposive mechanism" exemplified by both machine and nervous system. Like its analogue in nature, the nervous system, the computing machine is designed for the purpose of successfully adapting to changing purposes. The "general purpose" computer, as it is called, is intended to satisfy the performance requirements of tasks that its designers cannot fully foresee. "The nervous system," von Neumann explains, "is supposed to perform . . . under conditions which were unforeseeable while the nervous system evolved. . . . Now in all so-called purposive computing mechanisms you also have this attribute, that you want to make a mechanism know full in advance that you do not know what it will be used for."[113]

The successful design of the flexible, all-purpose computer is closely coupled with the concept of "logical automata," which also informs the McCulloch-Pitts model of nervous nets. Developed by the British mathematician Alan Turing in his theory of universal digital computation, logical automata create a conceptual bridge between mental behavior and the mechanization of such behavior in machines. The theory of logical automata states the possibility of mechanically simulating any operation, including mental processes, which can unambiguously be described in a discrete number of words.[114] For von Neumann, who develops his own version of automata theory, the electronic circuitry in a computing machine (automata in the metal), like the circuits in the nervous system (automata in the flesh), can be designed to perform any process that is operationalized in a limited series of words. The all-purpose computer can anticipate the performance of tasks that arise and are defined linguistically in the future.

By the time Norbert Wiener publishes the widely read *Cybernetics, or*

Control and Communication in the Animal and the Machine (1948), and the Macy conference series begins to recognize itself as the progenitor of the new field of cybernetics, the conceptual intimacies between computing machines and the human brain and nervous system have grown dense and seemingly indisputable. While thinkers like von Neumann apply the formal logics of nervous and mental activity to the engineering of new electronic technologies, Wiener, McCulloch, and others are busy refiguring mental and nervous processes and pathologies in light of the cybernetic machines. Wiener, in close collaboration with the neurophysiologist Arturo Rosenblueth, transposes the "pathology" of a negative feedback apparatus — "wild oscillation" — to an understanding of the disorder of the human nervous system called an "intention tremor."[115] (When Wiener's granddaughter later develops the disorder, the cybernetician is led to muse: "If I were a superstitious man, this experience . . . might make me suppose that a disease has a vicious personality and wished nothing more than to revenge itself on the scientist who pursued it.")[116]

In *Cybernetics of the Nervous System* (1965), which Wiener coedits while he is a visiting professor at the Central Institute for Brain Research in Amsterdam, cybernetics and information theory are used to theorize problems of neuronal function and structure, pattern recognition, memory, learning and self-organizing systems, and to advance the recently established field of artificial intelligence.[117] In "Perspectives on Neurocybernetics," Wiener's contribution to the volume, he speculates that long-term, deeply held memory, the kind to which "we refer in psychoanalysis," may be assumed to have "identifiable physico-chemical correlates," operating like "engrams burnt into the very intimate structure of mental and nervous organization." Wiener speculates that statistical mechanics (the probabilistic techniques of quantification that form the mathematical foundation of cybernetics) may offer a fruitful method for investigating and representing the neurophysiology of mental activity and the physical correlates of memory.[118]

Wiener concludes his essay with the observation that "the remaking of neurophysiology on a mechanistic basis," which neurocybernetics enables, is only half the challenge of future research and theory. There must also be a remaking of physics through a new level of interaction with the biological sciences. In the "new unified physics of the future," Wiener prophesies, biology's and physiology's "world of life" will become the studied object and inspirational teacher of the world of physics.[119]

For a biologically oriented psychiatrist like Warren McCulloch, cybernetics offers a confident method for linking "psychology and physiology in the understanding of diseases called 'mental.' "[120] Cybernetics, he writes in 1955, "has helped to pull down the wall between the great world of physics and the ghetto of the mind."[121] Cybernetic thinking refigures mental processes of perception, knowing, and memory (and their dysfunctions) as automated mechanisms of communication and control (and their disorders). As no other science before it, cybernetics promotes an integration of the mind/body dualism through the materialist metaphors of communication theory, although, as McCulloch points out, "*matter* for us [cyberneticians] *is far less material than it was once.*"[122] Cyber-materiality—or the brain "matter" of which the mind is composed—is already a semiotic, a linguistic and logical, structure, already saturated with the immateriality of symbolic circuitry. Cybernetics promises, in the words of Steve Heims, that "messages and signals have a material form, yet can be true and false and contain ideas. Thus the unnatural Cartesian dualism (mind and matter) could be transcended. The ultimate theory of madness, its cause, characterization, and cure, would then be formulated in terms of nervous nets constituting automata and in terms of communication to, from, and within such nets."[123]

In cybernetics, the theoretical unity of mind and body is secured through the notion of circular feedback between physical and psychological information circulating within the organism, and between the organism and its environment. Behavior, in the words of the cybernetically influenced psychiatrist Jurgen Ruesch, "can be understood only if both the biophysical and the symbolic processes are encompassed in one overall system."[124] Cybernetics tries to be that system. By modeling the brain as an information-processing device in which mental activity is analogous with information flows regulated by internal control mechanisms, cybernetics opens the conceptual door to notions of mental disorder as a problem in communication: a breakdown or deviation in the control mechanisms regulating information circuits in the nervous system.

For McCulloch, the cybernetic picture of mental disturbances is welcome scientific ammunition against the "pseudoscientific system" of psychoanalysis.[125] McCulloch's ambition since the early days of his brain research on monkeys has been to replace the Freudian neurosis with the dysfunction of neural activity, to translate the immateriality of the unconscious into the physiology of nerve pathways in the brain.

But in its more generous formulation, cybernetics does not dismiss psychoanalytic insights; it simply, complexly, transforms the language in which the unconscious is heard to speak. Here cybernetics interacts with psychoanalysis to reimagine its concepts through cybernetic notions of information, circular feedback, and communication. Norbert Wiener, who holds quite ecumenical attitudes toward psychoanalysis, encourages a rethinking of the libido or the unconscious through models not of psychic or erotic energy (which so influence Freud's own conceptual imaginary) but of the circuiting and exchange of information.[126] Just as in the history of engineering, where technological and theoretical attention shifts from nineteenth-century machines powered by energy to twentieth-century machines powered by information (i.e., electronic signals), so, too, Wiener suggests, a truly contemporary twentieth-century psychiatry must shift its attention from energy-based to information-based models of psychophysiological processes.[127] "What is gradually replacing concepts of psychological energy, libido, and specific drives is modern information theory," announces Roy Grinker, an early theorist of war neuroses, in 1967.[128] The unconscious is not necessarily killed by cybernetic thinking; rather, it is disassembled, reassembled, and reanimated through the sciences of information and communication.

In fact, as one participant recalls, it was not uncommon during the Macy cybernetics meetings for Norbert Wiener, "to the awe and amusement of the rest of us," to occasionally fall asleep during a discussion. Head on shoulder, snoring convincingly, Wiener would then suddenly "explode out of deep sleep into full sentences which had direct and incisive relevance to the discussion that had been going on around his sleeping head."[129] It becomes part of cybernetic legend that Norbert Wiener solved problems as he slept, dreaming in code, waking out of dark worlds of information. And perhaps, really, he did.

Despite considerable time and energy expended, we are relatively
incompetent when it comes to the description, prediction, and
control of human behavior. Perhaps what is most urgently needed
to understand such conditions is an improved set of models.
—NATHAN KLINE[130]

The ultimate model of a cat is of course another cat, whether it be
born of still another cat or synthesized in a laboratory.—ARTURO
ROSENBLUETH, NORBERT WIENER, AND JULIAN BIGELOW[131]

Despite the enthusiasm among some of the early cyberneticians for a scientific psychiatry guided by the insights of neurophysiology and the information sciences, the dominant paradigm of postwar U.S. psychiatry
initially develops in quite different directions: toward broadly humanistic, psychoanalytic, and social approaches to mental disease and therapeutic intervention.[132] In 1950, the Group for the Advancement of Psychiatry (GAP), a self-appointed and influential group operating within
the APA, declares that the professional responsibilities of psychiatry extend beyond the care of the institutionalized mentally ill into the realms
of "social action" and the "conscious and deliberate wish to change society."[133] And even as the cybernetic gaze narrowly considers the physiological intricacies of neuronal activity and the circular causality between
brain function and mental behavior, the Macy Foundation is simultaneously promoting the expansion—in the name of international order
and world peace—of a humanistic global psychiatry.

In 1948, Frank Fremont-Smith of the Macy Foundation, and Margaret
Mead and Lawrence Frank (who later participate in the cybernetics meetings), help establish the World Federation of Mental Health. Funded in
part by the Macy Foundation and the U.S. and British governments, the
World Federation calls for bringing the psychiatrist and the social scientist into the "closest possible contact with the administrator and political leader," expanding the mental health agenda from the promotion
of healthy individuals to "the larger task of creating a healthy society."[134]
Now that human nature is known to be "much more plastic and flexible"

than previously recognized, the World Federation suggests that the "sciences of man offer the hope of a new approach to the problem of war and a world community." Echoing on a global scale NIMH director Robert Felix's advocacy of the production of "positive mental health" for all, the World Federation promotes the active management of mental health and disease at an international level. In a World Federation proposal to study how best to facilitate technological change within a given society, mental health itself is conceived as a "technology" that can ease social adjustments to other kinds of technological change.[135] "The concept of mental health is co-extensive with world order and the world community," the World Federation declares, positioning world mental health as a prophylactic against future global convulsions.[136]

Warren McCulloch reacts with characteristic bluntness to his colleagues' ambitions for bettering global psychic dis-orderings. After reading the World Federation's statement, he writes to Fremont-Smith, "I would take no issue with your specific suggestions except that it seems to me that all of them are leveled at psychological and sociological evils whose biological chemical and physical roots are still almost unknown."[137] Yet for all of McCulloch's confident dismissal of such projects, the cybernetic visions developed by McCulloch, Wiener, Rosenblueth, and others—in which neurophysiology crossed with electrical engineering and information theory promises a rigorous method for modeling mental processes—circulate at the margins of Cold War psychiatry's psychosocial and psychodynamic mainstream. Interest in empirical and experimental research and in scientific modeling and methods is initially limited to a relatively small number of psychiatrists working at a handful of institutions that support basic research and a scientific approach to mental illness.

The New York State Psychiatric Institute (NYSPI) is one of those institutions. Founded in 1895 with the mission to study the "cause and conditions that underlie mental disease," and to serve as the central pathology laboratory for all mental hospitals in New York State, the NYSPI becomes by the 1950s a multidisciplinary site for scientifically minded psychiatric research.[138] In 1952, a young psychologist at the NYSPI, Joseph Zubin, argues publicly for the greater use of scientific modeling in the study of psychopathology, or "abnormal" psychological processes. In "On the

Powers of Models," Zubin observes that "only recently has the notion been accepted that the model need not be actual reality, but that a working representation would suffice."[139] Citing Norbert Wiener's *Cybernetics* as an example, Zubin describes the usefulness of abstract mathematical models: "The mathematical model is a quantitative or qualitative abstraction of the process or event under study which may serve as a basis for predicting the future course of similar processes or events. . . . [I]n the mathematical model, no one-to-one correspondence need exist between the model and reality." Since psychopathology generally lacks the kind of precise concepts around which rigorous models are built, Zubin encourages borrowing such concepts from the more exact sciences — specifically, neurology and biochemistry. Recognizing the power of models already borrowed from physiology (i.e., homeostasis) and engineering (i.e., feedback mechanisms), he evokes a future science of psychopathology that has lost its "fear" of importing and elaborating models from its scientific neighbors.[140]

"No substantial part of the universe is so simple that it can be grasped and controlled without abstraction," write Norbert Wiener and Arturo Rosenblueth in 1945. "Abstraction consists in replacing the part of the universe under consideration by a model of similar but simpler structure."[141] Zubin's call for more model making in psychopathology challenges the profession to deploy the growing powers of abstraction in its efforts to "grasp and control" the symptomatic universe of psychic disorders. The essay also anticipates Zubin's next career move: director of the biometrics department at NYSPI, where the development of quantifiable methods for precisely measuring mental phenomena becomes a research priority.

Perhaps more than any other event in psychiatry in the 1950s, the introduction of psychopharmacological drugs for the treatment of institutionalized mental patients intensifies interest in the scientific modeling of psychic disease. Chlorpromazine (brand name Thorazine, a synthetic drug manufactured by Smith, Kline, and French Laboratories) and reserpine (brand name Serpasil, isolated and manufactured in a pure form in 1952 by Squibb and Sons) appear to exhibit dramatic, observable effects on patients' mental and emotional processes. The introduction of these drugs in mental institutions in the early to mid-1950s is greeted in many quarters of the psychiatric profession with enormous optimism. The enthusiasm for the new drugs is not hard to understand: the range of accepted treatments for institutionalized mental patients is limited, stark, and conducted with at best variable rates of success. Outside psychotherapy, which by the early 1950s comprises a routine part of most institutionalized care, common treatments for patients are the insulin coma, where the patient is rendered unconscious for long periods of time; electroshock therapy, where the patient is shocked to the point of seizure by an electrical current; and psychosurgery, where frontal lobotomy, or the surgical removal of part of the brain, is the most common procedure.[142]

A welcome alternative to such brutal "therapeutics," the new drugs and their observed efficacy at the same time highlight a disturbing ignorance about the precise mechanisms by which psychopharmacology works to transform mental states. The drugs' effectiveness in alleviating some symptoms—and sometimes worsening or proliferating others—powerfully suggests that altering the neurochemistry of the brain is linked to the alteration of mental "behavior." But precisely how mental activity, orderly or disorderly, may be circuited through brain biochemistry remains virtually unknown.

The desire to construct empirically grounded theoretical models of brain-behavior interaction in the face of a profound ignorance about psychopharmacology's mechanisms of action is one impetus behind a series of five "Neuropharmacology" conferences, organized by Frank Fremont-Smith and the Macy Foundation from 1954 to 1959. Less well known than Macy's cybernetics conferences—though overlapping with them in both time and invited participants—the neuropharmacology meetings bring together pharmaceutical industry representatives, psychiatrists, pharmacologists, NIMH officials, neurologists, biochemists, and government representatives from the Department of Defense, the Office of Naval Research, and the U.S. Army. Transactions of the meetings are published in a five-volume set edited by Harold Abramson, a guest at the Macy cybernetics meetings and a research psychiatrist at the Biological Laboratory at Cold Springs Harbor.[143] Participants include Ralph Gerard, also a participant in the Macy cybernetics conferences, and the psychiatrist Roy Grinker. Conference presentations range from "Experimentally Induced Psychoses in Man" to "Functional Organization of the Brain" and "Effect of LSD-25 on Snails." Most of the research investigates the psychopharmacological effects on animal and human behavior of serotonin, reserpine, chlorpromazine, mescaline, and lysergic acid diethylamide (LSD).

The widespread research interest in LSD in the 1950s is compelled by the drug's dramatic capacity to produce effects that mimic or simulate psychotic symptoms. LSD creates drug-induced "model psychoses," viewed by psychiatric researchers like Abraham Wikler as "one important way in which psychiatry can be made 'experimental.' "[144] The ability to produce a model of psychosis with LSD, and then to block or turn it off via other pharmaceutical drugs, offers a seductive laboratory for hypothesizing the common neurochemistry underlying the action of each drug, with possible implications for understanding the neurochemistry of psychosis itself. The discovery that chlorpromazine can temporarily "turn off" the mind-altering effects of LSD and mescaline only amplifies experimental interest in the "model psychoses."[145] The Central Intelligence Agency's interest in the hallucinogenic effects of LSD — for example, as a possible weapon in the wartime interrogation of prisoners — is not a secret: Harold Abramson conducts extensive research on LSD throughout the 1950s and is "deeply involved in promoting LSD research on their [the CIA's] behalf."[146] According to Steve Heims, Abramson and the Macy Foundation meetings actually become for a time a conduit for CIA funding of LSD-related research. Frank Fremont-Smith and the Macy Foundation also sponsor two conferences in 1956 and 1959 on the use of LSD in psychotherapy, which, along with the neuropharmacology meetings, bring CIA-sponsored drug researchers together with government officials interested in their findings.[147]

The neuropharmacology meetings specify and extend a set of issues raised in another conference series, "Problems of Consciousness," sponsored by the Macy Foundation and held once each year from 1950 to 1954.[148] With considerable overlap in participants, the two conference series share a focus on the theoretical modeling of mental phenomena, both "normal" and "abnormal."[149] While presentations at the neuropharmacology meetings are largely limited to psychopharmacological experiments on humans and animals, "Problems of Consciousness" takes on a wider range of multidisciplinary topics—hypnosis, schizophrenia, consciousness and the "chemistry of time"—and involves more participants from the social sciences. Talcott Parsons is an invited participant at three of the five "Problems of Consciousness" meetings and delivers a presentation in 1953 entitled "Consciousness and Symbolic Processes." Parsons suggests that consciousness can be modeled as a complex communication system, with an integrated set of communicative subsystems sending messages and signals across subsystem boundaries.[150]

At the same 1953 meeting, Roy Grinker of the Institute for Psychosomatic and Psychiatric Research takes over as chair of the "Problems of Consciousness" conference series. His opening remarks encourage conference participants to engage directly with cybernetic models of mental behavior. Relying on a theory of communication based on "modern mechanics of servomechanisms and neuronal feedback concepts of neurophysiology (cybernetics)," Grinker describes consciousness as a system of interactions "in terms of a field in which there is an exchange of information."[151] Consciousness is modeled as a feedback process involving internal and external information flows.

In presenting this concept of consciousness, Grinker also proposes a theory of the process of modeling itself. Making models, he suggests, is intimately connected to the historically specific machines of the time, machines which are themselves modeled after models of the internal processes of human action, which are themselves modeled after the machines of that era. In reflecting on how the scientist, like the schizophrenic, imaginarily employs the latest technological inventions of the day—the scientist for making models and the schizophrenic for making delusions—Grinker elaborates: "Man invents a mechanical device because of some need to master an element in nature. The mechanics that he utilizes are derived from somatic anatomic-physiologic processes within his own brain. When he tries to make a model of some of his internal processes he utilizes the mechanical devices which he has himself made. Progress in conceptual thinking of man about man is a feedback mechanism. . . . [I]t is achieved by psychological analogies of projections of somatic processes."[152] Explaining how Freud's models of the distribution and discharge of psychic energy are developed in relation to the mechanics of steam and gas engines, Grinker states that a contemporary model of consciousness "corresponds with our most recent electronic inventions." Calling for interdisciplinary research on consciousness that is concerned not with "energy transactions" but with "communication processes within and without the organism," Grinker envisions a cross-disciplinary future in which "psychology will be of the same weight as physiology."[153]

Grinker's cybernetic approach to consciousness does not necessarily promote a narrow biological reductionism. Rather, it launches a kind of "informational" reductionism in which the life sciences, together with the social, mental, and physical sciences, are incited toward cross-disciplinary communication by modeling a diversity of phenomena— human, social, machine, biological— as information and communication systems.

The explicit interest in cybernetic models among Cold War psychiatrists extends to the influential work of Nathan Kline, director of research in the 1950s at Rockland State Mental Hospital in New York (where Warren McCulloch begins his career in neuropsychiatry). Kline, known as a founder of psychopharmacology in the United States for his indefatigable promotion of the new drugs to both the U.S. government and a broader public, conceives of the notion of the cyborg at a U.S. Air Force symposium in 1960. Together with his colleague Manfred Clynes, whose work at Rockland State on computers, biocybernetics, and the quantitative measurement of emotional communication helps establish Rockland as an internationally renowned psychiatric research center, Kline imagines the role of psychopharmacology in enhancing and adapting cybernetic man-machine systems to new environments.[154] Kline and Clynes argue that cyborg research, while originating out of problems that might arise in outer space, can contribute to "a clearer understanding of man's needs in his home environment."[155] Their sentiments are echoed in the concluding remarks at the 1960 Air Force symposium, delivered by Lieutenant Colonel Bernard Flaherty: "What was discussed here is not only space oriented. It has implications throughout the field of mental health. . . . While *the possible use of special devices to further automate man* . . . is still in the speculative stage, it offers interesting opportunities for research that will benefit not only space travel but general medicine as well."[156]

In the years before Kline speculates on the psychopharmacologics of the new cyborg, he is busy building the research facility at Rockland State into a multidisciplinary site specializing in drug research, including the on-site development and testing of new psychopharmaceuticals.[157] One of the earliest drugs that Kline tests on patients at Rockland is iproniazid, a chemical derivative of the rocket propellant used by Germany to fuel the v-2 rocket (the same German rockets targeted by wartime cybernetic models of antiaircraft artillery fire).[158] In 1956, in the published proceedings of what Kline describes as "the first major conference on the use of several new pharmaceuticals in the field of mental disease," he reports on the findings of experimental research on reserpine conducted with seven hundred human subjects, most of them patients institutionalized at Rockland State.[159] Kline gives the new drug to a wide array of patients — diversely diagnosed as psychotics, alcoholics, disturbed adolescents, and neurotics — and concludes that reserpine affords a promising treatment in a "great variety" of psychic disorders.[160]

In spite of support from organizations like the Macy Foundation or hospitals like Rockland State and the New York State Psychiatric Institute — where the department of experimental psychiatry is primarily occupied with drug research[161] — the emerging field of psychopharmacology does not immediately receive a friendly embrace from all quarters. At the NIMH, where psychiatric research is for the first time being organized and sponsored at a national level, the interest in drug treatments is considered a passing "fad," and requests to sponsor psychopharmacological studies are met with skepticism. Only when Nathan Kline joins up in the mid-1950s with the philanthropist Mary Lasker to directly lobby Congress for a $2 million annual appropriation for psychopharmacology research is the NIMH forced to pay attention to the new field.[162] The first director of the NIMH Psychopharmacology Service Center launched with the congressional money recounts: "The NIMH reluctantly accepted the extra money and I was hired to run the new program, I believe because no more senior or distinguished individual was available or interested."[163]

Despite its reluctant support, in 1956 the NIMH joins with the National Academy of Sciences and the American Psychiatric Association to cosponsor a huge conference called "Psychopharmacology: Problems in Evaluation." Attended by over one thousand participants, including representatives from the pharmaceutical industry and the Federal Drug Administration, the conference marks the growing importance of psycho-pharmacology to psychiatric practice and research. In his introductory remarks, conference chair Ralph Gerard (participant in both the Macy-sponsored "Cybernetics" and "Neuropharmacology" meetings) attributes the timing of the conference to the urgent need for the development of rigorous, reliable methods for objectively evaluating the effects of the new drugs. The aim of the conference is to help establish more standardized procedures for clinical drug evaluations, given that, as Gerard explains, "the methods [currently] available for the careful and scientific study of the effectiveness of a drug therapy [are] unsatisfactory."[164] Participants advocate the implementation of a standardized research design with blind and double-blind controls, in which neither patient nor doctor knows which drug, if any, the patient is taking.[165]

Another major stumbling block to a confident scientific method is the "deplorable effect [of] the lack of a common nomenclature and terminology" on both the conference proceedings and the possibility of objective and effective drug research. The hope is expressed that in the near future "as the physiological laboratories develop more delicate and different methods for making measurements," some progress on the standardization of psychiatric language might follow.[166]

PERFORMING CYBERPSYCHIATRY

Science is concerned with the test of performativity. As a cultural project, modern Western science has never been content only to represent nature but desires also and always to act upon it.
—HILARY ROSE[167]

Donald Klein, grandson of a Ukrainian faith healer and great-grandson of a wonder-working rabbi, is also profoundly discontent by the late 1950s with the language of psychiatric diagnosis. His interest in pharmaceutical dissection—or the "use of patterns of drug response as dissecting tools"[168]—is linked to a desire to circumvent the existing diagnostic system and develop a new psychiatric nomenclature that more accurately matches specific patient populations (i.e., diagnostic groups) with specific drug effects. In Klein's words, "The development of effective psychopharmacological agents confronted the psychiatric profession with the inadequacy of its diagnostic system for the provision of rational indications . . . for drug therapy." Klein's research mission is to demonstrate the usefulness of psychiatric diagnostic language when linked to the "prediction of treatment outcome," particularly the "outcome" of psychopharmacological drug treatment.[169]

So when Klein and his colleague Max Fink at Hillside Hospital begin drug research on institutionalized mental patients in 1958, they ignore diagnostic labels and administer the antidepressant imipramine to almost every patient at Hillside. As Klein recalls, "Max and I decided that all these medications were really new and nobody understood them. And Max was at the time a diagnostic nihilist. He did not believe that diagnosis meant anything. . . . And, further, he took the stand that we were sitting with all these drugs — antipsychotics, antidepressants — and didn't know what they were, and therefore the only way to learn anything about them was to use them as widely as possible and observe their effects."[170] In search of patterns of drug effects that can suggest new and more reliable diagnostic entities, Klein and Fink identify a group of fourteen patients whose reaction to the drug imipramine features a dramatic reduction in "episodic anxiety" or "'panic' attacks." They report an impressive 100 percent favorable "medication management" rating for the group as a whole.[171] The group of institutionalized mental patients exhibits the first pharmaceutically dissected appearance of a "disorder" that will, two decades later, be recognized in the official psychiatric diagnostic language as "panic disorder."

Klein and Fink are not alone in their impatience with the language of psychiatric diagnosis. In 1965 the Psychopharmacology Research Branch of the NIMH and the American Psychiatric Association cosponsor a conference calling for a "reexamination of the bases of psychiatric diagnosis."[172] Announcing the "increasing dissatisfaction with the traditional system of psychiatric diagnosis" and the need for "new objective systems" of classification, conference organizers bring together psychiatrists, behavioral scientists, mathematicians, and statisticians to collectively address the future of psychiatric naming. One computer expert suggests that if psychiatrists and statisticians could be coupled through the computer, the complexities of diagnosis could be more readily handled.[173]

Max Fink—a conference presenter along with Donald Klein, Roy Grinker, and Joseph Zubin—argues that neurophysiological tests should soon be able to "provide objective measures to classify psychiatric populations according to differences in biochemical organization of the central nervous system."[174]

One major goal of the conference is to urge methods of classification that address the issue of "treatment specificity," or the matching of specific diagnostic groups with specific treatments, including the growing array of available drugs.[175] The proliferation of psychopharmaceutical drugs in the 1960s lends urgency to the call for a more scientific psychiatry and a more instrumental psychiatric language. "Psychiatry is a technology," one conference participant states, and its classification system needs to better guide psychiatry's technological reach.[176] Psychopharmacology appears to offer the best postwar promise for the "mass approach" to mental health envisioned twenty years earlier by the first director of the NIMH. For psychiatrists trying to prescribe the new medications as well as researchers trying to study them, the current diagnostic system provides little help in administering the new mass solution to mental distress.

In 1969, Donald Klein coauthors the eight-hundred-page *Diagnosis and Drug Treatment of Psychiatric Disorders*, which he calls "one of the initial attempts to refocus American psychiatry on the importance of careful descriptive diagnosis as useful, rather than an empty exercise in formalistics."[177] The book becomes the "most influential textbook of clinical psychopharmacology in the U.S."[178] Klein and his coauthors argue in the revised edition of the textbook that a defining criterion of diagnostic validity should be the accurate prediction of treatment response. This approach to diagnosis would "utilize prognosis as the cutting edge for diagnosis, and attempt to tease out from the various diagnostic classifications those syndromal aspects that are crucial for prognosis and treatment response." According to this logic, diagnosis becomes "the key to correct treatment."[179] Without a diagnostic system that differentiates meaningfully between patient subpopulations with similar reactions to treatment, rational choice of treatment will lie forever beyond the reach of psychiatric knowledge.

If the problem of diagnostic classification is intensified by the apparent effectiveness of the new drugs, researchers continue to wrestle with their extensive ignorance regarding how the drugs actually work. In 1969, Donald Klein gathers with some twenty other psychiatrists, neurologists, surgeons, and clinical psychologists at the first annual "Cerebral Function Symposium," to tackle the problem of theorizing the relation between brain behavior and the biochemistry of psychoactive drugs.[180] Sponsored by seven pharmaceutical companies—including Eli Lilly, Geigy Pharmaceutical, and Hoffman-LaRoche—the symposium hopes to stimulate the development and testing of new models linking drug action and behavioral effects.[181]

At the symposium, Klein introduces his "cybernetic" model of drug-behavior interaction.[182] Foregrounding the "normalizing" effects of certain drugs on "deranged control mechanisms" in the central nervous system, his cybernetic model suggests that therapeutic drugs work to normalize existing regulatory control processes in the brain. The reparative effects of the drugs can be understood by analogy with the system regulating temperature in a furnace or refrigerator.[183] Positing the existence of "neural detectors" in the brain that continually test and automatically regulate biochemical activity, Klein hypothesizes that the detectors themselves can become defective: drugs operate by returning the defective regulators to their normal and normalizing control functions.[184] Acknowledging that "this is all quite speculative," Klein nonetheless emphasizes that his cybernetic model would succeed in resituating the mechanisms of psychopharmacology squarely in the realm of neurophysiological function, far outside the reference frames of psychoanalytic language. "This type of theorizing implies that behavioral drugs act on control mechanisms rather than at levels often considered in energy, libidinal, or drive terminology."[185]

Klein concludes his cybernetic theory of drug action with a summary of the implications of such a model for psychiatric diagnosis more generally:

There is distinct heuristic value in this emphasis on the possibility of reparative drug action since it fosters *the use of clinical drug effects as the basis for a drug-relevant psychiatric typology*. That is patients would be grouped on the basis of patterns of drug-induced changes. . . . *Responses to medication would be used as dissecting tools to distinguish various subpopulations* and . . . commonalities within each subpopulation. Hopefully, these commonalities may . . . serve the practical purpose of providing rational indications and contraindications for drug therapy.[186]

In both the 1969 and 1980 editions of the widely read *Diagnosis and Drug Treatment*, Klein and his coauthors elaborate this cybernetic model of drug-brain feedback circuits, citing the urgent need for a "drug-relevant" language of psychiatric classification.[187]

5

Panic Xanax: A Patient Diary

Instructions: Please fill out a page in the diary each evening after taking your last capsule. Since it is very important that you do not miss even one capsule, if you get in the habit of filling out your diary regularly, it may help you to remember your medication. — PATIENT DIARY, the Upjohn Company

And what might I forget? — PATIENT

It was happening again. Maria could feel her chest tightening, her head getting light. **She was breathing too fast**.[1] Across the table, Adam was cheerful and talkative as she struggled to calm herself, hoping it would pass. **And then it happened: her heart started beating faster**. Maybe it's just the thrill of the occasion, she thought nervously—dinner with Adam to celebrate her birthday. **Her heart accelerated so fast she could feel the pounding in her chest. She thought Adam must notice. Then the flushing sensation. . . . She couldn't breathe properly**. She wanted to escape, to run outside, get fresh air, but Adam continued calmly talking as the room started to shimmer and recede around her. **Beads of sweat broke out on her forehead; a rushing sensation in the bottom of her stomach. Everything became detached. She felt dizzy, lightheaded, and then that panicky feeling—that mental panic**.

In 1983, David Sheehan, M.D., publishes *The Anxiety Disease*, a bestselling medico-mythic story of Maria, a twenty-four-year-old woman who suffers from panic attacks and spells of floating terror. "This book is about Maria's people—their plight, their descent into terror, their peculiar experiences. It is also about the beginnings of the liberation of these people. And their journey to freedom."[2] A practicing psychiatrist at Massachusetts General Hospital in Boston when he writes the book, Sheehan grasps with remarkable clarity Donna Haraway's insight that "the boundary between science fiction and social reality is an optical illusion."[3] The fictional Maria is composed from the clinical details, stories, and symptoms of Sheehan's patients, reassembled into a narrative that oscillates between medical monograph and Harlequin romance. A curious instance of social realities imploding into medical science's fictions, Maria's story is a marketable mix of psychological trauma, heterosexual fantasy, medical mystery, and triumphant pharmaceutical cure. She is a composite of clinical facts recombined into a fiction whose truth appears no less scientific even though she never really existed at all.

Woven together with statistics on disease incidence, quizzes for self-diagnosis, symptom checklists, and a description of the seven progressive stages of the disease (ending with depression and thoughts of suicide), *The Anxiety Disease* takes a fateful turn when boyfriend Adam stumbles across an article in a science magazine, "Panic Attacks Can Kill." The once skeptical Adam goes to the nearest medical school library, searches the computer databases, and reviews the most recent scientific research on panic. A newly informed Adam then brings Maria to a doctor who understands her disease. She learns about the biochemical basis of panic and meets the real hero of the story—pharmaceutical medication. Her "journey to freedom" is now phrased in the medicalized discourse of a four-target plan for recovery. The first step is "Target 1: Biological," when a choice is made between available drug treatments. Sheehan recommends alprazolam, brand name Xanax, as the most rapid, effective, and least toxic drug choice: "It appears to be the safest to use, and it is the easiest for the physician to prescribe, regulate, and monitor."[4]

Sheehan is no stranger to Xanax, or to the Upjohn Company, which manufactures the drug. In 1981, together with James Coleman of Upjohn, Sheehan conducts the first Xanax-panic study in the United States at the Hypnosis and Psychosomatic Medicine Clinic at Massachusetts General Hospital. As an outpatient clinic for patients suffering from symptoms of panic, hysteria, anxiety neurosis, and agoraphobia, the Psychosomatic Clinic employs a range of treatments from hypnosis to psychopharmacology. The 1981 Xanax study, funded by Upjohn, enrolls thirty-two patients from the Psychosomatic Clinic. Almost immediately, Sheehan recalls, the drug's effectiveness was dramatically clear:

> Well, that stuff [Xanax], I mean it worked instantly. . . . I remember that there were two sisters in the group. . . . They took the meds and they were scared out of their minds. . . . So, I'm still in my office, it was like late at night, fall was coming, and 2 or 3 hours later I got this phone call. The sisters have arrived home. . . . And they said, "Dr. Sheehan you'll never guess what happened." And I said, "What happened?" And they said well we got on the subway . . . [and] they

got off the train in the suburb where they lived. One of them said her sister was quite obviously sedated . . . but she said she was so calm that she couldn't remember how long it was. And she felt—she said this is the first time in years that I have felt the way I feel like this. She said you cannot imagine. I've got no anxiety. It's gone. It's just gone. She said, I'm cured. . . .

. . . [T]he group [of patients] when they met on subsequent visits were literally—they said do you realize what this means? . . . [T]hey said we can't tell you or communicate to you what a major impact this is going to have on everyone's life. . . . They wanted to buy stock—they wanted to know who is the name of the company that made the drug. They wanted to buy stock in the company. I mean, it was incredible.[5]

Sheehan begins writing *The Anxiety Disease* less than a year later, acknowledging his debt to colleagues at the Upjohn Company, who have "set an example of how industry can forge a constructive, responsible alliance with academic medicine."[6] The idea for the book emerges out of the TV screen. In 1982, Sheehan is asked by ABC to write a short news piece on panic disorder, a new psychiatric diagnostic label. After the piece airs on national TV, the senior Mr. Scribner (of the publishing house) contacts Sheehan and suggests that he write a book. Sheehan begins to take notes during sessions with patients who, when he tells them he's writing a book, open up with more stories. Some even bring him their own written notes. At the same time, he begins reading up on how to write a successful romance novel. In the summer of 1982, Sheehan writes *The Anxiety Disease* in three weeks. Without scratching out a sentence. The book has sold more than a half million copies and has been translated into several languages.[7]

Despite the significant role he plays in popularizing Xanax as a cure for panic, Sheehan never comes to believe in the existence of panic disorder. In his published research, Sheehan insists that what psychiatry starts to call panic disorder in 1980 is part of a larger disease pattern that includes hysteria, agoraphobia, and other anxiety states. In a 1982 article on the history of disease classifications for anxiety and hysteria, he writes: "Hysteria has been a parent disorder—the hub of the neurotic wheel. In an attempt to strike some order into the confusing plethora of symptoms, different symptoms were splintered off and elevated to the category of disease in their own right. These stepchildren of hysteria include anxiety neurosis, hypochondriasis, agoraphobia, anxiety-hysteria, *panic disorder*, generalized anxiety disorder, hysterical personality."[8] Sheehan invents the label "endogenous anxiety" (anxiety that comes from inside) to name a "prototypical psychosomatic disorder" composed of panic attacks, dizzy spells, breathing difficulty, chest pains, and heart palpitations.[9] Someday, he predicts, panic disorder will be recognized as simply one "piece of all this bigger piece" of a psychosomatic anxiety disease.[10]

If Sheehan resists the particular way that panic is carved out and incorporated into the 1980 psychiatric classification system, he fully embraces the contemporaneous move within psychiatry to approach mental illnesses like panic using a medical disease model. One of Sheehan's aims in *The Anxiety Disease* is to persuade a readership of patients and doctors alike that the "central force in the anxiety disease appears to be a physical one. The proposed model suggests that at the center of this disease, feeding it like a spring, is a biological and probably a biochemical disorder."[11] The Department of Psychiatry at Massachusetts General Hospital, and the Hypnosis and Psychosomatic Medicine Clinic where Sheehan works while he's writing the book, are perfect sites for his medicalized approach. Since its founding by Stanley Cobb with Rockefeller Foundation money in the 1930s, the department is dedicated to the coupling of psychiatry and medicine. Exploring the complex circuiting of psyche with soma has for decades been a guiding motive of much of the department's psychiatric research. And panic and anxiety have repeatedly provided symptomatic scenes for psychosomatic medicine to pursue its interest in the networkings of mind and body, of medicine and psychiatry. Of mental distress and military research. Of the medical clinic and corporate capital. Integrating circuits, advancing in observable complexities.

It's late night, November 1942, and 114 bodies are delivered to the emergency room of Massachusetts General Hospital, victims of one of the most famous and fatal episodes of collective panic — the Cocoanut Grove Club fire, which kills 491 people. *Newsweek*'s description of the scene at the popular nightclub reads: "Every available table was taken. . . . [A] girl, her hair ablaze, hurtled across the floor screaming 'Fire!' That shriek heralded catastrophe. Some 800 guests, insane with panic, lunged in a wild scramble to get out. . . . Flames flashed with incredible swiftness. . . . The revolving doors jammed as the terror-stricken mob pushed them in both directions at the same time."[12] The ferocity of the fire is attributed to the combustible decorations in the Cocoanut Grove simulating a tropical environment.[13] Among survivors, lung injuries from the noxious fumes resemble those from certain war gases. More than a third of the victims die while trying to escape through the main exit, a revolving door that quickly jams. Nearly two hundred corpses are found piled up behind the exit.

At Massachusetts General Hospital, the "civilian defense" mode of emergency response — planned and rehearsed in those anxious years in anticipation of possible mainland U.S. war casualties — is activated. As part of the integrated response, the psychiatric staff arrives quickly on the scene.[14]

Psychiatrists' work on the Disaster Ward at Massachusetts General, where survivors of the Cocoanut Grove Club fire are treated, is discussed by Stanley Cobb in a special 1943 issue of *Annals of Surgery*. (Color photographs of the burn victims accompany Cobb's article, financed by a grant from the Macy Foundation.) Cobb reports that in monitoring the survivors for "problems of psychiatric study and management," the psychiatric staff was particularly interested to observe the "physiological features of grief" among those who lost friends or family in the fire.[15] Psychiatrists identified pupil dilation, heat waves to the head, flushing, sweating, and sighing as one possible "nucleus of a physiologic disturbance . . . form[ing] the background for the 'emotional distress.'"[16] Within the tangled circuits of psychic and somatic disturbance, the empirical outline of observable physiological patterns is becoming, just barely, intelligible.

Soon after the Cocoanut Grove Club fire, Cobb and an interdisciplinary group of colleagues in psychiatry, cardiology, and neurology at Massachusetts General conduct a series of studies under contract with the Office of Scientific Research and Development (OSRD), the wartime agency overseeing the mobilization and funding of science for military purposes.[17] Much of the research is restricted by the military and never published. The focus of the studies that are published is the problem of "neurocirculatory asthenia," a diagnostic label introduced during World

War I to designate a set of symptoms—heart palpitations, shortness of breath, fatigue, nervousness, dizziness—associated with cases of "shell shock" or "war neuroses."[18]

In 1944, in a study comparing patients on medical wards diagnosed with neurocirculatory asthenia, and patients in psychiatric units diagnosed with anxiety neurosis, Cobb and his colleague, a cardiologist, conclude that the two diseases—one purportedly located in the heart, the other in the mind—may indeed be the same affliction.[19] Also in 1944, Mandel Cohen, a psychiatrist at Massachusetts General, is lead author of a study in which men diagnosed with neurocirculatory asthenia, based on their complaints of dizziness, heart palpitations, chest discomfort, nervousness, and difficulty breathing, are subjected to vigorous physical training (first by a "kindly" athletic trainer and then by a "coercive" army sergeant) and to a series of painful electric shocks; their reactions are compared with those of healthy soldiers.[20] Cohen also participates in a 1950 follow-up study, funded by the Medical Department of the U.S. Army, of 173 patients diagnosed twenty years earlier with neurocirculatory asthenia.[21] In *The Anxiety Disease*, Sheehan cites Mandel Cohen's work as early evidence of the biological nature of the disease from which Maria suffers.[22]

Into these historical densities of psychosomatic disturbances taking shape at Massachusetts General Hospital walks a young sociologist and professor at Harvard University. Fascinated by the new field of psychosomatic medicine, in search of his own social scientific version of integrated circuits, Talcott Parsons in the late 1930s conducts fieldwork at Massachusetts General Hospital and Tufts Medical Center. As part of his research, he performs the role of an attending physician. "Equipped with a white coat and the (albeit nonmedical) legitimate title of doctor," Parsons recalls, he impersonates a medical doctor. In addition to "canvassing the literature" on medicine, he decides "to approach it through the methods of participant observation and interview. The semi-public character of medical practice in the modern hospital made a good deal of the former possible, such as . . . making ward rounds, observing operations, going on the home visit service. . . . (Perhaps, with current concern over ethical aspects of research, this mild deception of patients would now be regarded as unethical.)"[23]

Writing later of the psychosomatic features of the relationship between the personality and the human organism, Parsons theorizes that all behavior is mediated by "physiological mechanisms," including the communication systems involved with complex behaviors like personality.[24] For Parsons, the relation between somatic and psychic health is circuited through the problem of how the control of behavior is organized: while the "mind" is a level of organization above the somatic and in some sense controls it, the communication system through which the mind operates is itself mediated by physical processes.[25] Mind and body becoming matter all the way down. Mental communication and material control becoming integrated all the way through.

PANIC DIARY

(She's sleepless. Again. The circadian rhythm cracks, opening her inside out into dark circuits of story, electric and nonrandom. Night hard-wired with signal, noise, and static flesh. In that spectral space, she reaches as always for either a pill or a book. A pill or a book, those two different forms of story.)

I wake this morning barely slept but live-wired, anxious for my first visit to the Anxiety Research Unit at Massachusetts General Hospital. I scan through the personal diary I kept during the first months of the panic attacks. The scrawled, repetitious litany of symptoms, thermometer readings, pulse rates, vacillating self-diagnoses. Page after scribbled page.

I take the train downtown to Massachusetts General, arriving early for my appointment with Dr. M. I wander into a small, philanthropically funded museum gallery in the hospital lobby. Irene and Philip Faneuil Art Gallery, the sign reads. *You stand before the sun not blinking. Watching. We and the birds. We and the women and the sun. The figure of the woman is nothing but black edges outlined. And white space, static on both sides of her edges, inside and out, a white noise inside and out along her edges standing before her standing in front of the sun.* I blink. I'm standing before a painting, patterns of black line, orange color, white space. "Joan Miró — Woman and Birds in Front of the Sun," the gold plate on the wall reads. I'll have to remember to write that down. I blink. I take the elevator to the seventh floor.

Room 717, Psychosomatic Medicine Unit, reads the sign on the door. I enter. No one is there, and I stand hesitantly in front of the receptionist's empty desk. A young man approaches. He does not speak to me as he leans over and writes down my name, which he already knows, on the receptionist's calendar. Then he introduces himself. Tom. The research assistant. Blond, tall, a little awkward. Still learning.

We enter Tom's small office. On the desk is a Word-a-Day calendar with the drug company name "Merrel Dow, Inc.," at the bottom (remember to write that down). The word for today, September 14, is "buddhavista: spiritual wisdom, one who will probably become a Buddha." Tom gives me a medical research consent form to read quickly and sign. The form explains the purpose of the research study in which I am volunteering to participate: to test the effects of alprazolam (Xanax) in comparison with imipramine (Tofranil) and a placebo. The drug treatment for each volunteer research subject is randomized, assigned by lot, and the research will be double-blind; "neither you nor the investigator will know which drug you are receiving," the form reads. I sign in the space provided.

Tom then walks me down several short hallways to Dr. M.'s office. HOLLYWOOD — IS IT REAL OR IS IT FICTION? asks a silver-framed poster on the wall. Dr. M. is in his late thirties, dark haired, casual and only somewhat friendly. He explains, apologizing, that we'll have to go through a number of checklists. But afterward I'll be given a more open-ended interview, more "true to reality," he says to me with a slight, knowing smile.

In response to the questions that Dr. M. reads monotonously from sheets of paper on his lap, I tell my story. How the panic attacks began. My confusion and fear about heart trouble. The insomnia, the spells of dizziness and weakness, the anxiety and elevated heart rate in between the actual episodes of full-blown panic. He listens. He nods. My hands clasp and unclasp. My foot taps. I tell him I'm not currently taking any medication, though I once took Xanax for several months, soon after the attacks began.

DR. M.: Are you afraid of bad things happening?
PATIENT: Well, not more than most people, I don't think. I mean, I worry about nuclear war.

DR. M.: Well, you live in Boston. You have to worry about nuclear war. It's politically right.

[She smiles. He chuckles and puts a check on the page.]

DR. M.: Do you ever have feelings so bad you want to kill yourself?

PATIENT: [pause] No.

[He doesn't put a check next to that question.]

After almost an hour of questioning, Dr. M. leans back in his chair and summarizes, "Well, you have panic disorder and some depressive experience. No major depression. You're lucky. You've fought through it. Now, do you have any questions for me?"

I'm surprised by the abrupt transition. Am I in? Am I accepted into the research study? I start to reply, "Well, no, I'm not sure —"

Dr. M. says with his half smile, "Yes, you get to be the aggressor for a while."

I don't ask any questions.

Dr. M. tells me I'm a good candidate for the research program. He'll see me next week, unless something unusual shows up in the physical exam or my blood tests. I'm in. My heart beats faster in my chest.

Because, as I enter this research scene, I am not currently suffering from panic. I was diagnosed with panic disorder two years ago, took Xanax for several months, and then found other practices of calming and cure. Breath. Dream. Memory. Writing. I am here at Massachusetts General Hospital trying to research this research program on panic disorder. Drawing on my own past experiences, I am performing the role of a panicky woman, trying to get access, as a participant observer, to the sick role as it plays out in the social and psychic fields of a corporate-sponsored clinical drug trial. This is a self-chosen theater in which I recount my panic stories in public for purposes other than submission to their cure. For other purposes than free access to a drug in exchange for the selective details of my dis-ease. Pills and stories. Stories for pills. Pills for stories. Inside every pill there's a story, and I'm here to try to imagine how best to tell this one.

(It's a story circuited through the TV screen. A young white girl in braids and braces sits on the couch next to her mother. She calmly tells the TV talk show host and the home viewing audience about her first attack of panic. The sudden terror, pounding heart, sweaty palms, shortness of breath — the same dramatic symptoms her mother experienced in her twelve-year battle with panic disorder. The camera turns to a gray-suited man, Dr. Jerrold Rosenbaum, chief of the Psychopharmacology Unit at Massachusetts General Hospital, where clinical research on panic has been conducted since the mid-1970s. He calmly describes panic as a biochemically based disease, with genetic vulnerability passed through the family. Before the commercial break, the talk show host assures viewers who might be suffering from this disabling disorder that they are not alone. For more information, viewers should phone the toll-free number of the Anxiety Research Unit at Massachusetts General Hospital. Studio audience applause. A quick shot of the young girl smiling. The phone number flashes again. Break to commercial.

Over three hundred people, more than two-thirds of them women, phone the Anxiety Research Unit within two weeks of the airing of the TV talk show on panic disorder.

I am one of the three hundred people who phone.

Screened first by a survey sent in the mail, then by a twelve-item questionnaire conducted during a twenty-minute telephone interview, a handful of subjects with appropriate symptom profiles are selected as possible participants in Massachusetts General Hospital's clinical research program on panic disorder. The study is sponsored by the Upjohn Company, manufacturer of Xanax, a popular antianxiety drug approved for the market in 1981.

She doesn't know what a neural network is, really. But she knows what it's like to receive a televised relay of screened information, to phone the Anxiety Research Unit and respond to a voice across the electric circuits: "On a scale of one to ten: How severe was your most recent attack?" "Yes or no: Any thoughts of suicide?" "Never, sometimes, frequently, a lot of the time: Fear that something is wrong with your mind?" The voice on the phone tells me that if I am accepted as a program participant, I will receive one of three possible medications: Xanax, Tofranil, or a placebo. The voice mentions that almost half of the patients who take the placebo respond favorably to it — "the best situation you could have going," he says cheerily. Participation in the program is free. I "pay" for the treatment by supplying information that will help them achieve their research goals. Each participant is required to come to Massachusetts General Hospital for regular visits over a four-month period. A psychiatrist controls the drug dosage and monitors patient progress. Over the phone, we make an appointment for my first visit, when I'll be given a full psychological and physical exam. I don't know what a neural network is, really, but I know I'm getting deeply entangled.)

Dr. M. leads me to an exam room down the hall and leaves me waiting. The research assistant, Tom, enters with a woman, her black hair going to gray, though she looks quite young. Tom says, "We're going to give you an electrocardiogram. You'll need to take off your shirt and brassiere. I can leave if you'd like me to." I say, "I'd prefer if you leave."

The woman performs the EKG.

Tom returns and takes my blood pressure, struggling quietly to get a proper reading. Then he draws a sample of my blood.

Back in Tom's office, he hands me a pale blue notebook titled "PA-TIENT DIARY," with a set of xeroxed instructions. He'll see me next week —and I should bring the diary with me, remembering to fill it out each night.

I leave the Psychosomatic Medicine Unit and take the elevator down to the hospital lobby, exiting through the revolving doors.

MAKING DISEASE

> The diagnostic criteria described for hysteria will delineate a
> syndrome that is very similar from patient to patient [and] is
> associated with a highly uniform chronic course. . . . These
> conclusions, derived from the results of several systematic studies,
> strongly suggest that the syndrome we have been describing and
> studying is a valid and recognizable disorder. — SAMUEL B. GUZE[26]

> I assert, to begin with, that "disease" does not exist. . . . What does
> exist is not disease but practices. — FRANÇOIS DELAPORTE[27]

Panic disorder officially appears on the psychiatric diagnostic scene in 1980 with the publication of the third edition of the *Diagnostic and Statistical Manual of Mental Disorders* (or *DSM-III*). Organized around the experience of "panic attacks" or the "sudden onset of intense apprehension, fear, or terror, often associated with feelings of impending doom," the definition of panic disorder — like all disorders in the new DSM — is operationalized by a set of specific diagnostic criteria. The carefully enumerated criteria for a panic attack include (1) difficulty breathing, (2) heart palpitations, (3) chest pain or discomfort, (4) choking or smothering sensations, (5) dizziness, (6) feelings of unreality, (7) tingling in feet or hands, (8) hot and cold flashes, (9) sweating, (10) faintness, (11) trembling or shaking, and (12) fear of dying, going crazy, or doing something uncontrolled. To be diagnosed with panic disorder, a person must experience a minimum of three panic attacks within a three-week period, and each attack must involve at least four of the twelve specified symptom criteria.[28]

The styleless style of scientific objectivity and empirical precision characterizing the 470-page text of the 1980 DSM-III gives little hint of the passionate controversy and resistance that met this new edition of the U.S. psychiatric classification system.[29] As the professional language for communicating about mental disorder across a broad range of settings — from therapeutic sites to clinical and research sites to hospitals, insurance companies, the FDA, pharmaceutical companies, and the courts — the DSM's power of naming translates directly into multiple currencies of social, institutional, and economic power. The historic role of the American Psychiatric Association in authoring each revised edition of the DSM signals psychiatry's place at the top of a professional hierarchy of mental health care workers. Conflicts within the APA over the design of the 1980 DSM suggest, in turn, transformations in the power structure of U.S. psychiatry itself.

Robert Spitzer, chair of the APA task force that oversees the construction of the DSM-III, calls the radical changes in its form and content a "signal achievement for psychiatry" and an important advance toward the "fulfillment of the scientific aspirations of the profession."[30] The introduction to the 1980 edition states that the DSM-III reflects "an increased commitment in our field to reliance on data" in diagnosing mental disorders. In contrast to previous classification systems, the DSM-III defines diagnostic entities through an empirically based and "atheoretical" method; unsubstantiated theories of causality are avoided. Most important, the operationalizing of each diagnostic category through explicit diagnostic criteria promises a new "common language" for researchers and clinicians to "communicate about the disorders for which they have professional responsibility."[31]

For others, the changes in the *DSM-III* mark a dramatic move toward a "remedicalization of American psychiatry," and a brazen attempt to shift psychiatry from a "clinically-based biopsychosocial model to a research-based medical model" of mental disease.[32] With the publication of the 1980 *DSM-III*, the postwar ascendancy of psychoanalytic and psychosocial approaches to mental health—approaches emphasizing the unconscious meaning of an individual's symptoms, and the relation between psychic disorders and environmental stressors—undergoes a stunning reversal: psychiatric researchers, previously a relatively marginalized group, replace clinicians as the most powerful force in the profession. Researchers' most basic assumptions and tools—a medical model of disease and diagnosis, and the empirical tests and techniques on which that model relies—become central to psychiatric thinking.[33] Notions of anxiety as an expression of unconscious conflict, a central tenet of psychoanalytic thought, become the unsubstantiated theories excised by the *DSM-III*. Views of mental disorder as reactions to life situations and social conditions are replaced by the empirical visibility of observable behavioral symptoms that become the *DSM-III*'s new focus.

The rising influence of research psychiatry in the APA is not only a "palace coup" or the culmination of the work of an "invisible college" of researchers insinuating their way toward power over several decades.[34] It is true that the core membership of the *DSM-III* task force appointed by Robert Spitzer is weighted heavily toward psychiatric researchers, including Donald Klein, director of research and development at the New York State Psychiatric Institute, whose early drug experiments are credited with establishing panic as a distinct mental disorder. And Spitzer himself, director of the Biometrics Department at the NYSPI, is deeply engaged with problems of research methodology and technique, suggesting in a controversial address to the APA in 1976 that mental disorder "should be defined as merely a subset of medical disorder."[35] But the palace gates are opened as well by forces outside the psychiatric profession, and the struggling camp of U.S. psychiatric researchers attempting to rationalize and standardize the disorderly field of psychic symptoms are allied with a number of developments that help to create the conditions of possibility for the new empirical language of the *DSM-III*.

By the 1970s both the federal government and the insurance industry are pressuring psychiatry to codify its classification system. A 1978 report by President Carter's Commission on Mental Health condemns the lack of progress in psychiatric research and the inadequate data on treatment outcomes or incidence rates for mental illness, calling for more professional accountability and scientific standards of assessment. The health insurance industry begins to limit reimbursements for psychiatric illness, with Blue Cross complaining in 1975 that "compared to other types of [medical] services there is less clarity and uniformity of terminology concerning mental diagnoses [and] treatment modalities."[36] Psychiatry in the 1970s is coming under growing pressure to develop a diagnostic classification system that can produce useful statistics — one of the original missions of psychiatric nosology — to state and federal governments and other administrative agencies.

But one of the most potent forces for change comes from the emergent promise of psychopharmacological drugs to provide effective treatments for mental distress. And here psychiatric research is destined to play a leading role. After the birth of thousands of deformed infants is linked to pregnant women's use of the sleeping pill thalidomide, the government legislates a new standard of drug "efficacy": the 1962 Kefauver-Harris Act requires drug companies to conduct randomized, controlled clinical drug trials to test the safety *and the efficacy* of all new pharmaceuticals. The addition of an efficacy standard to the FDA drug approval process places front and center the issue of "specificity" in drug-disease interactions. For clinical drug trials to provide evidence of efficacy, the drug needs to be directed at a specific problem — that is, a specific disease or disorder — for which the drug provides a specific solution.[37] Without well-defined categories of disease, the efficacy tests for new drugs risk producing inconclusive research based on blurry diagnostics.

With the press for more efficacious drug medications bolstering calls for more empirically oriented psychiatric research, with the demands of the FDA's efficacy requirements placing drug companies in the business of clinical drug trials, and with insurance industry and government criticisms of psychiatry's inability to accurately count mental disease or account for itself, research psychiatry in the 1970s is well positioned to make a bid for power. And the psychiatric classification system is one strategic battlefield on which that power bid plays out.

The difficulties facing psychiatric research are legion, and while unresolved, they are by the early 1970s at least sharply defined. The problem of diagnostic reliability stands at the center of the storm. The reliability of the psychiatric classification system — or the degree of consensus between diagnosticians over how to name a disease — is famously low. In a series of articles published at the time of Robert Spitzer's appointment as *DSM-III* task force chair in 1974, Spitzer and his colleagues in the Biometrics Department at the NYSPI argue repeatedly that improving the reliability of the diagnostic classification system is key to moving the system toward that other sought-after scientific virtue: validity, or the measure of fit between a diagnostic category and what it purports to represent, in short, the realness of a classification system.[38] For researchers, the specter of unreliability raises an even more fundamental issue: without reliable diagnostic categories, there is no reliable research.

At the heart of the research process is the ability to select homogeneous research populations — subjects who suffer (reliably) from the same problem. This abstract collective subject, the "research population," presents a persistent methodological crisis for psychiatric researchers.[39] Without some fundamentally reliable measure of patients' "sameness," researchers can't gather useful data about the course of a disease or the efficacy of a specific treatment. Without being able to reliably establish experimentally equivalent patient groups, researchers can't compare or exchange data across research settings. Without reliable diagnoses, researchers don't have a common language for identifying or communicating about the very object they study.

From the point of view of research psychiatry, the language of mental disorders needs to be reliably standardized; it needs to pass the tests (in order to perform the tests) of a methodical science. Other technoscientific developments in the 1970s give reason for optimism: electronic computers are facilitating statistical analysis and the management of large databases, and researchers are developing "psychometric" techniques for quantifying symptom behavior.[40] Structured interviews (which standardize the information a diagnostician receives from a patient through a uniform set of questions) and rating scales (uniform criteria by which diagnosticians measure the intensity of, or changes in, symptoms) are being tested and revised. Much of Spitzer's work in the Biometrics Department at the NYSPI in the 1960s and 1970s is focused on improving structured interviews for psychiatric diagnoses. These developments promise to help control the "information variance" arising from different diagnostic practices between clinicians and between different institutional settings.[41]

But the rallying cry for Spitzer and a small but insistent group of psychiatric researchers is the necessity for uniform diagnostic criteria to operationally define each disease category. "The use of operational criteria for psychiatric diagnosis is an idea whose time has come!" Spitzer announces in 1978.[42] In "Research Diagnostic Criteria: Rationale and Reliability," Spitzer and his coauthors describe the successful development of a set of research diagnostic criteria (the "RDC") forged in a collaborative study sponsored by the NIMH. The purpose of the RDC is to "enable investigators to select relatively homogeneous groups of subjects who meet specified diagnostic criteria." The key data for making diagnostic judgments come from an examination of the research subject using a "focused clinical interview or a structured interview guide and rating scales designed specifically for eliciting information relevant to these categories."[43] Without the guidance of "explicit criteria" like the RDC, Spitzer argues, the diagnostician is forced to rely on "his own concept of the disorder," introducing uncontrollable subjective variables into the diagnosis.[44] Specific, standardized criteria protect against this subject-bound variance. As part of the NIMH-sponsored study, successive revisions of the RDC are constructed, based on data from a series of reliability studies conducted at several research sites, including Massachusetts General Hospital, the New York State Psychiatric Institute, and Washington University Medical School at St. Louis.

Although Spitzer and other key *DSM-III* task force members are closely involved with developing and promoting the RDC, the diagnostic criteria they produce are initially intended only for research purposes.[45] In 1975, Spitzer and his colleagues report that diagnostic criteria will be included in the *DSM-III* only as "*suggested* specific criteria," intended not to replace but *"merely to supplement* the narrative definitions" of mental disorders.[46]

But in fact the RDC end up serving as the template for a radical restructuring of the DSM classification system.[47] The 1980 DSM-III introduces specified diagnostic criteria as the centerpiece of its objective, empirical, descriptive, and atheoretical approach to diagnosis. The "comprehensive and systematic description" of each disorder by means of specific criteria, according to one task force member, provides "uniform rules of definition" that should "help stem the tide of insubstantial, unreliable or at best minimally generalizable data that has come to characterize publications in the field."[48] Psychiatric research and clinical diagnosis are together launched toward a future of more empirically verifiable and data-driven decision making.

The 1978 research diagnostic criteria identified by Spitzer and his colleagues mark the first appearance in psychiatric literature of the term "panic disorder"—as one of twenty-five distinct, criteria-specific disorders.[49] In 1980, when panic disorder is incorporated into the DSM-III's psychiatric language, most of the RDC for the new disorder are included in the DSM-III description. But the RDC's cluster of specific criteria defining panic disorder actually first appears—under a different diagnostic name—several years earlier, in a 1972 article titled "Diagnostic Criteria for Use in Psychiatric Research." Published by a group of research psychiatrists based at Washington University in St. Louis (later known as the "St. Louis group"), the article becomes one of the most frequently cited publications in the psychiatric literature of the 1970s.[50] Appearing in the influential *Archives of General Psychiatry*, the article by Feighner and his coauthors argues for the usefulness of diagnostic criteria in defining mental disease and presents criteria-based definitions for fourteen different mental illnesses, including homosexuality and alcoholism. In psychiatry, the criteria become famously known as the "Feighner criteria."

One of the fourteen syndromes identified by Feighner and his coauthors is "anxiety neurosis," first named and described by Sigmund Freud in 1895.[51] Freud's defining symptoms—chronic nervousness and recurrent anxiety attacks involving difficulty breathing, heart palpitations, chest pain or discomfort, and choking or smothering sensations—

are incorporated into the 1978 RDC (and then the 1980 DSM-III) under the new label "panic disorder."[52] Despite the Feighner group's emphasis on empirical validation, only one study is cited validating the diagnostic label of "anxiety neurosis": a 1950 study of neurocirculatory asthenia conducted by Mandel Cohen at Massachusetts General Hospital under contract with the U.S. Army.[53]

Another empirically precise diagnostic entity defined by the Feighner group is "hysteria." The specific criteria for hysteria include a list of fifty-nine symptoms, clustered in ten different groups—by far the most elaborate criteria of the fourteen disorders identified in the article. For validation studies of the hysteria diagnosis, Feighner et al. cite three studies, all published by coauthors of the Feighner article.[54]

In fact, hysteria has, in the twenty years preceding the Feighner criteria, been the diagnosis deployed by a small network of research psychiatrists to hone its arguments for the necessity of specified diagnostic criteria and the possibility of producing reliable and valid psychiatric diagnoses.[55] In his 1967 essay "The Diagnosis of Hysteria: What Are We Trying to Do?" Samuel Guze explains that research on hysteria has tried to establish standardized methods for defining a mental disorder and for constructing a scientifically valid diagnostic system.[56] At the heart of these efforts to define hysteria is the development of specified diagnostic criteria.

The choice of hysteria as a test for the psychiatric powers of standardized diagnostic techniques is not mere whimsy. With its 2,500-year history as a recognized disease and an equally long record of contentious debate over what precisely "it" is, hysteria emerges as an exemplary object for establishing the existence of a uniform psychiatric disease whose validity can empirically be confirmed. Surrounded for centuries by a fascinating ambiguity, and known as the "great imitator" for its ability to mimic or impersonate "real" physiological disorders, hysteria offers the perfect challenge to a psychiatry trying to ground itself in the precise measurements and verifiable methods of "real" science. And since a scientific approach to psychiatry in the years 1950–70, when most of the U.S. research on hysteria is conducted, is mostly a marginalized effort, sidelined by more dominant psychoanalytic paradigms, the hysteric takes on a particular appeal. As a central figure in the founding of Freud's psycho-analytic methods, she offers up — to those who now dream of a different kind of psychiatry — a seductive symbolic terrain on which to wage the battle for a uniform, objective language of mental disease.

The battle is launched in 1951 with the publication of "Observations on Clinical Aspects of Hysteria."[57] Based on a study of fifty women diag-nosed with hysteria in a hospital setting, and three sets of control subjects (including fifty women workers at the Ford Underwear Company and at General Electric, assigned to the study by their foreman), the authors conclude that hysteria "presented a characteristic clinical picture" and could be adequately identified "following the standard procedure used in the general field of diagnostic medicine."[58] More pointedly, they assert that "this method [of diagnosis] can be applied by any physician without the use of special techniques, dream analysis or prolonged investigation of psychological conflicts." While acknowledging the current lack of fac-tual data about hysteria's cause, the authors emphasize that questions of causality can be addressed only by "scientific investigation, rather than by the use of nonscientific methods, such as pure discussion, speculation . . . or the use of such pretentious undefined words as 'unconscious' . . . and 'Oedipus complex.'"[59]

The diagnostic technique used in the 1951 study of hysteria relies on patient interview data recorded on a 106-item standardized questionnaire form. The structured interview tries to systematize the way patients re-port their symptoms, particularly, the authors note, in light of hysterics' propensity to speak in "imprecise, vague, exaggerated, colorful and dra-matic" terms.[60] The standardized questionnaire and the statistical meth-ods for evaluating the interview data are borrowed from a research project on neurocirculatory asthenia conducted by Dr. Mandel Cohen and others at Massachusetts General Hospital; Cohen is also a coauthor of the 1951 hysteria study. Both the hysteria study and the research on neurocircu-latory asthenia use statistical tests of significance and quantified data to present their findings to an audience of mostly medical doctors (both studies are published in the prominent *Journal of the American Medical Association*).[61]

The picture of hysteria emerging from the 1951 study identifies ten primary symptoms, purportedly experienced by over 75 percent of the diagnosed hysterics, including anxiety attacks, heart palpitations, headaches, anorexia, sexual indifference, and crying easily.[62]

In the early 1960s, Samuel Guze and Michael Perley, both psychiatrists in the St. Louis group, cite the 1951 hysteria study as one of three "quantitative" studies on hysteria.[63] Guze and Perley also report findings from their own study suggesting that "when the diagnosis of hysteria is based upon the [specified] criteria," clinical evidence points to the existence of a "valid and distinct clinical syndrome."[64] In 1969, Guze and two colleagues at St. Louis pronounce hysteria an established "quantitative concept."[65] In 1972, the Perley-Guze criteria become the basis for the diagnosis of hysteria described in the famous essay by Feighner et al. that tries to establish the usefulness to psychiatry of specified diagnostic criteria.

But curiously, by 1980, hysteria disappears from the diagnostic scene. This valid and distinct quantitative concept, repeatedly verified empirically across twenty years of psychiatric research, is missing from the 1980 *DSM-III*. In "Hysteria Split Asunder" (1978), Robert Spitzer explains that hysterical symptoms, notorious for their ability to mimic physical disease, will be disassembled and redistributed into several different *DSM-III* diagnostic categories, each defined by its simulation of "real" physical conditions.[66] "The differentiation between 'real' and 'hysterical' symptoms has been among the most difficult diagnostic tasks for physicians," Spitzer recounts.[67] Deciding what, if anything, constitutes the "real" of hysteria has been somewhat challenging as well.

Does Spitzer remember that this is not the first time that hysteria exits from the symptomatic stage? On December 31, 1899, a young woman patient of Sigmund Freud's terminates the psychoanalysis in which they have been engaged for three months. In the first weeks of the new century, Freud writes his famous case study of the hysterical patient he names "Dora." Out of his therapeutic failure, Freud mines sufficient material for a theoretical success, fashioning from the woman's dreams, and from the meaning of her dramatic departure from the analysis, a compelling story of the hysterical figure. Faced with the evident failure of his new technique of dream analysis, Freud emphasizes the hysteric's stubborn insistence on performing, not simply recalling, her past trauma. "Thus she *acted* an essential part of her recollections and phantasies instead of reproducing it in the treatment," the jilted doctor writes. Since one of Dora's past traumas provoked a fantasy of revenge, she vengefully quits the psychoanalyst's office. "For how could the patient take a more effective revenge than by demonstrating upon her own person the helplessness and incapacity of the physician?"[68]

But the helpless physician quickly recovers, constructing in his "Fragment of an Analysis of a Case of Hysteria" (1905) an elaborate architecture that joins repressed infantile experiences, fear of syphilis, love for the father, disgust at female genitals, and a daydreamed desire for a kiss from Freud, to build a compulsively intricate case study. (Some years later, in a footnote, Freud belatedly decides that the real defect of technique in Dora's case was his failure to guess that her homosexual love for a woman "was the strongest unconscious current in her mental life.")[69]

The *DSM-III* appears to not much notice the departure of hysteria from its diagnostic lexicon. Although the *DSM*'s scientific stance and adoption of specific criteria are historically rehearsed on the hysteric's stage, built on the suggestive empirical evidence of hysteria's "real" existence, its authors have larger ambitions than keeping track of the hysteric's precise whereabouts. And for those who miss her, there are substitutes. Panic disorder, entering through the diagnostic door just as hysteria leaves, is described in 1989 by the National Institute of Mental Health as a psychiatric condition that has "befuddle[d] physicians' diagnostic accuracy to this day."[70] Differentiating between the psychic signs of panic and the physiological symptoms of "cardiologic, neurologic, and other medical syndromes" is no easy task. Written to help doctors recognize panic disorder in a medical setting, the NIMH publication also reports, on a more cheerful note, that recent research has led to a "biological revolution in the field of panic disorder," making possible far more effective and reliable treatments.[71]

PANIC DIARY

The xeroxed instructions read: "1. Please complete this Diary each evening before going to bed." I hold the pale blue PATIENT DIARY from the Upjohn Company in my hands, flipping through the pages. PANIC DIARY in bold letters at the top of each page. MEDICATION DIARY printed in bold about halfway down. The instructions define a "panic attack" as "a discrete period (with a definite beginning and end) of sudden and intense discomfort, fear or worry, with *at least 3 of the 14* characteristic symptoms." (A reference list of the fourteen possible symptoms is printed at the bottom of each page.) The "duration" of an attack is defined as "the average length of time *in minutes* that an attack lasts." The "average intensity" of an attack is "a rating from 1 to 10 of how bad the attacks were, with 1 being the least and 10 the most anxious or uncomfortable you can imagine." The PANIC DIARY asks me to record the number, the average duration, and the average intensity of my panic attacks for that day. The MEDICATION DIARY asks me to write down the total number of blue capsules I've swallowed.

A patient diarist, I remember, this evening, this morning's scene: my first visit to the Anxiety Research Unit at Massachusetts General Hospital. I am in the exam room alone and waiting. I have just been diagnosed with panic disorder. I am now a subject, a reliable object, of research. The research assistant Tom enters the room and introduces the woman with him — Diana. Her hair is black, turning early to silver-gray. She wears a blouse, skirt, and sandals, bare legged. Tom says, "We're going to do an EKG. You'll need to take off your blouse and brassiere. If you prefer, I can leave." I say, "I'd prefer if you'd leave." He leaves.

> You don't give a damn if he never comes around. You never want to see him again. Fuck his round face and his blonde hair and his five feet ten inches lean body. . . . Fuck his screwed-up mouth and his skinny legs . . . fuck that lousy cynicism that covers his naiveté that's totally fake fuck his sexual uptightness fuck his scaredness fuck his egotism fuck everything he's ever done fuck everything he's ever said everything he's ever said is false stick it in a barrel and send it to me.[72]

Alone with Diana, I take off my shirt, my bra, my shoes, and my nylon stockings. I leave on my black skirt. I put on a blue paper smock, open down the front. Diana rolls clean white paper the length of the brown leather exam table. I lie down on the paper, bare legged. Diana holds a tube of gel and applies a small, cold gob to my right ankle. She applies a cold gob to my left ankle. She turns my right arm and applies a cold gob to my right wrist. I raise my left arm toward her so she won't have to reach. She applies a cold gob of gel to my left wrist. She pulls back the blue paper and applies four cold gobs of gel in a half circle below my left breast. She applies one cold gob below my right breast. She says, "This is an old machine, so we have to connect you at the ankles and wrists, too. I'm going to attach these straps to your legs and arms. I have to pull them pretty tight. Just tell me if it hurts."

7:30 A.M. This hurts. I awake barely slept and search for a place in the waking noise and sleepy rush to connect with feeling for you—crash. Feeling broken (but let's not break up we say) I am returned to my self barely and alone. This hurts. I lie quite alone.

Diana wraps the white rubber strap around my right ankle. She pulls it tight. She wraps the second strap around my left ankle and pulls tight. Does it hurt yet? Her face is pale and slightly freckled, her black hair thick, turning early to silver-gray. She wraps the third strap around my right wrist. I raise my left arm toward her across my chest so she won't have to reach. She wraps the fourth strap around my left wrist. She pulls tight. She says, "I'm going to do the first reading just from your ankles and wrists for thirty seconds." She attaches a thin wire to each of the four straps on my ankles and wrists.

I ask, "Will this be sending electricity through my body?" Diana says, "No, this will just measure the electricity going through you already."

4:00 A.M. We are at a restaurant. It is like a diner and late night. We are walking down the aisle when a large gray man comes from behind and takes my left wrist. He is threatening me. With my right hand, I angrily scratch my nails across the top of his hand that holds mine. I am not yet afraid. You become afraid. You say to me—you cannot believe I really scratched him—you say that your mother taught you never to do that. Now I am scared. The man follows us down the aisle. He grabs me. He sticks a blunt knife through my hand. Enormous pain. We are standing in front of a booth with red seats. You are sitting down. You do not help me at all. The man sticks a second knife through my thigh. I am so scared and in pain. No one is coming to help me and I feel this man gripping my body in total control I cannot run.

I hear Diana turn a knob. I stare at the wall to my left. It is white mostly. Her face was slightly freckled, her thick black hair soft, going early to silver-gray. Her hands were cold and gentle.

Until recently, the root of panic disorder was assumed to be strictly psychological. . . . Traditional psychoanalytic theory held that the attacks were the result of accumulated anxiety over unconscious conflicts. . . . Today, researchers are looking to the body, not just the mind, for clues to the mysteries of panic attacks and panic disorder. It seems to run in families, and this may provide support for those who believe the condition is triggered by physical, perhaps inheritable, problems.[73]

I hear a click. Diana says, "Now I'm just going to attach this cup here," and she presses a small rubber cup attached to a wire below my left breast. She clicks a knob on, then off. She moves the cup three times in a half circle below my left breast. Click on, click off. Click on, click off. Click on. Does it hurt yet? Her hands are cold and gentle. Diana moves the rubber cup below my right breast. "Okay, now we're going to do a reading for a full sixty seconds," she says. I turn my head to the left and stare at the wall mostly white.

Her hands [1] were going around and around [2] a frying pan, scraping flecks [3] of black into cold, greasy dishwater. [4] The timid, tucked-in look of the scratching [5] toe—that was what Pauline was doing the first time [6] he saw her in Kentucky. [7] The tenderness welled up [8] in him, and he sank to his knees, [9] his eyes on the foot of his [10] daughter. Crawling on all fours [11] toward her, he raised [12] his hand and caught the foot [13] in an upward stroke. [14] Pecola lost her balance and [15] was about to careen to the floor. [16] Cholly raised his other hand to her [17] hips to save her from falling. He put [18] his head down and nibbled at the back [19] of her leg. His mouth trembled at the firm [20] sweetness of the flesh. [21] He closed his eyes, letting his fingers [22] dig into her waist. [23] The rigidness of her shocked [24] body, the silence of her [25] stunned throat, was better than Pauline's easy laughter [26] had been. The confused [27] mixture of his memories [28] of Pauline and the doing of a wild [29] and forbidden thing excited [30] him, and a bolt of desire ran down [31] his genitals, giving it [32] length, and softening the lips [33] of his anus. [34] Surrounding all this lust [35] was a border of politeness. [36] He wanted to fuck [37] her—tenderly. [38] But the tenderness would [39] not hold. The tightness [40] of her vagina was more than he could [41] bear. His soul seemed to slip down [42] to his guts and fly out [43] into her, and the gigantic thrust [44] he made into her [45] then provoked the only [46] sound she [47] made—[48] a hollow [49] suck of [50] air in [51] the back [52] of her [53] throat. Like the rapid loss of air from a circus balloon. He was conscious of her wet, soapy hands [54] on his wrists, the fingers clenching, but whether her grip was from a hopeless but stubborn struggle to be free, or from some other emotion, [55] he could not tell. Removing himself from her was so painful to him he cut it short and snatched his genitals out of her vagina. She appeared [56] to have fainted. Cholly stood up and could see only her greyish panties, so sad and limp around [57] her ankles. Again the hatred mixed with tenderness. [58] The hatred would not let him pick her up. [59] The tenderness forced him to cover her. [60][74]

Diana turns off the machine. She removes the cup from below my right breast. She removes the first rubber strap from my right ankle. She removes the second rubber strap from my left ankle. She removes the third rubber strap from my right wrist. I raise my left arm toward her across my chest so she won't have to reach. She removes the fourth rubber strap from my left wrist. I ask, "Do you do this all day?" She replies, "No. Just when there's a woman patient who asks for me."

So when the child regained consciousness, she was lying on the floor under a heavy quilt, trying to connect the pain between her legs with the face of her mother looming over her.[75] Something down deep breaks and I am wet all over. Dear Daddy I dream you naked in a loft Lower East Side New York and raining on the Lower East Side wet and you naked daddy save me from the story dear papa I leave you in the rain and hop in a car. Three blue women, big, friendly, we ride across wet bridges away from the Lower East Side. Quite a passage. Wet. Weeping. Down deep and wild. Regain consciousness on kitchen floor—quilted mama face looming pain—between legs and floored mama—face looming pain consciousness—face between legs mama—loom connection—face pain.

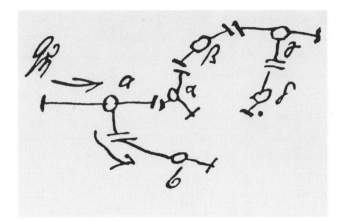

Repressing a painful memory—neuronal activity. Sigmund Freud, *Project for a Scientific Psychology*, 1895.

Holding a small square of clean white gauze, Diana wipes the gel from my right ankle. She uses two gauze squares to wipe off my left ankle. She uses one gauze square to wipe off my right ankle. She uses one gauze square to wipe off my right wrist. I raise my left arm toward her across my chest so she won't have to reach. She wipes my left wrist with one gauze square. She says, "Here's some more if you want to clean yourself off better," and places several clean white gauze squares on the exam table next to my right shoulder.

> With all its complications, panic disorder in the United States is estimated to cost billions of dollars annually in health care expenses, disability benefits and lost wages. As the disorder is more widely recognized, studied and treated, more precise cost figures will become available.[76]

I sit up. Diana walks to the small sink and begins washing the four white rubber straps. I take one gauze square and wipe below my left breast. It takes three gauze squares to clean off all the gel. I ask, "Can I get dressed now?" Diana answers, "Sure, it's all over."

I stand up. I put on my bra and shirt, then my stockings and shoes. Diana is washing her hands in the sink. She dries her hands with a paper towel, then throws it in the blue metal trash can. Then she walks to the brown leather exam table and pulls off the white paper, crumples it, and throws it in the blue metal trash can.

I put on my bra, then my shirt, then my stockings and shoes. Does it hurt yet you—touch me, touch my left breast do—you know how I long a woman—at my left breast you cup—me, mostly white I am—hurting, bare-legged, and electric black gone—early to silver-gray. I put on my bra, then my shirt, then my stockings and shoes. It's all over. You are the first woman Diana ever to make love with me last. Never leave me please don't ever leave me I love you hold me love me hold me don't ever leave me when I want to put my head on someone's shoulder I will love you forever. Does it hurt yet? Do the straps pull too tight?

"The American Psychiatric Association diagnostic manual indicates that one predisposition to panic disorder may be childhood separation anxiety (excessive anxiety concerning separation from people, places or things to whom a child is attached)."[77]

Diana leaves the exam room.

"In contrast, biological theories propose that a physical defect in the regulation of the autonomic nervous system exists."[78]

Diana leaves the exam room. She closes the door behind her. On the back of the door hangs a live body. From a hook on the back of the door, from a coat hanger rising from her back, hangs a live woman body. She is laughing. She has no body below her breasts. From the back of the door hangs a live woman half body laughing with both hands she is rubbing wild and furious in round brown-nipple circles her breasts. She is trying to come. Her mouth is open and laughter coming out shaking her breasts she rubs in wild circles her brown nipples. She is laughing. She is not mad. She has no body below her breasts.

> There is little doubt that in the near future this model will help us better to unravel the mysteries of the anxiety disease and will lead us to a better understanding of its causes. It will help us to find more accurate laboratory tests to aid us in diagnosing it. Above all, it will guide us to newer, safer, more rapid and effective treatments. We have already come a long way in controlling it. The rest is only a matter of time.[79]

I am laughing. I am not mad. I was waking. I remember. It is wild. It was morning. It's all over. I leave the exam room, laughing mad, and learning how to pass the time.

> The moods of the waters of the river were always delightful to watch.
> For me, as a mathematician and a physicist, they had another
> meaning as well. How could one bring to a mathematical regularity
> the study of the mass of ever shifting ripples and waves, for was not
> the highest destiny of mathematics the discovery of order among
> disorder? — NORBERT WIENER[80]

> The validation (or invalidation) of black holes, quarks, cold fusion,
> and mental disorder diagnoses have not, and will not, be answered by
> an unambiguous empirical finding. Empirical results . . . do not speak
> for themselves. — ALLEN FRANCES[81]

If the 1980 DSM-III stands as a threshold moment in which a new science of psychiatry — grounded in empirical methods, moving toward a medical model of disease, driven by data and not by unconscious conflicts — is born, then it's a strange and elusive empiricity that emerges in its wake. The new empirical form for psychiatric diagnosis exhibits curious symptoms of epistemological dizziness and ontological trembling.[82] Describing the DSM-III task force's work, Robert Spitzer recalls: "I think we knew that we often . . . were making up these criteria because they seemed really appropriate and useful. But there are very few instances where the actual choice was empirical. And most people don't appreciate that, but that is the fact."[83] The DSM-III's "atheoretical" approach to classification results in a delineation of 265 discrete mental disorders that are, as DSM-III task force member Theodor Millon explains, "in the main, only theoretical constructs." What the criteria-specific approach to classifying mental disorders really accomplishes, writes Millon, is "a significant *conceptual* step toward a future goal" when criteria of "appropriate specificity and breadth" will offer reliable and valid indices for identifying psychiatric syndromes. As a step toward a future empiricity, the DSM-III does not name "tangible entities" but rather "conceptual prototypes" — a paradigm shift away from the notion of a disease "entity" and toward a " 'prototypical' diagnostic model."[84]

In "Psychiatric Diagnosis as Prototype Categorization" (1980), Nancy Cantor and her coauthors explain that in moving away from older models of classification, the DSM-III employs a method of classification that helps "to emphasize, rather than obscure, the probabilistic nature of diagnostic categorization." This "prototype" model of classification enables the categorization of objects with shifting boundaries, inconsistent properties among different members of the same category, and statistically measurable but variable features from member to member: "Biologists, radiologists, and others engaged in taxonomic and diagnostic endeavors are increasingly embracing the more flexible (prototype) view that categorization can be probabilistic yet orderly." Using this prototype model, diagnoses can be made based on the "degree of fit between the patient's cluster of symptoms" and the "prototypes for various different categories."[85] Each disorder becomes, in a sense, a probabilistic model of that disorder. All the "empirical," criteria-specific syndromes named by the DSM-III are really operating, in Spitzer's words, as "hypotheses to be tested."[86]

In an important sense, then, the DSM-III departs from the dream of a reliable and valid psychiatric classification system and substitutes instead the desire for a reliable and probably valid classification system. The problem of validity—or the objective measure of a concept's "fit" with what it sets out to name—is historically coupled with the pursuit of reliability: as Spitzer and his colleagues assert in the early 1970s, constraints on the validity of the psychiatric classification system are set by its reliability (the strength of agreement or consistency among classified objects). Without reliable diagnoses, a valid system can't even be tested. The entire project of identifying specific DSM diagnostic criteria to increase diagnostic reliability is framed as a necessary step in the pursuit of validity.[87]

But as U.S. psychiatry bootstraps its way toward empiricity and operationalized definitions in the decade before DSM-III, discussions of validity take a decidedly pragmatic turn among many of those most closely involved with designing the new DSM. How to operationalize an appropriate measure of diagnostic validity in psychiatry has never been an easy, or settled, question.[88] With a lack of knowledge of (or consensus about) disease causation combined with an absence of techniques for empirically "locating" mental disorders, psychiatry has mostly only dreamed of what validity might mean. In the late 1960s, for Samuel Guze and others tracking a definitive diagnosis of hysteria, the model for validity is given by medicine, where a uniform etiology of disease and the uniform clinical and physiological course of the disease offer verifiable measures of a valid diagnosis. Arguing that it is "both necessary and possible" for psychiatry to establish its own rigorous classification system, Guze insists that valid diagnostic categories will form the basis for efficient communication, useful comparison, effective treatment, and the conduct of future research.[89] In 1972, Feighner et al. identify a five-step validation process (including laboratory studies and family studies) for mental disorders. While noting that, to date, "no psychiatric syndrome has yet been fully validated by a complete series of steps," the authors optimistically assert that "substantial" validation will become possible.[90]

In contrast, Spitzer and his colleagues in the 1970s propose that the validity of the classification system should be measured by its usefulness, or "the utility of [the] system for its various purposes."[91] Since two central purposes of diagnostic classification are the prediction of the course of disease, and the prediction of treatment response, validity is conflated with these future outcomes.[92] Or, in David Sheehan's words, the classification system becomes a kind of "latter day fortune telling system."[93] The notion of validity starts to float free of any measure of an actual correlation between the name and the thing (correlations made, for example, in medicine via the evidence of lesions, bacteria, fractured bones, blocked arteries); instead, validity is increasingly linked to predictive power, the ability to name not the thing but its future path. From an objective measure of realness to a pragmatic measure of predictive utility, the validity of psychiatric diagnoses becomes abstracted from any reality principle at precisely the moment the diagnostic classification system turns insistently empirical.[94]

In 1994, Allen Frances, task force chair of the fourth edition of the DSM, writes, "Most, if not all, mental disorders are better conceived as no more than (but also no less than) valuable heuristic constructs. . . . [T]hey are constructs with considerable *practical and heuristic value in predicting* course, family history, treatment response, and biological test results."[95] In the same year, the fourth edition of the DSM is published with the introductory claim that "more than any other nomenclature of mental disorders, DSM-IV is grounded in empirical evidence."[96] Empirical evidence for the valuable "constructs" named by the DSM-IV includes twelve field trials at over seventy different sites involving more than six thousand research subjects. The aim of the field trials is to "provide data on the performance characteristics (reliability, sensitivity, specificity, predictive power, internal consistency) of the criteria sets being considered."[97] This unprecedented massing of empirical evidence for DSM-IV criteria-specific diagnostic categories is funded by government (primarily NIMH) and philanthropic (the MacArthur Foundation) sources and is published in 1994 in a five-volume set accompanying the DSM-IV.

What precisely the empirically grounded constructs in the DSM-IV do name, if not valid disease entities, thus becomes a curious question. Both the 1980 and the 1994 editions of the DSM state explicitly that "there is no assumption that each mental disorder is a discrete entity with sharp boundaries (discontinuity) between it and other mental disorders, as well as between it and No Mental Disorder." Rather, mental disorder is conceptualized in both editions of the DSM as a "behavioral or psychological *syndrome or pattern* that occurs in an individual."[98] Historian Donald Lowe, in one of the few critiques of the DSM-III from outside the mental health professions, notes how the emphasis on symptom patterns, delinked from individual and social contexts, constructs a "closed system of labeling" that is simultaneously more systematic and less coherent than previous versions of the DSM. "The result is a one-level, free-floating ordering of syndromes or patterns, which is useful for . . . naming and classifying [illnesses] in terms of observable symptoms." This systematized incoherence of the diagnostic language, for Lowe, marks a "breakdown" in psychiatric discourse.[99]

But something more productive than a breakdown seems to be occurring as the DSM is transformed into a textual guide to pattern recognition, with each set of diagnostic criteria serving as a patterned prototype. Behind the DSM-III's move to empirically specify each mental disorder with a systematic, rule-bound set of symptom criteria lies another project, another desire perhaps more powerful even than the pursuit of scientific procedure, another dream at least as compelling and contagious as the reign of rational method.

In the years just before his appointment as chair of the DSM-III task force, Robert Spitzer experiments with the computer simulation of psychiatric diagnosis, looking for a way to replicate in the realm of code what clinicians and researchers perform in their daily practice.[100] The result is a series of computerized diagnostic programs — DIAGNO I, II, and III — developed in the late 1960s and early 1970s for use with an IBM computer system. Against the protests of those who believe that the subtleties of clinical judgment can never be translated into computerized, codable information, Spitzer and his colleague Jean Endicott state that, on the contrary, "any concept that can be operationally defined . . . can be coded for computer analysis."[101] Spitzer et al.'s experiments with computerized diagnosis attempt to formulate diagnostic categories in such a way that they can be translated into computerized data, transforming mental disorders into patterns of information that can be manipulated by computer algorithms. The specific diagnostic criteria for DSM-III mental disorders are in part a historical outcome of this pursuit of computer-simulated psychiatry.[102]

In 1975, DIAGNO III is "currently operational," installed for use at Rockland State Mental Hospital, home of Nathan Kline, cyborg psychiatrist and founder of U.S. psychopharmacology.[103] Spitzer and Endicott are particularly optimistic about the potential for linking psychopharmacology and automated computer systems, suggesting that "computer-assisted drug prescription" may become more effective than a clinician's prescription choice. They cite a computerized system, developed by Donald Klein and his colleagues at Hillside Hospital, that combines automated diagnosis and drug treatment: the computer classifies patients into specific diagnostic categories and then predicts their response to different drug treatments.[104]

In a 1974 article summarizing the computer project to date, Spitzer et al. argue that the ultimate obstacle to "simulat[ing] the diagnostic practices of expert diagnosticians" lies not with the technological constraints of the computer but "in the traditional diagnostic system itself."[105] In particular, the low reliability of the psychiatric classification system is hampering the development of valid diagnostic procedures for computers as well as clinicians.[106] And so the effort to computerize diagnosis turns into the drive to increase the reliability of psychiatric diagnosis. "Our current effort," Spitzer reports, "is in the direction of a change in the diagnostic system itself with emphasis on simplification, *explicit criteria*, and limiting the categories to those conditions for which validity evidence exists."[107] Spitzer and his colleagues, in collaboration with the NIMH, begin working on the Research Diagnostic Criteria (RDC) as the next, necessary step in improving diagnostic reliability. Jean Endicott — who works with Spitzer on the RDC and also as a core member of the DSM-III task force — recollects how, in shifting from automated computer diagnosis to developing the RDC, "We used to laugh and kind of say, okay, we'll stop trying to teach the computer to act like a clinician. *And we're trying to teach the clinician to apply logical rules, kind of more like a computer.*"[108] The explicit criteria developed for the RDC, which in turn become a model for the DSM-III, emerge out of this move away from computerizing diagnosis toward improving the reliability of psychiatric classification.

And back again to computerized diagnosis. In 1981, one year after the publication of the DSM-III, members of the St. Louis group develop the Diagnostic Interview Schedule (DIS). A structured interview that can be administered by nonclinicians, the DIS produces data that are then analyzed by a computer program capable of applying any of three different sets of specified diagnostic criteria (from the DSM-III, the RDC, or the Feighner criteria) to make an automated psychiatric diagnosis.[109] Led by Lee Robins, a medical sociologist with a background in survey research design, the St. Louis team develops the DIS under contract with the Division of Biometry and Epidemiology at the NIMH. The NIMH then uses the computer-automated DIS to carry out the Epidemiologic Catchment Area (ECA) study, the first large-scale U.S. survey of prevalence rates for specific mental disorders in the general population.[110] Celebrated as a landmark in U.S. psychiatric history, these state-sponsored epidemiological studies demonstrate that psychiatry at last can deliver on its deferred promise of statistical data to help inform the rational design of public mental health policy.

The DIS makes psychiatric diagnoses, Spitzer explains, "on the basis of algorithms that translate the DSM-III diagnostic criteria into inflexible rules which are then applied to the coded data after the interview has been completed."[111] In 1983 Spitzer concludes his presidential address to the American Psychopathological Association with the following provocation: "The DIS has put the proverbial ball in the clinician's court and the score is 40-love in favor of the DIS. The burden of proof is now on the clinician to show that advances in technology have not made the clinician superfluous in the task of diagnostic assessment."[112]

By 1994 and the publication of the *DSM-IV*, clinicians are not yet superfluous in diagnosing mental disorders. But the question of what exactly clinicians are diagnosing has become exceedingly troubled. Is it possible, as some critics suggest, that the transformations in diagnostic language introduced in the 1980 *DSM-III* provide a "common language" to talk reliably about mental disorders that don't precisely exist? Allen Frances, chair of the 1994 *DSM-IV* task force, suggests that *DSM* mental disorders are best understood as "prototypes" that facilitate "the probabilistic estimation of the resemblance of an individual member to the prototype."[113] Far from offering a specific word for a concrete thing, a "prototypical approach recognizes the fuzzy boundaries and heterogeneity within the *DSM-IV* criteria sets." Here the practice of diagnosis is not about naming discrete, definitive disorders embodied in individual patients. Francis et al. write in 1990: "A prototypic view of diagnosis *depends more on pattern recognition* and family resemblance than on . . . decision-tree logic."[114] Patterns of observable symptoms, practices of computable diagnosis—symptoms of a future psychiatry in which clinicians and computers together diagnose psychiatric disorders that are more reliable than real, more probabilistic than actually present? Indeed, Frances and others begin to advocate a "dimensional" model of psychiatric classification that presumes a continuous, shifting spectrum of symptoms with no clear boundaries or discrete, definitive nominal categories. A dimensional approach, considered a future possibility for the fifth edition of the *DSM*, could also permit a more rigorous mathematical modeling of symptom patterns, "based on quantification of attributes rather than assignment to categories."[115]

Is this one possible future a young Norbert Wiener sees, looking out from his office above the Charles River in Boston sometime in the 1920s, just downstream from Massachusetts General Hospital, already on his way toward a science of cybernetics and a daily dose of the drug Benzedrine but at the moment just studying *the problem of the waves*?[116] Seeing in their continuous, irregular motion the possibility of mathematical tools that rely more on *averaging and statistics*, on a *new physics of probability* in which the knower knows that only *imperfect knowledge* is attainable, in which the knower knows that the task is to *work not with a single, fixed universe but with many different universes simultaneously, each having some preassigned probability.* Looking back at the river waves thirty years later, Wiener in his memoir still sees in front of him the promise of a more general recognition of *the statistical nature of all science* and the *statistical and imperfectly precise nature of the quantities with which we operate.* Seeing that cybernetics has helped to establish this *general statistical point of view* in communication engineering, he sees the possibility of such a view extending productively in the future toward the *semi-precise sciences* like *sociology, economy, biometrics,* and the *very complicated study of the nervous system,* which could themselves begin to see how an imperfect, statistical knowledge *belongs to the very grammar of the use of mathematical methods* that lies at *the heart of the engineering of the future.*

PANIC DIARY

I am in a large hotel with a labyrinth of rooms. I am baby-sitting several children who tell me I must give them jelly beans. I say that I can't or won't. They go to their mother — she's young, high heels, hard red nails — who takes me into a small closet room where we lie down. She kisses my neck. A man in a suit and tie enters the room. He has a clipboard. He kneels down beside us and begins to take notes. He is the principal at my school. The woman begins to say to me over and over, "We have no real mother. We have no real mother." The children gather in the doorway, watching. I wake.

I return to Massachusetts General Hospital for my first appointment after being accepted into the Xanax study. I carry the pale blue PATIENT DIARY and its tongue-tied inventory of daily symptoms: "*Unexpected panic attack*: 1; *Duration*: 20 minutes; *Intensity*: 6." In Tom's office, he scans the diary without comment. I fill out two forms — the Sheehan Patient-Rated Anxiety Scale (with the word "Upjohn" printed in the upper corner), and the SCL-90 with questions about how I felt this week, and how I feel now at this moment.

I receive medication for the first time, bright blue capsules in a white plastic bottle. Tom gives me a xeroxed dosage schedule which is standard for every research subject for the first week, he explains. I should start out taking one capsule and increase the dosage to three capsules by next week's visit. After that, Tom says, my dosage will vary depending on my response. I look at the Word-a-Day calendar by Merrel Dow, Inc. Today's word, "Pas seul," a "dance or dance step for one performer. Solo dance." I notice for the first time that each page of the daily calendar is an advertisement for the drug Norpramin.

We walk down the hallway to the exam room. Tom takes my blood pressure three times each when I'm sitting, then standing. Then he takes my temperature.

I meet with Dr. M., who is cool, not friendly. When I say that tracking my panic in the diary seems to make my symptoms worse, he replies, "Yes, writing it all down forces you to look at your denial." We fill out twelve pages of forms. He apologizes for how long it takes. All the forms have the word "Upjohn" printed in the upper corner.

I've made a circle between 0 and 1 in response to one of the questions. When I hand the forms back to Dr. M., who scans each one quickly before laying it neatly on his desk, he sighs. "The computer people will go crazy. They hate answers like this. Do you mean one or zero?" He hands me back the form.

I ask him how long the research on panic has been going on at Mass General. He says that Dr. David Sheehan started research here in the mid- to late 1970s. He pulls out a prescription pad and writes: "*The Anxiety Disease* by David Sheehan, M.D." "He did real well on that," Dr. M. says, tearing off the slip of paper and handing it to me. He tells me that I can find the book in most bookstores.

I express some confusion over what constitutes a "panic attack" and how to record it in my diary. I explain that sometimes I experience three of the fourteen symptoms listed in the diary for a panic attack, but I don't feel like I'm dying, so to me it doesn't feel like panic. Dr. M. emphasizes consistency. "Decide how you define an attack and keep recording it that way," he explains.

"So if for me I have to feel terrified that I'm about to die in order for it to be a panic attack, that's okay?" I ask.

Sure, he replies. Then silence.

I take the elevator back down to the lobby floor.

Woman Dreaming of Escape. Joan Miró, 1945. © 2004 Successió Miró / ARS, New York / ADAGP, Paris. Reproduced by permission.

Her lips black and red inside her stomach and closed down toward her vulva she is with closed lips and transparently so, apparently, since you see her so. She curls into moon and full orange sun sometimes both at the same time, one on each arm. At another time she is dancing a black line in orbit tying herself up dancing somewhere between white moon curl and orange circle sun, dancing black and alone—pas seul—a black and curving line in solo and out, knotted in passing, in passage. These orbits. Between.

I blink. Then leave the gallery and Miró's sugggestive painting. Exiting through the spinning doors at Massachusetts General Hospital.

And each week I return, bringing my diary, making the short-distance rounds from the waiting room, to Tom's office, to the exam room, to Dr. M.'s office. Each week, as they increase my dosage, the bottle of pills gets bigger. Tom says they are giving me extra pills beyond the required dosage. Just in case. He reminds me that I have to bring back all the unused pills each week. FDA regulations. To ensure that I don't stockpile or sell them.

Each week there's a new word on Merrel Dow's Word-a-Day calendar, and each week there's the same word, "Norpramin," in bold along its edges.

Each visit becomes more routinized. My role as a voluntary subject of research becomes primarily monosyllabic and multiple choice: 1 2 3 4 5 6 7 (How bad was the panic attack?) Yes No (Did you experience sexual interest or a change in sexual interest?) Worse No Improvement

Some Improvement Better Much Better Very Much Better (How was your anxiety this week compared to last week?) In miles (How far would you go away from home, alone?)

Each week in the hospital lobby I stare hard at the Miró painting on the philanthropically funded wall. Seeking the shifting pattern. *You stand before the sun, the moon quartered in the upper left hand corner of your eye, you stand before that sun not blinking and your eyes go fire you shimmer with the heat you rise burning you become black you become bird beating wild you are now a blackbird flying just below orange sun circle rising it is dawn, only dawn and already you are flamed. Blackbird flying wing-tipped rising flame toward the sun and away.* Each week I exit, spinning, through the revolving doors.

Then one day Dr. M. leans forward in his chair. "So how close do you think you are to your baseline experience, before you started having problems?" he asks.

PATIENT: Well, I'm pretty far away because now I have to take drugs to get near my baseline.

DR. M. [smiling]: I know what you mean. But putting aside the drugs, how far away are you from your normal experience?

PATIENT: Well, not far. But sometimes I think with these drugs I'm maybe *more* calm than I ever was before? I mean, I think maybe now I'm *more* normal than I was ever before?

Dr. M. smiles and makes a note.

Later, she writes it all down. Everything she can remember. What she wore, what he wore, the patterns on the wall, the color of her blood, the contents of her dreams, the answers to questions they ask, the possibility of questions they never broach, the stories she tells, the stories they don't even begin to want to hear, the needles, the jokes, the straps around her wrists for the EKG. And the day when the research assistant Tom leaves the exam room for a moment and she picks up the bright green DSM-*III* on his desk and browses through the index. "Hysterical personality. *See* Histrionic personality disorder." She reads: "301.50 Histrionic Personality Disorder. . . . Individuals with this disorder are lively and dramatic and are always drawing attention to themselves. They are prone to exaggeration and often act out a role, such as the 'victim.' . . . Individuals with this disorder crave novelty, stimulation, and excitement and quickly become bored with normal routines. . . . Usually these individuals show little interest in intellectual achievement and careful, analytical thinking."[117]

Carefully, dramatically, she writes it all down, recording the entangled textures of her field.

THE "UPJOHN ILLNESS"

> Given the many revisions of psychiatric nosology during the past
> 30 years, it is clearly a mistake to think that mental illnesses are
> something that have an established reality and that the role of the
> drug company is to find the key that fits a predetermined lock, or the
> bullet that will hit a desired target. . . . [W]e are at present in a state
> where drug companies cannot only seek to find the key to the
> lock but can dictate a great deal of the shape of the lock.
> —DAVID HEALY[118]

> Contemporary neuropharmacology seeks to modify aberrant
> messages that occur in certain disease states.
> —THE UPJOHN COMPANY[119]

"Panic disorder's the same everywhere in the world. More or less," says James Ballenger in 1996.[120] Ballenger, a well-known psychiatric specialist on anxiety and panic disorders, gains his global view of panic after participating in one of the first multinational clinical drug trials in the history of U.S. psychiatry. The Cross-National Collaborative Panic Study, sponsored by the Upjohn Company from 1982 to 1987, is designed to test the safety and efficacy of Xanax in the treatment of panic disorder.[121] Involving nearly two thousand research subjects at twenty sites in fourteen countries across four continents, the Cross-National Study also aims to establish panic as a homogeneous global illness, and, as Upjohn reports, "to better differentiate panic disorders as a distinct disease category."[122] Ballenger, who travels around the world overseeing the Upjohn study, finds dramatic evidence of the disorder's universal, uniform existence: "For me to listen to people in South America, and then Scandinavia, and then Michigan, and then England, and then Italy—and they all described exactly the same thing. . . . [T]hey all have the same thing. That was a huge advance. A huge advance. It blew our minds."[123]

Upjohn's Cross-National Panic Study is celebrated as a model of cooperative collaboration between the pharmaceutical industry, the U.S. government (NIMH), and the academy, and as a welcome sign of things to come. "In the future," states Gerald Klerman in 1990 at an Upjohn-sponsored international conference on panic disorder, "the overlap among the roles of government, academia, and industry in drug development is likely to increase."[124] Klerman's career as an internationally esteemed U.S. psychiatrist itself embodies this trinity of academic-government-corporate relations. A prestigious professor of psychiatry (for many years at Massachusetts General Hospital and Harvard University), director of the NIMH from 1971 to 1975, and then director of the NIMH's parent agency, the sprawling Alcohol, Drug Abuse, and Mental Health Administration (ADAMHA), from 1977 to 1980, Klerman in 1982 agrees to serve as Upjohn's senior scientific advisor for the Cross-National Panic Study.[125] As lead author of the study's published findings, Klerman, like Ballenger, sees clear evidence of panic disorder's global reach: "The study demonstrated that panic disorder . . . is a clinical condition which can be ascertained in almost all nations," he writes in 1992—adding the brief qualifier, "if the inquiry procedures and diagnostic procedures are appropriate."[126]

The "appropriate" procedures employed by Upjohn's Cross-National Study hard-wire together the emergent techniques of U.S. scientific psychiatric with global corporate finance and management structures. The study's transnational research population is diagnosed using a structured interview commissioned by Upjohn from Robert Spitzer of the DSM-III task force.[127] Upjohn adopts a modified version of the Panic Attack Scale, developed by David Sheehan and Kathy Sheehan, as the standardized rating scale for measuring symptom changes from week to week. And Upjohn introduces the use of the "patient's weekly diary" in which 1,700 global research subjects record the number, duration, and intensity of their panic attacks each day.[128]

To monitor and ensure the uniform implementation of the study's protocol, Upjohn hires quality-assurance teams, composed of Upjohn employees and two independent psychiatric researchers, to visit each of the study's twenty international research sites.[129] Robert Spitzer, Donald Klein, David Sheehan, James Ballenger—all are members of Upjohn's traveling "Quality Assurance Program" (QAP). Sheehan, with a grant from Upjohn, develops a computer program for optically scanning all of the study's rating scales and outcome measures. The Biostatistics Unit of the Department of Psychiatry at Massachusetts General Hospital performs statistical analyses of the data. Gerald Klerman, the project's scientific advisor, and James Coleman, of Upjohn's Psychopharmacology Research Unit, cochair the steering committee overseeing the international study.

According to James Ballenger, the financial firm Smith Barney calls Upjohn's Cross-National Panic Study an "unprecedented scientific-business enterprise" and "the best business scheme they had ever seen."[130] And by 1988, when the prestigious *Archives of General Psychiatry* lavishly publishes a series of five articles on the findings from phase 1 of the Upjohn study—the editor in chief of the *Archives* is at the time working for Upjohn as chair of the Cross-National Study's ethics and safety oversight committee[131]—the business and science of Xanax for panic is booming. In 1987, Xanax leads all other Upjohn products in foreign sales growth.[132] By 1988, Xanax is the third most prescribed drug of all prescription drugs in the United States.[133] Xanax successfully replaces Valium as the most prescribed antianxiety drug in the United States, while worldwide sales of Xanax and Halcion (another central nervous system drug prescribed for insomnia) together account for almost half of Upjohn's annual earnings by the early 1990s.[134]

Upjohn notes, proudly and publicly, that the Cross-National Study "appears to have helped define a new central nervous system disorder—panic."[135] And Xanax appears to define, at least for the moment, the premier drug treatment for the new disorder. In the summer of 1987, Upjohn submits data from phase 2 of the Cross-National clinical drug trial to the FDA, with a request that the FDA grant an indication (a kind of "use" license) for Xanax in the treatment of panic disorder. In 1990, Xanax becomes the first drug to win an FDA indication for panic, another boost to Upjohn's profits in the burgeoning market for panic disorder treatments.

Yet even as Upjohn's transnational gaze discovers panic disorder almost everywhere, the validity of the new disorder remains in dispute among researchers and clinicians.[136] And even as Upjohn discovers panic almost everywhere *looking the same*, the official diagnostic picture of panic—the symptom pattern first identified in the DSM-III—shifts and mutates. In the DSM-III-R, a revision of the DSM-III published by the APA in 1987, the operational criteria for the diagnosis of panic disorder are redesigned.[137] A major issue is the uncertain boundaries between panic disorder and several other diagnostic categories, including agoraphobia, social phobia, and generalized anxiety disorder. Partly in response to these ongoing controversies, the 1994 DSM-IV criteria for panic disorder are again revised, with James Ballenger sitting on the Anxiety Disorders Work Group overseeing the changes. Calling the previous DSM-III-R criteria "pseudo-scientific" and "arbitrary," Ballenger pushes for a more "representative" picture of panic. But he has no doubt that the DSM-IV criteria will not be the final word: "Panic disorder is an arbitrary definition of severity. It's just sort of saying, okay, everybody that's on this line has it, and everybody that's short doesn't have it. And God didn't make that line, we're just drawing lines ourselves."[138]

The lines drawn around panic disorder are historically indebted not only to human manipulations but to the technique of "pharmaceutical dissection," Donald Klein's phrase for the differentiation of disease categories through the observation of drug effects. Klein's experimental observation in the early 1960s of "behavioral response patterns" among institutionalized mental patients who were given the antidepressant drug imipramine is regularly cited as early empirical evidence of panic disorder.[139] The effects of imipramine made visible the "boundary" between panic attacks and other, more diffuse, chronic anxiety states. Panic disorder as a differentiated pattern or syndrome emerged as an artifact of observable drug effects.

While "discovering" mental disorders through manipulating drug effects is not a new practice—dating back at least to Emile Kraepelin's late-nineteenth-century experiments with alcohol, caffeine, morphine, and tea—the contemporary proliferation of drug treatments and of pharmaceutical company ambitions creates unparalleled opportunities for drug-disease couplings. The multi-million-dollar circuiting of panic with Xanax in the 1980s is an exemplary instance of the enormous value, from the point of view of both psychiatry seeking "valid" disorders and drug companies pursuing marketable commodities, of pharmaceutical dissection as a technique for constructing the boundaries around particular symptom patterns (identified as distinct disease entities). The effects of a drug give visibility to a particular pattern of symptoms, which reliably disappears after administration of the drug, which then offers evidence of the validity of a particular diagnostic category.

With the patterns of panic and the patterns of drug activity locked in a kind of circular causality, with drug effects in a tight feedback relation with the empirical description and differentiation of mental disorders, psychiatry is set to enter brave new worlds of financial, research, and organizational hookups with the transnational pharmaceutical industry. The clinical drug trials required of pharmaceutical companies by the FDA only amplify the circuiting of specific drugs with specific disorders. The psychiatric classification system itself starts to operate as a functional code linking disease to its recommended drug treatment. Approaching validity as a measure of the disease category's power to predict treatment response only intensifies the feedback loops between drug effects and patterns of disorder. Between systems of classification and practices of commodification. And computers make possible even more automated forms of feedback: by the late 1990s, pharmaceutical companies, including Upjohn and Pfizer, develop computer software that matches a computerized diagnosis of a mental disorder with its recommended drug treatment, and distribute the software as a marketing tool.[140]

Clearly, Upjohn plays a lead role in globally promoting this act of pattern recognition — Xanax for panic. But a kind of circular causality is also at work between Upjohn's corporate agenda and the interests of the psychiatric profession and the U.S. government — the synergy among these three actors drives the extraordinary ascendancy of Xanax and panic disorder. For those who were there in the early 1980s, when Xanax-panic was just taking off, the sense of being moved by powerful, convergent forces was palpable. David Sheehan recalls:

> This was a giant — it was like all of a sudden — that's why everybody got so excited about it. It was like without realizing it, it was a — it turned out to be a major crossroads, a kind of galvanizing influence that just

got everybody out of all of these places to come together. Because all in their funny little ways saw instinctively that this is the way the current was flowing, and that everybody's interests were served at once. And so you were, what you were feeling was — everybody even used to joke about it when they were in the middle of it — it's like everybody was being swept along by forces beyond anybody's control.[141]

One of those forces is the globalizing desire to make the 1980 DSM-III into a universal language of mental disease. The Cross-National Study is a perfect vehicle, with Upjohn's interest in expanding the market for Xanax converging with U.S. psychiatry's pursuit of a hegemonic diagnostic language. The psychiatrist David Healy writes, "Klerman and others in designing the [Cross-National] alprazolam studies were at least as interested to see how the new DSM and American concepts such as panic disorder internationalized as they were to see how the drug worked."[142] Or in Sheehan's words: "Panic becomes the point man to get into Europe.... We get them involved [in the Cross-National study], but the price that they'll have to pay for getting involved is they'll have to buy into the DSM-III system. And if they buy into the DSM-III system to do these studies, then we've got them basically hooked into the whole damn thing."[143] The strategy largely works. The growing international hegemony of the DSM-III in the 1980s and beyond is in part indebted to the sustained communication between U.S. and non-U.S. (particularly European and Latin American) psychiatric researchers, funded and facilitated by Upjohn's Cross-National Study. As Myrna Weissman, a well-known psychiatric epidemiologist and the wife of Gerald Klerman, recounts: "One of the major outcomes of the [Cross-National] alprazolam studies was that it created a generation of young investigators throughout the world who had used DSM-III and who could talk to each other in the same language."[144]

While the globalization of a uniform psychiatric language may not have been on Upjohn's agenda when the Cross-National Study was launched, by the 1990s Upjohn is funding Myrna Weissman's international psychiatric epidemiology.[145] The standardized, universalizing psychiatric language that Upjohn helps to establish enables, for the first time, multinational epidemiological studies for rates of specific mental disorders. The feedback effects are clear: for a pharmaceutical company like Upjohn, epidemiological findings are a valuable form of global market research. In Weissman et al.'s "The Cross-National Epidemiology of Panic Disorder" (1997), annual prevalence rates for panic disorder in ten different countries in North America, the Caribbean, Europe, the Middle East, the Pacific Rim, and East Asia are found to be largely consistent, ranging from about 1 to 2 percent of the population.[146] Weissman's epidemiological research uses *DSM-III* diagnostic criteria and the DIS (used in the first nationwide epidemiological study of mental disorders sponsored by the NIMH in the early 1980s) to generate computer-automated diagnoses of interview data for the more than forty thousand subjects in the international study.

If the circuiting of interests between psychiatry, the drug industry, and the government grows increasingly "integrated" in the decade after the *DSM-III*, their interests are hardly integrated equally. By the mid-1980s, some psychiatric researchers are calling panic disorder the "Upjohn illness," and few would deny the drug company's central role in promoting panic as a distinct mental disorder and a significant public health problem.[147] "Upjohn in some ways created panic disorder," says Mark Pollack in 1995, a psychiatrist in the Psychopharmacology Unit at Massachusetts General Hospital who directed much of the research on anxiety disorders during the 1980s.[148] The more that psychopharmacological drugs are perceived — by both psychiatrists and a broader public — as magic bullets for mental disorders, the greater the incentive for pharmaceutical companies to help create the perception of mental disorders as specific targets the bullet can "hit." Pharmaceutical companies are in the business not just of making drugs but of making "views of illness."[149] And in contrast to academic psychiatry and the government, the companies' capability for "making" a drug — or a disease — is richly financed, transnationally organized, and largely hidden from public scrutiny. The boundary between making science and marketing products becomes profoundly blurred.

Upjohn's Cross-National Panic Study materializes the implosion of marketing and science with astonishing boldness. Under the direction of James Coleman and driven, as James Ballenger describes, "by Upjohn's wish to have [Xanax] registered in every country known to mankind,"[150] the company consolidates its marketing department, its research department, and its medical science liaison unit into a single program.[151] To speed up the funding flows, Coleman takes money from Upjohn's marketing budget and rolls it over into the study's research budget.[152] Drawing on an enormous fund for research (none of the U.S. psychiatrists involved in the study ever know exactly how large), Upjohn invites one hundred of the top international psychiatric researchers in the field to participate in the Cross-National Panic Study. In exchange for their participation, Upjohn awards them not only research money for the Xanax study but matching funds for a second research project of their choice, financed by Upjohn but designed and controlled by each investigator.[153] It was a "grandiose scheme," unsurpassed in its scope and ambition, says Ballenger, and "it was done in a way that has been unprecedented and will never be repeated, but it set the sort of stage for a lot of things in the future."[154]

One of the things the Cross-National Study sets the stage for is what David Healy calls today's "medico-pharmaceutical complex," a kind of technosocial integrated circuit in which "the notion that there is a pharmaceutical industry and an independent academic sector is somewhat illusory."[155] Here the knowledge base and information flows not only regarding the development of drugs, but also concerning the scientific foundations and elaborations of disease categories, are largely produced and controlled by pharmaceutical companies. If, in fact, the publication of the *DSM-III* ushers in the possibility of a new science of psychiatry—based on evidence, driven by data, transformed through standardized empirical techniques—then does it also accelerate a new science barely separable from corporate capital? James Ballenger estimates that the breakdown of money spent in the United States for drug development is 4 percent from the government, 1 percent from universities, and 95 percent from pharmaceutical companies, and "that fact dominates everything." Even more dramatically, when the federal government's support of the NIMH was decreasing in the 1980s, the government agency began *to accept money from pharmaceutical companies to fund its own basic research*.[156] If "scientific" evidence and data are the favored currency of contemporary psychiatry, then what information can be brokered, what knowledge exchanged, that isn't already trademarked by pharmaceutical company design?

In addition to heavily influencing the direction and production of research, Healy cautions, pharmaceutical companies also have control of the media through which information about drugs and mental disorders circulates. By means of advertising in psychiatric and medical journals, purchasing supplemental issues of journals to publish their corporate-sponsored research, sponsoring conferences on particular disorders and treatments, and even providing satellite-based electronic resources for the postgraduate education of psychiatrists, pharmaceutical companies control many of the channels of communication through which psychiatric knowledge is broadcast.[157]

But the most important channels of communication monopolized by the pharmaceutical industry may be those in the human brain and central nervous system itself. With cybernetic images of the brain as a communication/information device firmly established in both popular and scientific imaginaries by the late twentieth century, psychopharmaceutical drugs should perhaps themselves be analyzed as a form of "mass media" — standardized, corporately produced media that interrupt dysfunctional programming with more promising biochemical communications. More valued patterns of information. Broadcasting via the neural networks and transmission paths of today's informational brain, psychopharmacology promotes a kind of individualized, internalized, media(ted) culture in which communication and control operate through commodified, corporately designed and developed programming. Upjohn suggests that its central nervous system drugs like Xanax and Halcion "modify aberrant messages that occur in certain disease states."[158] Deviant messages, noisy static, undesired or undesirable information flows are met by an automated (re)channeling of communication, materialized by the mass-produced stories inside small white pills.

What other forms of cure might be communicated if a transnational pharmaceutical industry didn't control so many of the channels? What other stories might be swallowed if a "mass approach to mental health" — which the NIMH dreamed of in 1946 and began to deliver decades later in the form of psychopharmacological drugs — could be imagined and empirically tested for "efficacy" outside the major networks of drug company production?

And if Xanax does become a popularly prescribed form of mass media

Alprazolam

Chemical structure of Xanax
(alprazolam)

in the 1980s, what is the message it communicates? As with other mass media, although the broadcast of Xanax is standardized and highly regulated, its reception is never simply uniform: the drug elicits a range of felt effects in those who take it. For the more than 1,100 research subjects in phase 2 of Upjohn's Cross-National Study, speaking in the statistically aggregated chorus of a clinical drug trial, 70 percent feel that their panic attacks are gone after eight weeks on Xanax. In addition, after one week on Xanax, 58 percent of subjects feel sedated, with 20 percent experiencing fatigue and weakness and 16 percent experiencing impaired muscle coordination. Fifteen percent experience faintness or dizziness. Thirteen percent complain of headaches. Sixteen percent experience memory problems. Although some of these drug effects fade after several weeks on Xanax, approximately 15 to 30 percent of research subjects report that the memory problems, sedation, weakness, and fatigue persist for the duration of the eight-week study.[159]

For perhaps massively mediated reasons, Xanax's sedating story, incorporating the occasional blank screen of amnesia, is a really big hit. As one of the first "blockbuster" drugs to take its place alongside blockbuster movies in the pantheon of commercial popular culture, sales of Xanax peak just as psychotropic drugs start to circulate in more extended mass-media networks. In the 1990s, the FDA largely averts its regulatory gaze as pharmaceutical companies begin direct-to-consumer advertising for prescription drugs, including drugs for mental disorders.[160] Ads appear on television, in magazines, and eventually on the Internet. Whereas for decades the pharmaceutical industry focused its advertising and marketing efforts on physicians and psychiatrists, by 2000, drug companies are spending an estimated $2.5 billion annually on consumer advertising.[161] With more and more patients asking directly for brand-name drugs from their doctors, and research suggesting that mass-media marketing is significantly boosting prescription drug sales, the Pharmaceutical Research and Manufacturers of America affirms that the new drug ads communicate "important information" to consumers.[162]

And where is Upjohn in this story, as pharmaceutical companies multiply their channels of communication from biochemical messages in the brain, to thirty-second ads broadcast on ABC, NBC, CBS, Fox, and CNN? Faced with the simultaneous patent expiration in 1993 of Xanax and Halcion, its two best-selling drugs, and with pressures to rapidly globalize markets while downsizing production, Upjohn's own boundaries radically shift during the 1990s. After closing or reducing the size of almost half of its thirty-one factories and aggressively expanding its markets into China, India, and Central Europe in 1993, the company remains financially staggered.[163] In 1995, Upjohn ceases to exist as a valid and reliable entity: in the middle of a decade of spectacular mergers and acquisition battles within the worldwide pharmaceutical industry, Upjohn merges with the Swedish company Pharmacia to create "Pharmacia & Upjohn." In 1999, Pharmacia & Upjohn merges with the biotech giant Monsanto to create the Pharmacia Corporation, with a market value of $52 billion. (Relocating its new corporate headquarters in New Jersey, the Pharmacia Corporation purchases the former palatial headquarters of communications giant AT&T.)[164] In 2002, the Pharmacia Corporation is acquired for $60 billion by Pfizer Inc., the largest drug company in the United States, which, in 2000, merged with Warner-Lambert in what the *New York Times* calls a "widely admired . . . model of how to fully exploit an acquired portfolio of blockbuster drugs."[165] After the Pharmacia acquisition, Pfizer also becomes the largest drug company operating in Europe, Japan, and Latin America, controlling an estimated 11 percent of the global drug market.

And what happens to the "Upjohn illness" after Upjohn disappears from the scene? Patterns of panic continue to profitably integrate with patterns of corporate-developed drug activity, though Xanax is no longer the preferred treatment. In 1997, Pfizer receives an FDA indication for its blockbuster drug Zoloft in the treatment of panic. Zoloft is one of several antidepressants (including Paxil) that come to dominate the market for panic and anxiety treatments in the 1990s.[166]

Why would an antidepressant drug successfully treat an anxiety disorder? The validity of the boundaries between the different anxiety disorders, and between anxiety disorders and depression, continues to elude empirical proof or professional consensus. In fact, writes the psychiatrist Robert Kendell in 2002, "at present we have little evidence that the boundaries we have drawn between most of the 200 recognized syndromes are based on natural boundaries. We do not know, in other words, whether we are 'carving nature at the joints,' or even whether there are 'joints' . . . to be found."[167] Whether the boundaries around different mental disorders are real, or an artifact of drug effects, or a persuasive empirical probability, the boundaries around the market for treating mental disorders continue to expand exponentially. Whether Upjohn's Cross-National Panic Study trafficked in scientific facts, or drug-induced fictions, or their complex combination, the mental disorder Upjohn helped to create manages to outlive both its first corporate sponsor and the popularity of the small white pill that helped to produce it.

PANIC DIARY

Just last week I watch this video, *Total Recall*, where Arnold Schwarzenegger plays an ordinary guy who pays to get his dreams programmed so he can have a virtual vacation but things get crazy because instead of getting his dreams programmed Arnold learns that his entire mind's been programmed, all his memories erased, and he's not really an ordinary guy but a secret agent from Mars who works for a Big Corporation that's trying to crush the rebellion of masses of mutants and of poor people.

Last night I have a dream. It's a pretty nice dream in the woods, in a big two-story house, with a family and all that. Until I look in a mirror and see all my teeth crumbling in my mouth. I get scared and run downstairs and all of a sudden there's a TV camera crew in the kitchen. The people who were just in my dream are changing their makeup and costumes and getting ready to tape the next scene. One woman—she'd been my friend in the dream—says to me, "That was really funny, the part when you got afraid of the feminine." I start to panic because I thought I was some-place real or at least in a real dream and instead everybody's just actors, performing scripted scenes, then analyzing my dream. I lie down on the floor, fetal-like and terrified. A woman with a clipboard comes over to me and says quickly into her headset microphone, "WZBC-TV—We need to send this one back." She spins me around and I wake up. It's 6 A.M. I'm afraid to dream, afraid to be awake. The difference between these two states is radically unclear.

I wake at 8 A.M., groggy and reluctant. Last night, in preparation for today's visit to Massachusetts General Hospital, I swallow one of the blue plastic capsules. It's week eight of our research, and once each month they take a sample of my blood. Today, I need to have some of the blue capsule in my bloodstream. The first week of the study, I find the smooth white pill tucked into one end of the capsule. I swallow it. From its effects—the sedation and heavy calm that suffuses me within thirty minutes—I can tell that the drug is Xanax. Today, the smooth white pill is inside me.

I take a second blue capsule before heading to school. Calmly, with an unfamiliar absence of anxiety, I report to the seminar how my project on panic is taking shape. I'm able to listen to comments without my thoughts racing ahead, worrying over my response. Occasionally I get lost in a long sentence, forgetting my own beginning, unable to find my way back. My reaction is muted, unconcerned. I continue on. Theorizing out loud the transferential fields where doctor and patient, symptom and history, witch and inquisitor, research and dream, death and its denial, hold each other in passionate, sometimes violent, always irreducible embrace.

At noon, feeling really calm, I arrive at Massachusetts General Hospi-tal. I stare blankly at Joan Miró's *Woman and Birds in Front of the Sun.* I see bird, woman, insects. The sun today is red, not orange as I wrote last week. I take the elevator to the seventh floor.

I'm early. The waiting room of the Psychosomatic Unit is filled with more patients than usual. A man in a suit passes quickly through the waiting room, emerging from a hallway behind the receptionist's desk. He carries a plastic tray piled with fruit, chips, and a sandwich. Behind him a second man in a suit follows, saying, "And after the scientific pre-sentations, there were marketing presentations." They exit down another hallway.

In Dr. M.'s office, I tell him I'm doing well, really well. And feeling kind of scared, this drug is having such an effect. "Sometimes it's hard getting used to it. It's kind of existential," Dr. M. replies. "In truth, the fact of the matter is, it's like panic disorder is the result of the brain firing at the wrong time."

We go through several questionnaires. I have difficulty answering some of the questions. It's unclear to me what I'm supposed to compare my current health to — my feelings last week? Or before being on the drug at all? Or before having panic attacks? Dr. M. tells me the scale I'm being asked to respond with is *absolute*. I'm not supposed to be comparing my current state to any other state. Just answer the question on an absolute scale of 1 to 10.

DR. M.: Is there anywhere you would now be afraid to go?
PATIENT: Not out of the country.
DR. M.: Would you go to California?
PATIENT: Yes, if I had my supply of drugs.
DR. M.: Which drugs is that?

We both laugh and laugh.

DR. M.: Any change in your sleeping patterns?

I tell him how I'm dreaming vividly early in the morning. He says some people do report more vivid dreams. The drug probably changes our sleep patterns. Do I know about REM?

When I tell Dr. M. it's kind of upsetting to think a drug can make such a difference, he says that sometimes people feel *at a loss* without their panic. They are forced to face other interactive problems they have wanted to ignore. They feel *at a loss* without the panic to fill their mind.

In the exam room, Tom, the research assistant, takes my pulse. Then my temperature. He asks only two questions: How did you feel this week? How do you feel compared to the beginning of the study? I'm fine. I'm really doing fine.

I feel foggy, deeply tranquilized, as I roll up my sleeve and extend my bare arm for him to take my blood. Tom puts on white plastic gloves that snap as he pulls them up around his wrists. With one gloved finger he strokes the raised, thick, slightly blue stream of my vein. As always, I look away as he inserts the thin silver needle into my arm. He draws four vials of blood, deep red and beautiful, laid out on the tray in front of me. As he labels the vials he says, "You're a trooper," explaining that most women — "biological destiny, I guess" — are smaller than men, and often their veins are, too. So their veins can be hard to find. "You have great veins," he tells me, before taking off his gloves and washing his hands in the white porcelain sink.

COMMUNICATING THEORY

> Examine the two statements, "Help!" and "I need help." The first
> language is a cry; the second, a description. Only the cry, art, rather
> than the description, is primary. The cry is stupid; it has no mirror; it
> communicates.
>
>   I want to cry. — KATHY ACKER[168]

> Successful communication is the road to mental health.
>   — JURGEN RUESCH[169]

"Wrong theories are better than no theories," Donald Klein doggedly observes in a 1994 article describing his most recent theory of panic disorder.[170] An indefatigable theorist of panic and psychopathology for over four decades, Klein's latest ideas about the disorder eschew any "theoretical nostalgia" for the simplicity of a single necessary cause. The "mind-boggling" complexity of contemporary neuroscience, in which a neuron no longer looks like a simple binary on-off switch but like an "advanced computer," and brain receptor types and subtypes multiply explosively and are "all complexly looped in interacting, reverberating and damping circuits," presents for the theorist of mental disease a different challenge: a necessarily complex causality. With the brain operating less like a computer and more like a vast network of advanced computers communicating via "the intricacies of second and, possibly, third, fourth and fifth messenger systems," the best a theorist can do is hypothesize, test, evaluate, and expect to be quickly proved wrong.[171]

Ultimately, for Klein, the problem haunting theory construction is that "it requires knowledge of circuitry, and by and large our knowledge of circuitry is just outright primitive."[172] Even the pathology of a highly complex brain pathway could be deciphered if there were some persuasive knowledge of its function or purpose. But "without a functional framework, one is at a loss to understand the circuitry." Like a physicist making theories about a computer whose "strategic organization and goals" are unknown, the theorist of mental disease must fall back on trying to understand each "microcircuit" and how it may affect "contiguous circuitry."[173]

The importance that Klein attaches to knowledge of brain function is inextricably tied to his notion of mental disease, in which "something has gone wrong with the normal evolved functions of a biological system."[174] In the 1980s, Klein theorizes that panic disorder involves a biological dysfunction in the mechanism regulating "separation anxiety." The "evolutionary 'purpose'" of separation anxiety is to cause "the vulnerable infant to emit signals that will elicit retrieval" by a parent or others.[175] In panic disorder, the evolved "alarm" system for separation (whose function is to communicate distress) goes off too easily and too often; the cries of the panicked animal are maladapted to the actual level of threatened separation. The cry is a malfunctioning form of communication.

Even as an experimental program to selectively breed rats with high and low levels of separation anxiety—as measured by the "isolation cry" of the infant rat—is being developed at the New York State Psychiatric Institute, where Klein is director of research and development, Klein is busy constructing a new theory of panic disorder.[176] In the 1990s, he turns his attention to the biological function and dysfunction of the "suffocation alarm system."[177] Klein explains how both individual and collective panics may erupt when the brain's "suffocation monitor" mistakenly signals a lack of air, "thereby maladaptively triggering an evolved suffocation alarm system." The alarm system triggers breathlessness and a sense of smothering and choking—key symptoms in a panic attack—whose function is to communicate impending suffocation and motivate escape behavior.

As empirical support for his theoretical speculation, Klein cites an incident of "mass hysteria" among 990 women working at a telephone

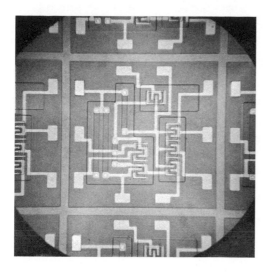

Integrating circuits

switchboard exchange. When the air conditioning fails, 250 of the women rapidly develop contagious symptoms of choking and hyperventilation, dizziness, and sweating; psychiatric evaluation diagnoses the symptoms as panic attacks.[178] Although in this instance the attacks were maladaptive to the situation, they demonstrate a potent evolutionary function of panic: to communicate the dangers of "a no-exit situation," or a situation where stagnant air "implies no exit." Klein concludes that theories like this, combined with an "active experimental" approach to panic and other psychopathologies, "may move us from symptoms to a grasp of deranged circuitry."[179] Perhaps.

The apparent biological reductionism in Klein's theory of mental disease masks the growing complexity of psychiatry's very notion of the "biological." Increasingly, many psychiatrists view biology and behavior, body and mind, soma and psyche, in intensely material, intricately wired circuits of relation and causality. Introductory remarks to the DSM-IV (1994) decry the "reductionistic anachronism of mind/body dualism" embedded in the very idea of "mental" (as distinct from "physical") disorder: a "compelling literature documents that there is much 'physical' in 'mental' disorders and much 'mental' in 'physical' disorders."[180] In 2002, psychosomatic medicine becomes for the first time an approved subfield of the American Board of Psychiatry and Neurology. And Klein sees the kind of "biopsychiatry" he practices and promotes as actually a theoretical synthesis of the exclusively biological approach of Emile Kraepelin with the exclusively psychological approach of Freud (as Klein notes that even Freud believed in the neurophysiology of neurosis, though the scientific limits of neurology at the time prevented him from pursuing it).[181] Translating the psychoanalytic notion of "separation anxiety" into the biological terms of an evolved control function is, for Klein, about theorizing panic disorder in multiple tongues, not about making claims for a strictly biological causality.

And yet, as U.S. psychiatry moves into the twenty-first century, "strictly" biological and genetic research on panic disorder proliferates, stimulated in part by the funding and research priorities of the Human Genome Project and the congressionally mandated Decade of the Brain (1990–2000), as well as the staked interests of a pharmaceutical industry invested in biological markers of mental disease.[182] The ability to experimentally produce panic attacks — to turn panic "on" and "off" — in a laboratory setting facilitates neurobiological research on the "neuronal circuitry" of the disorder. Panic in volunteer human research subjects is successfully provoked by a series of agents (sodium lactate, carbon dioxide, caffeine), and the experimental panic attacks are then "turned off" by the administration of a variety of drugs. As PET and SPECT scans and other neuroimaging techniques permit limited visualization of brain activity and blood flow, the dream of "establishing the unique brain signatures of psychiatric symptoms" promotes a growing body of image-based research on panic and other psychic disorders.[183] New hypotheses emerge. Perhaps an observed frontal brain asymmetry indicates a disturbed cortical processing in people with panic? Perhaps the "essential circuits of the anxiety responses" are located in the set of brain regions activated during attacks — perhaps panic lives in the supragenual anterior cingulate, the amygdala and parahippocampal gyrus, the orbito-frontal cortex, the insulae, or the cerebellum?[184]

Genetic research on panic disorder gathers momentum in the 1990s as "psychiatric genetics" is celebrated as an "exciting frontier that holds the promise of revealing the molecular basis of neuropsychiatry."[185] In 1997, the NIMH convenes a Genetics Workgroup that recommends that psychiatric genetics be fully integrated with medical genetics, and that the NIMH support the "growing partnership" between academic scientists and "their colleagues in pharmaceutical and biotechnology companies."[186] While some note that the insistent optimism of the early 1990s—when a revolution in psychiatry seemed just around the genetic corner—has given way a decade later to more modest and cautionary tales, the search for "anxiety genes" continues. But the early hope of finding a single gene tied to a specific disorder like panic fades. Instead, for complex diseases like panic, the search begins for "susceptibility genes," mediated by environment and participating in an exceedingly complex causality.

Myrna Weissman, who organizes some of the earliest genetic research on panic, reports that even though the studies are expensive and labor intensive—"going out and get[ting] the families, doing the interviews, getting the blood"—and not yet well funded, she thinks the chances are good of finding "some panic disorder that's genetic."[187] Panic is one of a handful of mental disorders considered especially promising candidates for genetic explanation: one large twin study of anxiety disorders estimates that the heritability of panic disorder is over 40 percent.[188] Authors regularly caution, however, that research is only in its early stages.

One repeatedly cited obstacle to a successful psychiatric genetics—for panic or any other disorder—is the "lack of validity of the classification of psychiatric disorders."[189] Researchers lament the ongoing uncertainty over what the boundaries around DSM disorders actually signify, some calling for a new " 'psychiatric genetic nosology' capable of classifying individuals in ways that correspond to distinct genetic entities."[190] The "search for susceptibility genes in psychiatry will create the need for a careful reexamination of the boundaries of our diagnostic categories," psychiatric researchers claim, with special attention to whether anxiety and depressive disorders constitute discrete disorders, and whether the anxiety disorders themselves (panic disorder, phobia, obsessive-compulsive disorder, etc.) are actually separate entities.[191]

For all the research activity and optimistically "wrong" theories produced about panic disorder, by the early twenty-first century, U.S. psychiatry achieves no theoretical consensus about what the disorder is or why it appears or where it comes from. Or how to cure it. Indeed, the problem of cure remains largely unspoken. Unaddressed in the far-flung realms of panic theory and research. While drug treatments are recog-

blinding research — not knowing, then learning, then forgetting again. A curious method.

ATIVAN   BUSPAR   CLOZARIL   ELAVIL   HALCION   HALDOL
KLONOPIN   LIBRIUM   MILTOWN   NEMBUTAL   NEURONTIN

Tom has me fill out two rating scales. The SCL-90 scale tracks my emotions, thoughts, and behavior over the last week. Any troublesome sexual fantasies? Thoughts of suicide? Belief that people were controlling your thoughts? Ideas or beliefs that you think no one else shares? I answer carefully, within the boxes provided, on a scale of one to five. Next I fill out the Sheehan Patient-Rated Anxiety Scale. Never, Sometimes, Frequently, A Lot of the Time. "Fear that something is wrong with your mind?" I check the appropriate box.

> "He recovered eventually, but, *entre nous*, he'll never really be the same." — Norpramin Word-a-Day Calendar

In the exam room, Tom performs the final physical exam. He takes my blood pressure when I'm sitting, then standing. He takes my temperature. He takes my pulse. Seated in a green vinyl chair, I pull up the sleeve on my left arm and prepare for him to take my blood. The key preparation for the taking of my blood is for me to look away. Always look away. I have learned this over the years. Let this always be a blind taking of my blood.

NARDIL NOZINAN ORAP PAMELOR PAXIL PERCOCET PERMITIL
PLACIDYL PROLIXIN PROZAC RITALIN SERAX SERENTIL SERZONE

But today I sit in the green vinyl chair and watch carefully as Tom lays out two glass vials and three short plastic tubes. He takes a long, thin needle and places it in the flexible needle holder. I watch as he presses the needle into the blue vein on my left arm. For a moment this hurts. Blood deep red a thin stream splashes against the back of the clear glass vial. I watch my blood fill the vial, pressing bubbled and froth-pink against the glass wall as it fills. With gloved fingers he removes the first glass vial now full red and attaches the next one. I keep watching. My blood deep red splashes against the back of the clear glass vial. I watch my blood fill the second vial. I watch him take my blood. This is not blind research. For a moment it hurts—jiggling the needle by accident, Tom removes the second glass vial and attaches the first short plastic tube. A thin stream red my blood splashes against the back of the tube.

He jiggles the needle again, accidentally. This hurts. I watch and the tube is not filling. The needle moves again inside my vein—I catch my breath—and the gloved hand quickly removes the plastic tube. Tom places a clean white gauze pad over the vein and pulls out the silk-thin needle. He says, "Sorry. We stopped getting blood." I press the gauze pad tight against my vein.

What will happen now? What happened?

I watched the taking of my blood. I did not look away. I watched the taking of my blood stop. Just between us, *entre nous*, I believe because I watched, the taking of my blood became more difficult.

But then the problem of my other arm. Of sustaining such a gaze on a silken solid silver needle, not blind to the taking of my blood. Because on my other arm was another blue vein slightly raised and pulsing and as Tom swabbed my right arm with an alcohol-soaked pad I forgot to watch. I just forgot. I went blind for the rest. I don't think really it was the pain. It hurts only a little to watch a solid silk silver needle penetrate your pulsing vein and, suddenly, get jerked around. The actual pain is very slight. No. I think I just forgot. I became interested in other things. I remembered dinner tonight—and he pricked the vein on my right arm, I could feel it—I needed to buy groceries on my way home. He removed the first plastic tube—I heard it pop softly as it disengaged—and put in another. I remembered the boxes of white gauze and bandages labeled and stacked in the brown cupboard to my left, and I forgot to watch, really, and while I was forgetting the next plastic tube filled and I heard Tom pop it out and insert the last tube. I remembered the time—5:05 P.M. there was a clock on the wall and I hoped to get home before 6:00 I'm so hungry. He popped out the final plastic tube and I felt a gauze pad against my arm with the needle inside and then he pulled out the needle and asked me to hold the gauze tight. He was finished taking my blood and had five full red containers on the tray in front of me.

I don't know really why I forgot to keep watching when he began to take blood from my right arm. But—*entre nous*—really, just between us, confidentially, it may have been because I remembered how many blue veins run through me. Perhaps I forgot to sustain my gaze because I remembered the raised blue veins behind my knees along my wrists translucent along my temple pulsing under my jaw down my neck and perhaps I just recalled—after that moment when my blood stopped flowing into the plastic tube and I imagined that if I refused to look away during the taking of my blood they would grow nervous, they would falter, because they count on that look away for the confident execution of these operations—perhaps I recalled what the stopping of this bloodletting might demand—my repeated and sustained gaze upon my flesh as they find new veins pulsing and blue to press into gently with their silk silver needles—the insistent attempts as they grow impatient and lose confidence—as they a little wild now press the needle into the veins behind my knees along my wrists down my neck as I twisting and trying to keep my gaze steady on this bloodletting and the silver needle slightly tearing the blue silk lining of the veins in my neck behind my knees along these wrists as I try to keep watching. To not look away.

Perhaps this is why I forgot. To keep watching. And let the last tubes fill red blood as I sat blind. *Entre nous*, this is a possibility. Although I may be wrong.

THORAZINETRANXENEVALIUMVESPRINVIVACTILWELLBUTRINX-
ANAXZOLOFTAMBIENBENZEDRINECYLERTDALMANEEFFEXORLU-
VOXMARPLANNORPRAMINPAXIMREMERONSEROQUELTOFRANIL

Half a block from Massachusetts General Hospital in the rain I want very much to have the slip of calendar with today's word *entre nous*—I want it in my pocket. So I walk back half a block and take the elevator to the seventh floor and enter the Psychosomatic Unit waiting room where it's 5:20 P.M. and the receptionist has left. I walk past the desk, down the hall to the exam room which is empty, and cross to the small desk and tear the page for January 25, *entre nous*. I slip the page into the pocket of my coat. I leave the exam room, take the elevator to the first floor, and exit through the spinning doors.

(She recovered eventually, but, *entre nous*, she'll never really be the same.)

EPILOGUE

history running back and forth

panic in the labyrinth

. . . you and I are caught in

a laboratory without a science

—ADRIENNE RICH[1]

This story opened with a fictional war of the worlds as high-tech Martians invaded the social imaginary, arriving via the electronic circuits of radio and creating a nationwide panic. The outbreak of terror led to a social scientific study of how collective panic might be more adequately theorized and effectively controlled; the findings were integrated a few years later into the actual prosecution of world war. The story ended with a real image of blood streaming from the body of a terrified research subject, sitting in the experimental laboratory of a corporate-sponsored clinical drug trial. Designed to test the effectiveness of the pill called Xanax for the problem called "panic disorder," the research program probed its subjects—our blood, our memories, our bodies—for information relevant to the scientific study of a pharmaceutical treatment. Is this, then, a story of the sadism of technoscience? Of mad technoscientists out to control the mad crowds and maddened body-minds caught in the maddening social laboratories of technoscience's mad reason?

Well, yes, in part. One of the multiple, messy origins of this project was to recount and account for the crazy practices I found inside the medical clinic, where sickness, "which had come to seek a cure, was turned into a spectacle."[2] And the spectacularly abstract and maddeningly reasonable language of that clinic was my early antagonist as I tried in my ethnographic notes—my panic diaries—to resist the translation of panicky symptoms into digitized computer data, to dramatize the weirdly unconscious and empirical cruelties of a corporate-driven psychiatric discourse.

And, yes, I do think it's possible we're entering the scary era of a "control society," led by the imaginary and material transformations of a globalizing technoscience, including information and communications technologies making possible the very infrastructures of globalizing capital. I do think we may be living in a historical moment in which newly flexible and liquid flows of terror, bodies, capital, blood, knowledge, desires, weapons, immiseration, and resistance are managed by increasingly automated and immanent techniques of technoscientific power—an emergent "informatics of domination."[3] In a control society, write Michael Hardt and Antonio Negri, power becomes "ever more immanent to the social field, distributed throughout the brains and bodies of the citizens."[4] Gilles Deleuze observes the "ultrarapid forms of free-floating control"—including pharmaceuticals and genetic manipulations—that may be displacing the "old disciplines" of hierarchy and classification.[5] Contemporary psychiatry and corporate psychopharmacology, in this story, can certainly be read as nodes in an emerging network of globalizing controls.

But at the same time, this story is not written, could not be written, outside the materialized abstractions or the intensifying communicative networks of a technoscientific social. It could not be written without or outside or (simply) against the hybrid, posthuman, and historically specific reassemblages of "bodies, memory, time, space, and unconscious desire that are given with . . . technoscience and transnational capitalism," in Patricia Clough's words.[6] These hybrid "other agencies"—of bodies spliced with machines, dreams cut through by electrochemical information—confound and reconfigure what might count as an "actor" in the technosocial theaters that I write about, and within which "I" am, really, being rewritten.[7] "Technoscience is a form of life, a practice, a culture, a generative matrix," Donna Haraway insists.[8] Its lively cultural force is certainly not my main focus in this panicky tale that attends anxiously to its rather deadly cultural powers. But other stories are being told, will be told, that interrupt and complicate the often scary, scared stories I tell here of an increasingly "informatic" control of unconscious spaces and of a psychiatric profession deeply wired into the financial and technoscientific circuits of a pharmaceutical industry while profoundly distanced from a technics, or ethics, of transformative cure.[9]

Yet the story I tell here is also something more and something other than a critique of technoscience, however much I find myself symptomatically entangled in its force fields. It is also a confabulating reenactment of history, a trauma in search of its missing event as I reconstruct the fantastic, storied origins of a psychic disorder that, they told me, is caused by a few faulty circuits inside. Isn't the psyche, though, precisely one place, one elusive and socially constituted process, through which the boundaries between "inside" and "outside" get made? And wouldn't one form that a politics of the psyche might take—one practice, you might say, of a PSYCHOpolitics—be a struggle over social perceptions of what's inside and what's out, and what passages might exist between? And what if this story is a little PSYCHOpolitical battle (because I was born out of the belly of military engagements, don't forget that I'm no stranger to hostile encounters, I don't shrink from the scene of armored invasion, though I tremble sometimes at the possibility of your touch), a small war of the worlds, this story, between their account of disorder and my attempt at a more contagious communication of dis-ease?

So if inside my dis-ease I encountered the outside, if I inhabited for some time a scattered archive and its historical traces of panicked crowds, a suggestible social, traumatized soldiers, a remote-controlled astronaut, mad Cold War daughters of functional fathers, electrified mental patients, the cry of a lab rat specially bred for anxious separation, all the fantastically mimetic theaters of my own fear—perhaps it was part of a PSYCHOpolitical strategy, this crazy reordering of a story of panic disorder? Fighting for a more complex circuiting of causalities, deepening the psychic openings inside out toward a different politics of perception. Performing terror on the way to a more suggestive and less fatal theater of the affective, emotional, and embodied effects of the social.

As I write these words (*ep-i-logue*, n., "A short poem or speech spoken directly to the audience following the conclusion of a play . . . often dealing with the future of its characters"), it feels like a dangerous and dangerously strange time to be performing panicky terrors. It feels, today, as if time itself is strange. As if time, and its relation to terror, are repeating themselves in some strange, historically or hysterically familiar ways. In chapter 3, I chronicled how, throughout the 1950s, a terrifying future was imaginarily imploded into a tremulous present as state-sponsored and mass-mediated theaters of atomic attack were repeatedly played out in civil defense propaganda, Cold War popular culture, and nationwide civil defense simulations. Today, as the so-called war against terrorism extends into an infinitely expanding battlefield, tightly choreographed theaters of threatening terrorist attack are reappearing as the militarization of social psychologies becomes, again, the business of government and, again, a dispersed target of PSYCHOpower.[10] Today the future is again staged in a panicky present tense, a terror-filled future-present productively performed in the blood-laced borderlands of psychic and political warfare.

"Seattle, May 12," the byline reads, and the news article reports at least 150 casualties when *a dirty bomb packed with radioactive agents* explodes in an industrial area of south Seattle in the spring of 2003.[11] *Plumes of toxic smoke fill the air for miles* as *firefighters in protective chemical suits milled through the scene . . . where overturned buses, police cars and fire engines could be seen, fake victims wandered in a daze, car fires smoldered and a few news helicopters flew overhead* in the *most extensive terrorism response training in the nation's history.* Organized by the Department of Homeland Security at a cost of $16 million and prepared for over an eighteen-month period, the simulated terrorist attack involves *8,500 medical, police, fire, rescue and other personnel across the country* and is to be followed the next day by *a covert biological attack on Chicago,* where volunteer victims will start to arrive in city hospitals *with flulike symptoms consistent with pneumonic plague.*

Terror is one symptom of imploding time; panic is, in part, a temporal disorder. I know this from living through panic attacks, when all the breathtaking somatic signs point to the psychic certainty that death has already arrived. You live, strangely, in death's aftershocks, gasping for air in the effort to grapple with the news. If making futures is a kind of technology, then making futures that arrive already over is another kind — panic and terror are futures technologies, practiced in the killing fields of manufactured time —

I didn't want it to end like this. Me, slightly ranting, as I feel my heart racing into a future, tense. You, a little nervous, worried that indeed she sounds a bit unbalanced. It's a strange time, I repeat, to be telling stories about terror. So why not just stop? Perhaps because a "story is *not* just a story. Once the forces have been aroused and set into motion, they can't simply be stopped at someone's request. Once told, the story is bound to circulate. . . . its effects linger on and its end is never truly an end."[12] At least that is my hope. As in performance, and disease, the efficacy of a story — "its only hope for survival" — is that "it catches on."[13] And when it does, can things ever really *be the same*?

NOTES

Prologue

1 Foucault, "Nietzsche, Genealogy, History," 88.
2 Foucault, *Madness and Civilization*, ix.

1. History, Memory, Story

1 Edgar Allan Poe, "The Tell-Tale Heart," in *Tales of Mystery and Imagination* (Secaucus, N.J.: Castle, 1983), 298.
2 Haraway, "A Game of Cat's Cradle," 62.
3 These details of the Iroquois Theater fire are taken from news reports in the *New York Times*, December 31, 1903, and January 1–2, 1904.
4 "Chicago Silently Mourns Its Dead," *New York Times*, January 1, 1904, 1.
5 "Nineteen Chicago Theatres Closed," *New York Times*, January 2, 1904, 1.
6 The Chicago fire marshal's annual report for 1903 describes the great, rolling sheet of flame that suddenly burst upward from the Iroquois Theater's stage toward the open vents at the back of the auditorium when stagehands opened the backstage doors to escape. Many people immediately suffocated in their seats from lack of oxygen. See Nat Brandt, *Chicago Death Trap: The Iroquois Theatre Fire of 1903* (Carbondale: Southern Illinois University Press, 2003), for a historical account of the disaster.
7 Quote by Samuel G. Nixon in the *New York Times*, December 31, 1903.
8 McDougall, *The Group Mind*, 36.
9 See also Le Bon, *The Crowd*; Park, *The Crowd and the Public*; Ross, *Social Psychology*; Sidis, *The Psychology of Suggestion*; and de Tarde, *The Laws of Imitation*.
10 Durkheim, *The Elementary Forms of Religious Life*. For a critique of the imperial presumptions and colonizing contexts of the "grand ethnography" on which Durkheim's work is based, see Connell, "Why Is Classical Theory Classical?"
11 Australian aboriginal cultures are Durkheim's primary focus, with indigenous cultures in the United States providing supplemental material. For his reference to the Iroquois, see Durkheim, *The Elementary Forms of Religious Life*, 86n8.
12 Clough, preface to *The End(s) of Ethnography*, xxiii. See also Artaud, *The Theater and Its Double*. Artaud, whose work becomes enormously influential in the 1960s in experimental theater and the new genres of performance art, also has a profound impact on cultural criticism of the last several decades, although he remains an obscure figure for most social scientists. For a wide-ranging consider-

ation of Artaud's legacy in terms of theory, politics, and performance, see Scheer, *Antonin Artaud: A Critical Reader.*

13   "Originary technicity" is Jacques Derrida's term for the writing technologies or devices that produce meanings; see Clough, *The End(s) of Ethnography*, xiv.

14   Clough, *The End(s) of Ethnography*, xxiii.

15   Artaud, *The Theater and Its Double*, 15.

16   Ibid., 17.

17   Ibid., 56.

18   Brown, *Politics out of History*, 89–90.

19   Deleuze, *Desert Islands and Other Texts*, 262.

20   Butler, "Performative Acts and Gender Constitution," 272.

21   Laurie Anderson, lyrics from "Same Time Tomorrow," in *Stories from the Nerve Bible* (Difficult Music BMI, 1994).

22   Foucault, *The Archaeology of Knowledge*, 129; italics in original.

23   Foucault, "Two Lectures," 204; italics mine.

24   Cantril, *The Invasion from Mars.*

25   See the official diagnosis for "panic disorder" in American Psychiatric Association, *Diagnostic and Statistical Manual of Mental Disorders*, 3rd ed., 231–32.

26   See Foucault, *The Birth of the Clinic*, 22–36.

27   Foucault, *The History of Sexuality*, vol. 1, 142–44.

28   Nikolas Rose, "Engineering the Human Soul," 352–53.

29   Ibid., 360.

30   Taussig, "Viscerality, Faith, and Skepticism," 281.

31   Healy, *The Anti-depressant Era*, 111, 113–14.

32   For a perfect, perverse example of how rationality mimes "madness" in the interests of the production of value, see Martin, "The Rationality of Mania."

33   Bernays was in fact the double nephew of Freud: his mother was Freud's sister, and his father was the brother of Freud's wife. See Bernays, *Crystallizing Public Opinion* and *Propaganda.*

34   Rauschning, quoted in Bernays, "Morale: First Line of Defense," 32.

35   Bernays, "Morale: First Line of Defense," 33–34.

36   Taussig, "Viscerality, Faith, and Skepticism," 290.

37   Baudrillard, *Forget Baudrillard*, 11–12, 15.

38   Baudrillard, *The Ecstasy of Communication*, 132.

39   Haraway, "Possible Worlds," 243.

40   Haraway, *Simians, Cyborgs, and Women*, 46.

41   I'm referring to Hitchcock's *Psycho* (1959), in which Norman, the psycho-killer, murders Marion, the secretary, in a symptomatic Cold War shower.

42   Sedgwick, *Touching Feeling*, 130.

43   Works in this genre that have most influenced my thinking include Baudrillard, *The Ecstasy of Communication* and *In the Shadow of the Silent Majorities*; Kroker and Cook, *The Postmodern Scene*; Pfohl, *Death at the Parasite Cafe*; and Virilio, *War and Cinema.*

44   Melley, *Empire of Conspiracy*, 5–6.

45 Sedgwick contrasts "paranoid" with "reparative" tendencies in social theory—noting that they are not mutually exclusive. See Sedgwick, *Touching Feeling*, 150.

46 Caruth, introduction to *Trauma: Explorations in Memory*, 5.

47 "Trauma studies" nominally joins together a wide, interdisciplinary range of work that is often quite heterogeneous. For a recent engagement with a wide breadth of the literature, see Cvetkovich, *An Archive of Feelings*, chap. 1; see also Caruth, *Unclaimed Experience* and *Trauma: Explorations in Memory*; Herman, *Trauma and Recovery*; Leys, *Trauma: A Genealogy*; and Young, *The Harmony of Illusions*.

48 Cvetkovich, *An Archive of Feelings*, 18.

49 Caruth, *Trauma*, 4.

50 If feminist hysteria studies was organized by an analytics of gendered power and sexual difference, trauma studies at its best can be said to extend that analytics to include the dynamics of war, genocide, population displacements, state-sponsored and stateless terror, and everyday traumas of systematic oppression. "Trauma discourse has allowed me to ask about the connections between girls like me feeling bad and world historical events," writes Cvetkovich (*An Archive of Feelings*, 3). Feminist hysteria studies, for the most part, located "girls feeling bad" in a more limited historical horizon. For influential work in psychoanalytic feminist hysteria studies, see Bernheimer and Kahane, *In Dora's Case*; Cixous and Clément, *The Newly Born Woman*; Gallop, *The Daughter's Seduction*; and Irigaray, *Speculum of the Other Woman*. For a historical overview and analysis of hysteria studies, see Micale, *Approaching Hysteria*.

51 Foucault, "Two Lectures," 203.

52 Ibid.

53 Cixous and Clément, *The Newly Born Woman*, 96.

54 The tormented psychoanalyst asks, "Why do the confessions extorted by torture have so much similarity to my patients' narratives during psychological treatment?" (Sigmund Freud, *Origins of Psychoanalysis*, quoted in Cixous and Clément, *The Newly Born Woman*, 12).

55 Irigaray, *This Sex Which Is Not One*, 29.

56 Caruth, *Trauma*, 4–5.

57 Gordon, *Ghostly Matters*, 22, 25.

58 Foucault, "First Preface to *Histoire de la folie à l'age classique*," 6. This sentence appears only in the first French edition of the book. Foucault deletes it from later editions.

59 Leys, *Trauma: A Genealogy*, 31. Leys narrates the analytic tensions between this "mimetic" paradigm of trauma, and a conflicting and often concurrent "antimimetic" paradigm that rejects the centrality of a suggestive-hypnotic rapport and argues for individualist notions of autonomy and responsibility.

60 Ibid., 32.

61 Ibid., 33.

62 Sulloway, *Freud, Biologist of the Mind*, 33.

63 Freud and Breuer, *Studies on Hysteria*, 6.

64 See Leys, *Trauma: A Genealogy*, chaps. 3 and 7.

65 Ibid., 119.

66 This rich literature extends far beyond what I'm delimiting as "scholarship," into the fields of science fiction, art, architecture, and literature. For a sampling of "cyber-scholarship," see Dyer-Witheford, *Cyber-Marx*; Edwards, *The Closed World*; Gerovitch, *From Newspeak to Cyberspeak*; Gray, *The Cyborg Handbook* and *Cyborg Citizen*; Haraway, "Manifesto for Cyborgs" and *Simians, Cyborgs, and Women*; Hayles, *How We Became Posthuman*; and Heims, *The Cybernetics Group*.

67 Hayles, *How We Became Posthuman*, 18. See also Hayles's discussion of the complexities of "information," both as a mathematically rigorous concept divorced from any notion of meaning, and as a suggestive metaphor that slips and slides in all kinds of meaningful (and ideologically loaded) directions, as cybernetics itself moves beyond mathematics into social, neurological, and political discourses (50–63).

68 Cvetkovich, *An Archive of Feelings*, 44.

69 Ibid., 43.

70 Park, *The Crowd*, 123.

71 Pfohl, *Death at the Parasite Cafe*, 43–45.

72 In the field of U.S. sociology, a number of texts from the late 1980s to the present have challenged stylistically and theoretically what might count as sociological discourse, drawing on developments in feminist, critical race and antiracist, queer, poststructural, psychoanalytic, and postcolonial theory. See Clough, *The End(s) of Ethnography* and *Feminist Thought*; Collins, *Black Feminist Thought*; Gordon, *Ghostly Matters*; Lemert, *Sociology after the Crisis*; Pfohl, "Twilight of the Parasites"; Seidman, "The End of Sociological Theory" and "The Political Unconscious of the Human Sciences"; and Orr, "Theory on the Market" and "Re/Sounding Race, Re/Signifying Ethnography." The journal *Qualitative Inquiry*, under the editorship of Norman Denzin, was a regular publication site for experimental and performative sociological writing. In 1990, Joseph Schneider, editor of *Social Problems*, devoted a special issue of the journal to emergent work in postmodern sociology; see *Social Problems* 37, no. 4 (November 1990).

73 Richman, "Anthropology and Modernism in France," 199. See also Hollier, *The College of Sociology*. Participants in the Collège included Georges Bataille, Michel Leiris, Roger Callois, and, briefly, Walter Benjamin.

74 For a discussion of Dada in the context of Situationist and poststructuralist practices emerging in the 1960s, see Plant, *The Most Radical Gesture*, 39–49.

75 Gordon, *Ghostly Matters*, 42.

76 Taussig, *The Nervous System*, 45.

77 Clough, *The End(s) of Ethnography*, 133.

78 Jennifer Natalya Fink, "Conclusion: Pushing through the Surface," 251.

79 New methods are particularly urgent if "social science [is] itself an enforcement of certain practices of reading and writing, similar to those promoted by mass media communication technologies" (Clough, *The End(s) of Ethnography*, 133).

80 Edwards, *The Closed World*, 14.

81 Gordon, *Ghostly Matters*, 37.

82 Haraway, *Simians, Cyborgs, and Women*, 162–63.

83 Ibid., 176.

84 I am using the term "performative writing" to refer to a broad range of politically engaged stylistic experiments with genre and form, that is, writing that recognizes and performs itself as a material practice *that can change shape* and can shape change. For explicit discussions of performative writing, see Phelan, "Introduction: The Ends of Performance"; Pollock, "Performing Writing"; and Sedgwick, "Teaching 'Experimental Critical Writing.' " For early influential examples outside sociology of writing-that-performs, see Ronnell, *The Telephone Book*; Trinh Minh-ha, *Woman, Native, Other*; and Williams, *The Alchemy of Race and Rights*.

85 Trinh, 20.

86 Park, *The Crowd*, 123.

87 Phelan, "Introduction: The Ends of Performance," 9.

88 Taussig, *The Nervous System*, 47.

89 Pfohl, *Death at the Parasite Cafe*, 98. See also Pfohl's discussion of collage, 97–101.

2. The Martian in the Machine

1 From the 1938 radio play by Howard Koch based on H. G. Wells's *The War of the Worlds* (1897), published in Koch, *The Panic Broadcast*, 68–69.

2 Irigaray, *Speculum of the Other Woman*, 136; italics in original.

3 All phrases in boldface in the next six paragraphs are quotes from the radio play adaptation of *The War of the Worlds*, in Koch, *The Panic Broadcast*, 33–80.

4 *New York Times*, October 31, 1938, quoted in Koch, *The Panic Broadcast*, 18–22.

5 John Houseman, CBS coproducer of the radio play, quoted in Koch, *The Panic Broadcast*, 85.

6 See Koch, *The Panic Broadcast*, 17–23; and Cantril, *Invasion from Mars*, 61–62.

7 Dorothy Thompson, "On the Record," *New York Tribune*, November 2, 1938, quoted in Koch, *The Panic Broadcast*, 92.

8 *Daily News*, October 31, 1938, quoted in Koch, *The Panic Broadcast*, 22.

9 "Preparedness vs. Panic Issue," *Variety*, November 2, 1938, quoted in Koch, *The Panic Broadcast*, 94.

10 Thompson, quoted in Koch, *The Panic Broadcast*, 92.

11 Cantril, *Invasion from Mars*, 159.

12 Koch, *The Panic Broadcast*, 13.

13 Reported in *Variety*, November 2, 1938, quoted in Koch, *The Panic Broadcast*, 95.

14 Koch, *The Panic Broadcast*, 86.

15 The audience for the CBS Mercury Theater increased from approximately 4 percent of the total radio listening audience to almost 8 percent. See Cantril, *Invasion from Mars*, 61, 56n5.

16 Robert K. Merton, introduction to *The Crowd: A Study of the Popular Mind*, by Gustave Le Bon, xxxiv.

17 Thompson, quoted in Koch, *The Panic Broadcast*, 93.

18 All phrases in boldface in the next two paragraphs are from the radio play in Koch.

19 Haraway, "Signs of Dominance," 135.

20 Park, *The Crowd*, 23–24.

21 For early and influential discussions of suggestibility, see Le Bon, *The Crowd*; Park, *The Crowd*; Ross, *Social Psychology*; McDougall, *Group Mind*; and Freud, *Group Psychology*.

22 Park, *The Crowd*, 18–20.

23 Sidis, quoted in Ross, *Social Psychology*, 26.

24 By the early 1920s, Le Bon's *The Crowd* was in its twenty-ninth edition and had been translated into sixteen languages. In 1960, Robert K. Merton called Le Bon a kind of "sociological prophet" in foreseeing issues that would continue to fascinate and trouble the discipline, including mass movements, the significance of popular culture, and the "role of the unconscious in social behavior" (Merton, introduction, xxxii, vii).

25 Le Bon, *The Crowd*, 27–34.

26 These race, class, and gender associations are drawn abundantly in Le Bon, *The Crowd*, 38–39, 46, 50, 81–82, 157–58. See also the remarkably racist and imperialist treatise by Le Bon, *The Psychology of Peoples*; and Sigmund Freud's parallels between the modern crowd and "primitive mental activity" in *Group Psychology*, 15, 69–70. For a critical history of how symptoms of individualized pathologies were transferred on to features of crowd behavior via popular beliefs in the existence of a racial or national "spirit," see Faber, "Suggestion: Metaphor and Meaning."

27 See Park, *The Crowd*, 47; Le Bon, *The Crowd*, 36–39, 54–55; and Ross, *Social Psychology*, 70–71. For a historical analysis of the reactionary and class-based conceptions of crowd psychology, see Leach, "Mental Epidemics."

28 Le Bon, *The Crowd*, 126.

29 McDougall, *Group Mind*, 36.

30 Freud, *Group Psychology*, 35–37. See also Freud's solution to the "riddle of suggestion" in the libidinal energy of what he calls group "love" (26–31).

31 Park, *The Crowd*, 45. In "Symbiosis and Socialization," Park writes: "In contrast with the organized or psychological crowd is the crowd in dissolution, i.e., the crowd in a state of panic" (10).

32 Park, *The Crowd*, 57–58.

33 Ibid., 57.

34 Ibid., 60–61.

35 Ibid., 80.

36 McDougall, *Introduction to Social Psychology*, 83; italics in original.

37 Irigaray, *Speculum*, 137; italics mine.

38 Cantril, *Invasion from Mars*, 147.

39 Cantril, foreword to *Invasion from Mars*, v.

40 Ibid., vii–viii.

41 "Anatomy of a Panic," *Time*, April 15, 1940, 58–59.

42 This and all following passages in boldface in this section are quotes from the interview protocol used in Cantril's study. The questionnaire is reprinted in Cantril, *Invasion from Mars*, appendix B, 213–22.

43 For a description of the rise of empiricism and "the objective method" in social psychology by one of its better-known practitioners, see Allport, "The Historical Background of Modern Social Psychology."

44 LaPiere, *Collective Behavior*, 455n2.

45 Cantril, *Invasion from Mars*, viii.

46 Ibid.

47 Ibid., x.

48 Ibid.

49 Ibid., 111, 112, 117.

50 Ross, *Social Psychology*, 63.

51 Ross, quoted in Karpf, *American Social Psychology*, 142.

52 Ross, *Social Psychology*, 63.

53 Cantril, *Invasion from Mars*, 55–56. One of the two surveys is done by George Gallup with the express purpose of measuring the audience for the broadcast of *The War of the Worlds*; the other is conducted by an industry research organization that regularly measures radio audience size.

54 Ibid., 58, 63.

55 Ibid., xii. The interviewers, all women, are identified as Mrs. Paul Trilling, Frances Ginevsky, Mrs. Richard Robinson, and Mrs. David Green.

56 Ibid., 88, 97; italics in original.

57 Ibid., 102–4. See table 3 on p. 104 for a summary of results. Owing to limited labor resources, only 460 of the 920 CBS interviews were analyzed by the Princeton Radio Research staff.

58 Ibid., 107.

59 Ibid., 117.

60 Ibid., 130–31, 131n3, 135n5. Cantril's seven criteria for measuring susceptibility to suggestion are insecurity, phobias, amount of worry, lack of self-confidence, fatalism, religiosity, and church attendance.

61 Ibid., 136–37.

62 Ibid., 202–5.

63 MacLeish, *Panic: A Play in Verse*, 9. The play, about the aftereffects of the 1929 stock market crash, was produced in New York City in 1935. The lead role of McGafferty, a powerful banker and industrialist, was played by nineteen-year-old Orson Welles.

64 Irigaray, *Speculum*, 143.

65 For a history of John D. Rockefeller's establishment of Standard Oil, see Collier and Horowitz, *The Rockefellers*, 15–29.

66 *The American Heritage Dictionary of the English Language* (Boston: Houghton Mifflin, 1980), 1123.

67 John D. Rockefeller was an early mastermind of the "corporate trust," a labyrinthine legal and financial structure designed to protect Standard Oil and its subsidiary companies from public scrutiny, and to enable the building of corporate monopolies. See Collier and Horowitz, *The Rockefellers*, 36–37.

68 "The Essential Value of Radio to All Types of Listeners," Rockefeller Archives Center (RAC), record group 1.1, series 200, box 271, folder 3234. For an earlier

draft of the proposal, see Hadley Cantril to John Marshall, December 31, 1936, RAC, record group 1.1, series 200, box 271, folder 3233.

69 "Essential Value of Radio"; italics mine.

70 Rockefeller Foundation Board Minutes, May 21, 1937, RAC, record group 1.1, series 200, box 271, folder 3233.

71 Rogers, *History of Communication Study*, 268.

72 Ibid., 272.

73 George Gallup to John Marshall, May 19, 1937, RAC, record group 1.1, series 200, box 271, folder 3234.

74 Rockefeller Foundation Board Minutes, May 21, 1937.

75 Rockefeller Foundation notes on "Princeton Project," RAC, record group 1.1, series 200, box 271, folder 3234. Cantril cites several reasons for the broadcast industry's lack of support for this kind of research, including the industry's approach to the radio listener as nothing more than a potential consumer, and its investment in a notion of "mass" popular appeal that recognizes no differences in "taste" between one socioeconomic group and another. "To indicate otherwise reduces the scope of the broadcaster's potential audience, and, hence, limits his [advertising] rates." See Cantril to Marshall, May 11, 1937.

76 For an intellectual and institutional biography of Lazarsfeld, see Rogers, *History of Communication Study*, 244–315.

77 Paul Lazarsfeld, "Princeton Radio Research Project," speech delivered in Columbus, Ohio, May 16, 1938, RAC, record group 1.1, series 200, box 271, folder 3236.

78 On the historical synergy between market research and the radio industry, see Rogers, *History of Communication Study*, 266–67.

79 Paul Lazarsfeld, "On the Use of Elaborate Personal Interviews for the Princeton Radio Research Project," presentation to senior staff members of the Princeton Project, June 1938, RAC, record group 1.1, series 200, box 271, folder 3236. See also Lazarsfeld, introduction to *Radio and the Printed Page*, xi–xviii.

80 Lazarsfeld, "Princeton Radio Research Project."

81 Rogers, *History of Communication Study*, 271.

82 Cantril, *Invasion from Mars*, xiii, 77, 103.

83 Ibid., xiii. Neither archival material nor Cantril's book makes clear where the funding for this study comes from—perhaps from Frank Stanton's research budget at CBS?

84 Ibid., xii. Regarding the General Education Board's $3,000 emergency grant to Cantril for the panic study, see Hadley Cantril to Robert Havighurst, November 21, 1938, RAC, record group 918, series 1, sub-series 3, box 361, folder 3723; Charles W. Duke to H. B. van Wesep, January 24, 1940, RAC, record group 918, series 1, sub-series 2, box 361, folder 3723; and "Princeton University Radio Research: Study of Public Reactions to the Orson Wells [*sic*] Broadcast, December 1, 1938–May 31, 1939, document dated June 21, 1939, RAC, record group 918, series 1, sub-series 2, box 361, folder 3723.

85 Cantril, *Invasion from Mars*, 55.

86 Rogers, *History of Communication Study*, 279.

87   Hadley Cantril, "Proposed Study of 'Mass Hysteria,'" RAC, record group 918, series 1, sub-series 2, box 361, folder 3723.

88   For a historical overview of the relation between the study of propaganda and the emergence of communications research, see Rogers, *History of Communication Study*, 203–43. For a history of the Rockefeller Foundation's role in promoting the new field of communications studies for understanding, and possibly deploying, propaganda techniques and public opinion control, see Brett Gary, *The Nervous Liberals*, 85–129.

89   Hadley Cantril to Robert Havighurst, November 21, 1938.

90   Cantril, *Invasion from Mars*, 131.

91   Ibid., 135–39.

92   Lazarsfeld, *Radio and the Printed Page*, 255–57.

93   T. W. Adorno, "On a Social Critique of Radio Music," paper presented to the staff of the Princeton Radio Research Project, October 26, 1939, RAC, record group 1.1, series 200, box 273, folder 3247. For an account of Adorno's relation to the Princeton Radio Research Project, see Rogers, *History of Communication Study*, 280–83. For an analysis of how this first piece of empirical research by Adorno influenced his later and better-known social critiques, see Gillian Rose, *The Melancholy Science*, 80–81, 97–98, 103.

94   Adorno, "Radio Music."

95   Rogers, *History of Communication Study*, 282–83.

96   Ibid., 222, 280.

97   Rockefeller Communications Group, "Research in Mass Communications," quoted in Gary, *The Nervous Liberals*, 103. For an analysis of the group's turn to national security issues and public opinion control, see Gary, *The Nervous Liberals*, 94–109.

98   Cantril, *Invasion from Mars*, 47.

99   Denning, *The Cultural Front*, 381.

100   For a discussion of Welles's and MacLeish's involvement in a community of performers, writers, and artists developing forms of antifascist theater in the late 1930s, see Denning, "The Politics of Magic: Orson Welles's Allegories of Anti-Fascism," in his *The Cultural Front*, 382–84.

101   Cantril, *Invasion from Mars*, 47.

102   This section is composed entirely of quotes from Cantril's *The Invasion from Mars*. The narrative of Miss Jane Dean appears in chapter 8, "The Individual Case," and all passages in regular type in this section are quotes from Hadley Cantril's descriptions in that chapter, 179–82. All passages in boldface in this section are quotes from seven different people interviewed for Cantril's study (in order of their citation), 89–90, 96, 158, 160, 99, 100, 91, 93.

103   Letter published in London's *Sunday Times* (February 1991), quoted in Alexander Cockburn, "The Press and the 'Just War,'" *The Nation*, February 18, 1991, 186.

104   MacLeish, *Air Raid: A Verse Play for Radio*, 34–35. The play was aired over the CBS network on October 27, 1938, with Orson Welles in the studio. Three days later, Welles's Mercury Theater performed *The War of the Worlds* on CBS.

105   Hadley Cantril, "Causes and Control of Riot and Panic," 669.
106   Ibid., 670, 675.
107   Sullivan, "Psychiatric Aspects of Morale." Sullivan opens the essay with a description of panic, which he defines as that "demoralization so complete that the term scarcely applies" (279).
108   Ibid., 288.
109   Park, "Morale and the News," 360.
110   Sullivan, "Psychiatric Aspects of Morale," 292–95. In his most "cold-blooded proposition," Sullivan suggests that people who "cannot reasonably be converted into trustworthy citizens of the nation at war" might best be dealt with by placing them "out of harm's way in a civilized version of the concentration camp" (294).
111   Shils, "Note on Governmental Research on Attitudes and Morale." For a historical analysis of the pursuit of specifically "democratic" techniques of managing publics and groups, see Nikolas Rose, *Inventing Our Selves*, 116–49.
112   Shils, "Note on Governmental Research," 472–73.
113   Park, "Morale and the News," 374–77.
114   Ibid., 366.
115   Angell, "Radio and National Morale," 353.
116   Wanger, "The Role of Movies in Morale," 380, 382–83.
117   Park, "Morale and the News," 363.
118   Ibid.
119   Sullivan, "Psychiatric Aspects of Morale," 288.
120   Shils, "Note on Governmental Research," 472.
121   Park, "Morale and the News," 366–67.
122   Stouffer, introduction to *The American Soldier*, 12.
123   Ibid., 37. See also Hyman, *Taking Society's Measure*, 72–74.
124   Stouffer, introduction to *The American Soldier*, 11. For comment on the classified nature of the Research Branch's activities, see Hyman, *Taking Society's Measure*, 79.
125   General Frederick Osborn, foreword to Stouffer, *The American Soldier*, vii.
126   Hyman, *Taking Society's Measure*, 64–65.
127   Ibid., 91.
128   Daniels, foreword to *Guide to the Reports of the United States Strategic Bombing Survey*, xvi–xvii.
129   Interview with German civilian, quoted in U.S. Strategic Bombing Survey (USSBS), *Effects of Strategic Bombing on German Morale*, 19. All subsequent quotes in boldface in this section are also from morale survey interviews in the same volume, 19–20.
130   See MacIsaac, *Strategic Bombing*, 4.
131   USSBS, *Effects of Strategic Bombing on German Morale*, iv. The full scope of the USSBS investigations included research into the total military, economic, and social effects of bombing and were conducted by specialists in rail transport and water, munitions, oil, machine tools, steel, civil engineering, and aircraft design and manufacturing. See MacIsaac, *Strategic Bombing*.

132 USSBS, *Effects of Strategic Bombing on German Morale*, 109.

133 Ibid., 24.

134 Hyman, *Taking Society's Measure*, 96.

135 Ibid., 92–93.

136 USSBS, *Effects of Strategic Bombing on German Morale*, 1.

137 Ibid., 1, 22. Explanations for this finding ranged from the problem of the mass exodus of civilians from the most heavily bombed cities — so that many civilians who suffered most were not interviewed — to the effects of apathy and indifference among a population subjected to persistent air raids.

138 Daniels, foreword to *Guide to the Reports*, xxiii.

139 USSBS, *Effects of Atomic Bombs on Hiroshima and Nagasaki*, iii.

140 Irigaray, *Speculum*, 134.

141 Wells, *War of the Worlds*, 242.

142 Ibid., 240.

143 Hyman, *Taking Society's Measure*, 123. For a more complete account of the methods used in the morale survey of Japanese civilians, see USSBS, *Effects of Strategic Bombing on Japanese Morale*, 9–13.

144 Wells, *War of the Worlds*, 240.

145 USSBS, *Effects of Atomic Bombs on Hiroshima and Nagasaki*, 33.

146 By the time of Japan's surrender, the U.S. air offensive, including both conventional and atomic bombings, had bombed five hundred targets, destroying an average of 43 percent of Japan's sixty-six largest cities, with an estimated 900,000 people killed and 1.3 million injured by the attacks. Over 8.5 million people were evacuated from cities as a result of the air attacks. See USSBS, *Effects of Strategic Bombing on Japanese Morale*, 1–2. This special report on the findings of the morale survey summarized the United States' approach to total war: "The war against Japan exemplified clearly a number of the distinguishing characteristics of modern warfare. The attack was directed against the nation as a whole — not only against the army, the fleet, the factories and the supply lines, but also against the entire population and its ability and will to resist" (9).

147 Wells, *War of the Worlds*, 245.

148 USSBS, *Effects of Atomic Bombs on Hiroshima and Nagasaki*, 20–21.

149 Ibid., 22. The morale survey concluded that the atomic bombings were not a decisive factor in Japan's decision to surrender. "From the standpoint of the politics of surrender — and by August 1945 politics was the key — the atom bombing of Hiroshima and Nagasaki was not essential. From its studies of Japanese resources, military position, and ruling class politics, the Survey estimates that the government would have surrendered prior to 1 November and certainly before the end of the year, whether or not the atomic bombs had been dropped" (USSBS, *Effects of Strategic Bombing on Japanese Morale*, 4).

150 Wells, *War of the Worlds*, 349.

151 USSBS, *Effects of Atomic Bombs on Hiroshima and Nagasaki*, 21.

152 Wells, *War of the Worlds*, 248.

153 USSBS, *Effects of Atomic Bombs on Hiroshima and Nagasaki*, 36.

154 Wells, *War of the Worlds*, 248–49.

155 USSBS, *Effects of Atomic Bombs on Hiroshima and Nagasaki*, 38.

156 Ibid., 41–43.

157 Wells, *War of the Worlds*, 243.

3. "Keep Calm!" for the Cold War

1 Anne Parsons, quoted in Breines, "Alone in the 1950s," 22–23. *Diary of a Mental Patient* is Parsons's title for the journal she kept after being hospitalized at the Yale Psychiatric Institute in the fall of 1963.

2 Caldicott, *Missile Envy*, 186–87.

3 Douvan and Withey, "Some Attitudinal Consequences of Atomic Energy," 112.

4 Wylie, "Panic, Psychology, and the Bomb," 37; italics in original.

5 In foregrounding the U.S. practice of dropping atomic bombs on its "self," I am not forgetting U.S. Cold War practices of dropping bombs on others, particularly the lands destroyed and the peoples sickened or killed by U.S. atomic testing in the Marshall Islands of the South Pacific.

6 Cottrell and Eberhart, *American Opinion on World Affairs in the Atomic Age*, xvii.

7 Osborn, foreword to Cottrell and Eberhart, *American Opinion*, xii–xiii.

8 For an account of the establishment of NORC and the State Department–sponsored surveys, see Hyman, *Taking Society's Measure*, 139–57; also Simpson, *Science of Coercion*, 54–55. According to Hyman, who worked at NORC in the early postwar years and conducted some of the State Department surveys, 104 different surveys were contracted by the State Department before congressional debate over the secret funding terminated the contract in 1957. Each survey questionnaire was designed and administered to a nationwide sample of 1,200 subjects after a planning session between NORC and State Department officials. The secrecy of the research did not extend to survey findings: after the State Department had seen the findings, NORC staff members were permitted to release them publicly. But the State Department's role in requesting, designing, and funding the topic-specific research was kept secret. The State Department also permitted NORC to "sell" additional survey questions to other clients for inclusion in the survey instrument, and to occasionally include questions of interest to the NORC staff. See Hyman, *Taking Society's Measure*, 150–51, 155.

9 Freed, *Death in Washington*, 34.

10 Hyman, *Taking Society's Measure*, 150. For more information about Hadley Cantril's research career in relation to U.S. intelligence efforts and covert psychological operations, see Simpson, *Science of Coercion*, 80–81. Simpson identifies a $1 million grant, covertly channeled through the Rockefeller Foundation, from the CIA to Cantril and his colleague Lloyd Free in 1956 to carry out public opinion research in countries "of interest" to the CIA. On the Rockefeller Foundation's sponsorship of national-security-related communications research and propaganda analysis, see Gary, *The Nervous Liberals*, 109–29.

11 Cottrell and Eberhart, *American Opinion*, 14, 19.

12 Ibid., 18, 22, 24, 27, 20, 59–60.

13   Ibid., xvi, 16.

14   Weart, *Nuclear Fear*, 110.

15   "The Evaluation of the Atomic Bomb as a Military Weapon: The Final Report of the Joint Chiefs of Staff Evaluation Board for Operation Crossroads," June 30, 1947, quoted in Oakes, *The Imaginary War*, 35.

16   Oakes, *The Imaginary War*, 35–36.

17   *Civil Defense for National Security* (Washington: Government Printing Office, 1948), quoted in Oakes, *The Imaginary War*, 36.

18   Office of Civil Defense, *Panic Control and Prevention*, 71–72.

19   Douvan and Withy, "Some Attitudinal Consequences," 109–11.

20   Ibid., 114–17.

21   Wylie, "Panic, Psychology, and the Bomb," 63; italics in original.

22   Ibid., 38.

23   Ibid., 63, italics in original.

24   Strauss, "Concepts, Communication, and Groups," 110–11.

25   Mills, *The Sociological Imagination*, 67.

26   Strauss, "Research in Collective Behavior."

27   Strauss, "The Literature on Panic," 327.

28   Mills, *The Sociological Imagination*, 100–118.

29   Merton and Lazarsfeld, *Continuities in Social Research*. One of the voices critical of Stouffer's original *The American Soldier* is C. Wright Mills, who writes: "These studies, it seems to me, prove that it is possible for social research to be of administrative use without being concerned with the problems of social science. The results must surely be disappointing to anyone who wishes to understand something of the American soldier who was in the war" (Mills, *The Sociological Imagination*, 53). See also the critical reviews published by Robert S. Lynd and Alfred M. Lee on the managerial and social control aspects of the studies, cited in Madge, *Origins of Scientific Sociology*, 319–20.

30   Stouffer, "Afterthoughts," 198.

31   For an excellent history of the bureau's transformation from the Princeton Radio Research Project into a national center of methodological innovation in the social sciences, see Hyman, *Taking Society's Measure*, 179–222.

32   In 1920, Robert Park observes that sociological research is at the same level of development that psychology was before the introduction of laboratory methods at the turn of the century. See Park and Burgess, *Introduction to the Science of Sociology*, 44–45. For a history of the emergence of a "scientific psychology" and its research methods, see Danzinger, *Constructing the Subject*. For a history of attempts at an "objective method" for social psychology, see Allport, "The Historical Background of Modern Social Psychology," 46–48. For an overview of research methods in social psychology in the mid-1950s, see Lindzey, *Handbook of Social Psychology*, chaps. 7–15.

33   Martin Scheerer, "Cognitive Theory," in Lindzey, *Handbook of Social Psychology*, 92.

34   Strauss, "The Literature on Panic," 326.

35   Milgram and Toch, "Collective Behavior," 581. The earliest example I found of a

laboratory experiment on panic is a 1944 essay by John R. P. French Jr., "Organized and Unorganized Groups under Fear and Frustration." For a review of experimental approaches to panic, see Schultz, *Panic Behavior*.

36 Mintz, "Non-adaptive Group Behavior," 150.

37 Henry Elsner Jr., introduction to Park, *The Crowd*, xix–xx.

38 Strauss, "Concepts, Communication, and Groups," 109; italics mine.

39 Mintz, "Non-adaptive Group Behavior," 158.

40 Ibid.

41 Ibid., 152.

42 Swanson, "A Preliminary Laboratory Study of the Acting Crowd."

43 Ibid., 522; italics mine.

44 Ibid., 523.

45 Ibid., 528.

46 Ibid., 523.

47 Office of Civil Defense, *Panic Control and Prevention*, 63, 76; italics mine.

48 Sherwood, "The Third World War," 19, 22.

49 Ibid., 27.

50 Boyle, "Washington under the Bomb," 20.

51 Murrow, "A-Bomb Mission to Moscow," 19.

52 "Operation Eggnog," editorial statement, *Collier's*, October 27, 1951, 6–10.

53 *Report of the Project East River, Part IX*, "Information and Training for Civil Defense," v.

54 Federal Civil Defense Administration (FCDA), *Annual Report for 1951*, 1–2.

55 Office of Civil Defense, *Panic Control and Prevention*, 7.

56 FCDA, *Annual Report for 1951*, 11. See *Survival under Atomic Attack* (Washington: U.S. Government Printing Office, 1950).

57 *Survival under Atomic Attack*, 12.

58 Ibid., 24–27, 31, 16–17.

59 FCDA, *Annual Report for 1951*, 14–15. The FCDA's motion picture program was organized in close collaboration with the film industry, which provided the capital, directed the films, and organized their distribution. The FCDA provided information and "technical consultation." The now famous Cold War film classic *Duck and Cover* (1951) was produced through this arrangement.

60 For a summary of the FCDA's media activities, see *Annual Report for 1951*, 10–15; see also FCDA, *Annual Report for 1952*, 43–49; *Annual Report for 1953*, 67–77; and *Annual Report for 1954*, 90–96.

61 Millard Caldwell, "Letter of Transmittal" to President Truman, April 18, 1952, in FCDA, *Annual Report for 1951*, v.

62 Ibid., vii. For an analysis of the demands of "total defense," see *Report of the Project East River, Part IX*, viii.

63 Caldwell to Truman, in FCDA, *Annual Report for 1951*, v.

64 *Report of the Project East River, Part IX*, 3.

65 *Report of the Project East River, Part IX*, i–v. See the discussion of "self-help defense" and the privatization of civil defense in McEnaney, *Civil Defense Begins at Home*, 7–8, 52–60.

66 Oakes, *The Imaginary War*, 47.

67 Legally restricted to the manipulation of psychological affairs beyond the U.S. borders, the Psychological Strategy Board's relations to *Project East River* remained unofficial and secret. See Oakes, *The Imaginary War*, 50–51.

68 Oakes, *The Imaginary War*, 51.

69 I use the phrase "psychological warfare" in the sense defined, for example, in a U.S. civil defense guide: "Psychological warfare consists of activities which communicate ideas and information intended to affect the minds, emotions, and actions of people. Its purpose is to reduce [or induce] morale and the will to fight" (Office of Civil Defense, *Panic Control and Prevention*, 8).

70 See Oakes, *The Imaginary War*, 62–71.

71 "Panic Prevention and Control," appendix IXB in *Report of the Project East River, Part IX*, 56–57.

72 Ibid., 55, 57–59, 62, 65.

73 *New York Times*, May 6, 1955.

74 FCDA, *Annual Report for 1955*, 77–78.

75 Ibid., 44, 6.

76 Ahlgren and Martin, "From Dante to Doomsday," 26.

77 For an account of Operation Doorstep, see FCDA, *Annual Report for 1953*, 58–60; Weart, *Nuclear Fear*, 132–33; and Ahlgren and Martin, "From Dante to Doomsday," 26, which includes images from the blast site.

78 FCDA, *Annual Report for Fiscal Year 1956*, 58.

79 For a brief discussion of the largely unwritten history of civil defense considerations in building the national U.S. interstate highway system, which was designed by the National System of Defense and Interstate Highways, see Castillo, "Thermonuclear Family Values," 63.

80 Miller, "Communication and the Information Theory," 29.

81 Wiener, *Human Use of Human Beings*, 110.

82 Fremont-Smith, "Orientation Address," 4–8.

83 See Frank Fremont-Smith, "History and Development of the Conference Program," Fremont-Smith Papers, Countway Library of Medicine, Harvard Medical School.

84 Heims, *The Cybernetics Group*, 164–65; also Fremont-Smith, "History of the Conference Program," 8–9.

85 Fremont-Smith, "History of the Conference Program," n.p.; Lawrence K. Frank was the executive who moved from Rockefeller to the Macy Foundation, bringing with him the idea of small, informal conferences for a cross-disciplinary nucleus of people who met over a several-year period.

86 Ibid.

87 Galdston, "The Conference as an Essay in Morale," in *Panic and Morale*, 1.

88 Social scientists participating in the preparatory conferences included Alvin Gouldner, Edward Shils, Steven Withey, Anselm Strauss, and Hans Zetterberg. See Galdston, *Transactions of the Conference on Morale*, 266.

89 Miller, "Communication and the Information Theory," 15–32.

90 Galdston, "Morale and Communication," in *Panic and Morale*, 11–12.

91   Ibid., 14–15.

92   Miller, "Communication and the Information Theory," 15–16.

93   Edwards, *The Closed World*, 223.

94   For an analysis of the military-industrial-academic triangles of research projects and personnel in which the Psycho-Acoustic Laboratory was situated, and a summary of George Miller's contributions to the emergence of cognitive science and the application of information theory to a "cybernetic psychology," see Edwards, *The Closed World*, 210–35.

95   Miller, "Communication and the Information Theory," 19–20.

96   Ibid., 20.

97   Ibid., 30.

98   Ibid., 31.

99   Roy Grinker, transcript of group discussion in Galdston, *Panic and Morale*, 127–29.

100 Ibid., 130; italics mine.

101 Fremont-Smith, "History of the Conference Program," n.p.

102 An important goal of Macy's sponsorship of cross-disciplinary meetings was the promotion and establishment of new interdisciplinary fields, with long-term research agendas and a core network of leading theorists, spokespeople, and researchers crystallizing out of the conference series. Warren McCulloch, who presided over the cybernetics conferences, became the first president of the American Society for Cybernetics, established in 1964; Heinz von Foerster, editor of the cybernetic conference transactions published by the Macy Foundation, was the chairman of the society's board of directors—see Fremont-Smith, "History of the Conference Program," 28. For a discussion of the relation between Macy sponsorship and the creation of new scientific subfields in post–World War II political economies of knowledge, see Heims, *The Cybernetics Group*, 166–67.

103 Lorente de Nó and John von Neumann are, respectively, the two presenters. See conference transcription, "Conference on Feedback Mechanisms and Circular Causal Systems in Biology and the Social Sciences," Fremont-Smith Papers.

104 "Conference on Feedback Mechanisms," 1; and Heims, *The Cybernetics Group*, 23–27.

105 Rosenblueth, Wiener, and Bigelow, "Behavior, Purpose and Teleology."

106 The philosophical implications of this modest essay are, according to Steve Heims, dramatic: "The Rosenblueth-Wiener-Bigelow ideas seemed to have vastly extended the realm accessible to exact science," suggesting that mathematical language could be applied to circular causality (previously believed to be impervious to precise quantification), and to a range of goal-oriented behaviors in human beings. See Heims, *The Cybernetics Group*, 16.

107 Wiener, *Cybernetics*, 10–11.

108 Ibid., 12–13.

109 Wiener, *Human Use of Human Beings*, 1.

110 Ibid., 3.

111 Ibid., 108–11. For a related discussion of cybernetics as the "science of form," see Bowker, "How to Be Universal," 110–11.

112 Wiener, *Human Use of Human Beings*, 8–9.

113 Fremont-Smith, "History of the Conference Program," n.p.

114 For a more elaborate discussion of the relation between cybernetics and behaviorism, see Edwards, *The Closed World*, 178–87. Edwards suggests that "the emerging cybernetic psychology was revolutionary because the tools it provided could be turned equally to the fully mathematized, behaviorist input/output description and the functionalist, internal-process description" (184).

115 Galdston, "Morale and Communication," in *Panic and Morale*, 7.

116 Office of Civil Defense, *Panic Control and Prevention*, 76.

117 Peterson, "Panic, the Ultimate Weapon?" 106–7, 109.

118 Ibid., 100.

119 Ibid., 105–7.

120 Ibid., 109.

121 FCDA, *Annual Report for Fiscal Year 1956*, 6–10.

122 Ibid., 2, 31, 26, 33, 39.

123 Ibid., 57–58. See FCDA, *Annual Report for 1955*, 78, for an estimate of the aggregate audience of over one-half billion viewers for the 1955 civil defense film program, based on figures predicting that each film would be seen by approximately 20 million people.

124 See Oakes, *The Imaginary War*, 58–59; and Weart, *Nuclear Fear*, 183, 157.

125 See Oakes, *The Imaginary War*, 149, 59.

126 I am indebted to the description of the film, which I later viewed at the National Archives in College Park, Maryland, offered in Oakes, *The Imaginary War*, 3–5.

127 *Alert Today—Alive Tomorrow*, quoted in Oakes, *The Imaginary War*, 5.

128 Talcott Parsons, "The Father Symbol," 40–41.

129 Sylvia Plath, "Daddy," in *Ariel* (New York: Harper and Row, 1961), 49.

130 Talcott Parsons, *Structure of Social Action*, vol. 1, 10–11, 6.

131 Alexander, *Modern Reconstruction of Classical Thought*, 7, 11; see also Bryan Turner and Robertson, "Introduction to Talcott Parsons," 1–21. For two influential critiques of Parsonian functionalism that articulate the broad disenchantment with Parsons's theory among sociologists in the 1960s, see Mills, *The Sociological Imagination*, 25–49; and Alvin Gouldner, *The Coming Crisis of Western Sociology*, 167–338.

132 For a historical analysis of Parsons's work and the post–World War II establishment of a theoretical canon in U.S. sociology, see Seidman, *Contested Knowledge*, 91–120. On the "Oedipal intensity" of the sociological canon, and an analysis of its efforts to rewrite the relation between sociological theory and nineteenth-century imperialist projects, see Connell, "Why Is Classical Theory Classical?"

133 See Talcott Parsons's introduction to part 2 of *The Structure of Social Action*, vol. 2, 474–86, for a summary of the traditions of positivistic versus idealistic empiricism, and his attempt to synthesize a solution to the methodological problem of a "frame of relation" in which to analyze human actions.

134 Talcott Parsons, *The Social System*, 3–23. For a succinct definition of "action," see Talcott Parsons and Edward Shils, *Toward a General Theory of Action*, 53.

135 Talcott Parsons, *The Social System*, 3; italics mine.

136 Ibid., vii. For a more extensive discussion of Parsons's work in relation to the Henderson seminars on Vilfredo Pareto (a social scientist with a background in mathematical physics), see Talcott Parsons, "On Building Social System Theory," 849–50. For a contextualization of Parsons's work in relation to the emergence of systems theory in the United States, see Lilienfeld, *The Rise of Systems Theory*, 196–99.

137 Talcott Parsons, *The Social System*, 20.

138 See Parsons's retrospective summary of the influence of this conference series in Talcott Parsons, "Field Theory and System Theory," 3. For published transactions of four of the conferences, see Grinker, *Toward a Unified Theory of Human Behavior*. An explicit formulation of the equivalence between Parsons's "theoretical frame of reference which I am accustomed to calling the 'theory of action'" and a "scheme for the analysis of *behavior* as a system" can be found in Talcott Parsons, "Social Structure and the Development of Personality," 81.

139 Talcott Parsons, "Field Theory and System Theory," 3–4, 8.

140 Ibid., 7, 9. See also Talcott Parsons, "Cause and Effect in Sociology," 52–53.

141 Talcott Parsons, "Field Theory and System Theory," 8.

142 Ibid., 6.

143 Talcott Parsons, "Building Social System Theory," 850; italics mine.

144 Alexander, *Modern Reconstruction*, 29–33.

145 Talcott Parsons, "The Superego and the Theory of Social Systems," "The Incest Taboo," and "The Father Symbol."

146 Talcott Parsons, "Building Social System Theory," 837.

147 Talcott Parsons, "Superego," 18, 33.

148 Ibid., 18–19, 20–29.

149 Talcott Parsons, "The Father Symbol," 38.

150 Ibid., 54, 41, 56.

151 Talcott Parsons, "The Incest Taboo," 72.

152 Anne Parsons, "Is the Oedipus Complex Universal?" 46.

153 Anne Parsons, quoted in Breines, "Alone in the 1950s," 11–12.

154 Breines, "Alone in the 1950s," 11–12.

155 Coser et al., introduction to Anne Parsons, *Belief, Magic, and Anomie*, xiv–xv.

156 Anne Parsons, "Expressive Symbolism in Witchcraft and Delusion," 185.

157 Talcott Parsons, *The Social System*, 384.

158 Anne Parsons, "Abstract and Concrete Images in Paranoid Delusions," 204–5.

159 Patient A, quoted in ibid., 205–6.

160 Patient B, quoted in ibid., 206.

161 Ibid., 201, 205, 209.

162 Anne Parsons, "Diffusion of Psychoanalytic Concepts," 285.

163 Ibid., 286–87.

164 Ibid., 288, 292.

165 Tiryakian, "Aftermath of a Thermonuclear Attack," 303.

166 Blumer, "Collective Behavior," in *Review of Sociology*, 132–33.

167 Ibid., 130. Use of the public/crowd/mass classification of collective behavior is a regular feature of Blumer's work and is incorporated in an early and influential

textbook in the emergent field; see Turner and Killian, *Collective Behavior*. See also Blumer, "Collective Behavior," in *Principles of Sociology*, 78–98.

168 Lindesmith and Strauss, *Social Psychology*, 456.

169 Turner and Killian, *Collective Behavior*, 12–13.

170 Blumer, "Collective Behavior," in *Review of Sociology*, 132.

171 Quarantelli, "Nature and Conditions of Panic," 267.

172 For other panic literature calling for more systematic empirical research and theoretical propositions, see Foreman, "Panic Theory"; Janis et al., "The Problem of Panic"; Quarantelli, "Behavior of Panic Participants"; and Tiryakian, "Aftermath of a Thermonuclear Attack." For an overview of panic research published in the 1950s and early 1960s, aimed at promoting more empirically rigorous investigation, see Schultz, *Panic Behavior*.

173 Quarantelli, "Behavior of Panic Participants," 187, 189.

174 Ibid., 187n1. For a brief history of the NORC Disaster Team research, see Hyman, *Taking Society's Measure*, 165–66.

175 Quarantelli, "Behavior of Panic Participants," 188; also Quarantelli, "Nature and Conditions of Panic," 269.

176 Quarantelli, "Behavior of Panic Participants," 189, 192–94.

177 Quarantelli, "Nature and Conditions of Panic," 275.

178 Janis et al., "Problem of Panic," 2; italics mine.

179 Janis, *Air War and Emotional Stress*, 1.

180 Ibid., 2–3, 7, 26–41.

181 Janis et al., "Problem of Panic," 1–2.

182 Ibid.

183 Foreman, "Panic Theory," 302–4.

184 Ibid., 299–300.

185 Ibid., 302.

186 Ibid., 303–4.

187 Ibid., 304.

188 Tiryakian, "Aftermath of a Thermonuclear Attack," 291–93.

189 Ibid., 292.

190 Ibid., 294–301.

191 Ibid., 298, 303.

192 Wiener, *Human Use of Human Beings*, 101.

193 Haraway, *Simians, Cyborgs, and Women*, 163.

194 See Heims, *The Cybernetics Group*; Bowker, "How to Be Universal"; and Pickering, "Cyborg History and the World War II Regime."

195 Haraway, "Signs of Dominance." See also Haraway, "The High Cost of Information." For a later reworking of her historical argument, see Haraway, "A Semiotics of the Naturalistic Field, from C. R. Carpenter to S. A. Altmann, 1930–1955," in *Primate Visions: Gender, Race, and Nature in the World of Modern Science* (New York: Routledge, 1989), 84–111.

196 Ruesch, "Social Communication and the Information Sciences," 899. See also Bowker, "How to Be Universal," 114–17.

197 Haraway, "High Cost of Information," 251.

198 Ibid., 250–52.

199 Wiener, *Human Use of Human Beings*, 96.

200 Ibid., 85–86.

201 Ibid., 94–95, 101.

202 Haraway, "Manifesto for Cyborgs," 83; italics in original.

203 Ibid., italics mine.

204 For biographical information on Norbert Wiener and his father, Leo, I am draw-
     ing from Heims, *John von Neumann and Norbert Wiener*, 1–25. Phrases in italics in
     this paragraph are excerpts from Norbert Wiener's autobiography, *Ex-Prodigy*,
     quoted in Heims, *John von Neumann*, 8–9.

205 Phrases in italics in this paragraph are from Wiener, *Human Use of Human
     Beings*, 69.

206 Morris Rosenfeld, quoted in Heims, *John von Neumann*, 3.

207 Wiener, *Human Use of Human Beings*, dedication page.

208 Ibid., 5.

209 Even, or even especially, the neurophysiological research conducted by the early
     cyberneticians involves a focus on reflex "feedback" occurring through electrical
     charges in the musculature; see Wiener, *Cybernetics*, 28–30.

210 Charles Dechert, "The Development of Cybernetics," 26–27.

211 Wiener, *Human Use of Human Beings*, 6. For a comprehensible but more tech-
     nical discussion of time series as a form of statistical analysis, and its application
     in communications engineering, see Norbert Wiener, *Time Series* (Cambridge:
     MIT Press, 1949), 1–4. It is through the concept of the time series that Wiener
     performs his consequential coupling of statistical mechanics and communica-
     tions engineering that lays the mathematical basis for cybernetics; see Wiener,
     Cybernetics, 16–18.

212 Le Bon, *The Crowd*, 68.

213 Bogard, *The Simulation of Surveillance*, 20.

214 FCDA, *Annual Report for 1955*, 32, 98.

215 Ibid., 33.

216 Ibid., 32. The FCDA's operational plan for local civil defense in the event of enemy
     attack involved a "thorough analysis of items such as the most probable tar-
     get area, probable damage and casualties, population distribution, industrial in- ·
     stallations, communications, transportation systems, evacuation routes, power
     and water facilities, medical resources, hospitals, jails, zoos, fire-fighting
     plans, potential assembly areas, feeding and welfare facilities, topography, pre-
     vailing winds, possible shelters, and many other items." The FCDA encouraged
     the development of operational plans in each of more than 180 critical target areas
     in the United States. See FCDA, *Annual Report for Fiscal Year 1956*, 27–28.

217 Oakes, *The Imaginary War*, 84.

218 Ibid., 85–86.

219 For example, local reports to the FCDA bomb damage assessment group—which
     estimated the hypothetical casualties and property damages during the Opera-
     tion Alert exercise—provided useful information for the FCDA's proposed de-
     velopment of "a system of automatic reporting of the time of attack, radius of

damage, and height and type of burst for every attacked area." See FCDA, *Annual Report for 1955*, 32, 92–93.

220 Ibid., 32.

221 All data on public participation are taken from FCDA regional reports in ibid., 182, 157, 165–66, 199.

222 Ibid., 165; Oakes, *The Imaginary War*, 86.

223 Oakes, *The Imaginary War*, 88–89.

224 Ibid., 87–89.

225 Ibid., 97–98.

226 Ibid., 102–3.

227 See FCDA, *Annual Report for 1955*, 35–37, for an evaluation of the 1955 exercises: "Although the exercise showed the Nation unprepared to cope with a thermonuclear attack, it concentrated the attention of the Nation on civil defense and provided Government agencies at all levels with valuable information on how to build a stronger civil defense program." The FCDA took the evaluations of Operation Alert exercises quite seriously, and the decision in 1958 to merge the FCDA with the Office of Defense Mobilization into a new agency, the Office of Civil and Defense Mobilization (OCDM), was based largely on problems in coordinating resource mobilization and information experienced during Operation Alert exercises in 1957. See FCDA, *Annual Report for Fiscal Year 1958*, 3.

228 Oakes, *The Imaginary War*, 92–93.

229 Ibid., 92, 95.

230 Ibid., 154.

231 Ibid., 163, 159.

232 Ibid., 160.

233 Ibid., 160, 158. One can see in Eisenhower's "logic" an early intuition of what will soon be formulated into the deterrence policy of mutual assured destruction, or MAD, which becomes institutionalized in the 1960s.

234 Val Peterson, National Security Council meeting, January 28, 1954, quoted in Oakes, *The Imaginary War*, 148.

235 Admiral Arthur Radford, National Security Council meeting, January 28, 1954, quoted in Oakes, *The Imaginary War*, 148–49.

236 Charles Wilson, Cabinet meeting, July 12, 1957, quoted in Oakes, *The Imaginary War*, 151.

237 Oakes, *The Imaginary War*, 151.

238 Frank Fremont-Smith et al., "The Human Effects of Nuclear Weapons Development," Report to the President, November 21, 1956, cited in Weart, *Nuclear Fear*, 135–36.

239 Anne Parsons, "Diffusion," 290n3.

240 Wiener, *Human Use of Human Beings*, 217.

241 Anne Parsons, quoted in Breines, "Alone in the 1950s," 18.

242 Ibid.

243 Anne Parsons to Jerome Frank, July 1, 1963, quoted in Breines, "Alone in the 1950s," 18–19.

244 A "training analysis" refers to a form of psychoanalytic treatment undertaken by

a candidate in training to become a psychoanalyst. The analysis is understood to be a necessary and central aspect of psychoanalytic training.

245 See Anne Parsons's acknowledgment to Dr. Grete Bibring's sponsorship in Anne Parsons, "Expressive Symbolism," 177. Talcott Parsons names Bibring as his analyst, and a "member of the original Freud circle in Vienna," in Talcott Parsons, "Building Social System Theory," 840.

246 Breines, "Alone in the 1950s," 12–14.

247 Anne Parsons, quoted in Breines, "Alone in the 1950s," 19.

248 Documentation of Anne Parsons's thinking on these issues exists in an eight-page letter to Betty Friedan, written in response to reading Friedan's *The Feminine Mystique*. See Breines, "Alone in the 1950s," 16–18.

249 Anne Parsons, quoted in Breines, "Alone in the 1950s," 19.

250 Anne Parsons, citing a communication from the Boston Psychoanalytic Institute, as quoted in Breines, "Alone in the 1950s," 19–20. Parsons, commenting on the institute's decision to expel her, writes: "It seems difficult to see why it was necessary to wait until six months after I had terminated a two-year analysis to communicate this to me. Being given the diagnosis of operable cancer after the time in which the operation could be carried out has passed must have about the same effect" (20).

251 Anne Parsons, "On Psychoanalytic Training for Research Purposes." Parsons writes: "Far from understanding the candidate as a person, the analyst may utilize his analysis to propagandize his own title to truth. . . . The analyst may, for example, stereotype aspects of the candidate's identity in his interpretations, either because he does not understand them or because they represent a threat to his own" (348).

252 Anne Parsons, quoted in Breines, "Alone in the 1950s," 23.

253 Haraway, "Signs of Dominance," 135.

254 Wiener, *Human Use of Human Beings*, 209–10.

255 For an overview of his mature theoretical system and the role played by a "cybernetic hierarchy of control," see Talcott Parsons, *Politics and Social Structure*, 5–33. In reviewing his own intellectual career, Parsons writes that "perhaps the most extensive convergence of all [in his lifelong theorization of the action system] has seemed to occur under the umbrella of the cybernetic conception, with its many associations and ramifications" (Talcott Parsons, "On Building Social System Theory," 870).

256 Haraway narrates the shift in the biological sciences from a pre–World War II discourse of "physiological functionalism" to the Cold War elaboration of "cybernetic functionalism." While her focus is on primatology, she offers a useful frame for studying a related transition in the social sciences; see Haraway, "Signs of Dominance," 187; and Haraway, *Primate Visions*, 93–111. The development of Parsonian "functionalism," particularly Parsons's shift from a concept of "homeostasis" analogous with organicist functionalism in the 1930s to notions of cybernetic feedback control in the 1950s, maps provocatively onto Haraway's analysis. See Talcott Parsons, "Cause and Effect," 51–54.

257 Haraway, "Signs of Dominance," 134–35.

258 In his analysis of cybernetics' strategies for becoming the "new universal science," Geof Bowker notes: "In the field of science studies, we have often taken laboratory science with its strategies to be the canonical science. . . . All sciences have gained enormous legitimacy from erecting barriers between 'inside' and 'outside.' However, there is also an effective strategy of making the inside and the outside converge—making people more like machines and machines more like people. . . . Instead of the laboratory being barricaded off from the world, the world will become a laboratory" (Bowker, "How to Be Universal," 123).

259 Talcott Parsons, "Some Reflections on the Problem of Psychosomatic Relationships in Health and Illness," 114.

260 This is not to say that the founding "fathers" of cybernetics were all equally hopeful about its applications as a science of society. Norbert Wiener clearly stated his reservations—partly based on the mathematical difficulties of obtaining adequately quantifiable data—regarding the use of cybernetics to solve social problems; see Wiener, *Cybernetics*, 34. But cybernetics stubbornly retained some of the ambitions of its conceptual predecessor, semiotics—that is, a desired unification of the social, biological, and humanistic sciences. The philosopher Charles Morris, a founding figure in semiotics, announced its dream of a common language uniting all the sciences: "The concept of sign may prove to be of importance in the unification of the social, psychological, and humanistic sciences in so far as these are distinguished from the physical and biological sciences. And since it will be shown that *signs are simply the objects studied by the biological and physical sciences related in certain complex functional processes*, any such unification of the formal sciences on the one hand, and the social, psychological, and humanistic sciences on the other, would provide the relevant material for the unification of these two sets of sciences with the physical and biological sciences"; see Morris, *Foundations of the Theory of Signs* (1938), quoted in Haraway, "Signs of Dominance," 167.

261 Talcott Parsons, "Psychosomatic Relationships," 114.

262 Talcott Parsons, "Theory in the Humanities and Sociology," 515.

263 "Thus the more general cultural patterns provide action systems with a highly stable structural anchorage quite analogous to that provided by the genetic materials of the species-type, focusing on the learned elements of action just as the genes focus upon the inheritable elements" (Parsons, *Politics and Social Structure*, 7). Parsons credits the analogy between culture and genetic codes to the biologist Alfred Emerson, who "put forward the conception that . . . the symbol was at the human cultural level the equivalent of the gene at the organic level" (Talcott Parsons, "Field Theory and System Theory," 5). See also Talcott Parsons, "On Building Social System Theory," 850, and "Theory in the Humanities," 514–16.

264 Talcott Parsons, "On Building Social System Theory," 870.

265 Talcott Parsons, *Politics and Social Structure*, 23; italics in original.

266 Talcott Parsons, "Cause and Effect," 55–56.

267 Parsons writes: "I refer to the idea that the degrees of freedom that make autonomous behavior possible are dependent on an individual's integration in a superindividual matrix" ("Cause and Effect," 57).

268 Dechert, "The Development of Cybernetics," 31; italics mine.

269 Talcott Parsons, "Psychosomatic Relationships," 123.

270 For Parsons's "precybernetic" formulation of sickness as deviance, see *The Social System*, 473–79. For later formulations shaped by cybernetic thought, see his "Definitions of Health and Illness in the Light of American Values and Social Structure" and "Some Reflections on the Problem of Psychosomatic Relationships in Health and Illness."

271 Talcott Parsons, "Definitions of Health and Illness," 259.

272 Ibid.

273 Talcott Parsons, "Psychosomatic Relationships," 114.

274 Another cybernetic social theorist, the psychiatrist Jurgen Ruesch, identified the terrain of "therapeutic communication" as not being limited to the professional psychotherapeutic relation but existing throughout all social settings: "Therapeutic communication can occur anywhere: at home, at work, on the playground, or on the ward. . . . Therapeutic communication is not a method invented by doctors to combat illness; instead, it involves the utilization of a universal function of man to support those in need, to dispel anxiety, to correct information, and to initiate action" ("Social Communication," 906).

275 Anne Parsons, letter to her parents, quoted in Breines, "Alone in the 1950s," 14.

276 Bogard, *The Simulation of Surveillance*, 89.

277 Anne Parsons to her parents, January 1964, quoted in Breines, "Alone in the 1950s," 27–29.

278 Breines, "Alone in the 1950s," 29.

279 According to Breines, Anne Parsons was "extremely productive throughout the winter of 1963 and 1964," writing numerous articles that were accepted for publication. Using a street address in New Haven, the city in which she was institutionalized, Parsons conducted professional correspondence without revealing her status as a mental patient — some people assumed she was on the faculty of Yale (29).

280 Anne Parsons, quoted in Breines, "Alone in the 1950s," 26–27.

281 Anne Parsons to Talcott Parsons, November 24, 1963, quoted in Breines, "Alone in the 1950s," 25.

282 Breines, "Alone in the 1950s," 26.

283 Anne Parsons, "Cultural Barriers to Insight and the Structural Reality of Transference," 321, 322–25, 330–31.

284 Breines, "Alone in the 1950s," 24–25.

285 The editors of Anne Parsons, *Belief, Magic, and Anomie*, are Rose Laub Coser, Renée Fox, Louisa Howe, Merton Kahne, Sidney Mintz, Jesse Pitts, and David Schneider.

286 Taussig, *The Nervous System*, 2.

287 Smelser, *Theory of Collective Behavior*, 13–14.

288 Ibid., 14.

289 Ibid., 1–2.

290 Smelser draws on the work of Talcott Parsons and Edward Shils, *Toward a General Theory of Action* (1951); see Smelser, *Theory of Collective Behavior*, 23–28.

291 Smelser, *Theory of Collective Behavior*, 23.

292 See Talcott Parsons and Smelser, *Economy and Society*.

293 Smelser, *Theory of Collective Behavior*, 23, 71. Smelser's model of social action in relation to strain is based on models of the organism's reaction to stress and is organized around the imperatives of functionalist adaptation (70n2).

294 Ibid., 8.

295 See Elsner, introduction to Park, *The Crowd*, xvi.

296 Kelley et al., "Collective Behavior in a Simulated Panic Situation."

297 Smelser, *Theory of Collective Behavior*, 386.

298 Kelley et al., "Collective Behavior," 20. The authors are referring to Alexander Mintz's 1951 laboratory study of panic.

299 Ibid., 22–24.

300 Ibid., 22.

301 All phrases in boldface through the end of this section are quotations, with punctuation removed, from Kelley et al.'s description of the experiment in "Collective Behavior," 27–28, 31–32.

302 Ibid., 27.

303 In this section, starting with "Boppy doppy doopy" and ending with "What can I do? I can repeat what I see," I am rewriting passages from Acker, *Blood and Guts in High School*, 68–69.

304 Haraway, "Manifesto for Cyborgs," 83.

4. Performing Methods

1 Grinker and Spiegel, *War Neuroses in North Africa*, 161–62.

2 Ibid., 161.

3 Ibid., 163, 165.

4 Ibid., 8, 12–13.

5 Ibid., 157–58.

6 Ibid., 298–99.

7 Kline and Clynes, "Drugs, Space, and Cybernetics," 347–48. The authors write: "For the artificially extended homeostatic control system functioning unconsciously, one of us (Manfred Clynes) has coined the Cyborg" (347–48). Thanks to Chris Hables Gray, editor of *The Cyborg Handbook*, who did the historical footwork to track down this origin story for the "cyborg."

8 Kline and Clynes, "Drugs, Space, and Cybernetics," 348, 345, 361.

9 Ibid., 347. See, for example, the description of the "ingenious osmotic pressure pump capsule" designed for the continuous injection of a drug at variable rates, without the participation of the organism: the "whole device can be buried in an animal, which can lead a reasonably normal life while the injection is going on" (348). (The original 1961 article shows a photograph of an experimental rat with the osmotic pressure pump "in situ" [351].)

10 Clynes, "An Interview with Manfred Clynes," 45.

11 Kline and Clynes, "Drugs, Space, and Cybernetics," 365.

12 Ibid., 369–70.

13 Otis Benson, preface to Flaherty, *Psychophysiological Aspects of Space Flight*, v–vi.

14 Bernard E. Flaherty, introduction to Flaherty, *Psychophysiological Aspects of Space Flight*, 1.

15 Klein and Fink, "Psychiatric Reaction Patterns to Imipramine," 432; and Klein, "Anxiety Reconceptualized," 235.

16 Klein and Fink, "Psychiatric Reaction," 432.

17 See Klein and Rabkin, "Specificity and Strategy in Psychotherapy Research and Practice," 306–7; also Klein, interview by author, March 29, 1996.

18 Klein, interview. Abraham Wikler, a codirector of the Lexington hospital and author of a three-hundred-page survey of psychopharmacology (1957) that became a landmark textbook in the emergent field, writes: "Implicit in the current interest in 'experimental psychiatry' is the recognition that drugs can be used as tools to detect and manipulate variables relevant to the determination of human behavior, normal or abnormal" (*The Relation of Psychiatry to Pharmacology*, 1–2).

19 Klein, interview.

20 Klein and Fink, "Psychiatric Reaction," 435.

21 Klein, "Anxiety Reconceptualized," 242. For additional reports on drug research conducted at Hillside hospital, see Klein, "Delineation of Two Drug-Responsive Anxiety Syndromes" and "Importance of Psychiatric Diagnosis in Prediction of Clinical Drug Effects."

22 Exact epidemiological figures vary. For a full discussion of the varying data and substantive debates surrounding the incidence of panic disorder and its closely related diagnostic kin, agoraphobia, see McNally, *Panic Disorder*, 26–42. The most oft-cited epidemiological figures come from the NIMH-sponsored Epidemiologic Catchment Area Study, which reports a lifetime prevalence of panic disorder at just under 2 percent of the population. Women reportedly suffer the disorder at rates about twice those of men; see Eaton, Dryman, and Weissman, "Panic and Phobia," 159–64.

23 Romanyshyn, *Technology as Symptom and Dream*, 29.

24 The collapse of public interest in nuclear conflict is reflected in a range of indicators, including newspaper and magazine coverage, nonfiction and fiction books, and films; see Weart, *Nuclear Fear*, 262, 267.

25 Ibid., 299. For a history of the emergence of the U.S. nuclear energy industry and the public debates over reactor safety, see pp. 280–327.

26 Schirra was the third astronaut sent into orbit under Project Mercury. John Glenn "manned" the first Mercury launch on February 20, 1962. See Swenson et al., *This New Ocean*, 461–85.

27 Romanyshyn, *Technology as Symptom and Dream*, 17.

28 Loren Eiseley, quoted in Romanyshyn, *Technology as Symptom and Dream*, 18.

29 See Romanyshyn, *Technology as Symptom and Dream*, 16–31.

30 American Psychiatric Association, *Diagnostic and Statistical Manual of Mental Disorders*, 3rd ed., 231–32.

31 Grinker and Spiegel, *Men under Stress*, vii.

32 Grob, "Forging of Mental Health Policy in America," 410.

33 Ibid., 412–13. For an excellent history of pre–World War II psychiatric practices *within* hospital psychiatry that established new epistemological and institutional foundations for the psychiatric management of everyday life and the "normal," see Lunbeck, *The Psychiatric Persuasion*, 46–77.

34 Grob, "Forging of Mental Health Policy," 421.

35 Grob, "Origins of DSM-I," 427.

36 American Psychiatric Association, *Diagnostic and Statistical Manual for Mental Disorders*, 1st ed., 2–7.

37 Before World War II, the classification system for mental disease was developed for use by the U.S. Bureau of the Census to gather statistics on patient populations in mental asylums. In 1918 the Association of Medical Superintendents of Asylums for the Insane published the first standardized psychiatric nosology, *Statistical Manual for the Use of Institutions for the Insane*, based largely on organic notions of mental disease.

38 Georges Raines, foreword to American Psychiatric Association, *Diagnostic and Statistical Manual*, 1st ed., vi–vii.

39 Grob, "Origins of DSM-I," 427. For a fuller account of the effects of World War II on U.S. psychiatry, see Grob, *From Asylum to Community*, 3–43.

40 Grob, "Origins of DSM-I," 427.

41 Grinker and Spiegel, "The Management of Neuropsychiatric Casualties in the Zone of Combat," quoted in Grob, "Origins of DSM-I," 427.

42 Grinker and Spiegel, *Men under Stress*, vii–viii.

43 Ibid., 427–28.

44 Grob, "Origins of DSM-I," 427–28. For a summary of the "continuum model" of mental disorder and its application to anxiety states, see Klerman, "History and Development of Modern Concepts of Anxiety and Panic," 5–6.

45 Felix, "Mental Disorders as a Public Health Problem," 405; italics mine.

46 Ibid., 402.

47 Kolb, "Research and Its Support under the National Mental Health Act," 407.

48 Felix, "Mental Disorders," 401.

49 Ibid., 402; italics mine.

50 Kolb, "Research and Its Support," 407.

51 Felix, "Mental Disorders," 404.

52 Kolb, "Research and Its Support," 407.

53 Weissman and Klerman, "Epidemiology of Mental Disorders," 706. Their specific reference to influential World War II Research Branch studies is to Samuel Stouffer et al., eds., *The American Soldier: Combat and Its Aftermath*, vol. 2 (Princeton: Princeton University Press, 1949).

54 Srole et al., *Mental Health in the Metropolis*.

55 Weissman and Klerman, "Epidemiology of Mental Disorders," 706. For a related description of how the "new epidemiology" in the post-1945 era reflected "an extraordinary broadening of psychiatric boundaries and a rejection of the traditional distinction between mental health and mental abnormality," see Grob, "Forging of Mental Health Policy," 417–18.

56 Grob, *Asylum to Community*, 21.

57   Grob, "Forging of Mental Health Policy," 423–25.

58   Cannon, " 'Voodoo' Death," 181.

59   Heims, *The Cybernetics Group*, 165–67. See also Benjamin White, *Stanley Cobb*, 220–23.

60   Benjamin White, *Stanley Cobb*, 220. The first Rockefeller-funded psychiatry service established in a general hospital was located at the University of Colorado. The Rockefeller Foundation's promotion of psychiatry as a branch of medicine also included financing full-time professors of psychiatry to teach at elite U.S. medical schools.

61   Ibid., 32–33, 217, 41.

62   Cobb, *Foundations of Neuropsychiatry*, 2–4.

63   Stanley Cobb, "Decennial Report of Psychiatric Service of the Massachusetts General Hospital (1934–1944)," quoted in Benjamin White, *Stanley Cobb*, 222.

64   Benjamin White, *Stanley Cobb*, 221.

65   Fremont-Smith, "History of the Conference Program." See also Heims, *The Cybernetics Group*, 166; and Benjamin White, *Stanley Cobb*, 41, 331.

66   Benjamin White, *Stanley Cobb*, 124–25, 185.

67   Fremont-Smith, "History of the Conference Program," n.p.

68   Letter, Frank Fremont-Smith to Stanley Cobb, December 15, 1937, Fremont-Smith Papers, Countway Library of Medicine, Harvard Medical School.

69   Heims, *The Cybernetics Group*, 65, 166. See also Fremont-Smith, "History of the Conference Program."

70   *Josiah Macy Jr. Foundation Six Year Review, 1930–1936*, 13–14, quoted in Heims, *The Cybernetics Group*, 164.

71   Heims, *The Cybernetics Group*, 166; and Benjamin White, *Stanley Cobb*, 38, 160–61.

72   Cannon, *The Wisdom of the Body*, 24.

73   Ibid., 323.

74   Ibid., 273–83.

75   For an overview of the role of psychiatry during World War II, written by the chief of the Neuropsychiatric Division of the U.S. Army Surgeon General, see Menninger, "Development of Psychiatry in the Army in World War II," 14–15; and Menninger, "Psychiatric Experience in the War, 1941–1946." For a review of psychosomatic medicine during World War II, see Lewis and Engle, *Wartime Psychiatry*, 139–41.

76   Grinker and Spiegel, *War Neuroses in North Africa*, 298.

77   Ibid., 278–79.

78   For a summary of other wartime literature on the use of "narcosynthesis," also called "narcoanalysis" and "narcosis therapy" by U.S. and British medical officers, see Lewis and Engle, *Wartime Psychiatry*, 364–68.

79   In addition to the wartime promotion of Grinker's and Spiegel's research, the Macy Foundation pursued its interest in "various aspects of psychosomatic problems" by sponsoring an international conference in 1943, "Traumatic War Neuroses," organized by Frank Fremont-Smith and chaired by the surgeon general of the U.S. Public Health Service. The foundation also provided funds to the Na-

tional Research Council to start a "Committee on Neuropsychiatry." Fremont-Smith became an active member of that committee's Subcommittee on War Neurosis. See Fremont-Smith, "History of the Conference Program."

80 Cannon, *Wisdom of the Body*, xiii; and Cannon, " 'Voodoo' Death," 179.

81 Cannon, " 'Voodoo' Death," 176–81.

82 Cannon, *Wisdom of the Body*, 25–26.

83 Ibid., 305.

84 Talcott Parsons, "On Building Social System Theory," 835.

85 Ibid.

86 Ibid., 836.

87 Ibid., 835.

88 Talcott Parsons, *The Social System*, 453.

89 Ibid., 478.

90 Talcott Parsons, "Propaganda and Social Control," 159, 162.

91 See Talcott Parsons, "Social Structure and Dynamic Process: The Case of Modern Medical Practice," chapter 10 of *The Social System*. Parsons explains: "The most important phase of this interest [in medicine] was concerned with a field study of medical practice which was carried out mainly in the Boston area several years ago. A variety of circumstances prevented the completion of that study and its publication in the intended form. Hence the opportunity has been taken for the formulation of some of the most important of the results in the context of their relevance to the present work" (428n2).

92 Ibid., 476–77, 431. See also Talcott Parsons, "Building Social System Theory," 838.

93 Talcott Parsons, *The Social System*, 477–78.

94 Ibid.

95 Emile Durkheim and Marcel Mauss, *Primitive Classification*, trans. Rodney Needham (Chicago: University of Chicago Press, 1963), 82, 84.

96 Heims, *The Cybernetics Group*, 32–33, 40, 133–34.

97 Fremont-Smith, "History of the Conference Program."

98 The essay is published the next year in the journal *Philosophy of Science* as Rosenblueth, Wiener, and Bigelow, "Behavior, Purpose and Teleology."

99 Fremont-Smith recalls how a comment by McCulloch at the 1942 meeting that "what we really need is a series of conferences on feedback mechanisms" initiates the cybernetics conference series. See Fremont-Smith, "History of the Conference Program."

100 As Paul Edwards explains in his history of the U.S. military's central role in the development of computers, the desire to automate mathematical computation — particularly the massive logistical enterprise of humans armed with desk calculators computing the ballistics tables needed to improve the accuracy of antiaircraft artillery systems during World War II — was the driving force behind the design of the first electronic digital computer, a military-funded project that von Neumann joined in 1944. See Edwards, *The Closed World*, 44–46, 49–52.

101 Heims, *The Cybernetics Group*, 41.

102 McCulloch and Pitts, "A Logical Calculus of the Ideas Immanent in Nervous Activity," 115–17. For analyses of the McCulloch-Pitts essay, see Heims, *The Cyber-*

netics Group, 20, 41–44; Edwards, *The Closed World*, 188–89; and Gerovitch, *From Newspeak to Cyberspeak*, 77–81.

103 McCulloch and Pitts, "Logical Calculus," 131.

104 Ibid., 130–31.

105 Ibid., 130, 132; italics mine.

106 Lettvin and Pitts, "A Mathematical Theory of the Affective Psychoses," 139.

107 McCulloch, "The Brain as a Computing Machine," 583.

108 Heims, *John von Neumann*, 185.

109 As a contemporary of McCulloch explains: "The *Logical Calculus*, McCulloch knew, was not even a caricature of any existing nervous process. Indeed he made that very clear at the time of writing. . . . There were some who took the work literally and went searching for the circuits of the brain. Warren tolerantly felt that it was a good thing, because then one might find what such real circuits might be and devise a model for them" (Lettvin, "Warren and Walter," 518).

110 Gerovitch, *From Newspeak to Cyberspeak*, 80.

111 Edwards, *The Closed World*, 44–46, 49–52.

112 Josiah Macy Jr. Foundation, *Conference on Feedback Mechanisms and Circular Causal Systems in Biology and the Social Sciences*, March 8–9, 1946, New York City, Frank Fremont-Smith Papers.

113 Von Neumann, in Macy Foundation, *Conference on Feedback Mechanisms*, 4–5.

114 For commentary on the role of "automata theory" in coupling the logics of mechanical/computer and mental processes, see Edwards, *The Closed World*, 16–17, 241–44; Heims, *The Cybernetics Group*, 20–21, 42–44; Heims, *John von Neumann*, 137, 211–13; and Maron, "On Cybernetics, Information Processing, and Thinking," 122–25.

115 Wiener, *I Am a Mathematician*, 253–54.

116 Ibid., 254.

117 Norbert Wiener and J. P. Schadé, eds., *Cybernetics of the Nervous System*, vol. 17, Progress in Brain Research (Amsterdam and New York: Elsevier, 1965). For a discussion of the contributions of cybernetics to the field of artificial intelligence, see Selfridge, "W. S. McCulloch and the Foundations of AI," 579–81; Edwards, *The Closed World*, 239–44, 271–73; and Maron, "On Cybernetics," 125–33.

118 Wiener, "Perspectives on Neurocybernetics," 402, 404.

119 Ibid., 407–8.

120 McCulloch, quoted in Heims, *The Cybernetics Group*, 133.

121 McCulloch, "*Mysterium Iniquitatis*," 987.

122 McCulloch, "The Past of a Delusion," 776; italics mine.

123 Heims, *The Cybernetics Group*, 133.

124 Ruesch, "Social Communication," 901.

125 See McCulloch's gleeful, vitriolic attack on the "confabulations" of Freudian theory in "The Past of a Delusion."

126 Stanley Cobb describes how Wiener "was equally interested in cerebral mechanisms and in psychoanalysis. He understood the possibilities of both approaches and saw no incompatibility" ("Norbert Wiener and Psychiatry," 15). See also Heims, *The Cybernetics Group*, 127.

127   Wiener, in Macy Foundation, *Conference on Feedback Mechanisms*, 60–63.

128   Roy Grinker, introduction to *Toward a Unified Theory of Human Behavior*, vii.

129   "Norbert Wiener, 1894–1964," editorial statement, *Journal of Nervous and Mental Disease* 140, no. 1 (January 1965): 3. For a social psychoanalytic reading of Wiener's mathematical activities and anxieties, see Pfohl, "The Cybernetic Delirium of Norbert Wiener," 114–28.

130   Kline, "Toward a Theory of Man," 106.

131   Rosenblueth, Wiener, and Bigelow, "Behavior, Purpose and Teleology," 23.

132   For a careful history of the hegemonic rise of psychosocial and psychoanalytic paradigms in postwar U.S. psychiatry, see Grob, *From Asylum to Community*, 24–43.

133   Group for the Advancement of Psychiatry, "The Social Responsibility of Psychiatry," GAP *Report* 13 (1950), quoted in Grob, "Forging of Mental Health Policy," 419.

134   World Federation statement in *International Congress on Mental Health, London 1948*, vol. 1, *History, Development and Organization*, quoted in Heims, *The Cybernetics Group*, 173.

135   Margaret Mead, ed., *Cultural Patterns and Technical Change* (1954), quoted in Heims, *The Cybernetics Group*, 174.

136   World Federation statement, quoted in Heims, *The Cybernetics Group*, 174. The hidden agenda of the federation's liberal consensus, Heims suggests, was the containment of communism and the "political conflicts generated by aggressive, expanding American capitalism impinging on indigenous societies" (174). For a discussion, see pp. 170–77.

137   Letter from Warren McCulloch to Frank Fremont-Smith, January 10, 1949, quoted in Heims, *The Cybernetics Group*, 175.

138   Kety, foreword to *The First Psychiatric Institute*, xv.

139   Zubin, "On the Powers of Models," 430.

140   Ibid., 432–33, 435.

141   Rosenblueth and Wiener, "The Role of Models in Science," 316.

142   For an overview of contemporary treatment techniques in the 1950s, see Sainz, "Clinical Applications of Chlorpromazine in Psychiatry," 39–40.

143   Harold A. Abramson, ed., *Neuropharmacology*, vols. 1–5 (New York: Josiah Macy Jr. Foundation, 1955–60). Abramson is also a participant in the Macy-sponsored Problems of Consciousness conferences, editing the published transactions from those meetings as well.

144   Wikler, *Relation of Psychiatry to Pharmacology*, 65.

145   See the discussion on the production of "model" psychoses in Wikler, *Relation of Psychiatry to Pharmacology*, 63–84. See also Healy, *The Antidepressant Era*, 113–16.

146   Heims, *The Cybernetics Group*, 167. For a bibliography of Harold Abramson's LSD-related research, see Wikler, *Relation of Psychiatry to Pharmacology*, 271–72.

147   Heims, *The Cybernetics Group*, 167–68.

148   Harold A. Abramson, ed., *Problems of Consciousness*, vols. 1–5 (New York: Josiah Macy Jr. Foundation, 1951–54).

149 Participants who attend both the "Neuropharmacology" and the "Problems of Consciousness" conferences include Harold Abramson (the Biological Laboratory, Cold Spring Harbor), who edits the ten volumes of transactions published for both conference series; Hudson Hoagland (Worcester Foundation for Experimental Biology), who chairs the second "Neuropharmacology" series; Henry Beecher (Department of Anesthesia, Harvard Medical School); Mary A. B. Brazier (Neurophysiology Laboratory, Massachusetts General Hospital); Seymour S. Kety (National Institute of Mental Health); and Roy Grinker (Institute for Psychosomatic and Psychiatric Research and Training, Michael Reese Hospital).

150 Talcott Parsons, "Consciousness and Symbolic Processes," 51–55.

151 Grinker, "Problems of Consciousness," 24.

152 Ibid., 22.

153 Ibid., 25, 28.

154 See Clynes, "Sentics."

155 Kline and Clynes, "Drugs, Space, and Cybernetics," 346.

156 Flaherty, conclusion to *Psychophysiological Aspects*, 375–76; italics mine.

157 See *Annual Report of the Rockland State Hospital*, vols. 26–28 (1956–58).

158 Healy, *The Antidepressant Era*, 61, 67–68.

159 Kline, "Clinical Applications of Reserpine." In rather dramatic contrast to his claims about the limited side effects of the new drugs, Kline describes the "turbulent phase" of reserpine therapy regularly observed in psychotic patients: "Many of the patients are frightened by the feeling that they have 'no control' over their impulses. Some feel that they 'do not know what they are going to do next,' and in point of fact may begin screaming and throw themselves to the floor. . . . Delusions and hallucinations increase and behavior not infrequently becomes more disturbed than prior to the beginning of treatment" (85). Kline advises that medication be continued, noting that the "turbulent phase" usually lasts *no more than two or three weeks*.

160 Ibid., 107.

161 Kolb and Roizin, *The First Psychiatric Institute*, 182–91. Paul Hoch, a guest at the second "Neuropharmacology" conference and listed as a regular participant thereafter, is the first director of the experimental psychiatry department at NYSPI.

162 Klein, interview by author.

163 Cole, "The ECDEU-NCDEU Program," 3–4.

164 Gerard, introduction to *Psychopharmacology*, 1–2.

165 See Seymour Kety, "Summary of the Conference," in Cole and Gerard, *Psychopharmacology*.

166 Ibid., 646–47.

167 Hilary Rose, "My Enemy's Enemy," 71.

168 Klein, "Delineation," 407.

169 Klein, "Importance of Psychiatric Diagnosis," 118.

170 Klein, interview.

171 Klein and Fink, "Psychiatric Reaction Patterns," 434–36.

172   Katz, Cole, and Barton, preface to *The Role and Methodology of Classification in Psychiatry and Psychopathology*, iii.

173   Cole and Katz, "Introduction and Overview," 6–8, 2.

174   Max Fink, "Neurophysiological Response Strategies," 537.

175   Katz, Cole, and Barton, preface, iii.

176   Hamilton, "Perspectives on the Conference," 554.

177   See Klein and Davis, *Diagnosis and Drug Treatment of Psychiatric Disorders*. The quote is from the second edition, Klein et al., *Diagnosis and Drug Treatment of Psychiatric Disorders*, 2d ed., xxxi.

178   Klerman, "Historical Perspectives on Psychopathology," 16–17.

179   Klein et al., *Diagnosis and Drug Treatment*, 2d ed., 9, 13, 1.

180   Ulett, foreword to *Drugs and Cerebral Function*, xi.

181   The other industry sponsors are CIBA Pharmaceutical Company, Ives Laboratories, Marion Laboratories, and Merck Sharp and Dohme Postgraduate Program.

182   Klein, "Psychotropic Drugs," 74. For further elaborations of his cybernetic model, see Klein et al., *Diagnosis and Drug Treatment*, 2d ed., 812–16; and Klein, "Cybernetics, Activation, and Drug Effects."

183   Klein, "Psychotropic Drugs," 74–76.

184   Ibid., 76–77; see also Klein et al., *Diagnosis and Drug Treatment*, 2d ed., 813.

185   Klein, "Psychotropic Drugs," 78.

186   Ibid., 79, italics mine; and Klein et al., *Diagnosis and Drug Treatment*, 2d ed., 816, with slight variations.

187   Klein et al., *Diagnosis and Drug Treatment*, 2d ed., 816.

5. Panic Xanax

1   All phrases in boldface in this paragraph are quotes from David Sheehan, *The Anxiety Disease*, 4–5. The paragraph describes one of the book's opening scenes.

2   Ibid., 7.

3   Haraway, "Manifesto for Cyborgs," 66.

4   Sheehan, *The Anxiety Disease*, 121.

5   David V. Sheehan, interview by author, Miami, Florida, April 14, 1996.

6   Sheehan, *The Anxiety Disease*, xi.

7   Sheehan, interview.

8   Sheehan and Sheehan, "Classification of Anxiety and Hysterical States," 236; italics mine.

9   Sheehan and Ballenger, "Treatment of Endogenous Anxiety," 58.

10   Sheehan, interview.

11   Sheehan, *The Anxiety Disease*, 82.

12   *Newsweek*, December 7, 1942, 43–44.

13   Faxon, "Problems of the Hospital Administration," 803.

14   Oliver Cope, foreword to special issue, *Annals of Surgery* 17 (June 1943): 803–4. In this special issue devoted to treatment of the Cocoanut Grove Club fire victims, Cope notes: "Had such a catastrophe taken place before Pearl Harbor, the hos-

pital would have been swamped. As it was, the injured found the staff prepared, for the war had made us catastrophe-minded" (801).

15 Cobb and Lindemann, "Neuropsychiatric Observations," 818, 822.

16 Ibid., 822.

17 Benjamin White, *Stanley Cobb*, 243–44. The OSRD studies include Cohen et al., "Studies of Work and Discomfort in Patients with Neurocirculatory Asthenia"; and Paul White et al., "Observations on Neurocirculatory Asthenia."

18 For a genealogy of these several diagnostic terms that precede the recent term "panic disorder," see Thomas Lewis, *The Soldier's Heart and the Effort Syndrome*; Skerritt, "Anxiety and the Heart," 20–21; and Klerman, "History and Development," 5–6.

19 Paul White et al., "Observations on Neurocirculatory Asthenia," 135–36.

20 Cohen et al., "Studies of Work and Discomfort," 934.

21 Wheeler et al., "Neurocirculatory Asthenia." One of the study's conclusions, that neurocirculatory asthenia is not necessarily an incapacitating disorder, leads its authors to recommend to their sponsor, the U.S. Army, that military disability for veterans diagnosed with the problem should be reconsidered (888).

22 Sheehan, *The Anxiety Disease*, 84.

23 Talcott Parsons, "Building Social System Theory," 835.

24 Talcott Parsons, "Definitions of Health and Illness," 260.

25 Ibid., 262.

26 Guze, "Diagnosis of Hysteria," 83.

27 François Delaporte, *Disease and Civilization: The Cholera in Paris, 1832*, trans. Arthur Goldhammer (Cambridge: MIT Press, 1986), 6.

28 American Psychiatric Association, *Diagnostic and Statistical Manual*, 3rd ed., 230–32.

29 For a critical history of the making of the 1980 DSM-III, see Kirk and Kutchins, *The Selling of DSM*; see especially pp. 97–119 for a history of the conflict within the APA. For a sampling of the literature critical of the DSM-III, see Faust and Miner, "The Empiricist and His New Clothes"; Kutchins and Kirk, "The Business of Diagnosis"; Kaplan, "A Woman's View of DSM-III"; Schacht, "DSM-III and the Politics of Truth"; and Wilson, "DSM-III and the Transformation of American Psychiatry." For commentary by DSM-III task force participants celebrating the new psychiatric language, see Bayer and Spitzer, "Neurosis, Psychodynamics and DSM-III"; Klerman et al., "A Debate on DSM-III"; Millon, "The DSM-III"; Millon, "On the Past and Future of the DSM-III"; Spitzer, "DSM-III and the Politics-Science Dichotomy Syndrome"; and Spitzer, Sheehy, and Endicott, "DSM-III: Guiding Principles."

30 Bayer and Spitzer, "Neurosis, Psychodynamics, and DSM-III," 187.

31 Spitzer, introduction to *Diagnostic and Statistical Manual*, 3rd ed., 1, 6–8.

32 Wilson, "DSM-III," 399–400.

33 In 1976, when the revision process for the DSM-III was well under way, Robert Spitzer and his associate Jean Endicott, also a core member of the DSM-III task force, proposed to the American Psychiatric Association that the new DSM state that mental disorders are a subset of medical disorders. The ensuing controversy

persuaded the task force to drop the proposal. See Spitzer, Sheehy, and Endicott, "DSM-III: Guiding Principles." For discussion of the controversy, see Millon, "Insider's Perspective," 805–6. In 1994 the battle is won in favor of Spitzer and Endicott's original proposal, with the fourth edition of the DSM stating, if somewhat circumspectly, that "the term *mental disorder* unfortunately implies a distinction between 'mental' disorders and 'physical' disorders that is a reductionistic anachronism of mind/body dualism." Grudgingly, the authors concede, "The term persists in the title of DSM-IV because we have not found an appropriate substitute," in American Psychiatric Association, *Diagnostic and Statistical Manual of Mental Disorders*, 4th ed., xxi.

34 See Kirk and Kutchins, *The Selling of DSM*, 97–103; and Blashfield, "Feighner et al., Invisible Colleges, and the Matthew Effect." For a sympathetic discussion of the "invisible college" of neo-Kraepelinians purportedly overtaking the language of psychiatric diagnosis, see Klerman, "Historical Perspectives on Psychopathology," 16–17.

35 See Spitzer and Endicott, "Medical and Mental Disorder," 16.

36 Quoted in Wilson, "DSM-III," 403. See also Klerman, "Historical Perspectives," 14–15.

37 See Healy, *The Antidepressant Era*, 103.

38 See Fleiss et al., "Quantification of Agreement in Multiple Psychiatric Diagnosis." Also see Spitzer and Fleiss, "A Re-analysis of the Reliability of Psychiatric Diagnosis"; and Spitzer, Endicott, and Robins, "Clinical Criteria for Psychiatric Diagnosis and DSM-III." For an astute critique of the "reliability" problem in psychiatry, see Kirk and Kutchins, *The Selling of DSM*, 28–49.

39 For a compelling history of how psychology establishes the homogeneous "treatment group" via experimental and statistical methods of abstraction, see Danzinger, *Constructing the Subject*, 113–17.

40 Klerman, "Historical Perspectives," 14–15.

41 Spitzer, Endicott, and Robins, "Clinical Criteria," 1187–88.

42 Spitzer, Endicott, and Robins, "Research Diagnostic Criteria," 781.

43 Ibid., 774.

44 Spitzer, Endicott, and Robins, "Clinical Criteria," 1188; and Spitzer, Endicott, and Robins, "Research Diagnostic Criteria," 773.

45 Spitzer, Endicott, and Robins, "Research Diagnostic Criteria," 774.

46 Spitzer, Endicott, and Robins, "Clinical Criteria," 1190–91; italics mine.

47 Wilson, "DSM-III," 404.

48 Millon, "Insider's Perspective," 807–8.

49 Spitzer, Endicott, and Robins, "Research Diagnostic Criteria," 778.

50 Feighner et al., "Diagnostic Criteria for Use in Psychiatric Research." The "St. Louis group" refers to a network of researchers trained at or employed by the Department of Psychiatry at Washington University School of Medicine in St. Louis, who become quite influential in the 1980s. For a history of the St. Louis group, see Healy, *The Creation of Psychopharmacology*, 293–97. See also Blashfield, "Feighner et al.," 1; and Guze et al., "Comments on Blashfield's Article."

51 The "anxiety attack" was a central component of the clinical picture that Freud

drew of "anxiety neurosis." Accompanied by the idea of the "extinction of life, or of a stroke, or of a threat," the anxiety attack, according to Freud, could "exhibit a great wealth of forms." Among the common symptoms of an attack, he listed disturbances of heart action (palpitations, arrhythmia, or tachycardia), disturbed breathing, attacks of sweating, shivering, vertigo, diarrhea, and ravenous hunger. See Freud, "On the Grounds for Detaching a Particular Syndrome from Neurasthenia under the Description 'Anxiety Neurosis,'" 93–94.

52 Feighner et al., "Diagnostic Criteria," 59. The authors of the RDC state that "panic disorder" is "similar to the Feighner category of anxiety neurosis, but has slightly different criteria for the number of attacks and duration of illness" (Spitzer, Endicott, and Robins, "Research Diagnostic Criteria," 778).

53 In discussing Cohen et al.'s early research at Massachusetts General Hospital on neurocirculatory asthenia, David Healy remarks: "Many of their patients would today be diagnosed as having panic disorder" (*The Creation of Psychopharmacology*, 293).

54 Feighner et al., "Diagnostic Criteria," 59–60. Four of the seven authors of "Diagnostic Criteria" are actively involved in hysteria studies at Washington University Medical School, St. Louis, in the previous twenty years: Eli Robins, Samuel Guze, Robert Woodruff, and George Winokur.

55 I am referring to the research efforts and published work spanning almost twenty years, much of it by the St. Louis group. This lineage of research on hysteria includes, in chronological order of publication, Purtell, Robins, and Cohen, "Observations on Clinical Aspects of Hysteria"; Perley and Guze, "Hysteria — the Stability and Usefulness of Clinical Criteria"; Guze and Perley, "Observations on the Natural History of Hysteria"; Guze, "The Diagnosis of Hysteria"; Farley, Woodruff, and Guze, "Prevalence of Hysteria"; and Woodruff, Clayton, and Guze, "Hysteria."

56 Guze, "The Diagnosis of Hysteria," 491–92.

57 Purtell, Robins, and Cohen, "Observations on Clinical Aspects," 902.

58 Ibid., 903, 909. Of the 267 hospitalized women patients examined as possible participants in the study, 91 of them — just over one-third — were diagnosed with hysteria by researchers (902). While much else about hysteria remains uncertain, it certainly was a popular diagnosis with mid-twentieth-century U.S. psychiatrists.

59 Ibid., 909.

60 Ibid., 904.

61 For the study on neurocirculatory asthenia coauthored by Cohen, see Wheeler et al., "Neurocirculatory Asthenia" (1950).

62 Purtell, Robins, and Cohen, "Observations on Clinical Aspects," 904.

63 Perley and Guze, "Hysteria"; and Guze and Perley, "Natural History of Hysteria." Together with an untranslated, eight-hundred-page treatise written by the French physician Pierre Briquet in 1859, and the 1909 lectures of Thomas Savill, the 1951 article is named as one of three studies that offer empirical evidence of hysteria as a "distinct disease entity."

64 Perley and Guze, "Hysteria," 425.

65 Woodruff, Clayton, and Guze, "Hysteria," 1245.

66 Hyler and Spitzer, "Hysteria Split Asunder." The DSM-III diagnostic categories into which hysteria is split include somatoform disorders, malingering, and factitious disorders.

67 Ibid., 1503.

68 Freud, *Dora*, 141–42; italics in original.

69 Ibid., 142n2.

70 National Institute of Mental Health, *Panic Disorder in the Medical Setting*, 13.

71 Ibid., 16.

72 Acker, *The Adult Life of Toulouse Lautrec*, 280.

73 Upjohn Company, *What You Should Know about Panic Disorder*, 6.

74 Morrison, *The Bluest Eye*, 128–29; numbers in brackets have been added to the text.

75 Ibid., 129; italics mine. The rest of this passage is not by Toni Morrison.

76 Upjohn Company, *What You Should Know*, 7.

77 Ibid.

78 Ibid.

79 Sheehan, *The Anxiety Disease*, 182–83.

80 Wiener, *I Am a Mathematician*, 33.

81 Frances et al., "DSM-IV Meets Philosophy," 211.

82 For a useful analysis of these issues of psychiatric epistemology, see Faust and Miner, "The Empiricist and His New Clothes"; and Sedler, "Foundations of the New Nosology," 218–38.

83 Robert L. Spitzer, interview by author, New York City, April 1, 1996.

84 Millon, "Insider's Perspective," 808.

85 Cantor et al., "Psychiatric Diagnosis as Prototype Categorization," 192.

86 Spitzer, quoted in Wilson, "DSM-III," 408.

87 Spitzer and Fleiss, "Re-analysis," 345–55.

88 For a discussion of the validity problem in psychiatry, see Kirk and Kutchins, *The Selling of DSM*, 28–30.

89 Guze, "The Diagnosis of Hysteria," 491–92.

90 Feighner et al., "Diagnostic Criteria," 57–58.

91 Spitzer and Fleiss, "Re-analysis," 341.

92 Donald Klein is one of the most persistent advocates of this notion of validity. Improvement in the diagnostic classification will come, he writes, not from the "search for natural trait clusters" but from the search for symptom information that will "allow maximum predictive ability" regarding prognosis and response to medication (Klein et al., *Diagnosis and Drug Treatment*, 2d ed., 7–13).

93 Sheehan, interview.

94 For a critique of the lack of validity in the DSM-III, see Vaillant, "The Disadvantages of DSM-III Outweigh Its Advantages," 545. Vaillant's comments were delivered as part of a public debate with Robert Spitzer and Gerald Klerman over the new DSM-III at the 1982 meetings of the American Psychiatric Association. See also Seller, "Foundations," 219–21.

95 Frances et al., "DSM-IV Meets Philosophy," 210; italics mine.

96 American Psychiatric Association, introduction to *Diagnostic and Statistical Manual of Mental Disorders*, 4th ed., xvi.

97 Frances et al., "Classification of Panic Disorders," 7.

98 American Psychiatric Association, introduction to *Diagnostic and Statistical Manual*, 3rd ed., 6; italics mine. The statements are repeated in 1994 in the introduction to *Diagnostic and Statistical Manual*, 4th ed., xxi–xxii.

99 Lowe, *The Body in Late-Capitalist USA*, 158.

100 See Spitzer and Endicott, "DIAGNO"; Spitzer and Endicott, "DIAGNO II: Further Developments"; and Spitzer et al., "Constraints on the Validity of Computer Diagnosis."

101 Spitzer and Endicott, "Computer Applications in Psychiatry," 835.

102 While much of this history is marginalized or forgotten, George Vaillant publicly stated in a debate with Robert Spitzer over the DSM-III at the 1982 American Psychiatric Association meetings that psychiatry "has more in common with the inevitable ambiguity of great drama than with *the DSM-III's quest for algorithms compatible with the cold binary logic of computer science*" (Vaillant, "Disadvantages," 544; italics mine).

103 Spitzer and Endicott, "Computer Applications," 823. Rockland State housed the central computer facility for the Multi-state Information System for Psychiatry Patients, which included DIAGNO III. Nathan Kline, director of research at Rockland State, had been interested since the 1960s in the application of computers in psychiatry. See Kline and Laska, *Computers and Electronic Devices in Psychiatry*.

104 Spitzer and Endicott, "Computer Applications," 824–25.

105 Spitzer et al., "Constraints on the Validity," 198, 202.

106 To address the problem of reliability through the use of computers, the Biometrics Department at NYSPI introduced in 1972 a computerized statistical procedure, "the kappa coefficient," as a quantified measure of diagnostic reliability. See Fleiss et al., "Quantification of Agreement in Multiple Psychiatric Diagnosis." For a thorough critique of this statistical measure, see Kirk and Kutchins, *The Selling of DSM*, 47–75.

107 Spitzer et al., "Constraints on the Validity," 203; italics mine.

108 Jean Endicott, interview by author, New York City, March 25, 1996; italics mine.

109 Spitzer, "Psychiatric Diagnosis," 276.

110 See Robins et al., "National Institute of Mental Health Diagnostic Interview Schedule"; Regier et al., "NIMH Epidemiologic Catchment Area Program"; and Robins and Regier, *Psychiatric Disorders in America*.

111 Spitzer, "Psychiatric Diagnosis," 281.

112 Ibid., 287.

113 Frances et al., "DSM-IV Meets Philosophy," 216.

114 Frances et al., "DSM-IV: Work in Progress," 1443; italics mine.

115 American Psychiatric Association, introduction to *Diagnostic and Statistical Manual*, 4th ed., xxii. For other advocates of dimensional models, possibly for use in the next edition of the DSM, see Kendell, "Five Criteria for an Improved Tax-

onomy of Mental Disorders," 12–13; Maser and Patterson, "Spectrum and Nosology"; and Widiger, "Categorical versus Dimensional Classification."

116 All phrases in italics in this paragraph are quotes from Wiener, *I Am a Mathematician*, 33–34, 255–60. For Wiener's discussion of his use of Benzedrine during his wartime research on prediction theory, see p. 249.

117 American Psychiatric Association, *Diagnostic and Statistical Manual*, 3rd ed., 313–15.

118 Healy, "Psychopharmacology in the New Medical State," 29–30.

119 Upjohn Company, *Upjohn Company Annual Report 1984*, 21.

120 James Ballenger, interview by author, Charleston, S.C., April 22, 1996.

121 For a sampling of the publications produced out of Upjohn's Cross-National Study, in chronological order of publication, see Klerman, Coleman, and Purpura, "Design and Conduct"; Ballenger et al., "Alprazolam in Panic Disorder and Agoraphobia"; Klerman, "Overview of the Cross-National Collaborative Panic Study"; Noyes et al., "Alprazolam in Panic Disorder and Agoraphobia"; and Klerman et al., "Drug Treatment of Panic Disorder: Comparative Efficacy of Alprazolam, Imipramine, and Placebo."

122 Upjohn Company, *Upjohn Company Corporate Annual Report 1987*, 22.

123 Ballenger, interview.

124 Gerald L. Klerman, "Introduction," *Journal of Psychiatric Research*, 2. The supplementary issue of the journal is sponsored by the Upjohn Company.

125 For commentary on the conflicts of interest between Klerman's paid position with Upjohn and his role as lead author of the Cross-National Study's findings, see Marks et al., "Drug Treatment of Panic Disorder: Further Comment," 796; and Breggin, *Toxic Psychiatry*, 348–50. For a limited defense of Klerman's role in the study, see Healy, *The Antidepressant Era*, 195.

126 Gerald L. Klerman et al., "Drug Treatment of Panic Disorder: Reply to Comment by Marks and Associates," 470.

127 Spitzer, interview. Called SCID-UP, the interview protocol used in the Cross-National Study is a slightly revised version of the SCID (Structured Clinical Interview for DSM-III), developed by Robert Spitzer and Janet Williams, with funding from the NIMH, for the purpose of making psychiatric diagnoses using diagnostic categories from the 1980 *DSM-III*.

128 Klerman et al., "Drug Treatment of Panic Disorder: Comparative Efficacy," 193.

129 Ibid.

130 Ballenger, interview.

131 Breggin, *Toxic Psychiatry*, 350–51. Daniel Freedman was the editor in chief.

132 Upjohn Company, *Upjohn Annual Report 1987*, 6.

133 Taggart, *The World Pharmaceutical Industry*, 155.

134 Cotts, "Xanax Panic," 208.

135 Upjohn Company, *Upjohn Company Annual Report 1985*, 17.

136 The debate between U.S. and European psychiatrists over the validity of the new "panic disorder" label is particularly fraught. See Jablensky, "European and American Concepts of Anxiety," 8. See also Gelder, "Panic Disorder: Fact or Fic-

tion?"; Marks, "Agoraphobia, Panic Disorder, and Related Conditions"; and Roth and Argyle, "Anxiety, Panic, and Phobic Disorders." For an overview of the validity problem for panic disorder, see Rosenberg et al., "Validation Criteria for Panic Disorder as a Nosological Entity."

137 See McNally, *Panic Disorder*, 4–11.

138 Ballenger, interview.

139 See Klein and Fink, "Psychiatric Reaction Patterns"; and Klein, "Delineation of Two Drug-Responsive Anxiety Syndromes."

140 Myrna Weissman works with the Upjohn Company to develop a software package for computerized diagnosis of mental disorders in primary-care settings (Myrna Weissman, interview with author, New York City, March 26, 1996). In 1996, Pfizer directly distributes its software program called PRIME-MD to primary-care physicians. According to Robert Spitzer, Pfizer's own market research shows that regional sales of its popular antidepressant Zoloft increase significantly after the company conducts local workshops to train primary-care physicians in how to administer PRIME-MD in their offices (Spitzer, interview).

141 Sheehan, interview.

142 Healy, *The Antidepressant Era*, 198.

143 Sheehan, interview.

144 Myrna Weissman, interview with David Healy, 532.

145 Weissman, interview.

146 Weissman et al., "The Cross-National Epidemiology of Panic Disorder," 307.

147 Healy, "New Medical State," 25.

148 Mark Pollack, interview with author, Boston, Mass., October 30, 1995.

149 Healy, "New Medical State," 18.

150 Ballenger, interview.

151 Sheehan, interview.

152 Ibid.

153 Ballenger, interview.

154 Ibid.

155 Healy, "New Medical State," 14. Healy's critique of the relations between academic psychiatry and the pharmaceutical industry is more measured than my own, and he presents a historical argument for the central role of FDA regulations in pushing pharmaceutical companies into the business of drug research. He also acknowledges the benefits from pharmaceutically sponsored research. For his summary of the Upjohn panic disorder story, see Healy, *The Antidepressant Era*, 191–99. For a more scathing critique detailing Upjohn's role in promoting Xanax for panic disorder, and Upjohn's financial wooing of the American Psychiatric Association in the 1980s, see Breggin, *Toxic Psychiatry*, 251–60, 348–52.

156 Ballenger, interview.

157 Healy, "New Medical State," 33.

158 Upjohn Company, *Annual Report 1984*, 21.

159 Klerman et al., "Drug Treatment of Panic Disorder: Comparative Efficacy," 195. Both the significant side effect profile for Xanax and the disputed equivalence between the efficacy of Xanax and of placebo are a focus of the highly public

critique of the Cross-National Study by British psychologist Isaac Marks and colleagues. See Marks et al., " 'Efficacy' of Alprazolam"; Marks et al., "Comment on the Second Phase"; and Marks et al., "Drug Treatment of Panic Disorder."

160 Bruce Mirken, "Ask Your Doctor," *San Francisco Bay Guardian*, October 23, 1996.

161 Stephen S. Hall, "Prescription for Profit," *New York Times Magazine*, March 11, 2001, 45. This is an astronomical increase from $35 million in 1987, and $357 million in 1995; see Mirken, "Ask Your Doctor," 46.

162 Quoted in Mirken, "Ask Your Doctor," 46. For an assessment of the effect of consumer advertising on prescription drug sales, see Robert Pear, "Marketing Tied to Increase in Prescription Drug Sales," *New York Times*, September 20, 2000.

163 Upjohn Company, *Upjohn Company Annual Report 1993*, 11.

164 Melody Petersen, "Medicine Merger: The Overview," *New York Times*, July 16, 2002.

165 Andrew Ross Sorkin, "Pfizer Said to Buy Large Drug Rival in $60 Billion Deal," *New York Times*, July 15, 2002.

166 See Ballenger, "Selective Serotonin Reuptake Inhibitors."

167 Kendell, "Five Criteria," 10.

168 Acker, "Models of Our Present," 64.

169 Ruesch, "Social Communication," 909.

170 Klein, "Testing the Suffocation False Alarm Theory," 3.

171 Ibid. 2.

172 Klein, interview.

173 Klein, "Testing the Suffocation False Alarm Theory," 2.

174 Ibid., 1.

175 Klein, "Anxiety Reconceptualized," 247.

176 The lab rat research was conducted by Dr. Susan A. Brunelli in the Developmental Psychobiology unit at NYSPI. See *New York State Psychiatric Institute 1993*, 36.

177 Klein, "False Suffocation Alarms, Spontaneous Panics, and Related Conditions"; and Klein, "Testing the Suffocation False Alarm Theory."

178 The study is conducted by J. C. Boulougouris et al., "Epidemic Faintness: A Psychophysiological Investigation," cited in Klein, "False Suffocation Alarms," 311–12.

179 Klein, "False Suffocation Alarms," 306, 314.

180 American Psychiatric Association, introduction to *Diagnostic and Statistical Manual*, 4th ed., xxi.

181 Klein and Wender, *Mind, Mood, and Medicine*, 19–20, 30.

182 For useful summaries and extensive bibliographies of recent neurobiological and genetic research on panic, see Gorman et al., "Neuroanatomical Hypothesis of Panic Disorder"; Hettema, Neale, and Kendler, "Review and Meta-analysis of the Genetic Epidemiology of Anxiety Disorder"; and Malizia and Nutt, "Brain Mechanisms and Circuits in Panic Disorder."

183 Daniel Goleman, "Behind the Veil of Thought: Advances in Brain Research," *New York Times*, June 13, 1995, C1.

184 Malizia and Nutt, "Brain Mechanisms," 65–66.

185 Smoller and Tsuang, "Panic and Phobic Anxiety," 1152.

186 Barondes, "Agenda for Psychiatric Genetics," 550.

187 Weissman, interview.

188 Cited in Smoller and Tsuang, "Panic and Phobic Anxiety," 1152–53.

189 Merikangas and Risch, "Will the Genomics Revolution Revolutionize Psychiatry?" 628.

190 Smoller and Tsuang, "Panic and Phobic Anxiety," 1153.

191 Ibid., 1158–59.

192 This entire passage is a transcription from my interview with Donald Klein, "psychiatrist."

Epilogue

1 Adrienne Rich, "Letters to a Young Poet," in *Midnight Salvage*, 25.

2 Foucault, *Birth of the Clinic*, 85.

3 Haraway, "Manifesto for Cyborgs," 79–85. For a consideration of the "informatics of domination" in relation to contemporary technomedicine, see Clarke et al., "Biomedicalization." For theorizations of the "control society," see Deleuze, "Postscript on the Societies of Control"; Hardt and Negri, *Empire*; and Parisi and Terranova, "Heat-Death."

4 Hardt and Negri, *Empire*, 23.

5 Deleuze, "Postscript," 4.

6 Clough, *The End(s) of Ethnography*, xxiii.

7 Ibid., xxv.

8 Haraway, *Modest_Witness@Second_Millennium.FemaleMan©_Meets_Onco Mouse™*, 50.

9 For examples of recent critical analyses of psychiatry and psychopharmacology that also point in more hopeful directions, see Metzl, *Prozac on the Couch*. Metzl, a psychiatrist and cultural theorist, calls on psychiatry to "develop a theory of itself and of its own complex constitution. Psychiatry needs to expose its own synapses and dendrites with the same vigor with which it has exposed those of its patients" (198). See also Bradley Lewis, *Moving Beyond Prozac*; and a wonderful feminist analysis of the "pharmorg" in Zita, *Body Talk*, 61–79.

10 See Orr, "Militarization of Inner Space."

11 Sarah Kershaw, "Terror Scenes Follow Script of No More 9/11's," *New York Times*, May 13, 2003, A21. All phrases in italics in this paragraph are quotes from Kershaw's article.

12 Trinh, *Woman, Native, Other*, 133.

13 Diana Taylor, "You Are Here," 166.

BIBLIOGRAPHY

Abramson, Harold A., ed. *Neuropharmacology*. Vol. 5. New York: Josiah Macy Jr.
    Foundation, 1959.
———, ed. *Problems of Consciousness*. Vol. 4. New York: Josiah Macy Jr. Founda-
    tion, 1954.
Acker, Kathy. *The Adult Life of Toulouse Lautrec by Henri Toulouse Lautrec*. In
    Portrait of an Eye: Three Novels. New York: Grove Press, 1975.
———. *Blood and Guts in High School*. New York: Grove Press, 1978.
———. "Models of Our Present." *Artforum* 22 (February 1984): 62–65.
Ahlgren, Carol, and Frank Edgerton Martin. "From Dante to Doomsday: How a
    City without People Survived a Nuclear Blast." *Design Book Review* 17 (winter
    1989): 26–28.
Alexander, Jeffrey. *The Modern Reconstruction of Classical Thought: Talcott Parsons*.
    Berkeley: University of California Press, 1983.
Allport, Gordon W. "The Historical Background of Modern Social Psychology."
    In *Handbook of Social Psychology*, vol. 1, ed. Gardner Lindzey. Cambridge:
    Addison-Wesley, 1954.
American Psychiatric Association. *Diagnostic and Statistical Manual of Mental
    Disorders*. 1st ed. Washington: American Psychiatric Association, 1952.
———. *Diagnostic and Statistical Manual of Mental Disorders*. 2nd ed. Washington:
    American Psychiatric Association, 1968.
———. *Diagnostic and Statistical Manual of Mental Disorders*. 3rd ed. Washington:
    American Psychiatric Association, 1980.
———. *Diagnostic and Statistical Manual of Mental Disorders*. 4th ed. Washington:
    American Psychiatric Association, 1994.
"Anatomy of a Panic." Review of *Invasion from Mars: A Study in the Psychology of
    Panic*, by Hadley Cantril. *Time*, April 15, 1940, 58–59.
Anderson, Laurie. *Stories from the Nerve Bible*. Difficult Music BMI, 1994.
Angell, James R. "Radio and National Morale." *American Journal of Sociology* 47,
    no. 3 (November 1941): 352–59.
Annual Report of the Rockland State Hospital. Vols. 26–28, 1956–58.
Artaud, Antonin. *The Theater and Its Double*. Trans. Mary Caroline Richards. New
    York: Grove Press, 1958.
Ballenger, James C. Interview by author. Charleston, S.C., April 22, 1996.
———. "Selective Serotonin Reuptake Inhibitors (SSRIs) in Panic Disorder." In
    Panic Disorder: Clinical Diagnosis, Management and Mechanisms, ed. David J.
    Nutt, James Ballenger, and Jean-Pierre Lepine. London: Martin Dunitz, 1999.

Ballenger, James C., Graham D. Burrows, Robert L. DuPont, Ira M. Lesser, et al. "Alprazolam in Panic Disorder and Agoraphobia: Results from a Multicenter Trial." *Archives of General Psychiatry* 45 (May 1988): 413–22.

Barondes, Samuel. "An Agenda for Psychiatric Genetics." *Archives of General Psychiatry* 56, no. 6 (June 1999): 549–52.

Baudrillard, Jean. *The Ecstasy of Communication*. Trans. Bernard and Caroline Schutze. New York: Semiotext(e), 1987.

———. *Forget Baudrillard: An Interview with Sylvere Lotringer*. New York: Semiotext(e), 1987.

———. *In the Shadow of the Silent Majorities, or The End of the Social*. Trans. Paul Foss, John Johnston, and Paul Patton. New York: Semiotext(e), 1983.

———. *Simulations*. Trans. Paul Foss, Paul Patton, and Philip Beitchman. New York: Semiotext(e), 1983.

Bayer, Ronald, and Robert L. Spitzer. "Neurosis, Psychodynamics and DSM-III." *Archives of General Psychiatry* 42, no. 2 (February 1985): 187–96.

Benjamin, Walter. *Illuminations*. Ed. Hannah Arendt and trans. Harry Zohn. New York: Schocken, 1969.

Bernays, Edward. *Crystallizing Public Opinion*. New York: Boni and Liveright, 1934.

———. "Morale: First Line of Defense." *Infantry Journal* 48 (May 1941): 32–35.

———. *Propaganda*. New York: H. Liveright, 1928.

Bernheimer, Charles, and Claire Kahane, eds. *In Dora's Case: Freud—Hysteria—Feminism*. New York: Columbia University Press, 1985.

Blashfield, Robert K. "Feighner et al., Invisible Colleges, and the Matthew Effect." *Schizophrenia Bulletin* 8, no. 1 (1982): 1–6.

Blumer, Herbert. "Collective Behavior." In *Review of Sociology: Analysis of a Decade*, ed. Joseph B. Gittler, 127–58. New York: John Wiley and Sons, 1957.

———. "Collective Behavior." In *Principles of Sociology*, 3rd ed., ed. Alfred McClung Lee. New York: Barnes and Noble Books, 1969.

Bogard, William. *The Simulation of Surveillance: Hypercontrol in Telematic Societies*. Cambridge: Cambridge University Press, 1996.

Bowker, Geof. "How to Be Universal: Some Cybernetic Strategies." *Social Studies of Science* 23 (1993): 107–27.

Bowlby, John. "Separation Anxiety." *International Journal of Psycho-Analysis* 41 (1960): 89–113.

Boyle, Hal. "Washington under the Bomb. *Collier's*, October 27, 1951, 20–21.

Brandt, Nat. *Chicago Death Trap: The Iroquois Theatre Fire of 1903*. Carbondale: Southern Illinois University Press, 2003.

Breggin, Peter. *Toxic Psychiatry*. New York: St. Martin's Press, 1991.

Breines, Winifred. "Alone in the 1950s: Anne Parsons and the Feminine Mystique." In *Talcott Parsons: Critical Assessments*, vol. 4, ed. Peter Hamilton. New York: Routledge, 1992. First published in *Theory and Society* 15 (1986): 805–43.

Brown, Wendy. *Politics out of History*. Princeton: Princeton University Press, 2001.

Butler, Judith. "Performative Acts and Gender Constitution: An Essay in Phenomenology and Feminist Theory." In *Performing Feminisms: Feminist Critical Theory and Theatre*, ed. Sue-Ellen Case. Baltimore: Johns Hopkins University Press, 1990.

Caldicott, Helen. *Missile Envy: The Arms Race and Nuclear War*. New York: Bantam Books, 1986.

Cannon, Walter B. " 'Voodoo' Death." *American Anthropologist* 44, no. 2 (April–June 1942): 169–81.

———. *The Wisdom of the Body*. New York: W. W. Norton, 1932.

Cantor, Nancy, Rita deSales French, Edward E. Smith, and Juan Mezzich. "Psychiatric Diagnosis as Prototype Categorization." *Journal of Abnormal Psychology* 89, no. 2 (1980): 181–93.

Cantril, Hadley. "Causes and Control of Riot and Panic." *Public Opinion Quarterly* 7 (winter 1943): 669–79.

———. *The Invasion from Mars: A Study in the Psychology of Panic*. Princeton: Princeton University Press, 1940.

Caruth, Cathy, ed. *Trauma: Explorations in Memory*. Baltimore: Johns Hopkins University Press, 1995.

———. *Unclaimed Experience: Trauma, Narrative, and History*. Baltimore: Johns Hopkins University Press, 1996.

Castillo, Greg. "Thermonuclear Family Values." *Design Book Review* 27 (winter 1993): 61–67.

Cixous, Hélène, and Catherine Clément. *The Newly Born Woman*. Trans. Betsy Wing. Minneapolis: University of Minnesota Press, 1986. Originally published as *La jeune née*. Paris: Union Générale d'Éditions, 1975.

Clarke, Adele, Laura Mamo, Jennifer Fishman, Janet Shim, and Jennifer Ruth Fosket. "Biomedicalization: Technoscientific Transformations of Health, Illness, and U.S. Biomedicine." *American Sociological Review* 68, no. 2 (April 2003): 161–94.

Clough, Patricia Ticineto. *Autoaffection: Unconscious Thought in the Age of Teletechnology*. Minneapolis: University of Minnesota Press, 2000.

———. *The End(s) of Ethnography: From Realism to Social Criticism*. 2nd ed. New York: Peter Lang Publishing, 1998.

———. *Feminist Thought: Desire, Power and Academic Discourse*. Oxford: Blackwell, 1994.

Clynes, Manfred. "An Interview with Manfred Clynes." By Chris Hables Gray. In *The Cyborg Handbook*, ed. Chris Hables Gray. New York: Routledge, 1995.

———. "Sentics: Biocybernetics of Emotion Communication." *Annals of the New York Academy of Sciences* 220 (July 9, 1973): 55–131.

Cobb, Stanley. *Foundations of Neuropsychiatry*. 3rd ed. Baltimore: Williams and Wilkins, 1944.

———. "Norbert Wiener and Psychiatry." *Journal of Nervous and Mental Disease* 140, no. 1 (January 1965): 13–15.

Cobb, Stanley, and Erick Lindemann. "Neuropsychiatric Observations." *Annals of Surgery* 117 (June 1943): 814–24.

Cockburn, Alexander. "The Press and the 'Just War.' " *The Nation*, February 18, 1991.

Cohen, Mandel E., Robert E. Johnson, Stanley Cobb, William P. Chapman, and

Paul White. "Studies of Work and Discomfort in Patients with Neurocirculatory Asthenia." *Journal of Clinical Investigation* 23 (1944): 934.

Cole, Jonathan. "The ECDEU-NCDEU Program." *Psychopharmacology Bulletin* 22, no. 1 (1986): 3–5.

Cole, Jonathan O., and Ralph W. Gerard, eds. *Psychopharmacology: Problems in Evaluation.* Washington: National Academy of Sciences, 1959.

Cole, Jonathan O., and Martin M. Katz. "Introduction and Overview of the Conference." In *The Role and Methodology of Classification in Psychiatry and Psychopathology*, ed. Martin M. Katz, Jonathan O. Cole, and Walter E. Barton. Washington: National Institute of Mental Health, 1968.

Collier, Peter, and David Horowitz. *The Rockefellers: An American Dynasty.* New York: Holt, Rinehart and Winston, 1976.

Collins, Patricia Hill. *Black Feminist Thought.* Boston: Unwin Hyman, 1990.

Committee on Statistics of the American Medico-Psychological Association in Collaboration with the Bureau of Statistics of the National Committee for Mental Hygiene. *Statistical Manual for the Use of Institutions for the Insane.* New York: National Committee for Mental Hygiene, 1918.

Connell, Robert W. "Why Is Classical Theory Classical?" *American Journal of Sociology* 102, no. 6 (1997): 1511–57.

Coser, Rose Laub, Renée C. Fox, Louisa P. Howe, Merton J. Kahne, et al. Introduction to *Belief, Magic, and Anomie: Essays in Psychosocial Anthropology*, by Anne Parsons. New York: Free Press, 1969.

Cottrell, Leonard S., Jr., and Sylvia Eberhart. *American Opinion on World Affairs in the Atomic Age.* Princeton: Princeton University Press, 1948.

Cotts, Cynthia. "Xanax Panic: The Pushers in the Suites." *The Nation*, August 31–September 7, 1992, 208–11.

Cvetkovich, Ann. *An Archive of Feelings: Trauma, Sexuality, and Lesbian Public Cultures.* Durham: Duke University Press, 2003.

Daniels, Gordon, ed. *A Guide to the Reports of the United States Strategic Bombing Survey.* London: Office of the Royal Historical Society, 1981.

Danzinger, Kurt. *Constructing the Subject: Historical Origins of Psychological Research.* Cambridge: Cambridge University Press, 1990.

Dechert, Charles. "The Development of Cybernetics." In *The Social Impact of Cybernetics*, ed. Charles Dechert. New York: Simon and Schuster, 1966.

Deleuze, Gilles. *Desert Islands and Other Texts, 1953–1974.* Ed. David Lapoujade and trans. Michael Taormina. New York: Semiotext(e), 2004.

———. "Postscript on the Societies of Control." *October* 59 (1991): 3–7.

Denning, Michael. *The Cultural Front: The Laboring of American Culture in the Twentieth Century.* New York: Verso, 1996.

de Tarde, Gabriel. *The Laws of Imitation.* New York: H. Holt, 1903.

Douvan, Elizabeth, and Stephen B. Withey. "Some Attitudinal Consequences of Atomic Energy." *Annals of the American Academy of Political and Social Science* 290 (November 1953): 108–17.

Dreyfus, Hubert L., and Paul Rabinow. *Michel Foucault: Beyond Structuralism and Hermeneutics.* Chicago: University of Chicago Press, 1982.

Durkheim, Emile. *The Elementary Forms of Religious Life*. Trans. Karen E. Fields. New York: Free Press, 1995.

Dyer-Witheford, Nick. *Cyber-Marx: Cycles and Circuits of Struggle in High-Technology Capitalism*. Urbana: University of Illinois Press, 1999.

Eaton, William W., Amy Dryman, and Myrna Weissman. "Panic and Phobia." In *Psychiatric Disorders in America: The Epidemiologic Catchment Area Study*, ed. Lee Robins and Darrel Regier. New York: Free Press, 1991.

Edwards, Paul. *The Closed World: Computers and the Politics of Discourse in Cold War America*. Cambridge: MIT Press, 1996.

Elsner, Henry, Jr. Introduction to *The Crowd and the Public and Other Essays*, by Robert Park. Chicago: University of Chicago Press, 1972.

Endicott, Jean. Interview by author. New York, March 25, 1996.

Faber, Diana P. "Suggestion: Metaphor and Meaning." *Journal of the History of the Behavioral Sciences* 32 (January 1996): 16–28.

Farley, J., Robert A. Woodruff, and Samuel B. Guze. "The Prevalence of Hysteria and Conversion Symptoms." *British Journal of Psychiatry* 114 (1968): 1121–25.

Faust, David, and Richard A. Miner. "The Empiricist and His New Clothes: DSM-III in Perspective." *American Journal of Psychiatry* 143, no. 8 (August 1986): 962–67.

Faxon, Nathaniel W. "The Problems of Hospital Administration." *Annals of Surgery* 117 (June 1943): 803–8.

Federal Civil Defense Administration. *Annual Report for 1951*. Washington: U.S. Government Printing Office, 1952.

———. *Annual Report for 1952*. Washington: U.S. Government Printing Office, 1953.

———. *Annual Report for 1953*. Washington: U.S. Government Printing Office, 1954.

———. *Annual Report for 1954*. Washington: U.S. Government Printing Office, 1955.

———. *Annual Report for 1955*. Washington: U.S. Government Printing Office, 1956.

———. *Annual Report for Fiscal Year 1956*. Washington: U.S. Government Printing Office, 1957.

———. *Annual Report for Fiscal Year 1958*. Washington: Government Printing Office, 1959.

Feighner, John P., Eli Robins, Samuel B. Guze, Robert A. Woodruff, George Winokur, and Rodrigo Munoz. "Diagnostic Criteria for Use in Psychiatric Research." *Archives of General Psychiatry* 26 (January 1972): 57–63.

Felix, Robert. "Mental Disorders as a Public Health Problem." *American Journal of Psychiatry* 106, no. 6 (December 1949): 401–6.

Fink, Jennifer Natalya. "Conclusion: Pushing through the Surface; Notes on Hybridity and Writing." In *Performing Hybridity*, ed. May Joseph and Jennifer Natalya Fink. Minneapolis: University of Minnesota Press, 1999.

Fink, Max. "Neurophysiological Response Strategies in the Classification of Mental Illness." In *The Role and Methodology of Classification in Psychiatry and Psychopathology*, ed. Martin Katz, Jonathan Cole, and Walter Barton. Washington: National Institute of Mental Health, 1968.

Flaherty, Bernard E., ed. *Psychophysiological Aspects of Space Flight*. New York: Columbia University Press, 1961.

Fleiss, Joseph L., Robert L. Spitzer, Jean Endicott, and Jacob Cohen. "Quantification of Agreement in Multiple Psychiatric Diagnosis." *Archives of General Psychiatry* 26 (February 1972): 168–71.

Foreman, Paul. "Panic Theory." *Sociology and Social Research* 37, no. 5 (May–June 1953): 295–304.

Foucault, Michel. *The Archaeology of Knowledge and the Discourse on Language.* Trans. A. M. Sheridan Smith. New York: Pantheon Books, 1972.

———. *The Birth of the Clinic: An Archaeology of Medical Perception.* Trans. A. M. Sheridan Smith. New York: Vintage Books, 1975.

———. "First Preface to *Histoire de la folie à l'age classique (1961).*" *Pli* 13 (2002): 1–10.

———. *The History of Sexuality, Volume I.* Trans. Robert Hurley. New York: Vintage Books, 1978.

———. *Madness and Civilization: A History of Insanity in the Age of Reason.* Trans. Richard Howard. New York: Vintage Books, 1965.

———. "Nietzsche, Genealogy, History." In *The Foucault Reader,* ed. Paul Rabinow. New York: Pantheon Books, 1984.

———. "Two Lectures." In *Culture/Power/History: A Reader in Contemporary Social Theory,* ed. Nicholas B. Dirks, Geoff Eley, and Sherry B. Ortner. Princeton: Princeton University Press, 1994.

Frances, Allen, Avram H. Mack, Michael B. First, Thomas A. Widiger, et al. "DSM-IV Meets Philosophy." *Journal of Medicine and Philosophy* 19, no. 4 (June 1994): 207–18.

Frances, Allen, Gloria M. Miele, Thomas A. Widiger, Harold A. Pincus, et al. "The Classification of Panic Disorders: From Freud to DSM-IV." *Journal of Psychiatric Research* 27, suppl. 1 (1993): 3–10.

Frances, Allen, Harold Alan Pincus, Thomas A. Widiger, Wendy Wakefield, et al. "DSM-IV: Work in Progress." *American Journal of Psychiatry* 147, no. 11 (November 1990): 1439–48.

Freed, Donald. *Death in Washington: The Murder of Orlando Letelier.* Westport, Conn.: Lawrence Hill, 1980.

Fremont-Smith, Frank. "Orientation Address." In *Transactions of the Conference on Morale—and the Prevention and Control of Panic.* New York: New York Academy of Medicine, 1951.

———. Papers. Countway Library of Medicine, Harvard Medical School.

French, John R. P., Jr. "Organized and Unorganized Groups under Fear and Frustration." In *Collective Behavior,* 2nd ed., ed. Ralph Turner and Lewis Killian. Englewood Cliffs, N.J.: Prentice-Hall, 1972. Originally published in Kurt Lewin et al., *Authority and Freedom.* Iowa City: University of Iowa Press, 1944.

Freud, Sigmund. *Dora: An Analysis of a Case of Hysteria.* New York: Macmillan, 1963.

———. *Group Psychology and the Analysis of the Ego.* Trans. James Strachey. New York: Bantam Books, 1960.

———. *The Interpretation of Dreams.* Trans. James Strachey. New York: Avon Books, 1965.

———. "On the Grounds for Detaching a Particular Syndrome from Neurasthenia under the Description 'Anxiety Neurosis.'" In *The Standard Edition of the Complete Psychological Works of Sigmund Freud, Vol. III (1893–1899)*, ed. and trans. James Strachey, with Anna Freud. London: Hogarth Press, 1962.

———. "Transference." In *Introductory Lectures on Psychoanalysis*, ed. and trans. James Strachey. New York: W. W. Norton, 1966.

Freud, Sigmund, and Josef Breuer. *Studies on Hysteria*. Trans. James Strachey. New York: Basic Books, 1957.

Galdston, Iago, ed. *Panic and Morale: Conference Transactions*. New York: International Universities Press, 1958.

———, ed. *Transactions of the Conference on Morale—and the Prevention and Control of Panic*. New York: New York Academy of Medicine, 1951.

Gallop, Jane. *The Daughter's Seduction: Feminism and Psychoanalysis*. Ithaca: Cornell University Press, 1982.

Gary, Brett. *The Nervous Liberals: Propaganda Anxieties from World War I to the Cold War*. New York: Columbia University Press, 1999.

Gelder, M. "Panic Disorder: Fact or Fiction?" *Psychology* 19 (1989): 277–83.

Gerard, Ralph W. Introduction to *Psychopharmacology: Problems in Evaluation*, ed. Jonathan O. Cole and Ralph W. Gerard. Washington: National Academy of Sciences, 1959.

Gerovitch, Slava. *From Newspeak to Cyberspeak: A History of Soviet Cybernetics*. Cambridge: MIT Press, 2002.

Gibson, William. *The Perfect War: Technowar in Vietnam*. Boston: Atlantic Monthly Press, 1986.

Gordon, Avery. *Ghostly Matters: Haunting and the Sociological Imagination*. Minneapolis: University of Minnesota Press, 1997.

Gorman, Jack, Justine Kent, Gregory Sullivan, and Jeremy Coplan. "Neuroanatomical Hypothesis of Panic Disorder, Revised." *American Journal of Psychiatry* 157, no. 4 (April 2000): 493–505.

Gouldner, Alvin. *The Coming Crisis of Western Sociology*. New York: Basic Books, 1970.

Gray, Chris Hables. *Cyborg Citizen*. New York: Routledge, 2002.

———, ed. *The Cyborg Handbook*. New York: Routledge, 1995.

Grinker, Roy R. "Inadequacies of Contemporary Psychiatric Diagnosis." In *Psychiatric Diagnosis*, ed. Vivan Rakoff, Harvey Stancer, and Henry Kedward. New York: Brunner/Mazel, 1977.

———. "Problems of Consciousness: A Review, an Analysis, and a Proposition." In *Problems of Consciousness: Transactions of the Fourth Conference*, ed. Harold A. Abramson. New York: Josiah Macy Jr. Foundation, 1954.

———, ed. *Toward a Unified Theory of Human Behavior: An Introduction to General Systems Theory*. 2nd ed. New York: Basic Books, 1967.

Grinker, Roy, and John Spiegel. *War Neuroses in North Africa*. New York: Josiah Macy Jr. Foundation, 1943.

———. *Men under Stress*. London: J. and A. Churchill, 1945.

Grob, Gerald. "The Forging of Mental Health Policy in America: World War II to New Frontier." *Journal of the History of Medicine and Allied Sciences* 41, no. 4 (October 1987): 410–46.

———. *From Asylum to Community: Mental Health Policy in Modern America.* Princeton: Princeton University Press, 1991.

———. "Origins of DSM-I: A Study in Appearance and Reality." *American Journal of Psychiatry* 148, no. 4 (April 1991): 421–31.

Guze, Samuel B. "The Diagnosis of Hysteria: What Are We Trying to Do?" *American Journal of Psychiatry* 124, no. 4 (October 1967): 491–98.

Guze, Samuel B., and Michael J. Perley. "Observations on the Natural History of Hysteria." *American Journal of Psychiatry* 119 (1963): 960–65.

Guze, Samuel B., John S. Strauss, Martin M. Katz, and R. E. Kendell. "Comments on Blashfield's Article." *Schizophrenia Bulletin* 8, no. 1 (1982).

Hamilton, Max. "Perspectives on the Conference." In *The Role and Methodology of Classification in Psychiatry and Psychopathology*, ed. Martin M. Katz, Jonathan O. Cole, and Walter E. Barton. Washington: National Institute of Mental Health, 1968.

Haraway, Donna. "A Game of Cat's Cradle: Science Studies, Feminist Theory, Cultural Studies." *Configurations* 2, no. 1 (1994): 59–71.

———. "The High Cost of Information in Post–World War II Evolutionary Biology: Ergonomics, Semiotics, and the Sociobiology of Communication Systems." *Philosophical Forum* 13, nos. 2–3 (winter–spring 1981–82): 244–78.

———. "Manifesto for Cyborgs: Science, Technology, and Socialist Feminism in the 1980s." *Socialist Review* 80 (1985): 65–108.

———. *Modest_Witness@Second_Millennium.FemaleMan©_Meets_OncoMouse™: Feminism and Technoscience.* New York: Routledge, 1997.

———. "Possible Worlds: An Interview with Donna Haraway." Interview by Avery Gordon. In *Body Politics: Disease, Desire, and the Family*, ed. Avery Gordon and Michael Ryan. Boulder, Colo.: Westview Press, 1994.

———. *Primate Visions: Gender, Race, and Nature in the World of Modern Science.* New York: Routledge, 1989.

———. "Signs of Dominance: From a Physiology to a Cybernetics of Primate Society, C. R. Carpenter, 1930–1970." In *Studies in History of Biology*, vol. 6, ed. William Coleman and Camille Limuges. Baltimore: Johns Hopkins University Press, 1983.

———. *Simians, Cyborgs, and Women: The Reinventions of Nature.* New York: Routledge, 1991.

Hardt, Michael, and Antonio Negri. *Empire.* Cambridge: Harvard University Press, 2000.

Hayles, N. Katherine. "Boundary Disputes: Homeostasis, Reflexivity, and the Foundations of Cybernetics." *Configurations* 3 (1994): 441–67.

———. *How We Became Posthuman: Virtual Bodies in Cybernetics, Literature, and Informatics.* Chicago: University of Chicago Press, 1999.

Healy, David. *The Antidepressant Era.* Cambridge: Harvard University Press, 1997.

———. *The Creation of Psychopharmacology*. Cambridge: Harvard University Press, 2002.

———. "Psychopharmacology in the New Medical State." In *Psychotropic Drug Development: Social, Economic, and Pharmacological Aspects*, ed. David Healy and Declan P. Doogan. London: Chapman and Hall Medical, 1996.

Heims, Steve J. *The Cybernetics Group*. Cambridge: MIT Press, 1991.

———. *John von Neumann and Norbert Wiener: From Mathematics to the Technologies of Life and Death*. Cambridge: MIT Press, 1987.

Herman, Judith. *Trauma and Recovery*. New York: Basic Books, 1992.

Hettema, John, Michael Neale, and Kenneth Kendler. "A Review and Meta-analysis of the Genetic Epidemiology of Anxiety Disorder." *American Journal of Psychiatry* 158, no. 10 (October 2001): 1568–78.

Hollier, Dennis, ed. *The College of Sociology (1937–1939)*. Trans. Betsy Wing. Minneapolis: University of Minnesota Press, 1988.

Hyler, Steven, and Robert L. Spitzer. "Hysteria Split Asunder." *American Journal of Psychiatry* 133, no. 12 (December 1978): 1500–1504.

Hyman, Herbert. *Taking Society's Measure: A Personal History of Survey Research*. New York: Russell Sage Foundation, 1991.

Irigaray, Luce. *Speculum of the Other Woman*. Trans. Gillian C. Gill. Ithaca: Cornell University Press, 1985. Originally published as *Speculum de l'autre femme*. Paris: Editions de Minuit, 1974.

———. *This Sex Which Is Not One*. Trans. Catherine Porter. Ithaca: Cornell University Press, 1985. Originally published as *Ce sexe quie n'en est pas un*. Paris: Editions de Minuit, 1977.

Jablensky, Assen V. "European and American Concepts of Anxiety." *Journal of Psychiatric Research* 24, suppl. 1 (1990): 8.

Janet, Pierre. *The Major Symptoms of Hysteria*. New York: Macmillan, 1929.

Janis, Irving. *Air War and Emotional Stress: Psychological Studies of Bombing and Civilian Defense*. New York: McGraw-Hill, 1951.

Janis, Irving, Dwight Chapman, John Gillin, and John Spiegel. "The Problem of Panic." *Civil Defense Technical Bulletin* TB-19-2 (June 1955): 1–8.

Josiah Macy Jr. Foundation. *Conference on Feedback Mechanisms and Circular Causal Systems in Biology and the Social Sciences*. March 8–9, 1946, New York. Frank Fremont-Smith Papers. Countway Library of Medicine, Harvard Medical School.

Kaplan, Marcie. "A Woman's View of DSM-III." *American Psychologist* (July 1983): 786–92.

Karpf, Fay B. *American Social Psychology: Its Origins, Development, and European Background*. New York: McGraw-Hill, 1932.

Katz, Martin M., and Jonathan O. Cole. "Reflections on the Major Conference Issues." In *The Role and Methodology of Classification in Psychiatry and Psychopathology*, ed. Martin M. Katz, Jonathan O. Cole, and Walter E. Barton. Washington: National Institute of Mental Health, 1968.

Katz, Martin M., Jonathan O. Cole, and Walter E. Barton, eds. *The Role and Method-*

ology of Classification in Psychiatry and Psychopathology. Washington: National Institute of Mental Health, 1968.

Kelley, Harold, John Condry Jr., Arnold Dahlke, and Arthur Hill. "Collective Behavior in a Simulated Panic Situation." *Journal of Experimental Social Psychology* 1, no. 1 (January 1965): 20–54.

Kendell, Robert E. "Five Criteria for an Improved Taxonomy of Mental Disorders." In *Defining Psychopathology in the 21st Century: DSM-V and Beyond*, ed. John E. Helzer and James J. Hudziak. Washington: American Psychiatric Publishing, 2002.

Kety, Seymour S. Foreword to *The First Psychiatric Institute: How Research and Education Changed Practice*, by Lawrence Kolb and Leon Roizin. Washington: American Psychiatric Press, 1993.

Killam, Keith F., and Eva K. Killam. "Central Action of Chlorpromazine and Reserpine." In *Neuropharmacology*, vol. 5, ed. Harold A. Abramson. New York: Josiah Macy Jr. Foundation, 1959.

Kirk, Stuart, and Herb Kutchins. *The Selling of DSM: The Rhetoric of Science in Psychiatry*. New York: Aldine de Gruyter, 1992.

Klein, Donald. "Anxiety Reconceptualized." In *Anxiety: New Research and Changing Concepts*, ed. Donald Klein and Jeremy Rabkin. New York: Raven Press, 1981.

———. "Cybernetics, Activation, and Drug Effects." *Acta Psychiatrica Scandinavia* 77, no. 341 (1985): 126–37.

———. "Delineation of Two Drug-Responsive Anxiety Syndromes." *Psychopharmacologia* 5 (1964): 397–408.

———. "False Suffocation Alarms, Spontaneous Panics, and Related Conditions: An Integrative Hypothesis." *Archives of General Psychiatry* 50 (April 1993): 306–17.

———. "Importance of Psychiatric Diagnosis in Prediction of Clinical Drug Effects." *Archives of General Psychiatry* 16 (January 1967): 118–26.

———. Interview by author. New York, March 29, 1996.

———. "A Proposed Definition of Mental Illness." In *Critical Issues in Psychiatric Diagnosis*, ed. Robert Spitzer and Donald Klein. New York: Raven Press, 1978.

———. "Psychotropic Drugs and the Regulation of Behavioral Activation in Psychiatric Illness." In *Drugs and Cerebral Function*, ed. W. Lynn Smith. Springfield, Ill.: Charles C. Thomas, 1970.

———. "Testing the Suffocation False Alarm Theory of Panic Disorder." *Anxiety* 1 (1994): 1–7.

Klein, Donald, and J. M. Davis. *Diagnosis and Drug Treatment of Psychiatric Disorders: Adults and Children*. 1st ed. Baltimore: Williams and Wilkins, 1969.

Klein, Donald, and Max Fink. "Psychiatric Reaction Patterns to Imipramine." *American Journal of Psychiatry* 119 (November 1962): 432–38.

Klein, Donald, Rachel Gittelman, Frederic Quitkin, and Arthur Rifkin. *Diagnosis and Drug Treatment of Psychiatric Disorders: Adults and Children*. 2nd ed. Baltimore: Williams and Wilkins, 1980.

Klein, Donald, and Jeremy G. Rabkin. "Specificity and Strategy in Psychotherapy Research and Practice." In *Psychotherapy Research: Where Are We and Where*

Should We Go? ed. Janet Williams and Robert Spitzer. New York: Guilford Press, 1984.

Klein, Donald, and Paul Wender. *Mind, Mood and Medicine: A Guide to the New Biopsychiatry.* New York: Farrar, Straus and Giroux, 1981.

Klerman, L. Gerald. "Historical Perspectives on Psychopathology." In *Contemporary Directions in Psychopathology: Toward the DSM-IV,* ed. Theodore Millon and Gerald L. Klerman. New York: Guilford Press, 1986.

———. "History and Development of Modern Concepts of Anxiety and Panic." In *Clinical Aspects of Panic Disorder,* ed. James C. Ballenger. New York: John Wiley and Sons, 1990.

———. "Introduction." *Journal of Psychiatric Research* 24, suppl. 1 (1990): 2.

———. "Overview of the Cross-National Collaborative Panic Study." *Archives of General Psychiatry* 45 (May 1988): 407–12.

Klerman, Gerald L., James H. Coleman, and Robert Purpura. "The Design and Conduct of the Upjohn Cross-National Collaborative Panic Study." *Psychopharmacology Bulletin* 22, no. 1 (1986): 59–64.

Klerman, Gerald L., George E. Vaillant, Robert L. Spitzer, and Robert Michels. "A Debate on DSM-III." *American Journal of Psychiatry* 141, no. 4 (April 1984): 539–53.

Klerman, Gerald L., et al. "Drug Treatment of Panic Disorder: Comparative Efficacy of Alprazolam, Imipramine, and Placebo. Cross-National Collaborative Panic Study, Second Phase Investigators." *British Journal of Psychiatry* 160 (1992): 191–202.

Klerman, Gerald L., et al. "Drug Treatment of Panic Disorder: Reply to Comment by Marks and Associates." *British Journal of Psychiatry* 161 (1992): 465–71.

Kline, Nathan. "Clinical Applications of Reserpine." In *Psychopharmacology,* ed. Nathan Kline. Washington: American Association for the Advancement of Science, 1956.

———. "Toward a Theory of Man." In *Psychiatric Research Report No. 2.* Washington: American Psychiatric Association, 1955.

Kline, Nathan S., and Manfred Clynes. "Drugs, Space, and Cybernetics: Evolution to Cyborgs." In *Psychopharmacological Aspects of Space Flight,* ed. Bernard E. Flaherty. New York: Columbia University Press, 1961.

Kline, Nathan, and E. Laska, eds. *Computers and Electronic Devices in Psychiatry.* New York: Grune and Stratton, 1968.

Koch, Howard. *The Panic Broadcast.* New York: Avon Books, 1967.

Kolb, Lawrence. "Research and Its Support under the National Mental Health Act." *American Journal of Psychiatry* 106, no. 6 (December 1949): 407–12.

Kolb, Lawrence, and Leon Roizin. *The First Psychiatric Institute: How Research and Education Changed Practice.* Washington: American Psychiatric Press, 1993.

Kroker, Arthur, and David Cook. *The Postmodern Scene: Excremental Culture and Hyper-Aesthetics.* New York: St. Martin's Press, 1986.

Kutchins, Herb, and Stuart A. Kirk. "The Business of Diagnosis: DSM-III and Clinical Social Work." *Social Work* 33, no. 4 (1988): 215–20.

LaPiere, Richard T. *Collective Behavior.* New York: McGraw-Hill, 1938.

Lazarsfeld, Paul. *Radio and the Printed Page: An Introduction to the Study of Radio and Its Role in the Communication of Ideas*. New York: Duell, Sloan and Pearce, 1940.

Leach, Eugene E. " 'Mental Epidemics': Crowd Psychology and American Culture, 1890–1940." *American Studies* 33 (spring 1992): 5–29.

Le Bon, Gustave. *The Crowd: A Study of the Popular Mind*. New York: Viking Press, 1960.

———. *The Psychology of Peoples*. New York: G. E. Stechert, 1912.

Lemert, Charles. *Sociology after the Crisis*. Boulder, Colo.: Westview Press, 1995.

Lettvin, Jerome. "Warren and Walter." In *Collected Works of Warren S. McCulloch*, vol. 2, ed. Rook McCulloch. Salinas, Calif.: Intersystems Publication, 1989.

Lettvin, Jerome, and Walter Pitts. "A Mathematical Theory of the Affective Psychoses." *Bulletin of Mathematical Biophysics* 5 (November 1943): 139–48.

Lewis, Bradley. *Moving Beyond Prozac, DSM, and the New Psychiatry: The Birth of Postpsychiatry*. Ann Arbor: University of Michigan Press, 2006.

Lewis, Nolan D. C., and Bernice Engle, eds. *Wartime Psychiatry: A Compendium of the International Literature*. New York: Oxford University Press, 1954.

Lewis, Thomas. *The Soldier's Heart and the Effort Syndrome*. New York: Paul B. Hoeber, 1920.

Leys, Ruth. *Trauma: A Genealogy*. Chicago: University of Chicago Press, 2000.

Lilienfeld, Robert. *The Rise of Systems Theory: An Ideological Analysis*. New York: John Wiley and Sons, 1978.

Lindesmith, Alfred, and Anselm Strauss. *Social Psychology*. Rev. ed. New York: Holt, Rinehart and Winston, 1956.

Lindzey, Gardner, ed. *Handbook of Social Psychology*. Vol. 1. Cambridge: Addison-Wesley, 1954.

Lowe, Donald. *The Body in Late-Capitalist USA*. Durham: Duke University Press, 1995.

Lunbeck, Elizabeth. *The Psychiatric Persuasion: Knowledge, Gender, and Power in Modern America*. Princeton: Princeton University Press, 1994.

MacIsaac, David. *Strategic Bombing in World War Two: The Story of the United States Strategic Bombing Survey*. New York: Garland, 1976.

MacLeish, Archibald. *Air Raid: A Verse Play for Radio*. New York: Harcourt, Brace, 1938.

———. *Panic: A Play in Verse*. Boston: Houghton Mifflin, 1935.

Madge, John. *The Origins of Scientific Sociology*. New York: Macmillan, 1962.

Malizia, Andrea L., and David J. Nutt. "Brain Mechanisms and Circuits in Panic Disorder." In *Panic Disorder: Clinical Diagnosis, Management and Mechanisms*, ed. David J. Nutt, James Ballenger, and Jean-Pierre Lepine. London: Martin Dunitz, 1999.

Margolis, Lester H., Ames Fischer, Robert N. Butler, and Alexander Simon. "Clinical Observations with Chlorpromazine." In *Psychopharmacology*, ed. Nathan Kline. Washington: American Association for the Advancement of Science, 1956.

Marks, Isaac. "Agoraphobia, Panic Disorder, and Related Conditions in the DSM-III and ICD-10." *Journal of Psychopharmacology* 1 (1987): 6–12.

Marks, Isaac, Metin Basoglu, Homa Noshirvani, John Greist, et al. "Drug Treatment of Panic Disorder: Further Comment." *British Journal of Psychiatry* 162 (1993): 795–96.

Marks, Isaac, John Greist, Metin Basoglu, Homa Noshirvani, et al. "Comment on the Second Phase of the Cross-National Collaborative Panic Study." *British Journal of Psychiatry* 160 (1992): 202–5.

Marks, Isaac, et al. "The 'Efficacy' of Alprazolam in Panic Disorder and Agoraphobia: A Critique of Recent Reports." Letter to the editor. *Archives of General Psychiatry* 46 (July 1989): 668–70.

Maron, M. E. "On Cybernetics, Information Processing, and Thinking." In *Cybernetics of the Nervous System*, vol. 17, ed. Norbert Wiener and J. P. Schadé. New York: Elsevier, 1965.

Martin, Emily. "The Rationality of Mania." In *Doing Science + Culture*, ed. Roddey Reid and Sharon Traweek. New York: Routledge, 2000.

Maser, Jack D., and Thomas Patterson. "Spectrum and Nosology: Implications for DSM-V." *Psychiatric Clinics of North America* 25 (2002): 855–85.

McCulloch, Warren. "The Brain as a Computing Machine." In *Collected Works of Warren S. McCulloch*, vol. 2, ed. Rook McCulloch. Salinas, Calif.: Intersystems Publication, 1989. Originally presented at the AIEE meetings, February 1949.

———. "*Mysterium Iniquitatis* of Sinful Man Aspiring unto the Place of God." In *Collected Works of Warren S. McCulloch*, vol. 3, ed. Rook McCulloch. Salinas, Calif.: Intersystems Publication, 1989. Originally published in *Scientific Monthly* 80, no. 1 (January 1955).

———. "The Past of a Delusion." In *Collected Works of Warren S. McCulloch*, vol. 2, ed. Rook McCulloch. Salinas, Calif.: Intersystems Publication, 1989. Originally presented at the Chicago Literary Club, January 28, 1952.

McCulloch, Warren, and Walter Pitts. "A Logical Calculus of the Ideas Immanent in Nervous Activity." *Bulletin of Mathematical Biophysics* 5, no. 4 (December 1943): 115–33.

McDougall, William. *The Group Mind: A Sketch of the Principles of Collective Psychology with Some Attempt to Apply Them to the Interpretation of National Life and Character*. New York: G. P. Putnam's Sons, 1920.

———. *An Introduction to Social Psychology*. 14th ed. London: Methuen, 1950.

McEnaney, Laura. *Civil Defense Begins at Home: Militarization Meets Everyday Life in the Fifties*. Princeton: Princeton University Press, 2000.

McNally, Richard J. *Panic Disorder: A Critical Analysis*. New York: Guilford Press, 1994.

Melley, Timothy. *Empire of Conspiracy: The Culture of Paranoia in Postwar America*. Ithaca: Cornell University Press, 2000.

Menninger, William C. "Development of Psychiatry in the Army in World War II." In *Wartime Psychiatry: A Compendium of the International Literature*, ed. Nolan D. C. Lewis and Bernice Engle. New York: Oxford University Press, 1954. Originally published in *War Medicine* 8 (October 1945): 229–34.

———. "Psychiatric Experience in the War, 1941–1946." *American Journal of Psychiatry* 103:577–86.

Merikangas, Kathleen Ries, and Neil Risch. "Will the Genomics Revolution Revolutionize Psychiatry?" *American Journal of Psychiatry* 160, no. 4 (April 2003): 625–35.

Merton, Robert K. Introduction to *The Crowd: A Study of the Popular Mind*, by Gustave Le Bon. New York: Viking Press, 1960.

Merton, Robert K., and Paul F. Lazarsfeld, eds. *Continuities in Social Research: Studies in the Scope and Method of "The American Soldier."* Glencoe, Ill.: Free Press, 1950.

Metzl, Jonathan. *Prozac on the Couch: Prescribing Gender in the Era of Wonder Drugs.* Durham: Duke University Press, 2003.

Micale, Mark S. *Approaching Hysteria: Disease and Its Interpretation.* Princeton: Princeton University Press, 1995.

Milgram, Stanley, and Hans Toch. "Collective Behavior: Crowds and Social Movements." In *The Handbook of Social Psychology*, vol. 4, 2nd ed., ed. Garner Lindzey and Elliot Aronson. Reading, Mass.: Addison-Wesley, 1969.

Miller, George A. "Communication and the Information Theory." In *Panic and Morale: Conference Transactions*, ed. Iago Galdston. New York: International Universities Press, 1958.

Millon, Theodore. "The DSM-III: An Insider's Perspective." *American Psychologist* (July 1983): 804–14.

———. "On the Past and Future of the DSM-III: Personal Reflections and Projections." In *Contemporary Directions in Psychopathology: Toward the DSM-IV*, ed. Theodore Millon and Gerald L. Klerman. New York: Guilford Press, 1986.

Mills, C. Wright. *The Sociological Imagination.* New York: Oxford University Press, 1959.

Mintz, Alexander. "Non-adaptive Group Behavior." *Journal of Abnormal and Social Psychology* 46, no. 2 (April 1951): 150–59.

Mirken, Bruce. "Ask Your Doctor." *San Francisco Bay Guardian*, October 23, 1996.

Morrison, Toni. *The Bluest Eye.* New York: Simon and Schuster, 1970.

Murrow, Edward R. "A-Bomb Mission to Moscow." *Collier's*, October 27, 1951, 19.

National Institute of Mental Health. *Panic Disorder in the Medical Setting*, by Wayne Katon. DHHS Pub. No. (ADM) 89-1629. Washington: U.S. Government Printing Office, 1989.

New York State Psychiatric Institute 1993. New York: New York State Psychiatric Institute, 1994.

Noyes, Russell, Jr., Robert L. DuPont, John C. Pecknold, Arthur Rifkin, et al. "Alprazolam in Panic Disorder and Agoraphobia: Results from a Multicenter Trial." *Archives of General Psychiatry* 45 (May 1988): 423–28.

Oakes, Guy. *The Imaginary War: Civil Defense and American Cold War Culture.* New York: Oxford University Press, 1994.

Office of Civil Defense, Sacramento, Calif. *Panic Control and Prevention: Instructor's Manual and Teaching Outline.* Sacramento: California State Printing Office, 1951.

Orr, Jackie. "The Militarization of Inner Space." *Critical Sociology* 30, no. 2 (spring 2004): 451–82.

———. "Panic Diary: (Re)constructing a Partial Politics and Poetics of Dis-ease."

In *Reconsidering Social Constructionism: Debates in Social Problems Theory*, ed.
James A. Holstein and Gale Miller. New York: Aldine de Gruyter, 1993.

———. "Re/Sounding Race, Re/Signifying Ethnography: Sampling Oaktown Rap."
In *Prosthetic Territories: Politics and Hypertechnologies*, ed. Gabriel Brahm Jr. and
Mark Driscoll. Boulder, Colo.: Westview Press, 1995.

———. "Theory on the Market: Panic, Incorporating." *Social Problems* 37, no. 4
(November 1990): 460–84.

Osborn, Frederick. Foreword to *American Opinion on World Affairs in the Atomic
Age*. Princeton: Princeton University Press, 1948.

———. Foreword to *The American Soldier: Adjustment during Army Life*. Studies
in Social Psychology, vol. 1, ed. Samuel Stouffer et al. Princeton: Princeton
University Press, 1949.

Overholser, Winifred. Foreword to *Psychopharmacology*, ed. Nathan Kline. Washington: American Association for the Advancement of Science, 1956.

Parisi, Luciana, and Tiziana Terranova. "Heat-Death." *C-Theory: Theory, Technology,
Culture* 23, nos. 1–2 (May 2000).

Park, Robert E. *The Crowd and the Public and Other Essays*. Trans. Charlotte Elsner.
Chicago: University of Chicago Press, 1972.

———. "Morale and the News." *American Journal of Sociology* 47, no. 3 (November
1941): 360–77.

———. "Symbiosis and Socialization: A Frame of Reference for the Study of
Society." *American Journal of Sociology* 45 (1939): 1–25.

Park, Robert E., and Ernest W. Burgess. *Introduction to the Science of Sociology*.
Chicago: University of Chicago Press, 1921.

Parsons, Anne. "Abstract and Concrete Images in Paranoid Delusions: A Comparison of American and South Italian Patients." Chapter 8 of *Belief, Magic, and
Anomie: Essays in Psychosocial Anthropology*. New York: Free Press, 1969.

———. "Cultural Barriers to Insight and the Structural Reality of Transference."
Chapter 14 of *Belief, Magic, and Anomie: Essays in Psychosocial Anthropology*.
New York: Free Press, 1969.

———. "Diffusion of Psychoanalytic Concepts." Chapter 13 of *Belief, Magic, and
Anomie: Essays in Psychosocial Anthropology*. New York: Free Press, 1969. Trans-
lated from Anne Parsons's Ph.D. diss., "La pénétration de la psychoanalyse en
France et aux Etats Unis," Paris, 1956.

———. "Expressive Symbolism in Witchcraft and Delusion: A Comparative
Study." Chapter 7 of *Belief, Magic, and Anomie: Essays in Psychosocial Anthropology*. New York: Free Press, 1969. Originally published in *Revue Internationale
d'Ethnopsychologie Normale et Pathologique* 1, no. 2: 99–119.

———. "Is the Oedipus Complex Universal? The Jones-Malinowski Debate Re-
visited." Chapter 1 of *Belief, Magic, and Anomie: Essays in Psychosocial Anthropology*. New York: Free Press, 1969. Originally published in Warner Muenster-
berger and Sidney Axelrad, eds., *The Psychoanalytic Study of Society*. Vol. 3. New
York: International Universities Press, 1964.

———. "On Psychoanalytic Training for Research Purposes." Chapter 15 of *Belief,
Magic, and Anomie: Essays in Psychosocial Anthropology*. New York: Free Press,

1969. Originally published in *Psychiatry: Journal for the Study of Interpersonal Processes* 27 (1964): 364–76.

Parsons, Talcott. "Cause and Effect in Sociology." In *Cause and Effect: The Hayden Colloquium on Scientific Method and Concept*, ed. Daniel Lerner. New York: Free Press, 1965.

——. "Consciousness and Symbolic Processes." In *Problems of Consciousness: Transactions of the Fourth Conference*, ed. Harold A. Abramson. New York: Josiah Macy Jr. Foundation, 1954.

——. "Definitions of Health and Illness in the Light of American Values and Social Structure." Chapter 10 of *Social Structure and Personality*. New York: Free Press, 1964. Originally published in E. Gartly Jaco, ed., *Patients, Physicians and Illness*. New York: Free Press of Glencoe, 1958.

——. "The Father Symbol: An Appraisal in the Light of Psychoanalytic and Sociological Theory." Chapter 2 of *Social Structure and Personality*. New York: Free Press, 1964. Originally presented at the annual meetings of the American Psychological Association, September 1952.

——. "Field Theory and System Theory: With Special Reference to the Relations between Psychobiological and Social Systems." In *Modern Psychiatry and Clinical Research: Essays in Honor of Roy R. Grinker, Sr.*, ed. Danila Offer and Daniel X. Freedman. New York: Basic Books, 1972.

——. "The Incest Taboo in Relation to Social Structure and the Socialization of the Child." Chapter 3 of *Social Structure and Personality*. New York: Free Press, 1964. Originally published in *British Journal of Sociology* 5, no. 2 (June 1954).

——. "On Building Social System Theory: A Personal History." *Daedalus: Journal of the American Academy of Arts and Sciences* 99, no. 4 (fall 1970): 827–81.

——. *Politics and Social Structure*. New York: Free Press, 1969.

——. "Propaganda and Social Control." In *Essays in Sociological Theory*, rev. ed. Glencoe, Ill.: Free Press, 1954.

——. "Social Structure and the Development of Personality: Freud's Contribution to the Integration of Psychology and Sociology." Chapter 4 of *Social Structure and Personality*. New York: Free Press, 1964. Originally published in *Psychiatry* 21, no. 4 (November 1958): 321–40.

——. *The Social System*. New York: Free Press, 1951.

——. "Some Reflections on the Problem of Psychosomatic Relationships in Health and Illness." Chapter 5 of *Social Structure and Personality*. New York: Free Press, 1964. Originally presented at the annual meeting of the American Psychosomatic Society, March 1960.

——. *The Structure of Social Action*. Vols. 1 and 2. New York: Free Press, 1937.

——. "The Superego and the Theory of Social Systems." Chapter 1 of *Social Structure and Personality*. New York: Free Press, 1964. Originally published in *Psychiatry* 15, no. 1 (February 1952).

——. "Theory in the Humanities and Sociology." *Daedalus: Journal of the American Academy of Arts and Sciences* 99, no. 2 (spring 1970): 495–523.

Parsons, Talcott, and Edward Shils. *Toward a General Theory of Action*. Cambridge: Harvard University Press, 1951.

Parsons, Talcott, and Neil J. Smelser. *Economy and Society*. Glencoe, Ill.: Free Press, 1956.

Perley, Michael J., and Samuel B. Guze. "Hysteria: The Stability and Usefulness of Clinical Criteria." *New England Journal of Medicine* 266, no. 9 (March 1, 1962): 421–26.

Peterson, Val. "Panic, the Ultimate Weapon?" *Collier's*, August 21, 1953.

Pfohl, Stephen. "The Cybernetic Delirium of Norbert Wiener." In *Digital Delirium*, ed. Arthur Kroker and Marilouise Kroker. New York: St. Martin's Press, 1997.

———. *Death at the Parasite Cafe: Social Science (Fictions) and the Postmodern*. New York: St. Martin's Press, 1992.

———. "Twilight of the Parasites: Ultramodern Capital and the New World Order." *Social Problems* 40, no. 2 (May 1993): 125–51.

Phelan, Peggy. "Introduction: The Ends of Performance." In *The Ends of Performance*, ed. Peggy Phelan and Jill Lane. New York: New York University Press, 1998.

Pickering, Andy. "Cyborg History and the World War II Regime." *Perspectives on Science* 3, no. 1 (1995): 1–48.

Plant, Sadie. *The Most Radical Gesture: The Situationist International in a Postmodern Age*. London: Routledge, 1992.

———. *Zeros + Ones: Digital Women + the New Technoculture*. New York: Doubleday, 1997.

Pollack, Mark. Interview by author. Boston, October 30, 1995.

Pollock, Della. "Performing Writing." In *The Ends of Performance*, ed. Peggy Phelan and Jill Lane. New York: New York University Press, 1998.

Princeton Radio Research Project. Papers. Rockefeller Archive Center, Tarrytown, N.Y.

Purtell, James J., Eli Robins, and Mendel E. Cohen. "Observations on Clinical Aspects of Hysteria: A Quantitative Study of 50 Hysteria Patients and 156 Control Subjects." *Journal of the American Medical Association* 146, no. 10 (July 7, 1945): 902–9.

Quarantelli, Enrico L. "The Behavior of Panic Participants." *Sociology and Social Research* 41, no. 3 (January–February 1957): 187–94.

———. "The Nature and Conditions of Panic." *American Journal of Sociology* 60, no. 3 (November 1954): 267–75.

Raines, Georges. Foreword to *Diagnostic and Statistical Manual of Mental Disorders*, 1st ed., by the American Psychiatric Association. Washington: American Psychiatric Association, 1952.

Regier, Darrel A., Jerome K. Myers, Morton Kramer, Lee N. Robins, et al. "The NIMH Epidemiologic Catchment Area Program." *Archives of General Psychiatry* 41 (October 1984): 934–48.

Report of the Project East River, Part IX. New York: Associated Universities, 1952.

Rich, Adrienne. *Midnight Salvage: Poems, 1995–1998*. New York: W. W. Norton, 1999.

Richman, Michele. "Anthropology and Modernism in France: From Durkheim to the Collège de Sociologie." In *Modernist Anthropology: From Fieldwork to Text*, ed. Marc Manganaro. Princeton: Princeton University Press, 1990.

Robins, Lee N., John E. Helzer, Jack Croughan, and K. S. Ratcliff. "National Institute of Mental Health Diagnostic Interview Schedule." *Archives of General Psychiatry* 38 (1981): 381–89.

Robins, Lee N., and Darrel A. Regier, eds. *Psychiatric Disorders in America: The Epidemiologic Catchment Area Study.* New York: Free Press, 1991.

Rogers, Everett M. *A History of Communication Study: A Biographical Approach.* New York: Free Press, 1994.

Romanyshyn, Robert. *Technology as Symptom and Dream.* New York: Routledge, 1989.

Ronnell, Avital. *The Telephone Book: Technology, Schizophrenia, Electric Speech.* Lincoln: University of Nebraska Press, 1989.

Rose, Gillian. *The Melancholy Science: An Introduction to the Thought of Theodor W. Adorno.* New York: Columbia University Press, 1978.

Rose, Hilary. "My Enemy's Enemy Is—Only Perhaps—My Friend." *Social Text* 14, nos. 1–2 (spring–summer 1991): 61–80.

Rose, Nikolas. "Engineering the Human Soul: Analyzing Psychological Expertise." *Science in Context* 5, no. 2 (1992): 351–69.

———. *Inventing Our Selves: Psychology, Power, and Personhood.* Cambridge: Cambridge University Press, 1996.

Rosenberg, R., J. O. Ottoson, P. Bech, M. Mellergard, et al. "Validation Criteria for Panic Disorder as a Nosological Entity." *Acta Psychiatrica Scandinavica* 83, suppl. 365 (1991): 7–17.

Rosenblueth, Arturo, and Norbert Wiener. "The Role of Models in Science." *Philosophy of Science* 12, no. 4 (October 1945): 316–21.

Rosenblueth, Arturo, Norbert Wiener, and Julian Bigelow. "Behavior, Purpose and Teleology." *Philosophy of Science* 10, no. 1 (January 1943): 18–24.

Ross, Edward A. *Social Psychology.* New York: Macmillan, 1908.

Roth, Martin, and Nick Argyle. "Anxiety, Panic, and Phobic Disorders: An Overview." *Journal of Psychiatric Research* 22, suppl. 1 (1988): 33–54.

Ruesch, Jurgen. "Social Communication and the Information Sciences." In *American Handbook of Psychiatry*, vol. 6, 2nd ed., ed. Silvano Arieti. New York: Basic Books, 1975.

Sainz, Anthony. "Clinical Applications of Chlorpromazine in Psychiatry." In *Psychopharmacology*, ed. Nathan Kline. Washington: American Association for the Advancement of Science, 1956.

Schacht, Thomas. "DSM-III and the Politics of Truth." *American Psychologist* 40, no. 5 (May 1985): 513–21.

Scheer, Edward, ed. *Antonin Artaud: A Critical Reader.* London: Routledge, 2004.

Scheerer, Martin. "Cognitive Theory." In *Handbook of Social Psychology*, vol. 1, ed. Gardner Lindzey. Cambridge, Mass.: Addison-Wesley, 1954.

Schultz, Duane, ed. *Panic Behavior: Discussion and Readings.* New York: Random House, 1964.

Sedgwick, Eve Kosofsky. "Teaching 'Experimental Critical Writing.'" In *The Ends of Performance*, ed. Peggy Phelan and Jill Lane. New York: New York University Press, 1998.

————. *Touching Feeling: Affect, Pedagogy, Performativity*. Durham: Duke University Press, 2003.

Sedler, Mark J. "Foundations of the New Nosology." *Journal of Medicine and Philosophy* 19, no. 4 (June 1994).

Seidman, Steven. *Contested Knowledge: Social Theory in the Postmodern Era*. Cambridge, Mass.: Blackwell, 1994.

————. "The End of Sociological Theory." In *The Postmodern Turn: New Perspectives on Social Theory*, ed. Steven Seidman. Cambridge: Cambridge University Press, 1994.

————. "The Political Unconscious of the Human Sciences." In *Difference Troubles: Queering Social Theory and Sexual Politics*. Cambridge: Cambridge University Press, 1997.

Selfridge, Mallory. "W. S. McCulloch and the Foundations of AI." In *Collected Works of Warren S. McCulloch*, vol. 2, ed. Rook McCulloch. Salinas, Calif.: Intersystems Publication, 1989.

Sheehan, David V. *The Anxiety Disease*. New York: Scribner, 1983.

————. Interview by author. Miami, Fla., April 14, 1996.

Sheehan, David V., and James Ballenger. "Treatment of Endogenous Anxiety with Phobic, Hysterical, and Hypochondriacal Symptoms." *Archives of General Psychiatry* 37 (January 1980): 51–59.

Sheehan, David V., and Kathy Sheehan. "The Classification of Anxiety and Hysterical States, Part I: Historical Review and Empirical Delineation." *Journal of Clinical Psychopharmacology* 2, no. 4 (1982): 235–44.

Sherwood, Robert. "The Third World War." *Collier's*, October 27, 1951, 19–31.

Shils, Edward. "A Note on Governmental Research on Attitudes and Morale." *American Journal of Sociology* 47, no. 3 (November 1941): 472–80.

Sidis, Boris. *The Psychology of Suggestion: A Research into the Subconscious Nature of Man and Society*. New York: D. Appleton, 1898.

Simpson, Christopher. *Science of Coercion: Communication Research and Psychological Warfare, 1945–1960*. New York: Oxford University Press, 1994.

Skerritt, Paul W. "Anxiety and the Heart — A Historical Review." *Psychological Medicine* 13 (1983): 17–25.

Smelser, Neil. *Theory of Collective Behavior*. New York: Free Press, 1962.

Smoller, Jordan, and Ming Tsuang. "Panic and Phobic Anxiety: Defining Phenotypes for Genetic Studies." *American Journal of Psychiatry* 155, no. 9 (September 1998): 1152–62.

Spitzer, Robert L. "DSM-III and the Politics-Science Dichotomy Syndrome: A Response to Thomas E. Schacht." *American Psychologist* 40, no. 5 (May 1985): 187–96.

————. Interview by author. New York, April 1, 1996.

————. Introduction to *Diagnostic and Statistical Manual of Mental Disorders*, 3rd ed., by the American Psychiatric Association. Washington: American Psychiatric Association, 1980.

————. "Psychiatric Diagnosis: Are Clinicians Still Necessary?" In *Psychotherapy*

Research: Where Are We and Where Should We Go, ed. Robert L. Spitzer and Janet B. Williams. New York: Guilford Press, 1984.

Spitzer, Robert L., and Jean Endicott. "Computer Applications in Psychiatry." In *American Handbook of Psychiatry*, 2nd ed., ed. Silvano Arieti. New York: Basic Books, 1975.

——. "DIAGNO: A Computer Program for Psychiatric Diagnosis Utilizing the Differential Diagnostic Procedure." *Archives of General Psychiatry* 18 (1968): 746–56.

——. "DIAGNO II: Further Developments in a Computer Program for Psychiatric Diagnosis." *American Journal of Psychiatry* 125, suppl. 8 (1969): 12–21.

——. "Medical and Mental Disorder: Proposed Definition and Criteria." In *Critical Issues in Psychiatric Diagnosis*, ed. Robert L. Spitzer and Donald F. Klein. New York: Raven Press, 1978.

Spitzer, Robert L., Jean Endicott, Jacob Cohen, and Joseph Fleiss. "Constraints on the Validity of Computer Diagnosis." *Archives of General Psychiatry* 31 (August 1974): 197–203.

Spitzer, Robert L., Jean Endicott, and Eli Robins. "Clinical Criteria for Psychiatric Diagnosis and *DSM-III*." *American Journal of Psychiatry* 132, no. 11 (November 1975): 1187–92.

——. "Research Diagnostic Criteria: Rationale and Reliability." *Archives of General Psychiatry* 35 (June 1978): 773–82.

Spitzer, Robert L., and Joseph L. Fleiss. "A Re-analysis of the Reliability of Psychiatric Diagnosis." *British Journal of Psychiatry* 125 (1974): 341–47.

Spitzer, Robert L., Michael Sheehy, and Jean Endicott. "DSM-III: Guiding Principles." In *Psychiatric Diagnosis*, ed. Vivan Rakoff, Harvey Stancer, and Henry Kedward. New York: Brunner/Mazel, 1977.

Srole, L., T. Langner, S. Michael, et al. *Mental Health in the Metropolis: The Midtown Manhattan Study*. New York: McGraw-Hill, 1962.

Stouffer, Samuel. "Afterthoughts of a Contributor to *The American Soldier*." In *Continuities in Social Research: Studies in the Scope and Method of "The American Soldier,"* ed. Robert K. Merton and Paul F. Lazarsfeld. Glencoe, Ill.: Free Press, 1950.

Stouffer, Samuel, Edward Suchman, Shirley Star, and Robin Williams, eds. *The American Soldier: Adjustment during Army Life*. Studies in Social Psychology, vol. 1. Princeton: Princeton University Press, 1949.

Strauss, Anselm. "Concepts, Communication, and Groups." In *Group Relations at the Crossroads*, ed. Muzafer Sherif and M. O. Wilson. New York: Harper, 1953.

——. "The Literature on Panic." *Journal of Abnormal and Social Psychology* 39 (1944): 317–28.

——. "Research in Collective Behavior: Neglect and Need." *American Sociological Review* 12, no. 4 (June 1947): 352–54.

Sullivan, Harry Stack. "Psychiatric Aspects of Morale." *American Journal of Sociology* 47, no. 3 (November 1941): 277–301.

Sulloway, Frank J. *Freud, Biologist of the Mind: Beyond the Psychoanalytic Legend*. New York: Basic Books, 1972.

Survival under Atomic Attack. Washington: U.S. Government Printing Office, 1950.

Swanson, G. E. "A Preliminary Laboratory Study of the Acting Crowd." *American Sociological Review* 18, no. 5 (October 1953): 522–33.

Swenson, Lloyd S., Jr., et al. *This New Ocean: A History of Project Mercury*. Washington: National Aeronautics and Space Administration, 1966.

Szasz, Thomas. *The Myth of Mental Illness: Foundations of a Theory of Personal Conduct*. New York: Harper and Row, 1974.

Taggart, James. *The World Pharmaceutical Industry*. London: Routledge, 1993.

Taussig, Michael. *The Nervous System*. New York: Routledge, 1992.

———. "Viscerality, Faith, and Skepticism: Another Theory of Magic." In *Magic and Modernity: Interfaces of Revelation and Concealment*, ed. Birgit Meyer and Peter Pels. Stanford: Stanford University Press, 2003.

Taylor, Diana. " 'You Are Here': The DNA of Performance." *Drama Review* 46, no. 1 (spring 2002): 149–69.

Tiryakian, Edward. "Aftermath of a Thermonuclear Attack on the United States: Some Sociological Considerations." *Social Problems* 6 (1959): 291–303.

Trinh, T. Minh-ha. *Woman, Native, Other: Writing Postcoloniality and Feminism*. Bloomington: Indiana University Press, 1989.

Turner, Bryan S., and Roland Roberston. "An Introduction to Talcott Parsons: Theory, Politics and Humanity." In *Talcott Parsons: Theorist of Modernity*, ed. Bryan S. Turner and Roland Robertson. London: Sage Publications, 1991.

Turner, Ralph H., and Lewis M. Killian. *Collective Behavior*. Englewood Cliffs, N.J.: Prentice-Hall, 1957.

Ulet, George A. Foreword to *Drugs and Cerebral Function*, ed. W. Lynn Smith. Springfield, Ill.: Charles C. Thomas, 1970.

Upjohn Company. *The Upjohn Company Annual Report 1984*. Kalamazoo, Mich.: Upjohn Company, 1985.

———. *The Upjohn Company Annual Report 1985*. Kalamazoo, Mich.: Upjohn Company, 1986.

———. *The Upjohn Company Annual Report 1987*. Kalamazoo, Mich.: Upjohn Company, 1988.

———. *The Upjohn Company Annual Report 1993*. Kalamazoo, Mich.: Upjohn Company, 1994.

———. *What You Should Know about Panic Disorder*. Pamphlet. Kalamazoo, Mich.: Upjohn Company, 1986.

U.S. Strategic Bombing Survey. *The Effects of Atomic Bombs on Hiroshima and Nagasaki*. Washington: GPO, 1946.

U.S. Strategic Bombing Survey, Morale Division. *The Effects of Strategic Bombing on German Morale*. Vol. 1. Washington: GPO, 1947.

———. *The Effects of Strategic Bombing on Japanese Morale*. Washington: Morale Division, 1947.

Vaillant, George E. "The Disadvantages of DSM-III Outweigh Its Advantages." *American Journal of Psychiatry* 141, no. 4 (April 1984): 542–45.

Virilio, Paul. *War and Cinema: The Logistics of Perception*. Trans. Patrick Camiller. London: Verso, 1984.

Wanger, Walter. "The Role of Movies in Morale." *American Journal of Sociology* 47, no. 3 (November 1941): 378–83.

Waring, Stephen. *Taylorism Transformed: Scientific Management Theory since 1945.* Chapel Hill: University of North Carolina Press, 1991.

Weart, Spencer R. *Nuclear Fear: A History of Images.* Cambridge: Harvard University Press, 1988.

Weissman, Myrna. Interview by author. New York, March 26, 1996.

———. Interview by David Healy. In *The Psychopharmacologists II: Interviews by Dr. David Healy.* London: Chapman and Hall, 1998.

Weissman, Myrna, Roger Bland, Glorisa Canino, Carlo Faravelli, et al. "The Cross-National Epidemiology of Panic Disorder." *Archives of General Psychiatry* 54 (April 1997): 305–9.

Weissman, Myrna, and Gerald Klerman. "Epidemiology of Mental Disorders." *Archives of General Psychiatry* 35 (June 1978): 705–12.

Wells, H. G. *The War of the Worlds.* New York: Charles Scribner's Sons, 1924.

Wheeler, Edwin O., Paul D. White, Eleanor W. Reed, and Mandel E. Cohen. "Neuro-circulatory Asthenia (Anxiety Neurosis, Effort Syndrome, Neurasthenia)." *Journal of the American Medical Association* 142, no. 12 (March 25, 1950): 878–89.

White, Benjamin V. *Stanley Cobb: A Builder of the Modern Neurosciences.* Boston: Francis A. Countway Library of Medicine, 1984.

White, Paul, Stanley Cobb, William Chapman, Mandel Cohen, and Daniel Badal. "Observations on Neurocirculatory Asthenia." *Transactions of the Association of American Physicians* 58 (1944): 129–36.

Widiger, Thomas A. "Categorical versus Dimensional Classification: Implications from and for Research." *Journal of Personality Disorders* 6, no. 4 (1992): 301–12.

Wiener, Norbert. *Cybernetics, or Control and Communication in the Animal and the Machine.* New York: Technology Press, 1948.

———. *Extrapolation, Interpolation, and Smoothing of Stationary Time Series.* Cambridge: MIT Press, 1949.

———. *The Human Use of Human Beings: Cybernetics and Society.* Boston: Houghton Mifflin, 1950.

———. *I Am a Mathematician.* New York: Doubleday, 1956.

———. "Perspectives on Neurocybernetics." In *Cybernetics of the Central Nervous System*, vol. 17, ed. Norbert Wiener and J. P. Schadé. New York: Elsevier, 1965.

Wikler, Abraham. *The Relation of Psychiatry to Pharmacology.* Baltimore: Williams and Wilkins, 1957.

Williams, Patricia. *The Alchemy of Race and Rights: Diary of a Law Professor.* Cambridge: Harvard University Press, 1991.

Wilson, Mitchell. "DSM-III and the Transformation of American Psychiatry: A History." *American Journal of Psychiatry* 150, no. 3 (March 1993): 399–410.

Woodruff, Robert A., Paula J. Clayton, and Samuel B. Guze. "Hysteria: An Evaluation of Specific Diagnostic Criteria by the Study of Randomly Selected Psychiatric Clinic Patients." *American Journal of Psychiatry* 115 (1969): 1243–48.

Wylie, Philip. "Panic, Psychology, and the Bomb." *Bulletin of Atomic Scientists* 10 (1954): 37–40.

Young, Allen. *The Harmony of Illusions: Inventing Post-traumatic Stress Disorder.* Princeton: Princeton University Press, 1995.

Zita, Jacquelyn. *Body Talk: Philosophical Reflections on Sex and Gender.* New York: Columbia University Press, 1998.

Zubin, Joseph. "On the Powers of Models." *Journal of Personality* 20, no. 4 (June 1952): 430–39.

———. "Perspectives on the Conference." In *The Role and Methodology of Classification in Psychiatry and Psychopathology*, ed. Martin M. Katz, Jonathan O. Cole, and Walter E. Barton. Washington: National Institute of Mental Health, 1968.

INDEX

Abramson, Harold A., 200–201, 311
n.143, 312 n.149

abstraction, 25, 122–23, 154, 199; panic
research and, 91–92; paranoid delusions and, 125–126

Acker, Kathy, 265

Adorno, Theodor W., 59–60, 289 n.93

advertising, drug, 260–261, 321 n.161

agoraphobia, 214, 254

Air Raid (MacLeish), 63, 289 n.104

Air War and Emotional Stress (Janis), 130

Alert TodayóAlive Tomorrow, 115–16, 117

alprazolam. *See* Xanax

American Institute of Public Opinion,
57, 61, 68

American Journal of Sociology (special
issue on morale), 67–70

American Psychiatric Association (APA);
DSM-III and, 224–225, 314 n.33; origins, 175; post–World War II expansion, 175–76; and the Upjohn Company, 320 n.155. *See also* psychiatry

American Soldier, The (Osborn), 70–71,
89

Anderson, Laurie, 9

Angell, James, 69

antidepressants, 262

antifascist theater, 289 n.100

anxiety attack. *See* panic disorder

Anxiety Disease, The (Sheehan), 213–16,
218

anxiety neurosis, 229–30; Freud on, 229–
30, 315 n.51; neurocirculatory asthenia
and, 218, 230; panic disorder and,
215–16, 316 n.52

archives, 9, 19, 53, 279

Artaud, Antonin, 6–8, 281 n.12

astronauts, 164, 169–70, 173–74

atomic bomb. *See* bombing; nuclear war

automata theory, 193, 310 n.114

autonomic nervous system, 184, 185, 239

Ballenger, James, 251, 253, 254, 257–58

Bates, Norman, 16

Bateson, Gregory, 108

Baudrillard, Jean, 15–16

"Behavior, Purpose, and Teleology"
(Rosenblueth et al.), 108–9, 189–90,
296 n.106

behaviorism, 169–72; cybernetics and,
111, 297 n.114

Belief, Magic, and Anomie (A. Parsons),
124–27

Bell Telephone Laboratories, 81, 104–5

Bernays, Edward L., 14, 282 n.33

biopower, 11, 13

biopsychiatry, 13, 267–68

Birth of the Clinic (Foucault), 11

Blumer, Herbert, 128, 298 n.167

Bogard, William, 140, 156

bombing: atomic bombs, 83–88, 95–
102; collective panic and, 83–88,
97–100, 112–16, 130, 132–34, 145–46;
cybernetics and, 108–9; of Germany,
71–73, 290 n.131; of Japan, 73, 74–77,
291 n.146; Operation Alert exercises,
140–46, 300 n.219, 301 n.227; survey
research on, 71–73, 74–77, 83, 84–
85. *See also* military; United States
Strategic Bombing Survey (USSBS)

Boston Psychoanalytic Institute, 122,
148–49, 157, 182, 302 n.250

crowds and, 5–6, 41–45, 95, 286 n.31; cybernetics and, 12, 23–24, 30, 107, 110–11; empirical science and, 12, 29–30, 61–62, 88–89, 90–95, 128–34, 159–60, 174; Freud on, 43; Macy conferences on panic and morale, 102–7, 110–11; as military weapon, 85, 131; morale and, 67–69, 86; Operation Alert exercises and, 140–46, 301 n.227; panic disorder and, 30, 174–75; production of, 14, 131–32; PSYCHOpower and, 12, 14; radio and, 36–40, 67; as reasonable behavior, 95, 90–92, 128–29; research on, 45–52, 90, 93–95, 113, 128–34, 160–62, 172–74, 293 n.35; sociology and, 10, 88, 128–34, 159–60, 174; suggestion and, 6, 41, 43–44, 50–53, 90, 128; technoscience and, 23–24; theater fires and, 5–6, 92, 216–17; World War II and, 66–73. *See also* crowd; mass hysteria; panic; panic disorder; *War of the Worlds*

Collège de Sociologie, 26, 284 n.73

Columbia Broadcasting Systems (CBS), 36, 39, 50, 55, 57

Columbia Bureau of Applied Social Research, 89–90, 293 n.31

Commission on Mental Health, 226

Committee on Experimental Neuroses, 183

communication: cybernetic control and, 12, 16, 107–8, 109–10, 134–40, 150–55; with the dead, 20, 53, 63; disease and, 7, 18, 19, 279; drugs and, 9, 259–60; human-machine, 110, 136, 139–40; and the social, 6–8, 18. *See also* mass communication studies

communication and information science: information theory, 29, 104–6, 121, 194, 284 n.67, 296 n.94; panic and morale and, 104–6, 110–11; social theory and, 151–52. *See also* cybernetics

"Communication and the Information Theory" (Miller), 104–5

computerized psychiatric diagnosis, 243–46, 255, 320 n.140

computers: antiaircraft artillery and, 309 n.100; central nervous system and, 24, 108, 190, 193–94; Electronic Numerical Integrator and Calculator (ENIAC), 192; mental processes and, 310 n.114; military support for, 192, 309 n.100; performance and, 29; use in psychiatry, 243–45, 255, 257, 318 n.103, 318 n.106, 320 n.140

Continuities in Social Research (Lazarsfeld and Merton), 89–90

control: of collective panic, 23–24, 29–30, 51–52, 66–68, 92–93, 131–132; "control society," 277–78; cybernetic feedback and, 16, 107–8, 109–10, 121, 134–40, 138–39, 150–55; of the future, 139–40; semiotics and, 135. *See also* social control

corporations: control of communication, 53, 63, 259; drug research and, 208, 214–15, 251–58; philanthropic activities, 53, 54, 57, 181–85; and public relations industry, 14–15; survey research and, 54–56. *See also* pharmaceutical industry; radio; Upjohn Company

Cottrell, Leonard S., 83

Cross-National Collaborative Panic Study (Upjohn), 251–53, 256–58, 319 n.121, 320 n.159

crowd: class associations and, 42, 286 n.26; collective panic and, 5–6, 41–45, 95, 286 n.31; gender associations and, 42, 286 n.26; laboratory experiments and, 93–95; nationalism and, 42–43, 286 n.26; the public vs., 44, 48–49; race associations and, 42, 286 n.26; radio audience as, 39–40; social psychology of, 41–45, 93–95; suggestion and, 5–6, 41–45, 94. *See also* collective behavior

Crowd, The (Le Bon), 42, 286 n.24

Crowd, The (Park), 44, 286 n.31

Cvetkovich, Ann, 19, 25, 283 n.50

cybernetics: artificial intelligence and, 310 n.117; behaviorism and, 111, 297 n.114; central nervous system and, 107–8, 170, 188–89, 193–94; circular causality in, 108, 189–90, 296 n.106; communication as control, 16, 107–8, 109–11, 134–40, 150–55; computer and, 190, 192–93; functionalism and, 121, 151, 302 n.256; and the future, 108, 109, 139–40; history of, 16, 107, 135; homeostasis and, 121, 190, 302 n.256; hypnosis and, 24, 189; information theory and, 23–24, 107; language and, 134–40, 152, 154–55, 163, 303 n.260; Macy Foundation and, 107–8, 110–11, 188–90, 193, 296 n.102; mathematical models and, 108–9, 192, 199, 300 n.211; McCulloch-Pitts model of neural nets, 190–92, 309 n.102; mental behavior and, 190–192, 194–95, 200, 202–3; mental disorder and, 24, 194, 195–96, 208; mind/body dualism and, 188, 195; model of drug action and, 208–9; neurocybernetics, 194–95; neurophysiology and, 189, 193, 194, 202, 300 n.209; panic and, 12, 23–24, 30, 107, 110–11, 259; psychiatry and, 24, 107, 196, 203, 204, 208–9, 255; psychoanalysis and, 196, 208, 310 n.125; psychology and, 296 n.94; psychopharmacology and, 24, 169–70, 200–201, 203, 204, 208–9, 255, 259; Rockland State Hospital and, 169–70, 189, 244, 318 n.103; social control and, 16, 23–24, 107, 110, 121, 150–55, 302 n.255; social theory and, 121, 151–54, 303 n.260; trauma and, 24–25; the unconscious and, 24, 196; as universal science, 23, 135, 151, 303 n.258, 303 n.260. *See also* cyber-psychiatry; cyborg; Wiener, Norbert

Cybernetics (Wiener), 108, 193–94, 199

Cybernetics of the Central Nervous System (Wiener and Schadé), 194–95

cyber-psychiatry, 205–9; computerized diagnosis and, 243–47, 255; drug-brain interaction and, 208–9; Klein and, 205–9; Kline and, 203–4, 305 n.7; mental disorder as communication problem in, 24, 195; pharmaceutical industry and, 255–57

cyborg, 30, 169–70, 203–4, 305 n.7

Dada, 26, 28, 284 n.74

Daddy (stories), 81–82, 116–18, 122–23, 126, 137–38, 149–50, 159–64

Day Called X, 144

Death at the Parasite Cafe (Pfohl), 26

Dechart, Charles, 153

Delaporte, François, 223

Deleuze, Gilles, 8, 278

Derrida, Jacques, 282 n.13

DIAGNO (I, II, and III), 244, 318 n.103

"Diagnosis of Hysteria" (Guze), 230

Diagnostic and Statistical Manual of Mental Disorders (DSM-I), 176

Diagnostic and Statistical Manual of Mental Disorders, 3rd ed. (DSM-III): ascendancy of research psychiatrists and, 225–227; computerized diagnosis and, 243–46, 318 n.102; critiques of, 224–25, 317 n.94; Cross-National Collaborative Panic Study (Upjohn) and, 256; development of, 223–32, 314 n.29; DSM-III-R, 254; empirical science and, 224–25, 226–27, 229, 240–42, 243; Feighner criteria and, 229–30; hysteria and, 232, 233, 250–51, 317 n.66; international hegemony of, 256; medical model of mental disorders and, 225, 314 n.33; probabilistic model of mental disorder and, 240–41, 246; reliability problems, 227–28, 241; Research Diagnostic Criteria (RDC) and, 228–29, 245; standardized diagnostic criteria and, 228–33; validity problems, 240–42, 255, 317 n.92, 317 n.94, 319 n.136. *See also* classification, psychiatric

Healy, David, 251, 256, 258, 316 n.53, 320
    n.155
Heims, Steve J., 189, 195, 201, 311 n.136
Henderson, L. J., 120, 121, 186, 298 n.136
Hillside Hospital, 170–72, 244, 306 n.21
Hiroshima, bombing of, 73, 74–77, 291
    n.146, 291 n.149
Hoch, Paul, 312 n.161
Hoffman-LaRoche, 208
Homeland Security, Department of, 280
homeostasis, 184, 187–88; cybernetics
    and, 190, 305 n.7
Human Genome Project, 268
Human Use of Human Beings (Wiener),
    108–9
Hyman, Herbert, 71, 292 n.8
hyperreality, 15–16
hypnosis, 21, 22, 182, 202; cybernetics
    and, 24, 189; suggestion and, 22, 41,
    42, 283 n.59
Hypnosis and Psychosomatic Medi-
    cine Clinic (Massachusetts General
    Hospital), 214, 216
hysteria: Dora's case, 232–33; *DSM-III*
    and, 232, 233, 250–51, 317 n.66; Freud
    on, 19, 22, 42, 232–33; panic disorder
    and, 215–16, 233; politics of knowl-
    edge and, 19–20; scientific psychiatry
    and, 230–33, 316 n.55, 316 n.63; *Studies
    on Hysteria* (Freud and Breuer), 22,
    42; trauma studies and, 19, 283 n.50.
    See also mass hysteria
"Hysteria Split Asunder" (Spitzer et al.),
    232

imipramine (Tofranil), 170, 71, 206, 220,
    222
informatics of domination, 277–78, 322
    n.3
information highway, 163
information theory, 29, 104–6, 121, 194,
    284 n.67, 296 n.94
integrated circuits, 25, 81–82, 150, 216,
    218, 267

intention tremors, 194
Invasion from Mars (Cantril), 45–52, 53,
    57–58, 61–62, 64–65, 84
Irigaray, Luce, 20, 34, 45, 52–53, 73
Iroquois Theater, 5–6, 281 n.6

Janis, Irving, 129, 131
Japan, bombing of, 74–77, 291 n.149, 292
    n.146
Josiah Macy Jr. Foundation. *See* Macy
    Foundation
Journal of Psychosomatic Medicine,
    183–84

Kefauver-Harris Act, 226
Kendall, Robert, 262
Klein, Donald, 170–72, 174, 205–9, 225,
    265–68, 317 n.92; and cybernetic
    model of drug action, 208–9; and
    computerized psychiatric diagnostics,
    244; panic disorder and, 172, 206,
    253, 254, 266–67, 270; pharmaceutical
    dissection and, 171–72, 205–6, 254
Klerman, Gerald, 252, 253, 256, 317 n.94
Kline, Nathan, 197, 203–4, 312 n.159; and
    computer use in psychiatry, 244, 318
    n.103; and the cyborg, 169–70, 203,
    305 n.7
Kraepelin, Emile, 254, 268
Kubie, Lawrence, 189

laboratory experiments, 8, 94, 151, 276,
    303 n.258; collective panic and, 90–
    93, 95, 113, 160–62, 293 n.35; panic
    disorder and, 266, 268
LaPiere, Richard, 46–47
Lasker, Mary, 204
Laswell, Harold, 61
Lazarsfeld, Paul, 61, 70; Macy cybernet-
    ics conferences and, 108; Princeton
    Radio Research Project and, 55–56, 57;
    Radio and the Printed Page, 59
Le Bon, Gustave, 42, 43, 140, 286 n.24
Lettvin, Jerome, 191, 310 n.109

Lewin, Kurt, 108
Leys, Ruth, 21, 22–23, 283 n.59
Likert, Rensis, 83, 86
lobotomy, 200
Lowe, Donald, 243
LSD research, 14, 171, 201
Lynd, Robert S., 61

MacLeish, Archibald, 52, 63, 66, 287
    n.63, 289 n.100, 289 n.104
Macy Foundation, 103; cybernetics and,
    107–8, 110–11, 188–90, 193, 296 n.102;
    homeostasis and, 184; psychosomatic
    medicine and, 181–85, 308 n.79; sup-
    port for government research, 103;
    war neuroses and, 168, 184–5, 308
    n.79; World Federation of Mental
    Health and, 197–98
Macy Foundation conferences: "Cere-
    bral Inhibition Meeting," 189–90;
    creation of interdisciplinary subfields,
    296 n.102; on cybernetics, 107–8,
    188–90, 190; Grinker and, 106–7,
    200, 202–3; history of, 103, 295 n.85;
    "Neuropharmacology," 200–201, 312
    n.149; on panic and morale, 102–
    7, 110–11; T. Parsons and, 121, 202;
    "Problems of Consciousness," 201–2,
    311 n.143, 312 n.149; and research on
    LSD, 201; "Traumatic War Neuroses,"
    308 n.79
madness, xi, 13, 277; PSYCHOpower and,
    14, 282 n.32
Madness and Civilization (Foucault), xi,
    13
Mama (stories), 116–18, 126, 137–38,
    149–50, 159, 162–64
market research, 12, 60; by pharmaceuti-
    cal industry, 256–57, 320 n.140; survey
    research and, 54, 55–56, 70
Marks, Isaac, 320 n.159
Marshall Islands, 115, 292 n.5
Massachusetts General Hospital, 228;
    history of Department of Psychiatry,

182, 183, 216, 217; neurocirculatory
    asthenia studies, 218, 230, 231; panic
    disorder studies, 219–23, 233–39,
    247–51, 262–65, 270–74; T. Par-
    sons' fieldwork at, 186, 218, 309 n.91;
    psychosomatic medicine and, 182–83,
    214–15, 216, 217–18, 220; Xanax panic
    study (1981), 214–15
mass communications studies: mar-
    ket research and, 55–56, 60; national
    security and, 61, 292 n.10; propaganda
    and, 58, 61, 289 n.88; Rockefeller
    Communication Seminar and, 60–61;
    suggestion and, 48–49
mass hysteria, 12, 37, 58, 61, 87–88, 130,
    266–77. See also collective panic
mass media, 6, 8; civil defense and, 98,
    100–2, 114–16, 297 n.123; collective
    panic and, 36–40, 67; drugs as, 259–
    60; panic disorder and, 215, 221–22;
    PSYCHOpower and, 15–17; suggestion
    and, 40, 48–49
mathematics: cybernetics and, 108–9,
    193, 199, 300 n.211, 303 n.260; models
    of brain behavior and, 190–91, 192
Mauss, Marcel, 188
McCulloch, Warren, 189, 191; critique
    of psychoanalysis, 196, 310 n.125; on
    cybernetics and mental disease, 195;
    Macy cybernetics conferences and,
    189, 190, 309 n.99
McCulloch-Pitts model of neural nets,
    190–92, 193, 309 n.102, 310 n.109
McDougall, William, 5–6, 42, 43
Mead, Margaret, 108, 197
medical disorder: mental disorder and,
    216, 225, 314 n.33 (see also psychoso-
    matic medicine); panic disorder as,
    216, 233
medico-pharmaceutical complex, 258
Melley, Timothy, 17–18
memory, 117, 221; cybernetics and,
    194, 195; performative writing and,
    27; psychopharmacology and, 24,

212, 260; PSYCHOpower and, 11, 13; technoscience and, 278; trauma and, 19, 20, 21–22, 273–74

mental disorders, xi; continuum model of, 177–78, 180–81, 307 n.44; cybernetic model of, 24, 194, 195–96, 208; drug-disease relationship and, 254–55, 256; epidemiology of, 179–80, 245, 256–57, 307 n.55; government management of, 11, 178–81, 197–98; medical model of, 216, 225, 314 n.33; and mental institutions, 175–78; social control of, 155. *See also* classification, psychiatric

mental health, 178–81; mass approach to, 178, 179, 207, 259; World Federation of Mental Health, 197–98, 311 n.136. *See also* National Institute of Mental Health

Mental Health in the Metropolis (Srole), 180

mental institutions, 175; A. Parsons and, 124–25, 148–50, 156–59; psychiatric classification system and, 176, 307 n.37

Men under Stress (Grinker and Spiegel), 177

Mercury Theater. *See* CBS Mercury Theater

Merton, Robert K., 89, 286 n.24

Milgram, Stanley, 90

military, 17, 25, 27–28, 68, 117; computer development and, 192, 309 n.100; cybernetics and, 108–9, 110, 135, 169–70; Operation Alert, 140–46, 300 n.219, 301 n.227; Operation Crossroads, 77, 83, 85–86, 87; Operation Cue, 100–101; Operation Doorstep, 101–2, 295 n.77; Operation Ivy, 115; panic and, 38, 67, 147, 157, 173–74; panic research and, 65–66, 130, 131–32, 133–34; psychiatry and, 167–69, 176–77, 181, 184–85, 217–18, 307 n.39, 308 n.75, 314 n.21; PSYCHOpower and, 14–15, 16–17; survey research and, 70–77,

83–85, 89, 293 n.29; and total war, 67–68, 69–70, 98, 99, 291 n.146. *See also* bombing; World War II

Miller, George, 102, 104, 296 n.94

Millon, Theodor, 240

Mills, C. Wright, 88, 293 n.29

mimesis, 6, 21, 22; PSYCHOpower and, 14–15

mind/body dualism, 15, 195, 267, 314 n.33

Minh-ha, Trinh, 28, 280

Mintz, Alexander, 90, 91

Miss Jane Dean (case study), 63–64

morale: *American Journal of Sociology* special issue on, 67–70; cybernetic approach to, 110–11; Macy conferences on panic and morale, 102–7, 110–11; panic and, 67–69, 86; survey research on, 70, 71–77. *See also* civil defense; United States Strategic Bombing Survey (USSBS)

Morale Division, U.S. War Department, 70, 180

Morris, Charles, 303 n.260

Murrow, Edward R., 96

Nagasaki, bombing of, 73, 74–77, 291 n.146, 291 n.149

narcosynthesis, 168–69, 185, 308 n.78

National Institute of Mental Health (NIMH), 11, 181, 204–5, 206, 233; genetic research, 268–69; origins of, 178–79; pharmaceutical industry support for, 258

National Mental Health Act, 178–79, 181

National Opinion Research Center (NORC), 84, 129, 292 n.8

National Research Council, 130, 183–84

national security; mass communications research and, 61, 292 n.10; panic and, 99–100, 112

National Security Council, 115, 145–46

Negri, Antonio, 278

neural nets, 192, 195

neurocirculatory asthenia, 217–18, 230, 231, 314 n.18, 316 n.53
neurocybernetics, 194–95
Neurological Supper Club (Harvard University), 184
"Neuropharmacology" conferences (Macy), 200–201, 312 n.149, 312 n.161
neuropsychiatry, 181, 182, 183, 268, 308 n.79; cybernetics and, 188–89
New York Academy of Medicine, 102, 104
New York State Psychiatric Institute, 198–99, 225, 228, 266, 312 n.161
NIMH. *See* National Institute of Mental Health
"Non-Adaptive Group Behavior" (Mintz), 90
NORC. *See* National Opinion Research Center
normalizing society, 11
nuclear war, 73–77, 82, 172–74; panic and, 84–88, 97–100, 112–16, 130–31, 132–34, 147, 157; simulation of, 95–97, 100–102, 140–46, 301 n.227

Oakes, Guy, 99–100, 141, 143–44, 146
"Observations on Clinical Aspects of Hysteria" (Purtel et al.), 230–31
Oedipal relations, 124, 231; sociological theory and, 119, 297 n.132. *See also* Daddy (stories)
Office of Civil Defense Planning, 86, 95
Office of Defense Mobilization, 301 n.227
Office of Public Opinion Research (Princeton), 84
Office of Scientific Research and Development (OSRD), 217, 314 n.17
Operation Alert, 140–46, 300 n.219, 301 n.227
Operation Alert (film), 143–44
Operation Crossroads, 83, 85–86, 87
Operation Cue, 100–101
Operation Doorstep, 101–2, 295 n.77
Operation Doorstep (film), 149

Operation Eggnog, 95–97
Operation Ivy (film),115
Osborn, Frederick H., 70–71, 83
OSRD (Office of Scientific Research and Development), 217, 314 n.17

panic, 8–11, 29; and the future, 101–2, 279–80; nuclear war and, 84–88, 97–100, 112–16, 130–31, 132–34, 147, 157; A. Parsons and, 147–48, 157; PSYCHOpower and, 12–13, 14, 17; and the social, 6, 43–44, 279. *See also* collective panic; panic disorder
Panic: A Play in Verse (MacLeish), 287 n.63
"Panic, Psychology, and the Bomb" (Wylie), 83, 87–88
Panic Attack Scale (Sheehan), 252
panic broadcast. See *War of the Worlds, The*
Panic Control and Prevention (Office of Civil Defense), 86, 95
panic diaries, 30–31, 219–23, 233–39, 247–51, 262–65, 270–74
panic disorder, 11, 224–25; antidepressants and, 262; *Anxiety Disease, The*, 213–16, 218; anxiety neurosis and, 215–16, 229–30, 316 n.52; collective panic and, 30, 174–75; Cross-National Collaborative Panic Study, 251–54, 256–58, 319 n.121, 320 n.159; cure for, 221, 269–70; cybernetics and, 24, 30, 259; debates over validity of, 215–16, 262, 319 n.136; diagnostic criteria for, 224, 229–30, 254; empirical science and, 12, 13, 174; genetic research on, 268–69, 321 n.182; history of, 171–72, 206, 229–30, 254, 314 n.18; hysteria and, 215–16, 233; mass marketing of, 213–15, 221–22, 257–58; neurocirculatory asthenia and, 217–18, 316 n.53; panic attacks, 9, 214–15, 223–24; pharmaceutical dissection of, 171–72, 206, 254; psychiatric classification of, 229–

30, 254; PSYCHOpower and, 13, 17;
psychosomatic medicine and, 216,
220; separation anxiety and, 239, 266;
Upjohn Company and, 251–58, 320
n.155; Xanax and, 11, 214–15, 262. *See
also* collective panic; panic
"Panic Theory" (Foreman), 130–31
paranoia, 17–18, 124–27
Pareto, Vilfredo, 298 n.136
Park, Robert E., 26, 44, 69; on panic, 43,
286 n.31; on psychic warfare, 67–68;
on suggestion, 41, 44, 46, 48
Parsons, Anne: *Belief, Magic, and Anomie*, 124–27; critiques of psychotherapy, 149, 156–58; critiques of U.S.
militarism, 147, 156; "Diary of a Mental Patient," 80, 148–49; as mental
patient, 80, 156–59; panic and, 147–48,
157; psychoanalysis and, 124, 126–27,
147–50, 157, 302 n.250; research on
mental disease, 124–26; suicide of, 159
Parsons, Talcott: abstraction and, 122–
23; cybernetic functionalism and, 151,
302 n.256; cybernetic theory of social
control, 121, 150–55, 302 n.255; on
father symbol, 118–19, 123; fieldwork
at Massachusetts General Hospital,
186, 218, 309 n.91; functionalism and,
119, 297 n.131, 302 n.256; on language
as control, 152; Macy conferences participant, 121, 201–2; on mental disease
as social deviance, 154–55, 188; on
A. Parsons, 124, 159; psychoanalysis
and, 122, 148, 187; psychosomatic
medicine and, 186–87, 218–19; on resistance, 154–55; systems theory and,
120–21
Patient Diary (Upjohn), 212, 233–34, 252
Paxil, 17, 262
performance, 28–29, 31, 166, 281 n.12;
empirical methods as, 29; healing
and, 22, 167–68, 280; hysteria and,
22, 232–33, 250; panic and, 29, 279;
sociology and, 26–27

performative writing, 26–29, 284 n.72,
285 n.84
Performing Hybridity (Fink), 27
Perly, Michael, 232
Peterson, Val, 112, 115, 146
Pfizer, 255, 261, 262, 320 n.140
Pfohl, Stephen, 26, 285 n.89, 311 n.129
pharmaceutical industry, 8, 31; clinical
drug trials and, 226, 255, 277; consumer advertising, 261, 321 n.162;
control of communication channels,
259, 261s; creation of mental disorders, 257–58; drug research and,
208, 222, 252, 320 n.155; marketing,
255, 257–58, 320 n.140; "Neuropharmacology" conferences (Macy) and,
200; psychiatric classification system
and, 226–27, 256. *See also* Upjohn
Company
pharmaceutical dissection, 171–72,
205–6, 254–55
Pharmacia Corporation, 261
pharmorg, 322 n.9
Phelan, Peggy, 28
phobias, 174
Pitts, Walter, 190, 191
Plath, Sylvia, 118
Pollack, Mark, 257
postmodern, 17, 26, 28, 284 n.72
power, xi, 8, 10, 11, 15, 278. *See also* biopower; PSYCHOpower; social control
PRIME-MD, 320 n.140
Princeton Radio Research Project, 53–
61; Adorno and, 59–60, 289 n.93;
Columbia Bureau of Applied Social
Research and, 89–90; Lazarsfeld and,
55–56, 59; market research and, 54–56,
60; Rockefeller Foundation support
for, 53–55, 60–61; *War of the Worlds*
and, 45–52, 287 n.57. *See also* Cantril,
Hadley; *Invasion From Mars*
"Problems of Consciousness" conferences (Macy), 201–2, 311 n.143, 312
n.149

Project East River Part IX, Report of, 98–100, 295 n.67
Project Mercury, 170, 173–74, 306 n.26
propaganda, 15, 58, 60, 289 n.88; democracy and, 61, 69, 99; fascism and, 14, 69
Prudential Life Insurance Company, 71
"Psychiatric Diagnosis as Prototype Categorization" (Cantor et al.), 240–41
psychiatric epidemiology. *See* epidemiology, psychiatric
psychiatry: ascendancy of research psychiatrists in, 226–29; computerized diagnosis in, 243–46, 255, 257, 318 n.102, 320 n.140; cybernetics and, 24, 107, 196, 203, 204, 208–9, 255; epidemiology of, 179–80, 245, 256–57, 307 n.55; epistemology of, 240–41, 307 n.33, 317 n.82; expansion of (post–World War II), 17578; genetic research and, 268–69, 321 n.182; global hegemony of, 256–57; medicalization of, 182–83, 225; military (in World War II), 167–69, 176–77, 179–80, 181, 217–18, 307 n.39, 308 n.75; pharmaceutical industry and, 255–59, 278; psychoanalytic paradigms in, 176–77, 197, 225; psychosomatic medicine and, 169, 181–83, 184–85; quantification of hysteria in, 230–32; research on LSD and, 14, 171, 201; Rockefeller Foundation and, 181–83, 216, 308 n.60; social, 180–81. *See also* classification, psychiatric; cyber-psychiatry; *Diagnostic and Statistical Manual of Mental Disorders* (DSM-III)
Psycho (Hitchcock), 282 n.41
Psycho-Acoustic Laboratory (Harvard University), 104, 296 n.94
psychoanalysis, 20, 182, 270; ascendancy of (post–World War II), 176–77, 197; of collective panic, 43; cybernetics and, 196, 208, 310 n.125; DSM-III and,

225; hysteria and, 19–20, 230–31, 232–33; A. Parsons and, 124, 126–27, 147–50, 157, 302 n.250, 302 n.251; T. Parsons and, 122, 148, 187. *See also* Freud, Sigmund; unconscious
psychological warfare, 19, 67–68, 99, 279, 283 n.54, 294 n.69
psychopharmacology, 14, 278; advertising, 260–61, 321 n.161; computerized psychiatric diagnostics and, 244, 255, 320 n.140; cybernetics and, 24, 200–1, 203, 204, 208–9, 255, 259; and the cyborg, 169–70, 305 n.9; discovery of panic attack and, 171, 206, 254; history of, 170, 199–200, 204–5, 306 n.18; as mass approach to mental health, 207, 259; as mass media, 259–60; "Neuropharmacology" conferences (Macy), 200–201, 312 n.149; pharmaceutical dissection and, 171–72, 205–6, 254–55; PSYCHOpower and, 13, 14, 17; research on mental patients and, 170–72, 204, 206, 312 n.159; scientific models of mental behavior and, 199–201; standardized psychiatric classification system and, 205, 206–7, 226, 255. *See also* drugs; pharmaceutical industry; Xanax
PSYCHOpower, 11–17; biopower and, 11–13; panic and, 12–13, 14, 17; psychopharmacology and, 13, 14, 17; PSYCHOpolitics and, 279
psychosomatic medicine, 267; Macy Foundation support for, 181–85, 217, 308 n.79; Massachusetts General Hospital and, 182, 186, 214, 216; origins of, 181; T. Parsons on, 186–87, 218–19; Rockefeller Foundation support for, 181, 182–83; war neuroses and, 169, 184–85
psychosurgery, 200
public, 44; and suggestion, 48–89
public opinion, 44, 61; research on, 55, 68, 83–85, 87

Quarantelli, Enrico, 129, 131

radio: and the crowd, 39–40; market research and, 54–56, 60; panic and, 36–40, 67; propaganda and, 37–38, 58, 60; social psychology and, 47–48; suggestion and, 40, 59; survey research and, 10, 50, 54–56, 57, 59, 288 n.75. See also *Invasion from Mars*; Princeton Radio Research Project

Radio and the Printed Page (Lazarsfeld), 58

Rand Corporation, 130

Reading, Pennsylvania, 81, 82, 115–16, 117, 143

real, 26–28, 48, 52, 213; empirical science and, 88, 174; hysteria and, 232; simulation and, 27, 140

reason: madness and, xi, 13, 14, 17, 20, 277; panic and, 38–39, 52, 62, 95, 128, 132

reliability, in psychiatry, 227–28, 241, 315 n.38

Report of the Project East River, Part IX, 98–100, 295 n.67

Research Center for Economic Psychology, 55

Research Diagnostic Criteria (RDC), 228–29, 245, 316 n.52

"Research Diagnostic Criteria" (Spitzer), 228–29

reserpine (Serpasil), 171, 199, 312 n.159

Robins, Lee, 245

Rockefeller Communication Seminar, 60–61

Rockefeller Foundation, 53; CIA research and, 292 n.10; mass communications studies and, 60–61; Princeton Radio Research Project and, 53–55, 60–61; propaganda and, 289 n.88; psychiatry and, 181–183, 216, 308 n.60; psychosomatic medicine and, 181, 182–83; public opinion research and, 83, 292 n.10

Rockland State Hospital, 169–70, 189, 203, 204, 244, 318 n.103

Romanyshyn, Robert, 172, 173–74

Rose, Hilary, 205

Rose, Nikolas, 11–12

Rosenbaum, Jerrold, 222

Rosenblueth, Arturo, 108, 189–90, 194, 197, 199, 296 n.106

Ross, Edward A., 41, 46, 48–49

Ruesch, Jürgen, 195, 265, 304 n.274

Salpêtrière Clinic, 22

Schirra, Walter M., 173, 306 n.26

science studies, 303 n.258

Sedgwick, Eve Kosofsky, 17, 283 n.45

semiotics, 135–36, 191, 303 n.260

Serpasil (reserpine), 171, 199, 312 n.159

Shadow, 40

Sheehan, David, 213–16, 218, 242, 252, 255–56

Shils, Edward A., 68, 295 n.88

simulation: of atomic attack, 95–97, 100–2, 140–46; of collective panic, 161–62; mass media and, 38–39, 142; psychiatric diagnosis and, 244–46; PSYCHOpower and, 13–14, 16; and the real, 27, 140

Smelser, Neil, 159–60

Smith, Kline, and French Laboratories, 199

social: communication and, 6–8; panic and, 6, 43–44, 279; suggestion and, 6–8, 22–23, 41–45

social control: cybernetics and, 16, 23–24, 107, 110, 121, 150–55; empirical methods and, 29–30, 51–52, 89; of panic, 23–24, 29–30, 51–52, 92–93, 131–32; T. Parsons on, 150–55, 187–88, 302 n.255

"Social Impact of Cybernetics" (symposium), 153

social psychiatry, 180–81

social psychology, 10; of the crowd, 41–45, 93–95; empirical methods for,

social psychology (*continued*)
45, 47, 51–52, 88–95, 128–32; market research and, 57; panic research and, 88–95, 128–133, 160–62; survey research and, 46–47, 70, 89–90; World War II morale studies, 70, 71–77. *See also* Cantril, Hadley; *Invasion From Mars*

Social Science Research Council (SSRC), 83, 84

Social Structure and Personality (T. Parsons), 159

Social System, The (T. Parsons), 120, 188

social systems theory, 118–23, 151–53, 154–55, 301 n.255

sociology, 10, 17–18, 297 n.132; panic research and, 88, 128–34, 159–60, 174; performance and, 26–28, 29, 284 n.72; psychoanalysis and, 20, 122

sodium pentothal, 168–69

Spectres of the Spectrum, 136

Spiegel, John, 168–69, 177, 184–85

Spitzer, Robert, 232, 241, 242, 253, 314 n.33, 319 n.127; computerized psychiatric diagnosis and, 243–46; *DSM-III* and, 224–25, 240, 317 n.94; standardized diagnostic criteria and, 228–29

Srole, Leo, 180

Stanton, Frank, 55, 57, 70

Statistical Manual for the Use of Institutions for the Insane (AMSAI), 307 n.37

St. Louis group (University of Washington), 229–30, 245, 315 n.50; research on hysteria and, 230–32, 316 n.55

storytelling, 22, 25, 28, 280; Daddy (stories), 81–82, 116–18, 122–23, 126, 137–38, 149–50, 159–64; dreams (stories), 102, 117–18, 154, 235, 237, 247, 262–63; Mama (stories), 116–18, 126, 137–38, 149–50, 159, 162–64; panic diaries, 30–31, 219–23, 233–39, 247–51, 262–65, 270–74

Stouffer, Samuel, 70, 89–90, 180, 293 n.29

Strauss, Anselm, 88, 90, 91, 94–95, 295 n.88

stress, 177, 305 n.293

Structured Clinical Interview for DSM-III (SCID), 319 n.127

Studies on Hysteria (Freud and Breuer), 22, 42

subjugated knowledge, 19

suggestion: and the crowd, 5–6, 41–45, 94; empirical methods and, 10, 50–52, 128, 132; hysteria and, 22; mass media and, 40, 48–49; narcosynthesis and, 168–69, 185; panic and, 6, 41, 43–44, 50–53, 90, 128; propaganda and, 58; PSYCHOpower and, 15; and the social, 6–8, 22–23, 41–45; trauma and, 21–23, 283 n.59; war neuroses and, 22, 168–69

Sullivan, Harry Stack, 67, 68, 290 n.107, 290 n.110

surrealism, 26, 28, 127

survey research, 45–52, 83–84; in *The American Soldier*, 70–71, 89, 293 n.29; market research and, 54–55, 60–61; on morale, 70, 71–77; National Opinion Research Center (NORC) and, 84, 129, 292 n.8; on panic, 49–51, 61–62; psychiatric epidemiology and, 179–80, 307 n.53; radio and, 10, 50, 54–56, 57, 59, 288 n.75; secret government use of, 84, 292 n.8; social engineering and, 70–71, 89; social psychology and, 46–47, 70, 89–90; U.S. Strategic Bombing Survey, 71–77, 290 n.31, 291 n.146, 291 n.149; U.S. War Department and, 70–73. *See also Invasion From Mars*; Princeton Radio Research Project

Survey Research Center (University of Michigan), 87, 114

Survival City, Nevada, 100–101

"Survival under Atomic Attack" (FCDA), 97–98

Swanson, G. E., 93

Taking Society's Measure (Hyman), 71, 292 n.8

Tarde, Gabriel, 48

Taussig, Michael, 13, 15

technoscience, 16, 23–26, 277–78; panic as technoscientific object, 23–24; performance and, 29; sadism of, 277; social reality and, 27–28; trauma and, 24–25

thalidomide, 226

"Theatre and the Plague, The" (Artaud), 7

Theory of Collective Behavior (Smelser), 159–60

Thompson, Dorothy, 37–38

Thorazine (chlorpromazine), 171, 199

Tiryakian, Edward, 128, 132–34

Toch, Hans, 90

Tofranil (imipramine), 170, 71, 206, 220, 222

Total Recall, 262

total war, 67–68, 69–70, 98, 99, 291 n.146

trauma, 18–25; memory and, 19, 20, 21–22, 273–74; politics of knowledge and, 19–20; psychosomatic medicine and, 184–86, 308 n.79; and the social, 23; studies, 18–19, 283 n.47, 283 n.50; suggestion and, 21–23, 283 n.59

Trauma (Leys), 21

Traumatic Shock (Cannon), 185–86

Turing, Alan, 193

unconscious, 34, 231; cybernetic model of, 24, 196; cyborg and, 169, 305 n.7; *DSM III* and, 225; A. Parsons on, 126–27; social science and, 27. *See also* dreams

United States Strategic Bombing Survey (USSBS), 71–77, 290 n.131, 291 n.146, 291 n.149

Upjohn Company, 11, 251–62; computerized psychiatric diagnostics and, 320 n.140; creation of panic disorder, 257–58; Cross-National Collaborative Panic Study, 251–53, 256–58, 319 n.121, 320 n.159; patient diary, 212, 233–34, 252; Xanax-panic study (1981), 214–15. *See also* Xanax

U.S. Air Force, 163; and the cyborg, 169–70; war neuroses research, 168, 177

U.S. Army, 176, 218, 314 n.21

U.S. Public Health Service, 171, 178–79

USSBS. *See* United States Strategic Bombing Survey (USSBS)

U.S. War Department, 70–73, 180, 309 n.100

Vaillant, George E., 318 n.102

validity, in psychiatry, 241–43, 255, 317 n.92, 317 n.94, 319 n.136

Valium, 253

von Neumann, John, 190, 192, 193, 296 n.103, 309 n.100

"Voodoo Death" (Cannon), 185–86

Wanger, Walter, 69

War in the Air (Wells), 71

war neuroses: civilian psychiatry and, 176–78; Macy Foundation and, 168, 184–85, 189, 308 n.79; narcosynthesis and, 168–69; psychosomatic medicine and, 184–85; suggestion and, 168–69

War Neuroses in North Africa (Grinker and Spiegel), 167–69, 177, 184–85

War of the Worlds, The (radio broadcast), 29–30, 35–40; Cantril study on, 45–52; panic and, 36–38. See also *Invasion from Mars*

War of the Worlds, The (Wells), 36, 74, 75, 76, 77

war on terrorism, 279–80

Washington University School of Medicine, 228, 315 n.50, 316 n.54

Weissman, Myrna, 256–57, 269, 320 n.140

Welles, Orson, 36–39, 40, 63, 289 n.100, 289 n.104

Wells, H. G., 39, 71, 73–74
Wiener, Norbert: on abstraction, 199;
    Benzedrine use, 246, 319 n.116; *Cyber-
    netics*, 108, 193–94, 199; dreams, 196,
    311 n.129; founding of cybernet-
    ics, 108, 190; *Human Use of Human
    Beings, 102, 109–10*; information
    theory and, 105; on language, 134, 136;
    on machine-human relations, 108–
    9, 136, 139; military research, 108–9;
    on neurocybernetics, 194; on and
    new physics of probability, 246–47;
    relation to father, 137–38; on study
    of society, 110, 247, 303 n.260; on the
    unconscious, 196. *See also* cybernetics
Wikler, Abraham, 201, 306 n.18
Williams, Janet, 319 n.127
Winokur, George, 316 n.54
Wisdom of the Body (Cannon), 184
Withey, Steven B., 83
Woman Dreaming of Escape (Miró), 219,
    249
World Federation of Mental Health,
    197–98, 311 n.136
World War II: communications research
and, 61; computer development and,
192, 309 n.100; origins of cybernetics
and, 108–9; panic research and, 66–
67, 88; psychiatry and, 176–77, 179–80,
307 n.39, 308 n.75; survey research
and, 70–77, 179–80 (*see also* United
States Strategic Bombing Survey);
as total war, 67–68, 69–70, 98, 99,
291 n.146; war neurosis and, 167–69,
184–85
writing, performative, 26–29, 284 n.72,
285 n.84
Wylie, Phillip, 83, 87–88

Xanax (alprazolam), 9; clinical drug
trials for, 221–23, 247–251, 251–53,
256–258, 263–265, 270–74, 319 n.121;
effects of, 260, 263, 320 n.159; as mass
media, 259–60; panic disorder and,
11, 251, 255–56, 262, 320 n.155; sales
of, 253, 260–61; Xanax-panic study
(1981), 214–15

Zoloft, 262, 320 n.140
Zubin, Joseph, 198–99, 207

Selected historical materials from chapters 3 and 4 appeared in different form in "The Militarization of Inner Space," *Critical Sociology* 30, no. 2 (2004): 451–82. Selected historical materials from chapters 4 and 5 appeared in different form in "Performing Methods: History, Hysteria, and the New Science of Psychiatry," in *Pathology and the Postmodern: Mental Illness as Discourse and Experience*, ed. Dwight Fee (London: Sage, 1999), 49–73; and in "The Ecstasy of Miscommunication: Cyberpsychiatry and Mental Dis-ease," in *Doing Science + Culture*, ed. Roddey Reid and Sharon Traweek (New York: Routledge, 2000), 151–76. Several pages from the "Panic Diary" sections in chapter 5 appeared originally in "Theory on the Market: Panic, Incorporating," *Social Problems* 37, no. 4 (1990): 460–84; and in "Panic Diary: (Re)constructing a Partial Politics and Poetics of Dis-ease," in *Reconsidering Social Constructionism: Debates in Social Problems Theory*, ed. James Holstein and Gale Miller (New York: Aldine de Gruyter, 1993), 441–82.

Jackie Orr is an associate professor of sociology at Syracuse University.

Library of Congress Cataloging-in-Publication Data

Orr, Jackie

Panic diaries : a genealogy of panic disorder / Jackie Orr.

p. cm.

ISBN 0-8223-3610-3 (cloth : alk. paper)

ISBN 0-8223-3623-5 (pbk. : alk. paper)

1. Panic disorders — Social aspects. 2. Panic disorders — History.

3. Panic disorders — Treatment. I. Title.

[DNLM: 1. Panic Disorder — etiology. 2. Panic Disorder — therapy.

3. Panic Disorder — history. 4. Socioeconomic Factors.

WM 172 075p 2005]

RC535.O77 2005

362.2′6 — dc22 2005025676